CHEFS, RESTAURANTS, AND CULINARY SUSTAINABILITY

FOOD AND
FOODWAYS
SERIES EDITORS:
JENNIFER JENSEN WALLACH
AND MICHAEL WISE

OTHER TITLES IN THIS SERIES

Chefs, Restaurants, and Culinary Sustainability

EDITED BY CAROLE COUNIHAN
AND SUSANNE HØJLUND

The University of Arkansas Press
Fayetteville
2025

978-1-68226-264-1 (cloth)
978-1-68226-265-8 (paperback)
978-1-61075-830-7 (e-book)

29 28 27 26 25 5 4 3 2 1

Manufactured in the United States of America

Designed by William Clift

♾ The paper used in this publication meets the minimum requirements of the
American National Standard for Permanence of Paper for Printed Library Materials
Z39.48–1984.

LIBRARY OF CONGRESS CATALOGING-IN-PUBLICATION DATA

Names: Counihan, Carole, 1948– editor. | Højlund, Susanne, editor.
Title: Chefs, restaurants, and culinary sustainability / edited by Carole Counihan,
    Susanne Højlund.
Description: Fayetteville : The University of Arkansas Press, 2025. | Series: Food
    and foodways | Includes bibliographical references and index. | Summary: "This
    volume explores how chefs around the world approach culinary sustainability.
    Building on empirical data collected from a wide range of cultural, historical,
    political, and economic settings, the contributors to this collection provide
    an engaging examination of how chefs in diverse culinary contexts tackle the
    increasingly urgent societal and environmental need for a more secure food
    future"— Provided by publisher.
Identifiers: LCCN 2024021724 (print) | LCCN 2024021725 (ebook) |
    ISBN 9781682262641 (cloth) | ISBN 9781682262658 (paperback) |
    ISBN 9781610758307 (ebook)
Subjects: LCSH: Food service—Moral and ethical aspects. | Food service—
    Social aspects. | Cooks—Political activity. | Ethnic restaurants. | Cooking—
    Environmental aspects. | Social responsibility of business. | Food habits. | Food
    security. | Sustainable development.
Classification: LCC TX911.3.E84 C68 2025 (print) | LCC TX911.3.E84 (ebook) |
    DDC 647.95068—dc23/eng/20240910
LC record available at https://lccn.loc.gov/2024021724
LC ebook record available at https://lccn.loc.gov/2024021725

CONTENTS

FOREWORD

"Never let a serious crisis go to waste." Whether this phrase is attributed to Winston Churchill or to one of the various avatars of neoliberal capitalism (Mirowski 2014), it has now spread across the political spectrum, and in anthropology, with echoes of Victor Turner, it is a reminder that unusual times offer the possibility of reassessing the assumptions of what is normal. The COVID pandemic provided one such crisis, which has raised ongoing questions about food access, labor, supply chains, and the meaning of "essential (low-paid) workers" in our contemporary post- or mutant-neoliberal economy (Callison and Manfredi 2020).[1] The extended period in which eating in public was one of the commonsense things that was suddenly no longer possible led to questions about what a sustainable normality might look like for the restaurant industry, and whether we should perhaps simply "let it die," as Tunde Wey (2020) has suggested.[2] Wey notes that the restaurant industry is not distinctive in this regard, but part of a larger, deeply problematic system that has prompted us, in the wake of the pandemic, to think about "what can rise from the rubble" (Rosner 2020).

In their introduction to this collection, Højlund and Counihan note the closing of Noma, a restaurant that was synonymous with a version of high-end environmental sustainability. When I read about Noma in January of 2023, it was shortly before reading about the much less heralded closing of a small restaurant called Café Miranda in Rockland, Maine. Over the past half a dozen years, Café Miranda had become a favorite spot for me and my family on summer trips to the "mid-coast," a cozy place with a mix of traditional and more unusual Mediterranean-inflected dishes with indoor/outdoor service just off the main street. The owner, Kerry Altiero (2023), in an article in the *Boston Globe*, describes the forty-year run of Café Miranda as a passion project, a deeply meaningful community-that-becomes-family, a theme that David Beriss and I found running through many of the contributions to our collection of anthropological studies of restaurants (Beriss and Sutton 2007). Like our contributors, Altiero notes the contradictions of this family—between the love and joy on the one hand and the hyperexploitation and self-exploitation on the other—that such restaurant passion projects frequently entail: "We ran it so efficiently, and we put so much soul and so much heart into it, and we made a difference in the community, in the history of Maine. And what happened is that that model is toast. It's gone."[3] Similarly, the closing of Noma suggested that environmental sustainability and social sustainability had come crashing into each other, and that the myth of New Nordic cuisine more broadly was exactly that, a myth. As one reporter noted (West-Knights 2022), "the best restaurant in the world relied heavily on unpaid labour to produce its food." Even those workers who were paid described working in the Copenhagen restaurant industry as a "kidnapping from life." Abusive relationships that get passed on from head chefs to sous-chefs and on down can be seen as a "dark flipside of the restaurant-as-family metaphor" (West-Knights 2022). The ongoing sexual abuse that has only begun to be addressed in the wake of #MeToo is another.[4]

Café Miranda owner Kerry Altiero ends his article with a plea for a new model of restaurants, "one that works, and is sustainable." But what is sustainable? This book, as the first collection of its kind to address restaurant sustainability from a (primarily) anthropological perspective, provides diverse answers. Sustainability is "a complex process involving the construction of norms that translate into operational practices, rather than a definitive end point" (Gvion). "Sustainable food seeks to nourish all bodies, create jobs with living wages, and apply practices that will not further damage the environment, ensuring that future generations will be able to feed themselves" (Black). "Just sustainability . . . emphasizes the importance of social justice alongside environmental needs" (Navarro). We learn that, "As a refutation to a resource extraction–based economy, Indigenous peoples practice and honor their sustainable relationships. A Cherokee word that describes a sustainable relationship is *digadatsele'i* or 'we belong to each other' " (Gora).

But this collection also explores the competing and contradictory aspects of sustainability, as Elizabeth Hoover describes the trade-offs between buying "local" and buying "Native foods" for the Tocabe restaurant, and David Beriss and Lauren Darnell note the different raced visions of sustainability in New Orleans, arguing that any serious debate about sustainability must include culture. Running through all the empirically grounded perspectives of the different contributions is the sense "that sustainability is something you do, and it has to be understood, learned, and trained in practice," though it should not simply be defined individually as "a big box of possible actions" (Højlund and Bech). It is based on "relational values [that] often emerge from specific contexts" (Talib and Trubek) and on an "ethics of care" that extends beyond the human

(Matta). Much of it involves remembering and revaluing specific ingredients that have been forgotten through processes of commodity fetishism, racism, and colonialism, and thus sustainability must involve "decolonizing the table . . . by repopulating it with the tastes of its Indigenous cuisines" (Fontefrancesco and Zocchi). All these examples point to the importance of an anthropological perspective that not only stresses context but also highlights the importance of considering the social and the sensory dimensions of sustainability, as well as the cultural, as key aspects of a vision that imagines commensality as a regenerative and revivifying practice (Sutton 2021). As Santiago Rosero and Joan Gross note, in Ecuador, "people organize parties to collect wasted food, turn it into soup, and eat and dance together."

Restaurants are full of contradictions, between public and private, "home" and business, gift and commodity, which perhaps is why they have been dubbed prototypical "third spaces" (Beriss and Sutton 2007). While Tunde Wey suggests that they provide a particular lens on the "intersection of capital, finance, social life, food production [and] sustenance" (Rosner 2020), this complexity means that for some, restaurants might become images of a better, noncommodified life (though often specifically in times of crisis).[5] Hospitality is a sacred trust, the central value in many societies, and, as anthropologists well know, a practice full of contradictions and even hostility, a word to which it is etymologically closely related. This led philosopher Jacques Derrida to coin the playful term "hostipitality" to capture "the troubling analogy in their common origin" (2000, 15).[6] This collection provides a sophisticated and engaging way in to the ongoing contradictions of an industry that seems to show both the worst aspects of capitalist commodification of life and sustenance and our greatest potential for bridging differences and making connections that might challenge this deeply unsustainable system, helping us find ways to emerge from the rubble of ongoing crisis with possibilities for sustainable and regenerative futures.

DAVID SUTTON

Notes

1. See, e.g., Gunderson 2020 on the way that public restaurant space during the early days of COVID was conceptualized to the benefit of San Francisco's elite and at the expense of the homeless population.
2. See also Rosner 2020.

3. At the time of writing, the owner of Café Miranda had announced plans to open a food truck in the fall of 2023.
4. See the discussion of changes in the James Beard Award instituted since 2022 to address sexual abuse and lack of diversity, and their mixed results, at https://www.nytimes.com/2023/06/13/podcasts/the-daily/james-beard-awards.html.
5. See Lee 2020 on how some restaurants worked to help feed laid-off restaurant workers during COVID.
6. See also Mishan 2023; Sutton 2024.

References

Altiero, Kerry (as told to Kelly Horan). 2023. "The Old Restaurant Model Is Toast." *Boston Globe*, February 9. https://www.bostonglobe.com/2023/02/09/opinion/old-restaurant-model-is-toast/.

Beriss, David, and David Sutton, eds. 2007. *The Restaurants Book: Ethnographies of Where We Eat*. Oxford: Berg.

Callison, William, and Zachary Manfredi, eds. 2020. *Mutant Neoliberalism: Market Rules and Political Rupture*. New York: Fordham University Press.

Derrida, Jacques. 2000. "Hostipitality." *Angelaki: Journal of Theoretical Humanities.* 5 (3): 3-18.

Gunderson, Ariana. 2020. "The Illegitimate Tent: Private Use of Public Space at a San Francisco Restaurant." *Food and Foodways* 28 (4): 321–31.

Lee, Alicia. 2020. "Chefs Across the US Are Transforming Their Restaurants into Relief Centers for Laid-Off Restaurant Workers." CNN, March 20. https://www.cnn.com/travel/article/coronavirus-restaurant-workers-relief-trnd/index.html/.

Mirowski, Philip. 2014. *Never Let a Serious Crisis Go to Waste: How Neoliberalism Survived the Financial Meltdown*. London: Verso.

Mishan, Ligaya. 2023. "When Did Hospitality Get So Hostile?" *New York Times T Magazine*, February 10. https://www.nytimes.com/2023/02/10/t-magazine/restaurants-hostile-eating-out.html?searchResultPosition=1.

Rosner, Helen. 2020. "The Case for Letting the Restaurant Industry Die." *New Yorker*, May 22. https://www.newyorker.com/culture/annals-of-gastronomy/the-case-for-letting-the-restaurant-industry-die.

Sutton, David. 2021. "Revivifying Commensality: Eating, Politics, and the Sensory Production of the Social." In *Moveable Gardens: Itineraries and Sanctuaries of Memory*, edited by V. Nazarea and T. Gagnon, 133–60. Tucson: University of Arizona Press.

———. 2024. "The Hospitality Illusion." *Gastronomica* 24 (2): 1–5.

West-Knights, Imogen. 2022. "Fine Dining Faces Its Dark Truths in Copenhagen." *FT Magazine*, June. https://www.ft.com/content/a62a96b8-2db2-44ec-ac80-67fcf83d86ef.

Wey, Tunde. 2020. "Let It Die." https://mailchi.mp/0968a99c87a8/dont-bail-out-the-restaurant-industry.

PREFACE AND ACKNOWLEDGMENTS

This book began in 2019 when Susanne called me on Skype and said, "I have an idea for a new project." By then I had learned that Susanne's ideas were always worth listening to and that she was an inspiring, affable, and efficient collaborator. She had hosted me as a visiting professor at Aarhus University in 2014 for a month when we hashed out ideas about taste with students and colleagues, which led to our edited book *Making Taste Public: Ethnographies of Food and the Senses* (2018). When Susanne proposed we do a new edited collection together exploring how chefs and restaurants construct and practice culinary sustainability, I said, "Of course!" I thank you, Susanne, for your stimulating ideas and your friendship. I thank my family—brothers, sister, children, grandchildren, and above all, my husband, Jim Taggart—for their love and support.

CAROLE COUNIHAN

Ideas are never produced on one's own. After having worked with, visited, and developed a friendship with Carole (and her husband, Jim), it is not surprising that from good dialogues with clever friends, new ideas come to one's mind. I would call it synergy. With our years of inspiring collaboration within food culture research—and based on shared interests in taste, cooking, food culture, and food activism—it was natural to ask the following question: How do chefs around the world respond to the new demands for sustainable cooking? Our idea was that instead of imagining and speculating about this, instead of idealizing, moralizing, and politicizing, there was a need for exploring it empirically in local contexts. Before we set up new ideals and standards for sustainable restaurant practices, we need to know more about what enables and what inhibits these practices. It has been a great inspiration to learn about this from our authors. I thank all the dedicated researchers, chefs, educators, and colleagues who have taken part in this project over the last several years. A special thanks to my family for always supporting me in trying to understand how food, taste culture, and culinary practices are interwoven.

SUSANNE HØJLUND

Here we are, several years after the first seeds were planted with a book based on the work of a wonderful group of scholars. In the meantime, the COVID-19 pandemic struck with a vengeance and upended everyone's plans—personal and scholarly—those of our contributors among them. They forged on with their research, met our evolving deadlines, and assiduously responded to our suggested revisions. Their empirical research shows chefs reducing waste, lightening their environmental footprint, and fostering social and economic reproduction through buying local, practicing veganism, enhancing taste, and cooking free meals from products rescued from the waste system. We thank our contributors for their provocative original contributions to understanding culinary sustainability, and we thank David Sutton for reflecting upon them in the foreword. At the University of Arkansas Press, we thank David Scott Cunningham, David Cajias Calvet, Janet Foxman, Food and Foodways series editors Jennifer Jensen Wallach and Michael Wise, and the anonymous reviewers for their feedback and good ideas.

CAROLE COUNIHAN AND SUSANNE HØJLUND

CHEFS, RESTAURANTS, AND CULINARY SUSTAINABILITY

INTRODUCTION

Chefs, Restaurants, and Culinary Sustainability

SUSANNE HØJLUND AND
CAROLE COUNIHAN

Introduction

Worldwide we are in what has been named a "polycrisis" involving climate change, loss of biodiversity, the COVID-19 pandemic, inflation, food insecurity, conflict, and war (Altieri 2022). The food system is affected by it all, and as such it figures as both a problem and a solution. It is a problem because "the global food system is a leading driver of climate change" (Altieri 2022). It is a solution, because the food system is populated with people who have the ability to respond to the crisis through changed practices. The restaurant industry is a huge player in this system, reaching approximately $3 trillion in sales in 2017 (Cravy 2018). Until the COVID-19 pandemic dealt it a severe blow, it had been in steady and consistent growth for several decades, and it still is expected to expand all over the globe in the coming years, with total industry employment reaching almost fifteen million by the end of 2022 (National Restaurant Association 2022).

Restaurants of many types and cuisines, from snack shacks to fine dining, are part of the explosive development worldwide. Engaged chefs, restaurant workers, and food makers are central drivers in this growth, and they cannot simply build on former practices and traditions. The future food makers and restaurateurs have to think and act in new ways.

They have to address the polycrisis. We posit that they can do so through the frame of sustainability by developing alternatives to traditional culinary practices. Our mission here is to explore some of those alternatives and show how sustainability can be a productive guideline within the food system.

Increasing amounts of literature and political statements address what sustainability is or ought to be, how it is threatened, and how it can be used to rethink and rebuild the food industry. As a result of the increased industrialization during the twentieth century, the discussion about sustainable development has been ongoing for many years (Purvis, Mao, and Robinson 2019). The United Nations report *Our Common Future* is most often mentioned as a main document laying the groundwork for the concept of sustainability as "meet[ing] the needs of the present without compromising the ability of future generations to meet their own needs" (1987, 16). Sustainable development is here explained as a "three pillar model" with economic, environmental, and social dimensions. The three pillars are actually often represented as three overlapping circles, each part of one another, and in the middle shaping sustainability together (Barbier 1987). This model has been criticized for being too rigorous, for not taking culture into account, and for not making visible how the three parts of sustainability impact one another (Purvis, Mao, and Robinson 2019). It has also been criticized as being too broad, vague, universalizing, unmeasurable, too late to save the planet, and as being a crutch for "greenwashing" (Dernbach and Cheever 2015).

Nevertheless, it is an influential model that has shaped the background for the seventeen Sustainable Development Goals (SDGs) developed in 2015 at a United Nations conference in Rio de Janeiro, Brazil (United Nations 2015). These have garnered great interest, especially for their visual representation of relevant topics and their ability to create direction and guidelines for actions toward sustainability. In general, most discussions of sustainability are either at an abstract, philosophical level ("how did the concept develop and which discourses shaped it") or at a moral, activist level ("we ought to be more sustainable"). The first approach often ends with the conclusion that definitions of sustainability are multifaceted and blurred (e.g., Béné et al., 2019; Brightmann and Lewis 2017); the second approach often describes goals to reach without taking into the account the many obstacles people meet when acting in practice. The *EAT-Lancet Report* is an example of a such a generalist approach, outlining the principles for a diet that is needed for a sustainable future of both planet and people: "A planetary healthy plate should consist by volume of approximately half a plate of vegetables and fruits; the other half, displayed by contribution to calories, should consist of primarily whole grains, plant protein sources, unsaturated plant oils, and (optionally) modest amounts of animal sources of protein" (EAT-Lancet Commission 2019, 9). Although the report mentions once the need to consider "local and regional realities" (9), it never addresses how to do so to actually achieve this recommended dietary transition. Moreover, sustainability is often treated as a universalist concept as if it is the same for everyone, no matter where they live on the planet. But, as Ben Purvis, Yong Mao, and Darren Robinson (2019) caution, sustainability is "inherently political . . . and we should be careful to avoid reproducing models without carefully considering their theoretical basis and the embedded ideology within them." Therefore, it is important to define sustainability clearly in any given social and historical context.

There is currently a strong need for producing and sharing knowledge about sustainability that can contribute to uncovering the problems, potentials, and inspiration for action within the food system. "Food system" is, though, another abstract term, which has to be defined in relation to specific contexts (Smetana, Bornkessel, and Heinz 2019) where diverse visions of sustainable futures are interpreted and enacted (Heatherington 2014; Orlando 2011).

Restaurants provide a specific frame for analyzing sustainability. A few articles and reports, produced for the restaurant sector, building on interviews with chefs and restaurateurs, discuss barriers and challenges for working with sustainability in practice (Higgins-Desbiolles, Wijesinghe, and Moskwa 2015; Kasim and Ismail 2011; National Restaurant Association 2018). These studies mainly focus on challenges and problem solving, and to a lesser degree on making a theoretical contribution to the field. Our contribution to the current debates on restaurant sustainability is empirical research revealing how people in diverse culinary contexts interpret the concept and take action in relation to it. We aim to move from the theoretical and philosophical discussions of the concept to ethnographic insights, shedding light on how people engaged in local food systems understand the demand for sustainable change and adapt their practices accordingly. Thus, we decided to learn from chefs themselves about their approaches to sustainability.

Our Approach to Restaurant Sustainability

Recognizing that change has to come from human beings, we invited researchers within the field of restaurant studies to share their work on chefs in specific cultural, historical, political, and economic settings and to place them in the context of relevant cross-disciplinary scholarly literature. Inspired by the "three pillar model," our authors have considered sustainability as a process with social, economic, and environmental dimensions, but at the same time they have challenged and enhanced this definition by focusing on how people bring it to action in local contexts.

We asked contributors for reflections on questions such as: How do chefs and other food professionals in restaurants, cafeterias, and institutional kitchens understand and practice sustainability? How do they interpret the term? Is sustainability a business model, a social movement, a driver for tourism, or a means of local development? What are the motivations, the challenges, the potentials, the ideologies? Do restaurateurs seek to reduce waste, promote community, or educate customers? Which tactics do they deploy: managing food waste, planning a circular economy, connecting to local producers, gardening, foraging, developing new menus, reorganizing the kitchen, or developing new technologies, for example? How has the coronavirus pandemic affected sustainability efforts, not to mention the very survival of restaurants? What new definitions and forms of sustainability have emerged?

Hence, we approach sustainability not through defining it as a fixed concept, but through empirical, qualitative research on a wide range of chefs working in many types of restaurants in diverse locales across the globe. We focus on chefs because they have an enormous impact on people's food consumption and thereby on the health and biodiversity of the planet. Our contributors investigate diverse chefs' stories and perspectives through interviews, observations, and media analysis. They cover chefs who work in school cafeterias, culinary classrooms, workplace canteens, research laboratories, and humble and fancy farm-to-chef, vegan, and ethnic restaurants. These studies represent wide geographical, racial, and ethnic diversity with cases from Denmark, France, Norway, Colombia, Ecuador, Israel, Kenya, and the United States—including African American, Native American, and white chefs in Philadelphia, New Orleans, Connecticut, and Vermont.

Our contributors document chefs carrying out a wide range of different roles and responsibilities to advance sustainability. These chefs educate themselves and others about forgotten foods, local ingredients, vegan dishes, and delicious tastes. They teach children and youth to cook from scratch and eat healthily and they mentor other chefs. They reduce food waste and forge relationships with farmers and fishers to source ingredients. They build alliances with community members to promote food security and food sovereignty and become activists against cultural and culinary erasure, environmental degradation, waste, inequality in the food system, and food insecurity. We propose to label this practical work of restaurants toward sustainable futures as culinary sustainability.

Defining Culinary Sustainability

Culinary sustainability consists of the ways that cooking, cuisine, and kitchen work foster cultural, social, economic, and environmental survival and reproduction. It is rooted in both cultural and biological diversity. Culinary sustainability involves not only safeguarding environmental resources but also critically evaluating the intertwined cultural habits, economic imperatives, labor and client relationships, power dynamics, and daily activities of feeding and eating that shape the human use of the environment. Culinary sustainability consists of the embodied practices of chefs as they cook, forge tastes, rescue forgotten or disparaged foods, source locally, and promote vegetarian, organic, and traditional dishes with a complex sustainability agenda in mind. Central to our inquiry is just sustainability, the belief that food equity, security, and sovereignty are critical to successful environmental, economic, and social survival (Agyeman, Bullard, and Evans 2015).

Chefs' efforts for culinary sustainability are partial, incremental, evolving, and responsive to socioeconomic forces. Their impacts are usually small, with the possible exception of research chefs (see Deutsch's chapter in this volume), but nonetheless they are significant in raising awareness and providing models for action. They demand a continual balancing act between costs and returns. Some chefs aim for culinary sustainability by reducing waste, rescuing food destined for the dump, and using disregarded ingredients. Others aim to redress food insecurity by relying on community networks to cover costs and providing inexpensive or free food to poor and hungry folks. Indigenous and African American chefs aim for food sovereignty and cultural survival by highlighting their own traditional foods. Some chefs tout their efforts at sustainability and use it as a brand to define their identity and attract customers, while others downplay it and focus on the taste, healthiness, or distinctiveness of their cuisine. Some see culinary sustainability as an individual pursuit while others emphasize that it is a collective responsibility carried out through alliances with producers, policymakers, and community members.

The Book

We have grouped the fifteen chapters into four sections highlighting four important and overlapping themes that emerged in chefs' promotion of culinary sustainability: taste, kitchen practices, social relations, and activism. Together they emphasize a sensory, a practical, a relational, and a cultural-political dimension of culinary sustainability. These themes run throughout the book but are particularly prominent in the chapters in their sections.

Culinary Sustainability and Taste

The first section highlights the role of taste in an array of chefs' sustainable practices. Good tastes can increase consumption of healthy local foods and reduce waste while strengthening diverse traditions and communities. In chapter 1, anthropologist Rachel E. Black describes her ethnographic study of renowned chef Dan Giusti's Brigaid project to transform school food in New London, Connecticut, by introducing good tastes generated through cooking from scratch, using quality ingredients, and incorporating student feedback. The project heightened social, economic, and environmental sustainability by nourishing students, decreasing waste, sourcing from local farmers, and developing a more skilled kitchen work force.

In chapter 2, anthropologists Ana María Ulloa and Laura Garzón underscore the role of the senses, especially taste, in advancing culinary sustainability in chef Eduardo Martínez's Mini-Mal restaurant in Bogotá, Colombia. Colombia suffers from unequal distribution of land and resources, marginalization of peasant farming, and high food insecurity, creating challenges to attaining sustainability that Mini-Mal countered in several ways. It introduced to its urban clientele important and overlooked foods and flavors from the countryside, paid fair prices to farmers and validated their work, and expanded knowledge of rural and Indigenous foodways across Colombia. Taste served as the engine to reproduce biodiversity, uphold cultural diversity, and support creativity as the restaurant featured unknown or denigrated agricultural products from marginalized regions.

In chapter 3, cultural studies scholar Jonatan Leer explores the role of taste in a very different setting, the upscale vegan restaurant Bellies in Stavanger, Norway. Although fully aware that increasing plant consumption contributes to environmental sustainability, Bellies downplayed its vegan identity in its self-presentation and marketing, instead focusing on serving clients sensorily rich and tasty dishes. The story of Bellies reveals the significant role of contemporary chefs in advancing sustainability by serving delicious vegan food and the conundrum they face about if and how to advertise it.

In chapter 4, Ole G. Mouritsen and Klavs Styrbæk, a gastrophysicist and a chef, also aim to enhance sustainability through taste, but they focus very specifically on the taste of umami. They face head on the challenges of attaining culinary sustainability in a world that adores meat but where plant consumption is far more sustainable. Rather than interrogating the cultural and sensory significance of umami, they take it for granted and have collaborated over many years to figure out how to use umami taste to increase the consumption of what they consider unpalatable plant foods. They have developed an umami "taste and texture rack" of condiments and sauces to transform vegetables and legumes into delicious dishes by "umamification," which they demonstrate with the recipe for a vegetarian Bolognese sauce for pasta. This chapter shows how a chef and his collaborator take a concrete, food-focused approach and use the science of taste to nudge people's food consumption toward a more sustainable vegetarian diet.

Culinary Sustainability and Kitchen Practices

Chapters in the second section highlight how chefs are engaged in varied and evolving kitchen practices to advance economic, social, and environmental sustainability in response to consumer preferences, economic exigencies, and sourcing opportunities. In chapter 5, anthropologist Raúl Matta describes four Parisian chefs' discontent with the wasteful and environmentally damaging mainstream restaurant industry and their everyday efforts toward culinary sustainability. He interviewed a chef working at the staff canteen of the Paris Institute for Advanced Study, one working at an informal eatery catering to the staff of the Centquatre arts center, and two working at small neighborhood restaurants in the Paris suburbs. Although they admitted that their sustainability measures had limited scope and impact and that larger sociopolitical policy changes were needed, they believed that their small efforts were nonetheless important in propagating fair work conditions, quality local food, and trust from clients and suppliers, which are key to social, economic, and environmental sustainability.

Vegan restaurants are the focus of chapter 6, where sociologist Liora Gvion explores how chefs in modest vegan establishments in Tel Aviv, Israel, think about sustainability. For them it is an ad hoc, complex, and evolving process. They procure fresh local food and limit the use of industrial food where economically and logistically feasible. However, they compromise to please customers or to help the bottom line—for instance, by using industrially produced meat substitutes and by purchasing cheaper imported products. Ultimately, they define vegan food as healthy for bodies and the environment and its consumption as thus inherently sustainable.

Anthropologists Susanne Højlund and Nanna Hammer Bech shift the focus in chapter 7 from chefs preparing food in restaurants to training programs for student chefs. They conducted anthropological fieldwork at four Danish culinary schools to explore how students and teachers learn about sustainability and define their roles in the green transition. They found no dominant paradigm of sustainability; rather, it is a new and challenging frame with many definitions grounded in personal experiences of the teachers and students and constantly reformulated through kitchen craftsmanship.

In chapter 8, food studies scholar and chef Jonathan Deutsch examines a sector of professional cooking that is often overlooked but is extremely influential—research chefs or "Culinologists®" who work behind the scenes in laboratories or experimental kitchens developing products for the food industry. Deutsch interviewed ten research chefs about their complex challenges in promoting more sustainable food practices while also attaining "supply chain consistency, regulatory compliance, consumer satisfaction, and profitability." They found that more environmentally sustainable practices were often less economically sustainable, but they used their kitchen craft to forge successful strategies such as upcycling and educating consumers about industrial food production and the higher costs of environmentally friendly products.

Research chefs and all the professional chefs featured in this book were enmeshed in complex social relations with coworkers, bosses, suppliers, and clients that had to be maintained and that were instrumental to the survival of their entire enterprise, whether it be designing packaged brownies in a cooking lab, establishing supply networks with local farmers, or sustaining culturally diverse communities. In chapter 9, food systems scholar Sarra Talib and anthropologist Amy Trubek examine the importance of farm-to-chef social commitments in helping Vermont restaurants survive the COVID-19 pandemic. When these restaurants saw global supply chains failing them and prices rising, they pivoted to sourcing from local farmers whom they knew well, trusted, and were able to communicate with directly, enabling them to keep their restaurants stocked, their staff employed, and local farmers in business. Vermont chefs were able to continue feeding their community during the COVID-19 lockdown by experimenting with curbside takeout, meal kits, partial opening, and delivery. They maintained their social, economic, and environmental sustainability in spite of the pandemic and increased their already existing commitment to local provisioning and community food networks.

In chapter 10, anthropologist David Beriss and executive director of the Made in New Orleans foundation Lauren Darnell explore the sustainability of New Orleans restaurants, particularly those featuring seafood, in the aftermath of the COVID-19 pandemic. They interviewed a dozen African American and white chefs about their perceptions of sustainability and seafood in Louisiana. Seafood has always been essential to New Orleans culinary culture, but access to affordable seafood has been uncertain because of oil spills, hurricanes, pollution, overfishing, and the pandemic. In the interviews, white chefs focused on threats to the seafood catch whereas Black chefs focused on threats to New Orleans culinary culture, revealing divergent definitions and practices of sustainability, particularly in regard to the role of community.

In chapter 11, anthropologist Elizabeth Hoover relies on her decade of research with twenty-eight Native American chefs to explore Indigenous food sovereignty and just sustainability. She gives several examples of how Native chefs introduced underutilized species and traditional foods to support Indigenous producers and farming practices and to safeguard the agrobiodiversity of their homelands. They also aimed to support their communities socially and economically through their restaurants by creating jobs, mentoring young chefs, providing gathering places, and reproducing Indigenous culinary culture. Their businesses centered simultaneously on food justice and culinary justice—making food widely accessible and establishing the inherent worth of the cuisine of oppressed peoples. Hoover's chapter demonstrates that sustaining diverse communities is an essential force in movements for food justice and sustainability, a theme explored further in the next section.

Culinary Sustainability and Diversity, Equity, and Activism

Many chefs discussed in this book had an activist component in their approach to sustainability. The last four chapters examine diverse ways—whether implicit or explicit, individual or collective—that chefs practice food activism, "efforts to promote social and economic justice by transforming food habits" (Counihan 2019, 1). In chapter 12, ethnic studies scholar Marilisa Navarro analyzes six articles published from 2020 to 2022 in the daily newspaper the *Philadelphia Inquirer*. These articles highlighted the food activism of Black chefs and restaurateurs in Philadelphia, such as organizing community food drives, preparing free box lunches for hundreds of children when schools closed during the pandemic, developing cooking lessons for kids, mentoring other chefs in the restaurant business, and exalting African American and African-diasporic cultural foods. These chefs fostered just sustainability by advancing community food security, Black entrepreneurship, Black collaboration, and mutual aid.

Black Philadelphia chefs' food activism was a long-term strategy that was further stimulated by the COVID-19 pandemic. Chapter 13 describes a more formal and institutionalized form of food activism— the Slow Food Cooks' Alliance, which was founded in 2009 to advance Slow Food's overriding goals of "good, clean, and fair food," that is, food that is tasty, culturally meaningful, healthy, nonpolluting, and economically just. Anthropologists Michele Filippo Fontefrancesco and Dauro Mattia Zocchi studied the Cooks' Alliance in Kenya by conducting ethnographic life history interviews with eleven chefs working in diverse settings, including school and office canteens and upscale and humble restaurants. The chefs fostered environmental, economic, and cultural sustainability by reintroducing neglected and forgotten local products marginalized during the colonial period. They heightened awareness of and pride in Kenyan culinary culture, propagated traditional cooking practices, and enhanced the local farming economy.

In chapter 14 cultural historian L. Sasha Gora studies sustainability in the few Indigenous restaurants in the United States through accounts in local and national newspapers and chefs' own self-representations. She uncovers outsiders' quizzical and exoticizing attitudes toward Indigenous foods, which insiders in contrast promote as contributing to what Gora calls Indigenous culinary sustainability. This involves reciprocity between humans and nature, the exaltation of Native cuisine and its forgotten ingredients, the employment of Natives in the restaurants, and Indigenous food sovereignty—all of which face obstacles from lack of access to land and water, environmental degradation, economic marginalization, and cultural disruption.

In chapter 15, journalist and chef Santiago Rosero teams up with anthropologist Joan Gross to discuss Rosero's efforts in Ecuador to utilize food rescued from the waste system to create delicious meals, improve restaurant sustainability, and feed hungry people. Rosero also holds workshops to teach others about "optimization cooking," which minimizes waste by using otherwise discarded raw materials such as overripe produce, peels, and stems. The goal is to serve as a model for other restaurants and patrons to follow in enhancing sustainability.

Conclusion

The research presented in this book demonstrates that chefs around the world are working intensively in common actions to create more sustainable food systems. Culinary sustainability points to work that happens within specific contexts where people are preparing, cooking, presenting, and serving food and developing multiple meanings and practices of sustainability. The various chapters show that it is a complex frame and an ongoing process that affects many levels of food work. There is no universal definition of sustainability (Farley and Smith 2020), and no single path to effect it. Nevertheless, there is a growing awareness that many current practices should not continue and that new practices must be developed.

Since we began this project, this awareness has grown and a lot has already happened. The Danish restaurant Noma and other leading high-end restaurants have relinquished the expensive and exhausting fine-dining model. "It's unsustainable," Noma's chef René Redzepi said of the model that he helped create. "Financially and emotionally, as an employer and as a human being, it just doesn't work." He developed awareness that economic and environmental sustainability cannot be envisioned and enacted without social sustainability (Moskin 2023). Running a fine-dining kitchen simply has too many human costs and consequences to be sustainable. In relation to the theme of this book, the interesting aspect is that this is not just a single chef questioning the sustainability of fine dining, but rather a growing movement.

The Chefs' Manifesto is another example of how chefs see themselves as activists and powerful advocates for sustainable cooking. This is an initiative, related to the UN Sustainability Goals, that is explained at their website: "The Chefs' Manifesto is a chef-led project that brings together 1100+ chefs from around the world to explore how they can help deliver a sustainable food system."[1] Other chefs have intensified their collaboration with farmers and food producers in order to develop regenerative practices. In the growing regeneration movement sustainability is not enough.[2] Thinking in regenerative terms it becomes clear that a better culinary future includes action that, in effect, gives more back to the Earth than it takes— not merely avoiding the "unsustainable" but participating in repair work. The concept of One Health is embracing this strategy by guiding us to think about the interdependency between humans and the planet, and to address the point that healthy food for people should also be healthy for the planet (Dye 2022). All in all, there is a movement toward a more collective and activist approach to sustainability, more new concepts and thought models to learn from, and more and more chefs who engage in these activities. Culinary sustainability is an ongoing practice that forces chefs to continue to learn, collaborate, and innovate—in their respective social and cultural contexts. We hope this book can continue to inspire this work.

Notes

1. https://sdg2advocacyhub.org/chefs-manifesto.
2. https://www.regenerators.co/what-we-do, https://futurefoodinstitute.org/academy/boot-camps/regeneration-tracks/kitchens/.

References

Agyeman, Julian, Robert Bullard, and Bob Evans, eds. 2015. *Just Sustainabilities: Development in an Unequal World*. Cambridge, MA: MIT Press.
Altieri, M. A. 2022. "Agroecology, Climate Change Induced Polycrisis and the Transformation of Food Systems." https://www.e-ir.info/2022/04/20/agroecology-climate-change-induced-polycrisis-and-the-transformation-of-food-systems/.

Barbier, E. B. 1987. "The Concept of Sustainable Economic Development." *Environmental Conservation* 14 (2): 101–10. https://doi.org/10.1017/S0376892900011449.

Béné, Christopher, Peter Oosterveer, Lea Lamotte, Inge D. Brouwer, Stef de Haan, Steve D. Prager, Elise F. Talsma, and Colin K. Khoury. 2019. "When Food Systems Meet Sustainability: Current Narratives and Implications for Actions." *World Development* 113(C): 116–30.

Brightmann, Marc, and Jerome Lewis. 2017. *The Anthropology of Sustainability. Beyond Development and Progress.* London: Palgrave Macmillan.

Counihan, Carole. 2019. *Italian Food Activism in Urban Sardinia: Taste, Place, and Community.* Oxford: Bloomsbury.

Cravy. 2018: "The Restaurant Industry: A Global Perspective." Medium, October 2. https://medium.com/@CravyHQ/the-restaurant-industry-a-global-perspective-26cea1b91701.

Dernbach, John C., and Federico Cheever. 2015. "Sustainable Development and Its Discontents." *Journal of Transnational Environmental Law* 4 (2): 247–87. https://doi.org/10.1017/S2047102515000163.

Dye, C. 2022. "One Health as a Catalyst for Sustainable Development." *Nature Microbiology* 7 (4): 467–68.

EAT-Lancet Commission on Food, Planet, Health. 2019. *Summary Report: Food. Planet. Health. Healthy Diets from Sustainable Food Systems.* https://eatforum.org/content/uploads/2019/07/EAT-Lancet_Commission_Summary_Report.pdf.

Farley, Heather M., and Zachary A. Smith. 2020. *Sustainability: If It's Everything, Is It Nothing?* 2nd ed. London: Routledge. https://doi.org/10.4324/9781351124928.

Heatherington, Tracey. 2014. "Tasting Cultural Ecology: Foodscapes of Sustainability in the Mediterranean." *Gastronomica: The Journal of Critical Food Studies* 14 (2): 16–26.

Higgins-Desbiolles, Freya, Gayathri Wijesinghe, and Emily Moskwa. 2015. *A Taste of Sustainability: Case Studies of Sustainable Cafes in Australia.* Melbourne: University of South Australia, Analysis and Policy Observatory. https://doi.org/10.13140/RG.2.1.1200.6882.

Kasim, Azilah, and Anida Ismail. 2011. "Environmentally Friendly Practices among Restaurants: Drivers and Barriers to Change." *Journal of Sustainable Tourism* 20 (4): 551–70.

Moskin, Julia. 2023. "Noma, Rated the World's Best Restaurant, Is Closing Its Doors." *New York Times,* January 9. https://www.nytimes.com/2023/01/09/dining/noma-closing-rene-redzepi.html?searchResultPosition=4.

National Restaurant Association. 2018. *The State of Restaurant Sustainability.* https://restaurant.org/nra/media/downloads/pdfs/sustainability/restaurant_sustainability_research_report_2018.pdf.

———. 2022. *State of the Restaurant Industry.* https://restaurant.org/state-of-the-industry/.

Orlando, G. 2011. "Sustainable Food vs. Unsustainable Politics in the City of Palermo: The Case of an Organic Farmers' Market." *City & Society* 23 (2): 173–91.

Purvis, Ben, Yong Mao, and Darren Robinson. 2019. "Three Pillars of Sustainability: In Search of Conceptual Origins." *Sustainability Science* 14:681–95.

Smetana, S., S. Bornkessel, and V. Heinz. 2019. "A Path from Sustainable Nutrition to Nutritional Sustainability of Complex Food Systems." *Frontiers in Nutrition* 6:39.

United Nations. 1987. *Our Common Future: Report of the World Commission on Environment and Development*. https://sustainabledevelopment.un.org/content /documents/5987our-common-future.pdf.

———. 2015. *The 17 Goals*. https://sdgs.un.org/goals.

PART I

Culinary Sustainability and Taste

CHAPTER ONE

Chefs Creating Tasty and Sustainable School Food in the United States

RACHEL E. BLACK

Introduction

"When we were getting ready to launch Brigaid, a lot of people were skeptical about having chefs come run school kitchens. They thought we would make fancy food that would cost too much money. People were really wary of having us here. I knew we had a lot to prove in those first few months." These were the words of Dan Giusti—former chef de cuisine at Noma in Copenhagen, often touted as the world's best restaurant and pioneer of the hyperlocal New Nordic Cuisine movement—when we first met in 2016 to talk about Brigaid, his pilot project to transform school food in New London, Connecticut.

In discussions of school food in the United States, the question of taste is rarely addressed, much to the detriment of the success and sustainability of school feeding programs. Micah Trapp has argued for the consideration of "the right to taste," which is critical for the "social processes of nourishment" and which can provide a way of looking at the intersections between taste and food aid (2018, 17). The Brigaid pilot project reveals the politics of taste involved in feeding children and its more tangible outcomes; in particular, this research shows the important and often-overlooked ties between taste and sustainability. Much scholarly attention has been given to the politics (Gaddis 2019; Levine 2010; Ruis 2017) and nutrition of school food (Dunifon and Kowaleski-Jones 2003; Jaime and Lock 2009) in the United States and to how to fix the broken National School Lunch Program (NSLP) (Poppendieck 2010). However, the Brigaid case offers a unique perspective for understanding the role of chefs and the place of taste within the frameworks set out by the United States Department of Agriculture (USDA) in the NSLP and how a focus on taste can lead to more sustainable school food.

The definition of sustainability here does not mean the sustaining of a broken food system and an even more dysfunctional school feeding program. Sustainability is employed with a social justice focus that pushes back against the inequalities of late capitalism—sustainable food seeks to nourish all bodies, create jobs with living wages, and apply practices that will not further damage the environment, ensuring that future generations will be able to feed themselves. Following this line of reasoning, school food should sustain students' bodies and health, first and foremost, but it also has the potential to sustain the local economy through the creation of a skilled school-kitchen workforce and through support for local farms. School food can also be more environmentally sustainable through waste reduction, and here is where food that tastes good to kids can play an important role. Taste is defined here as the sensual, corporeal experience of food that validates individuals' experience. Taste is not taken as a concept tied to an ideal way to eat but rather as a subjective choice and judgment that gives children agency over their own experiences and bodies (Leer and Wistoft 2018). This chapter takes into consideration the challenges and contradictions that are present in definitions of sustainable food systems and seeks to give a central place to the social conception of sustainability from the perspectives both of labor in school kitchens and the culturally appropriate nature of school food (Béné et al. 2019).

Methods

During the fall semester of 2016, I began following the launch of the Brigaid program in the New London School District, from three schools at first to a total of five by the end of the school year in June 2017. Initially, I started this research with my students as part of a course on sustainable food systems. We met with Dan Giusti and he told us more about his vision for Brigaid. We asked him how we could contribute to the pilot project, and we decided together on a community-engaged ethnographic project to document the early months of the initiative. Dan wanted to understand how students were receiving and adapting to the new food being offered and to the presence of chefs in their lunchrooms. My students were trained in the basics of participant observation, and all of them made several observations of lunch lines and the cafeterias. Along with these observations, I conducted over forty hours of participant observation in the kitchens and cafeterias of two of the first Brigaid schools (a middle school and the only high school in the district). We used semistructured interviews to gather information about school food from teachers, chefs, administrators, and parents (n=12). In addition, I volunteered as a cook once a week for three months at the middle school and high school, which provided me with ample opportunities to observe kitchens, lunch lines, and cafeterias. The informal conversations I had with chefs, cooks, school staff, and children during my shifts gave me insights into how people saw the changes that were taking place. In 2021 and 2022, I did follow-up interviews with the director of child nutrition programs for the school district and the Brigaid chef who is currently in charge of the district. Both of these individuals were involved in the pilot and continue to be central to Brigaid's work in New London. Brigaid has since expanded to school districts in New York, California, and Colorado.

During the initial phase of my research, I interviewed Dan Giusti on several occasions. In one of our first interviews, Giusti told me how he decided to leave his prestigious position of chef de cuisine at Noma to feed children in the United States, where he is from originally: "I was tired of feeding only a few fortunate people. I wanted to feed more people and I wanted to put my skills as a chef to good use." Giusti chose New London to launch his business because the school superintendent was particularly supportive of the program, the district was a manageable size for a pilot, and the Community Eligibility Provision (CEP) was already in place for the NSLP—the schools could serve all students free of charge under the CEP model.[1] In 2015, Feeding America (2015) estimated that the rate of food insecurity in New London County was 11.8 percent, which amounted to 31,670 food-insecure people, and the rate of child food insecurity was 16.8 percent or 8,930 children. For the city of New London, the rate of food insecurity was much higher, at 21 percent (Gunderson et al. 2018), well above the 11.9 percent average for the state of Connecticut. Given these historic poverty rates, school food has been a critical source of nourishment for many children in New London. Giusti and the Brigaid crew are responsible for feeding more than 3,300 children each day on a budget of $3.93 per child for lunch and $2.11 for breakfast (US Federal Register 2022). Brigaid provides hot breakfasts, lunches, and dinners.

All of this falls largely under the purview of some of the biggest federal meal programs in the United States. The National School Lunch Program (NSLP) and School Breakfast Program (SBP) are federally assisted meal programs administered by the United States Department of Agriculture through the Food and Nutrition Service. The NSLP alone cost $14.2 billion in 2019 and is part of the largest title, "Nutrition," in the Farm Bill, which is an omnibus multiyear law that covers agriculture and food programs. The NSLP was first established in 1946 and in 2016 it served 30.4 million children in public and nonprofit private schools.

Brigaid's Philosophy and Early Days in New London

When Giusti first came to tour the schools in New London, they were serving reheated industrially prepared foods in polystyrene foam containers. Giusti observed that the half-defrosted corn muffins were soggy in their plastic wrap and that the students threw away most of the whole apples that they were served at each meal. He saw the opportunity to improve the overall taste of the food, reduce waste, and increase consumption of nutritious food; Giusti was on a mission to bring back scratch cooking and tasty food that kids would want to eat.

Guisti's first argument was that children cannot get good nutrition if they do not eat the food on their plate. His assumption was that if kids weren't eating it, the food must taste bad or look undesirable. Chefs who are used to serving demanding customers in fine dining restaurants are trained to consider the taste and aesthetics of food as a priority. They just need to adjust these parameters to meet the aesthetics and tastes of children. In addition to tasting good, food also needs to look good, even in a school cafeteria (Hagen 2021; Paakki et al. 2019). This is particularly true given the relationship between the visual cues that children take from food and a potential tendency toward neophobia, a reluctance to try new foods (Bäckström, Pirttilä-Backman, and Tuorila 2004). Much American school food is monochromatic and the central ingredients are indiscernible. Giusti has attempted to make sure that the food is colorful, that its freshness is apparent, and that children can understand what they are eating from looking at it. This may sound simple, but it turned out to be much more complicated than anyone had first imagined, particularly given the budgetary constraints, the need to reorder the kitchen spaces in schools, and the reskilling of labor.

The chefs had to work to expand the taste vocabulary of the children, who were used to a diet of highly processed foods, and to challenge the taste stronghold that school food industries have carefully cultivated over the years by engineering cheap foods apparently palatable to kids. Although the food that had previously been served in New London met the USDA dietary guidelines, it rarely featured fresh fruits and vegetables. As Jennifer Gaddis attests, USDA school food guidelines are supposed to be updated every five years, and industry has a strong influence in this process (2019, 109). One of the central challenges of reclaiming school food is trying to limit big industry's influence in shaping what food is served and what it tastes like. This process is not simple and it takes time for children to accept novel foods; Brigaid chefs have learned to listen to children and gain their trust. This is an approach that has been successfully applied in other school districts (Black 2017). Unfortunately, listening to and working with kids is rarely the norm when it comes to school food.

Giusti hired mostly chefs who came from a fine-dining background, not chefs who had cooked in institutional settings. Trained at the Culinary Institute of America and coming straight from one of the world's most lauded restaurants, Giusti put his name and network to use and was able to attract top candidates who might not otherwise have considered working in a school kitchen. Other star chefs have tried to make their mark on school food with limited success. Most notably, Jamie Oliver used his fame to try to transform school food in Britain. Oliver's 2005 documentary *School Dinners* brought to light the poor quality of food being served in British schools (Naik 2008), but he was unable to effect notable change. He chalked this up to the fact that eating well was viewed as a posh preoccupation of the middle class (Furness 2015). The initial reaction of the New London community toward the idea of having chefs in their schools mirrored this view that public assistance was not meant to be fancy or pleasurable. Giusti had to prove that chefs could have a place in school kitchens and reach a broad clientele.

Chefs and Taste

For many children, school lunch might be the only nutritious meal they receive in a day. In addition, many studies have shown that if children are not eating well they cannot focus and learn (Anderson, Gallagher, and

Ritchie 2018; Hinrichs 2010). Connecting learning outcomes to nutrition reveals how providing palatable school food that children want to eat is critical to social sustainability and the overall success of educational programs.

In a review of the literature focusing on the palatability of school food, Kayla Guerrero, Annemarie Olsen, and Karen Wistoft (2018) pointed out that collaborations of chefs with school food-service workers were some of the most successful efforts at improving children's intake of fruits and vegetables by adjusting taste in response to student feedback (Cohen et al. 2012; Thorsen et al. 2015; Zellner and Cobuzzi, 2017). Brigaid also had to break free of what Alison Hayes-Conroy and Jessica Hayes-Conroy (2013) call "hegemonic nutrition": an approach to food education and eating focused on rigid health norms and simplified understandings of nutrition that leave little room for taste. Brigaid chefs have had to navigate the minefield of "hegemonic taste" and the larger effects of the NSLP nutrition guidelines and the school lunch industry in imposing an untasty agenda of health that does not speak to the ethnic and racial diversity of students in the New London School district. Negotiating and cocreating the taste of school lunch (Galler, Gonera, and Varela 2020) have been important for the economic, environmental, and social sustainability of Brigaid's school food programs.

From the start Brigaid has given students daily informal opportunities to provide feedback on the food. Brigaid chefs also actively solicit this input when they circulate in the cafeteria to chat with students and ask them what they think of the day's offerings. The chefs take the student feedback seriously and do their best to respond to what the children tell them in a collaborative and iterative process. Defining what tastes good is a daily dialogue among cafeteria staff, chefs, and children—it is a process of trial and error. Most importantly, this is an exercise in building trust. Leveraging their excellent rapport with the cafeteria staff, many of whom had worked in the schools for years, the Brigaid chefs have also earned the trust of the students over time. I observed that if a cafeteria worker, chef, or cook encourages a student by saying, "Try it. I think you will like this dish," the children show a willingness to at least taste new foods. Although they have taken time to develop, the personal relationships and processes of dialogue and trust have helped Brigaid gain traction in New London schools. I observed a school chef circulate in the cafeteria during lunch. The children came up to tell her what they liked and did not like about the day's lunch. The roasted chicken was a hit, but one little girl told the chef that the house-made applesauce looked like vomit. The kids are harsh critics and rarely do they mince words. The cooks and chefs listen to the children and respond to their feedback and requests by eliminating unpopular dishes, adjusting seasonings, and developing new recipes.

Children are co-constructing taste. When students learn about food production, this leads to more successful school food programs. When they understand the impact of waste on the environment, this can lead to a reduction of plate waste, one of the central forms of waste in school food programs (Wilkie, Graunke, and Cornejo 2015). Brigaid has brought in barrels into which students deposit organic waste from their plates, causing them to hopefully think twice about leaving food uneaten. The food scraps from the barrels are rerouted from the waste stream to a local pig farm to supply feed for hogs. Although the New London School District has not conducted before-and-after plate waste studies, observations on the part of cafeteria staff indicated that initially, plate waste did not decrease, but as children adapted to the new scratch-cooked offerings, they began to eat more and waste declined. Staff noticed fewer scraps going to the pig farm. Although Brigaid was not putting into place a specific pedagogical strategy, the Brigaid chefs and cafeteria staff were keenly observing and talking to children and adapting their ways of doing food to respond to this feedback. For New London, the move away from prepared food also helped reduce waste related to packaging—they were no longer buying individually wrapped buns, burritos, and precut fruit. Brigaid was also able to improve the environmental sustainability of their school food programs by purchasing reusable plates and cutlery, doing away with the old Styrofoam boxes. Not only was this positive from the environmental perspective; it also improved the overall atmosphere and dining experience for the students. Chefs are trained to reduce waste in the kitchen because that always hurts the bottom line. By improving the appeal of school food, chefs were able to reduce plate waste as the children began to accept and enjoy the meals prepared for them at school.

A Better School Eating Experience

There are other structural issues that cause waste that are much harder to overcome than simply reducing packaging. Matteo Boschini et al. (2020) found that both a short lunch period and an unpleasant cafeteria environment led to greater waste. American schools have been opposed to lengthening the lunch period because they do not want to lose instructional time. Although Brigaid has been unsuccessful in getting the New London School District to lengthen its lunch period, it has improved the physical environment of school cafeterias. For example, at the middle school, a colorful mural of vegetables was painted on one of the central walls, and at the high school, a hydroponic garden was installed on a wall in order to grow lettuce. This got students talking and thinking about food in new ways while they were eating and integrated lunch into their social and academic learning.

While Brigaid has tried to create a pleasant environment for eating and to engage students in a dialogue about food, its main focus has been on taste. The idea of pleasure does not often enter into the discourse on school food in America, which is dominated by notions of controlling the body and ensuring its "proper" growth (Poppendieck 2010) and meeting the minimum requirements for nutrition and nothing more. The NSLP has decoupled the idea of nutrition from enjoyment and pleasure. Much of the literature on school food focuses on nutrition and the increased intake of specific foods such as whole grains and vegetables (Cho and Nadow 2004). Only a few studies have prioritized the palatability of school food as a key factor in improving child nutrition (Story 2009) and reducing food waste. When we talked to Giusti, he compared this pushback against pleasure in food to the ways in which public housing is delivered, which he described as follows: "It should meet the basic needs that humans have for shelter. It should not include anything beyond these bare necessities." Perhaps this is why a school lunch program produced by chefs initially seemed excessive to some members of the community. Part of Brigaid's mission has been to recenter the work and role of chefs in schools as problem solvers and responsive professionals in their relations with both school administrators and children.

There is no one "good" when it comes to school food and this is the treacherous water that the Brigaid chefs must navigate each day. For the chefs, "good" is a process that is mediated among the USDA guidelines for school food, their own "cheffy" sensibilities, and ultimately the tastes of children. A critical part of this process is getting feedback from students.

The Care Work of Feeding Children: Reskilling Labor and Reorienting Cooking

For Brigaid chefs, scratch cooking is critical in the production of taste and care. Here school food escapes from industrial food's hijacking of taste and meaning: baked goods are liberated from the mushy condensation of plastic packaging, and "mystery meat" produced in a faraway factory is banished from the menu. Companies such as Tyson and General Mills, multinational corporations that are big players in the American school food industry, contribute to a landscape of bland, placeless food, such as boneless chicken wings, chicken tenders, and tater tot coins. When these companies attempt to make "ethnic food," the dishes lack authenticity, leaving out critical spices and herbs. For example, Tyson touts its "Wokin' Orange All-In-One Entrée" as an "ethnic creation with a bit of spice," but it is not clear what ethnic group inspired this dish. The sweet orange sauce and reference to wok cooking seem to suggest something Asian or Chinese but with little semblance to any recognizable dishes from Chinese cuisines.

The New London school district is very ethnically and racially diverse: for the period 2018–22 it was 45 percent white, 13 percent Black, 34 percent Hispanic, 6 percent two or more races, 3 percent Asian, and 1 percent Other (National Center for Education Statistics 2024). Navigating taste in a heterogenous population is another big challenge for Brigaid chefs. Scratch cooking allows chefs to use herbs and spices, source some meat from local producers, and adjust recipes to meet the tastes of students as a way of making school food palatable for its specific constituents. As best they can, the Brigaid staff are creating meals that respond to their students' tastes, which are unique to the specific ethnic mix of this school district. An example is a lunch recently served at the middle school: *sinangag* (garlic fried rice), *ginsang repolyo* (vegetable stir-fry), and chicken adobo—an example of a Filipino-focused meal. The children readily tried and liked this meal. As Brigaid expands to new school districts in other parts of the country, it adjusts its recipes according to each area's ethnic makeup and develops new recipes that speak to local tastes and the availability of ingredients.

Chef Ryan explained that after five years of being in New London schools, he can see an increase in children's acceptance of the food that Brigaid serves and what kids are willing to try. In particular, he noted that children who have only eaten Brigaid food in school are good eaters and are more willing to try new foods—Brigaid has been able to shape their thinking about school food and their taste buds from the beginning of their school careers. It also helps that these kids are young and more adaptable. This finding is in keeping with the literature on children's food acceptance and neophobia, which indicates that early and repeated childhood exposure to novel foods is key for children to accept them (Dovey et al. 2008).

Children are not the only people in New London schools who are learning about food. Brigaid chefs have helped to reskill school cafeteria workers so that they will be able to continue preparing tasty food for the children they know and care for. This reskilling strengthens local economies, fosters advancement in school kitchens, and brings a sense of pride to the work of feeding children. This contributes to the economic sustainability of school food because it keeps federal funding in the local economy, rather than putting it back into the large national industry that provides prepared school meals (Gaddis 2019).

Brigaid has shown that scratch cooking is actually more cost effective than reheating prepared industrial food. This is in keeping with the findings of the Tisch Center Food, Education and Policy study of a scratch cooking pilot program in the Bronx (Trent, Ahmen, and Koch 2019). On a tight budget, Brigaid chefs and staff are able to produce a meal consisting of a protein, a vegetable, and a dessert that meet the dietary guidelines set out by the USDA (2012). A recent lunch menu at one of the elementary schools included pasta Bolognese with a house-made whole wheat focaccia, a side of garlic broccoli, and house-made applesauce for dessert. Five types of sandwiches were also on offer. In addition to their culinary skills, not only are chefs from fine dining trained to have a focus on taste, but they must consider food and labor costs at all times. Applying these principles of taste and efficiency that come from the restaurant industry to school food is an excellent model for producing delicious food at lower cost. However, the Brigaid chef is only one part of this equation: each school already had its own food-service staff who make each meal happen.

When Brigaid first started operating in the New London School District and reorganizing the kitchens, many of the long-time lunch staff worried that they would lose their jobs. These cafeteria staff jobs were already precarious: they were mostly low paying and part time with no benefits. A return to self-operating kitchens and an end to outsourcing are central steps in fixing the school food problem (Gaddis 2019). These are all elements of the solution that Giusti also understood from the start. He has underlined the importance of building a strong community, and he has done this largely by maintaining the staff who had been part of the New London schools for many years.

Brigaid's way of working required reskilling the labor of the school kitchens; elderly "lunch ladies" went from reheating prepared food to scratch cooking. This process was not without its tensions and challenges:

there were people who initially did not want to do the work and those who found it too hard. However, the kitchen staff that I worked alongside during my time as a volunteer cook told me about the new meaning that scratch cooking had given their work. They felt they were engaged in caring for the children at an entirely new level. They experienced for the first time the quality of the food and felt a personal investment in the process of transforming raw ingredients into meals. One day while I was working alongside Carolina, she expressed her pride in the pasta Bolognese and garlic bread we had prepared that morning. While we were serving the food to the children, she turned to me and said, "I am so glad they like the food. It feels so good to make them happy and serve them a healthy and delicious hot lunch. This is the only hot meal some of these kids will get today." The cooks in the two Brigaid schools where I worked became increasingly personally and emotionally engaged in cooking and feeding children (Fine 1996).

Brigaid cooks and chefs are engaging in care work that is tied to student well-being in a holistic sense. As Gaddis (2019, 137) notes, an economy of care is created when lunch ladies cook, but greater value needs to be assigned to this care work that has remained invisible: "Farming, cooking, and eating are all relational acts that connect humans to each other and to the natural environment. . . . The NSLP is a culturally, economically, and environmentally significant public institution that ordinary people can and should reclaim as part of a larger movement to build socially just, ecologically sustainable, democratically controlled solidarity economies." Most of the kitchen staff that I worked with also had other jobs to make ends meet and many were the main breadwinners in their multigenerational households. As the kitchen workers have developed their culinary skills, they have attained value as skilled labor and some have transitioned from hourly wage cooks to salaried chefs at schools. This is good for the economic sustainability of New London.

Feeding Community

The Brigaid chefs and cooks are not only feeding children. More and more of the school staff are starting to buy lunch and eat in the cafeteria because the food is good. The Brigaid program raises funds to pay its chefs by offering catering services for school meetings and through a community meal each Wednesday. Giusti explained that the idea behind the community meal was to show people that they could produce a really tasty meal for five dollars. "Try to get the same value at McDonald's," bragged Giusti, who wanted to create a healthy, affordable, and convenient alternative to the many fast-food restaurants that surround the schools in New London. Each week Brigaid announces the community meal menu via social media. For five dollars, diners get a main course, a side, a dessert, and a nonalcoholic beverage. The doors of the cafeteria open at 5 p.m. and there is immediately a long line. Community meals at the middle school generally feed about two hundred community members. Children race about as people from all corners of the community gather at the long tables to enjoy a meal; there is a positive vibe as laughter and conversation fill the air. When buying dinner tickets, some diners buy an extra meal and leave the ticket for whoever needs it—a sign of solidarity. The Brigaid community meal has become one more option for accessible food in a community that suffers from high rates of food insecurity and few affordable yet nutritious options that fit the time-impoverished lives of many people. These meals have also been a way to demonstrate to the community that the food served at the school can be tasty, unpretentious, and nutritious.

Often the Brigaid chefs will prepare themed meals that speak to the various ethnic groups in the community. For example, meals have included an Indian-themed menu featuring chicken tikka masala, southern comfort food with chicken stew and biscuits, and Peruvian chicken accompanied by *solterito* (bean salad) and *arroz chaufa* (Peruvian fried rice). In this way, the community meal becomes a cultural exchange and a moment of national and ethnic pride for some community members. The Brigaid chefs delve more into ethnic cuisine at the community meals because these meals are not obligatory for children and do not have to please everyone. The community meal has helped win over the initial naysayers who questioned the place of chefs in school kitchens.

Conclusions

Community meals and Brigaid's catering services speak to this company's entrepreneurial spirit and the resourcefulness of a private business to solve funding issues and foster social development and the good of the community. However, do private companies like Brigaid undermine or encourage the system-wide change that is needed to transform the NSLP and other school food initiatives? Without deeper policy engagement with the dysfunctional elements of school food, such as the stranglehold of big businesses that provide ultraprocessed school food, a disconnect from local food, and the deskilling of the local labor force, programs such as the ones Brigaid runs are unlikely to cause a sea change. Dan Giusti has been vocal about what he sees as the issues surrounding school food, but he has yet to engage with policymakers who might bring about a transformation, and this is not necessarily the purview of his work. Without more qualitative and quantitative data to support Brigaid's success and proof that this model can scale up, chefs will likely remain outliers in solving the sustainability issues inherent in school food.

The early public skepticism about Brigaid in the New London School kitchens revolved around the idea that chefs running the new food service would impose an aesthetic of taste that did not match up with its audience. There is a popular perception that chefs make fancy food and this is not what low-income kids need and not what public assistance should deliver. However, Brigaid has shown that, working with children to shape the taste of school food, chefs can improve its consumption and its social and economic sustainability. Brigaid is focusing on taste in order to ensure the general well-being of children. In this process, it is also reskilling the workers who are critical in transforming school food from industrial prepared meals to scratch meals prepared with care. This element of the Brigaid program pushes back against the corporate industry providing reheatable ultraprocessed foods to schools and brings agency and pride back to food-service workers. These skilled workers keep federal aid money in the local community and create a valuable skilled labor force contributing to the social, environmental, and economic sustainability of the school food business.

Brigaid founder Dan Giusti has used his fame as a chef in the world of haute cuisine to attract the talent and attention that is needed to aid in this transformation. Giusti's company is an interesting example of an innovative private approach to feeding children and rethinking the National School Lunch Program. However, more research is needed to understand the broader impact of such programs, whether they can influence policymakers to address structural issues that plague the NSLP, and what the potential is for such programs to scale up to a national level. What is certain is that chefs are well positioned to contribute solutions to the complex problems surrounding the sustainability of school lunch and they are putting taste at the center of their solutions.

Notes

1. "The Community Eligibility Provision (CEP) allows schools in high-poverty areas to offer USDA school meals to all students at no charge if a large share of students are directly certified. CEP can be used by a single school, a group of schools, or the entire school district if the share of directly certified students, called the Identified Student Percentage (ISP), is at least 40 percent." https://www.ers.usda .gov/amber-waves/2018/september/high-poverty-schools-are-more-likely-to -adopt-the-community-eligibility-provision-of-the-usda-school-meal-programs/.

References

Anderson, Michael L., Justin Gallagher, and Elizabeth Ramirez Ritchie. 2018. "How the Quality of School Lunch Affects Students' Academic Performance." *Education Digest* 83 (6): 61–64.

Bäckström, Adam, A.-M. Pirttilä-Backman, and Hely Tuorila. 2004. "Willingness to Try New Foods as Predicted by Social Representations and Attitude and Trait Scales." *Appetite* 43 (1): 75–83.

Béné, Christophe, Peter Oosterveer, Lea Lamotte, Inge Brouwer, Stef de Haan, Steve Prager, Elise Talsma, and Colin Khoury. 2019. "When Food Systems Meet Sustainability—Current Narratives and Implications for Actions." *World Development* 113 (January): 116–30. https://doi.org/10.1016/j.worlddev.2018.08.011.

Black, Jane. 2017. "Revenge of the Lunch Lady." *HuffPost*, February 9. https://highline .huffingtonpost.com/articles/en/school-lunch/.

Boschini, Matteo, Luca Falasconi, Clara Cicatiello, and Silvio Franco. 2020. "Why the Waste? A Large-Scale Study on the Causes of Food Waste at School Canteens." *Journal of Cleaner Production* 246: 118994. https://doi.org/10.1016/j.jclepro.2019 .118994.

Cho, Hyunyi, and Michelle Zbell Nadow. 2004. "Understanding Barriers to Implementing Quality Lunch and Nutrition Education." *Journal of Community Health* 29 (5): 421–35.

Cohen, Juliana F., Liesbeth A. Smit, Ellen Parker, Austin, S. B., A. Lindsey Frazier, Christina D. Economos, and Eric B. Rimm. 2012. "Long-Term Impact of a Chef on School Lunch Consumption: Findings from a 2-year Pilot Study in Boston Middle Schools." *Journal of the Academy of Nutrition and Dietetics* 112 (6): 927–33. https://doi.org/10.1016/j.jand.2012.01.015.

Cook, Daniel T. 2009. "Semantic Provisioning of Children's Food: Commerce, Care and Maternal Practice." *Childhood* 16 (3): 317–34.

Dovey, Terence M., Paul A. Staples, E. Leigh Gibson, and Jason C. G. Halford. 2006. "Food Neophobia and 'Picky/Fussy' Eating in Children: A Review." *Appetite* 50 (2–3): 181–93.

Dunifon, Rachel, and Lori Kowaleski-Jones. 2003. "The Influences of Participation in the National School Lunch Program and Food Insecurity on Child Well-Being." *Social Service Review* 77 (1): 72–92.

Feeding America. 2015. "Map the Meal Gap." Accessed June 15, 2021. http://map .feedingamerica.org/county/2015/overall/connecticut/county/new-london.

Fine, Gary. 1996. "Justifying Work: Occupational Rhetorics as Resources in Restaurant Kitchens." *Administrative Science Quarterly* 41 (1): 90–115.

Furness, Hannah. 2015. "Jamie Oliver Admits School Dinners Campaign Failed because Eating Well Is a Middle Class Preserve." *Telegraph* (London), August 24.

Gaddis, Jennifer E. 2019. *The Labor of Lunch: Why We Need Real Food and Real Jobs in American Public Schools*. Berkeley: University of California Press.

Galler, Martin, Antje Gonera, and Paula Varela. 2020. "Children as Food Designers: The Potential of Co-creation to Make the Healthy Choice the Preferred One." *International Journal of Food Design* 5 (1–2): 25–31. https://doi.org/10.1386/ijfd_00015_3.

Guerrero, Kayla, Annemarie Olsen, and Karen Wistoft. 2018. "What Role Does Taste Play in School Meal Studies? A Narrative Review of the Literature." *Journal of Child Nutrition & Management* 42 (1): 123–38.

Hagen, Linda. 2021. "Pretty Healthy Food: How and When Aesthetics Enhance Perceived Healthiness." *Journal of Marketing* 85 (2): 129–45.

Hayes-Conroy, Alison, and Jessica Hayes-Conroy. 2013. "Expansions of Consciousness. Introduction." In *Doing Nutrition Differently*, edited by Alison Hayes-Conroy and Jessica Hayes Conroy, 1–22. London: Ashgate.

Hinrichs, Peter. 2010. "The Effects of the National School Lunch Program on Education and Health." *Journal of Policy Analysis and Management* 29 (3): 479–505.

Jaime, Patricia Constante, and Karen Lock. 2009. "Do School Based Food and Nutrition Policies Improve Diet and Reduce Obesity?" *Preventive Medicine* 48 (1): 45-53.

Leer, Jonatan, and Karen Wistoft. 2018. "Taste in Education: A Critical Review Essay." *Food and Foodways* 26 (4): 329–49. https://doi.org/10.1080/07409710.2018.1534047.

Levine, Susan. 2010. *School Lunch Politics: The Surprising History of America's Favorite Welfare Program*. Princeton, NJ: Princeton University Press.

Naik, Asmita. 2008. "Did Jamie Oliver Really Put School Dinners on the Agenda: An Examination of the Role of the Media in Policy Making." *Political Quarterly* 79 (3): 426–33.

National Center for Education Statistics. 2024. "Education Demographic and Geographic Estimates." Accessed June 17, 2024. https://nces.ed.gov/Programs/Edge/ACSDashboard/0902820.

Oliver, Jamie. 2005. *School Dinners*. Channel 4.

Paakki, M., I. Aaltojärvi, M. Sandell, and A. Hopia. 2019. "The Importance of the Visual Aesthetics of Colours in Food at a Workday Lunch." *International Journal of Gastronomy and Food Science* 16: 100131. https://doi.org/10.1016/j.ijgfs.2018.12.001.

Poppendieck, Janet. 2010. *Free For All: Fixing School Food in America*. Berkeley: University of California Press.

Story, Mary. 2009. "The Third School Nutrition Dietary Assessment Study: Findings and Policy Implications for Improving the Health of US Children." Supplement, *Journal of the American Dietetic Association* 109 (2): S7–S13.

Thorsen, Anne V., Anne D. Lassen, Elisabeth W. Andersen, Lene M. Christensen, Anja Biltoft-Jensen, Rikke Andersen, Camilla T. Damsgaard, Kim F. Michaelsen, and Inge Tetens. 2015. "Plate Waste and Intake of School Lunch Based on the New Nordic Diet and on Packed Lunches: A Randomised Controlled Trial in 8- to 11-Year-Old Danish Children." *Journal of Nutritional Science* 4:e20. https://doi.org/10.1017/jns.2015.3.

Trapp, Micah M. 2018. "The Right to Taste: Conceptualizing the Nourishing Potential of School Lunch." *Food and Foodways* 26 (1): 1–22.

Trent, R., D. Ijaz Ahmed, and P. Koch. 2019. *Cooking Outside the Box: How a Scratch Cooking Pilot in The Bronx is Reshaping Meals in New York City Schools*. Laurie M. Tisch Center for Food, Education & Policy, Program in Nutrition, Teachers College, Columbia University.

United States Department of Agriculture (USDA). 2012. "Nutrition Standards in the National School Lunch and School Breakfast Programs."

US Federal Registrar. 2022. Vol. 87, no. 142, Notice 44329, July 26.

Wilkie, Ann C., Ryan E. Graunke, and Camilo Cornejo. 2015. "Food Waste Auditing at Three Florida Schools." *Sustainability* 7 (2): 1370–87.

Zellner, Debra A. and Jennifer L. Cobuzzi. 2017. "Eat Your Veggies: A Chef-Prepared, Family Style School Lunch Increases Vegetable Liking and Consumption in Elementary School Students." *Food Quality and Preference* 55 (January): 8–15. https://doi.org/10.1016/j.foodqual.2016.08.007.

CHAPTER TWO

Restaurant Sustainability as a Form of Cultural Awareness
A Colombian Experience

ANA MARÍA ULLOA AND LAURA GARZÓN

Introduction

On the twentieth anniversary of the restaurant Mini-Mal in December of 2021, there was a talk offered by Miguel Durango, an agricultural engineer, and Petronila Suarez, an elderly woman from San Andres de Sotaviento, an Indigenous Zenú reservation located within the departments of Cordoba and Sucre in Colombia's Caribbean region. Miguel and Petronila took turns explaining some of the products they had brought that were characteristic of traditional Zenú agricultural and cooking practices. In front of them there was a table dressed with bright plantain leaves, in which colorful varieties of corn in different shades of yellow, purple, and gray stood out among an equally varied sample of local tubers, vegetables, fruits, and nuts. That day, Miguel told us about the sixteen varieties of corn that are present in the Indigenous reservation and are currently being introduced to a few restaurants in Bogotá (the country's capital), out of a total of twenty-four varieties that are today recognized in Colombia's Caribbean region. Their products follow agroecological principles: they are seasonal, they are not treated with chemical fertilizers, they are GMO free, and they are

Acknowledgments: Ana María Ulloa acknowledges support from "Fondo de Apoyo a Profesores Asistentes" (FAPA) from Universidad de los Andes for the data interpretation and writing of the chapter.

grown from native seeds (RECAR 2005). Food sovereignty is sought after through a model of family planting and harvesting where 70 percent of the produce goes to household consumption. For both Miguel and Petronila, as well as for the restaurant's owners, taking care of local food preparation is a powerful form of defending threatened Indigenous livelihoods, dispossessed farmers, and lands in dispute.

The talk was followed by a dinner prepared jointly by Petronila and Mini-Mal's kitchen staff. It included a delicate sesame-and-lemongrass broth, empanadas made from different types of corn filled with local vegetables and meats, a green bean salad, sesame balls, and other typical dishes. Celebrating twenty years of operation is not a minor feat for any restaurant, and Mini-Mal's tribute to Zenú cuisine and people speaks volumes about what this Colombian restaurant is all about. Mini-Mal is a small restaurant in Bogotá that seeks to explore new notions of Colombian cuisine and identity based on biodiversity, cultural diversity, and creativity. Its creative output is reflected in dishes that often include various unknown or disfavored local flavors and ingredients intended to be discovered or rediscovered by locals and tourists alike. Hence its motto, "surprisingly Colombian" (*sorprendentemente colombiano*). Its work follows Frédéric Godart, Sorah Seong, and Damon Phillips's definition of creativity as "an intentional configuration of cultural and material elements that is unexpected for a given audience" (2020, 490).

The restaurant started its operations in December 2001, first as a pop-up event promoting Bogotá's urban and popular culture as expressed in music, street art, daily objects, and food. The restaurant, led by the couple Antonuela Ariza and Eduardo Martínez, is located in a traditional neighborhood in Bogotá called Chapinero—a cultural hub in the city that today is populated with cafés, designer shops, theaters, restaurants, and libraries. This neighborhood is also known for its large Victorian-style houses, associated in the second half of the twentieth century with modernity and family life. In one such house, belonging to the family of one of Mini-Mal's founding members, the restaurant consolidated its operations. Its name was devised to signify multiple but related things: the process of infusing certain ingredients deemed worthless with renewed value, creation made with little, sustainability derived from the utmost use of resources, and the aesthetics of the humble and simple (Martínez, Ariza, and Romero 2021).

All these meanings are at the center of the restaurant's everyday activities, informing whom it buys ingredients and products from, whom it hires as staff, and what types of events it hosts and participates in, as well as the dishes and products it creates and sells. Its understanding and enactment of culinary sustainability go beyond buying, cooking, and marketing food that is produced from agroecological or organic models. The restaurant's owners share with other food activists a desire to resist the agroindustrial food system that predominates worldwide (Counihan 2019, 3), but their focus is mostly cultural. In their practice, culinary sustainability includes a process of cultural awareness recognizing the richness, elegance, and refinement of traditional regional culinary practices, preparations, and ingredients. By cultural awareness we do not mean the process of coming to learn about worldviews, values, or practices of a minority culture as it is discussed and designed in health care and education services, but a looser approach that does not entail a directed pedagogical strategy. Cultural awareness is part of a process of valuation of Colombia's cultural and natural diversity that unfolds as diners come to appreciate different culinary aesthetics. As we argue in this chapter, Mini-Mal's efforts toward sustainability over these past twenty years include the valuation of lesser-known agricultural or culinary products from marginalized regions to develop cultural, political, and sensory awareness of the power of food as transformative practice.

This Colombian restaurant puts culinary sustainability in action under particular circumstances. Colombia is a country of exuberant biodiversity but limited economic resources. It has rich and diverse culinary traditions but conservative tastes (Camacho 2017, 170). Its various agricultural traditions coexist with a deep-rooted agrarian problem over land tenure. Colombia's land ownership is extremely disproportional and one of the most highly concentrated in Latin America. Land reforms have been promoted in the country for decades as a remedy for low agricultural productivity and high rates of poverty; nonetheless, the problem of concentrated land ownership persists.[1] It is also a multicultural and multiethnic country where Indigenous, Black, and peasant communities are constantly threatened by long-standing practices of violence, displacement, and rural poverty amid an armed conflict. Moreover, it is a country where traditional practices of food production and consumption have been profoundly transformed, partly by the expansion of agribusinesses and cultivation of monocrops such as palm oil in Magdalena Medio and sugarcane in Cauca Valley, and also by mining, hydrocarbon exploitation, and other forms of extractivism, including tourism and bioprospecting (Hurtado-Bermúdez et al. 2021). It is in such a context that the restaurant's process of valuing the products, the workers, and the artisans of the land must be appreciated and understood.

In this chapter, we will go through the history of Mini-Mal as a precursor of what some have called New Colombian cuisine—driven by chefs who are eager to use the full range of local ingredients and techniques marrying tradition and innovation. We will focus on the food story of one of its founding members, chef Eduardo Martínez. In retelling his story, we will describe the concept of culinary sustainability Mini-Mal has subscribed to and helped build. We will explain, later on, how a politics of sustainability as promoted by the restaurant intersects with an aesthetics of diversity. Material from this chapter comes, first and foremost, from recorded semistructured interviews with chef Martínez about the restaurant's history as well as what they currently do, how they do it, and why. Second, we also reviewed the national press, documents from the restaurant's archive, different writings of people related to the restaurant gathered in their first cookbook (Martínez, Ariza, and Romero 2021), and national policy documents.

This work contributes to understanding the role of chefs and restaurants in promoting sustainability in the Latin American context where issues surrounding conflicts over land distribution, resource management, food access, and malnutrition are major societal problems. Culinary sustainability, as practiced by an urban restaurant such as Mini-Mal, is an opportunity for the valuation of lesser-known agricultural or culinary products from rural regions that are often marginalized. Moreover, as Eduardo has found out, Mini-Mal's work has also contributed to turning cooking into a potent practice for collective action.

An Agricultural Revolution in the Kitchen

Eduardo Martínez, the restaurant's executive chef, is a Colombian agricultural engineer for whom the kitchen became a revolutionary space. Long haired and casual in demeanor, Eduardo is a self-taught cook who pays keen attention to diverse landscapes, products, and people. We met in the course of different meetings held by a collective of people interested in studying and fostering traditional cuisines in Colombia. So before choosing Mini-Mal as a case study we were familiar with Eduardo's work and his perspective on the country's gastronomy.

His prior work as a student of agronomy and intensive travels to different rural areas of the country are central to how the restaurant ended up understanding and practicing sustainability. In particular, his prolonged stay in the Pacific region by the Anchicayá River in the late 1990s was a transformative experience for him as he learned from Afro-Colombians about sustainability in the humid tropics. This region, despite being currently identified internationally and nationally as a "biodiversity hot spot," is still equally portrayed as "a poor, forgotten, hot, humid forest crisscrossed by innumerable rivers and inhabited by black and indigenous groups" (Escobar 2008, 4). Eduardo's interactions with locals and vivid interest in rural development, amid a forceful emergence of Black identities of the 1990s, raised questions about the region's marginality, its agricultural practices in a complex environmental ecosystem, biodiversity and its sustainable use, and, later on, the visibility of local cuisines and their articulation with urban and modern cuisines (Martínez, Ariza, and Romero 2021).

In our conversation about his experiences in the Pacific region, Eduardo described his early interests as follows: "I think I have a persistent concern and it is creating methods for the kind of situations we have in Colombia, a country in the tropics. I was very passionate about seeing how these people have developed agriculture in this rain forest, with poor soils, and have succeeded. I always had this concern about what it is to live in this biodiverse country, what it means to do agriculture in the tropics."

Eduardo's curiosity had the fortune to be propelled by a number of events taking place in the 1990s. On the one hand, there were new developments happening in his discipline. The Faculty of Agronomy at Universidad Nacional, the foremost public university in Colombia, where he studied, was just starting to offer a new concentration on rural sustainability after a long-standing institutional history in favor of agrarian modernism and the introduction and proliferation of the Green Revolution in the second half of the twentieth century. Tropical agricultural science, as developed in Colombia, found important international allies that sought to promote the accelerated use of high-yield seeds, chemicals, and mechanization of agriculture in the name of science, modernization, state control, and economic development (Wayne 2017). Eduardo's generation, conversely, put in practice alternative agricultural models and ideas by thinking about rural sustainability in place of rural efficiency.

The emphasis on family economy and sustainability echoes some of the principles of agroecology as it arrived in Colombia at the end of the 1970s—seeing in traditional peasant practices an alternative to agroindustrial and chemical forms of production. With connections to agronomy, ecology, rural development, sociology, anthropology, and the environmental movement, agroecology became at once a science, a social movement, and an agricultural practice (León-Sicard et al. 2015, 40). Agroecology's plasticity would later serve Eduardo and his restaurant partners in their own comprehensive conceptualization of culinary sustainability as many things in one.

To live in the Pacific region in the second half of the 1990s, as Eduardo did, was an opportunity to be exposed to an effervescent social environment in which ethnic groups, activists, and others were working toward a new political understanding of the territory in relation to rural development, traditional productive practices, and cultural uses of natural resources (Escobar 1998). Colombia's Political Constitution of 1991 (a progressive constitution that recognizes a variety of civil, political, economic, social, and cultural rights, and establishes judicial mechanisms to guarantee them), the Rio Summit in 1992 (where the concept of sustainable development was launched), the Law 99 of 1993 (the Environmental Law), the Law 70 of 1993 (the Law on Black Communities, which granted them cultural and territorial rights), and the Convention on Biological Diversity all granted important institutional support to Eduardo's work on rural development (León-Sicard et al. 2015).

This framework made research on traditional production systems by river communities all the more important. Since these types of systems are more oriented toward local consumption, diverse cultivars, and extensive and itinerant use of the land, they are generally more sustainable. This is why Eduardo found himself making characterizations of traditional production systems, as he worked for a local NGO, and he ended up staying in the Pacific region to do his undergrad thesis on family-based production from a sustainability perspective.

Throughout his stay, Eduardo found in the kitchens of Black women an interesting and unexplored space for local affirmation and effective cultural appropriation of biodiverse ecosystems. Eduardo likes to tell the story of how he stumbled upon the importance of the work that women do in a kitchen for promoting sustainable agricultural models. For him it materialized first while he was talking to local fishers about the possibility of letting him try a piece of fresh tuna they had recently caught. He was surprised to find out that their whole catch was sold to Japanese ships and that with their earnings they would later buy cans of tuna and sardines in the local store. This is an example of the paradox of scarcity amid plenty, he thought.

While thinking about that fresh tuna he did not get to try, and trying to come up with an activity for local women who needed to devise a new project to get funds from an NGO, he proposed to them a simple activity: for women to acquire ingredients and for men to do the kitchen prep work. The only condition was that no food product could be bought from the local store. The women prepared an incredible banquet as described by Eduardo. "I remember that they made this long table with millions of things, all crafted very beautifully. In that area there is a tradition of basket weaving, so all the packaging of tamales and sweets was stunning. So, at the end I told them, 'It seems to me that the project is at this table, what should be strengthened is here.'" But, as with the fresh-canned tuna exchange, Eduardo wondered why in the two years he had been living in Buenaventura he had never seen any of this food. To that the women answered, "This type of food is what we make when we struggle to have something to eat. But we made it for you because you seem to appreciate it."

It was this day when the work of the kitchen became a serious business for Eduardo. From that point on, he felt there was mounting evidence about what was at stake in the cuisine of a community, and how the kitchen was the right place to enact biodiversity, sustainability, and new research methods and different discourses about Colombia's cuisine.

Beyond the City: A Restaurant with Rural Roots

The idea of the restaurant came years later. After having worked at different institutions interested in rural development and the environment, Eduardo—along with other peers, including his founding partner at Mini-Mal, artist Manuel Romero—established Equilibrio, a foundation responding to the wave of environmental and ecological movements and currents, the opening of markets for ecological or organic products, and the political support expressed in regulatory advances that were gaining strength in the region by the mid-1980s (León-Sicard et al. 2015). This foundation carried out numerous workshops and rural development projects with communities from various regions of the country (such as the Pacific, the Andean-Amazon piedmont, and the mountains of the Sierra Nevada). This work of assisting rural communities in different corners of the country seeking alternatives for sustainable development and territorial planning was the precursor to Mini-Mal as a city restaurant with rural roots. In an interview given to the local media in Bogotá, once the restaurant was already known and talked about, Eduardo made the following remark: "I did not get into cooking because I was disappointed with agronomy, on the contrary, it was because I wanted to deepen my understanding of the rural world" (Hernández 2013).

The transition from foundation to restaurant occurred in 2001. Theirs was a cultural project looking for a new home. The project was influenced by an urban and young scene developing in Bogotá around new aesthetic forms that gave expression to Colombian popular culture as found in music, language, literature, and graphic design. The founders of Mini-Mal sought to express similar popular and everyday aesthetics in the realms of food and design. At the end of 2001, they tried a pop-up operation where different artists, fashion designers, graphic and object designers, and DJs could showcase their work, while offering a simple menu consisting of a couple of sandwiches, soups, main courses, and desserts.

From the beginning Mini-Mal's founders sought to include traditional preparations and local ingredients in new ways. They used smoked trout, *pernil* (roasted pork leg), *queso paipa* (a semiaged cheese that was granted a denomination-of-origin status in 2011), and feijoa (pineapple guava), among others. Mini-Mal's first dessert, named *Estrella polar*, included a corn parcel made by a woman from a town close to Bogotá. The restaurant's take was to present it as a dessert (something unexpected) along with a sauce made out of *lulo chocoano* (a fruit grown in wet soils by Indigenous and Afro-Colombian communities) and vanilla ice cream. Its gesture, as its staff like to call it, was simple but meaningful. People, we were told, still fondly remember this dessert. From then on other dishes started to appear under the idea of "cultural pairings" using ingredients from different regions (Martínez, Ariza, and Romero 2021, 29). For instance, a typical dish at the restaurant might be a braised beef neck with Amazonian *tucupi*, lemon ants, fried cassava, *casabe* (cassava bread), and fresh greens. Mini-Mal's culinary creativity depended on a series of relationships the restaurant began establishing with different communities that provided ingredients and preparations that were unknown to the urban consumer of the time.

Mini-Mal has remained open as a restaurant and design store as of 2024. Eduardo, an amateur cook at first, decided to take his cooking skills seriously and became the executive chef. By 2002, Celmira Valencia, a woman from the Pacific region who had been working in different houses as a domestic worker in Cali, San Jose del Guaviare, and Bogotá, had joined the team as head cook. The same year Antonuela Ariza, an artist and cook of the utmost cultural and aesthetic sensibility, joined the team, and she still runs the restaurant's kitchen with Eduardo, her partner.

Mini-Mal is a bridge to other regions of the country through purchases, workshops, and other activities with small farmers, fishing communities, and traditional cooks in regions like the Pacific, the Amazon, the Caribbean, and the Andes. Having the experience of working in different kinds of rural development projects, the people who created the restaurant recognized from the beginning that turning the kitchen into a transformative practice would require several years of work. But also, from the start, they thought of Mini-Mal as a cultural connector of the city with the countryside. They started with a commitment to issues surrounding family economy, local knowledge, diverse agriculture, fair and responsible fishing, and regional diversity. These commitments translated into the commercialization of "products obtained through sustainable practices" and the commitment to "break down the barriers between the city and the countryside" (Martínez, Ariza, and Romero 2021, 51–52).

For instance, one of Mini-Mal's most cherished products is *aji negro*, also known as *tucupi*—an indispensable staple for Indigenous communities in the Amazon made out of bitter cassava (*Manihot esculenta*) with the addition of hot peppers. Preparing *tucupi* requires a very elaborate process to eliminate the poison contained in cassava roots and turn them into a thick and dark paste. There are different types of preparation across different ethnicities. It is a complex product, made traditionally by older women, that can showcase diverse flavors and colors. Additionally, it was the first Colombian product to be recognized in Slow Food's Ark of Taste in 2010.[2] The elderly Indigenous women from the Amazon now sell it directly to Mini-Mal (their first buyer) and other restaurants, earning much more than what they would get locally.

Progressively, Mini-Mal has enacted its commitment to sustainability by bridging the city and the countryside in different ways. First, it uses and showcases to an urban audience different flavors, ingredients, and preparations from different regions in the country. Second, inside and outside of the restaurant, and in the field, it validates the work of farmers and people in rural areas, through fair-price strategies, workshops, and different types of promotional events and conferences. Finally, it has also started serving as ambassador and cultural broker both nationally and internationally, demonstrating the importance of Colombia's culinary patrimony.

The Politics of Sustainability

Conscious consumers may believe that a restaurant is moving toward sustainability because it is buying products directly from farmers, recognizing the care it takes with the food itself, and reducing the intervention of intermediaries. The restaurant is therefore seen as ascribing to certain ideals (economic, ecological, and social) that are loosely associated with a sustainable approach, particularly as it refers to agricultural and other food production practices (organic and local food, green design, reduced energy and water consumption, recycling programs, and so forth). Hence when talking about sustainability in the hospitality industry there is a tendency to focus almost exclusively on ecological dimensions (Higgins-Desbiolles, Moskwa, and Wijesinghe 2019).

Yet, several authors have shown that the rapid application of the term sustainability in different fields comes precisely from its ambiguity and diversity of interpretations (Glavič and Lukman 2007; Naredo 2004). Thus spinning once more the concept of sustainability, we find in the work of Mini-Mal a model that goes beyond buying, cooking, and marketing food that is produced from agroecological or organic models. Their politics directly confronts the socioeconomic, environmental, and cultural conditions that support producers' craft.

"For me it would be a disgrace," Eduardo acknowledged, "if as a result of high demand in the city we were to buy *tucupi* [Mini-Mal's cherished ingredient] and the grandmothers in the Amazon ended up with not enough for themselves." To be sustainable is to look after socio-environmental and political conditions buttressing the cultural life that binds people and products together. It is to give value to the product for its sensorial attributes as well as to the producer for her or his skills.

At the center of the activities of the restaurant there is the valuation of local foods, regional culinary traditions, and the diet of peasants and the working class, which have been seen as poor in nutrition, simple, rudimentary and with no aesthetic refinement (Camacho 2017, 171). Theirs is a bet toward investing unknown or forgotten products (such as local tubers, fruits, or particular food preparations) with new meanings and expectations. For example, they have worked with *tomate de árbol*, also known as tamarillo in English, a fruit cultivated in Colombia and other Andean countries. In Colombia, despite its ubiquitous presence in local markets, it is a fruit that is partially denigrated, particularly among youth. Its bitter aftertaste makes it an easy target for detractors. It cannot be eaten raw and it needs to be cooked to become pleasant tasting. Knowing of its bad reputation, Angela Martínez, Eduardo's sister, decided to create a dessert that would feature whole cooked tamarillos and displaying an intensely bright red color. It came with fresh cheese and was named *Amor al rojo* (love of red).

This process of valuation does not happen solely at the dining table. As Claes-Fredrik Helgesson and Fabian Muniesa have argued, value is the "outcome of a process of social work and the result of a wide range of activities (from production and combination to circulation and assessment) that aim at making things valuable" (2013, 6). The Mini-Mal team recognized that their relationship with rural producers could not be sustained in terms of supply and demand alone. Just purchasing the farmers' products would not have a major impact on their lives.

The potential lies instead, Mini-Mal's managers argue, in the gesture of appreciation toward a product made with quality and in how relationships with suppliers strengthen with time. The restaurant has thus contributed to opening the market in Bogotá, the capital, to products such as *tucupi*, *copoazu* (a fruit), and *pirarucu* (the second-largest river fish) coming from rural communities in the Amazon; *albacora* (yellowfin tuna), *piangua* (ark clams), and *lulo chocoano* (a fruit) from the Pacific; or *casabe* (flatbread made of cassava, a staple for pre-Hispanic cultures in the Caribbean and South America) and *corozo* (a fruit) from the Caribbean. These products acquire value as they participate in chains of production, commercialization, elaboration, and consumption that involve multiple actors, not only the chef, in a network of social relationships.

"At the beginning we made super elementary gestures," said Eduardo, and this meant different things to different people. "For the lady from whom we bought the *envueltos* [the type of wrapped corn parcel mentioned above] in Choachí it was valuable that these were valued by people outside Choachí and that they were also served as a dessert; for the ladies who sold us the smoked tuna from Bahía Solano [it was valuable] to know that we were selling their product and that it was appreciated in the city." These valuations and new meanings soon were recognized by the urban consumer, who noticed said Eduardo, "that you could eat well in the city without the need for international cuisine." And moreover, that an *envuelto* well done was something to marvel at.

These are some of the elements that differentiate Mini-Mal from a restaurant that seeks to be sustainable offering healthy, organic, or agroecological food and only thinks about producers after the fact. In this respect, Eduardo remarks, "That is why I sometimes criticize the local boom, because if it is only for the product but there is no interest in what happens in the territory, it could really be any product. If you are not interested in what happens locally, you are not making a difference. The scenario in Latin America is different because the cultural and social challenges are different." Being in the Pacific area and in different rural territories affected by the Colombian armed conflict prior to his work as a chef led him to understand that a restaurant that commits to sustainability has to be based on gestures of appreciation that strive toward a cultural recognition of the dignity of people and the quality of their products.

The Aesthetics of Diversity

As a cultural project the restaurant has been closely involved with designers, artists, musicians, and DJs. The aesthetic sensibility of Manuel Romero (founding member) and Antonuela Ariza (head chef), both artists, has been central to Mini-Mal's project. In a brief text describing his take on the restaurant, Manuel writes, "In Mini-Mal we use food as a language to communicate stories, ideas, and feelings that invite us to recognize and value the presence of diversity in our geographic and cultural reality, and from there, to reflect on the way we see ourselves as a nation. This process has as its starting point and main argument the experience of flavor" (Martínez, Ariza, and Romero 2021, 226).

To center its valuation project in the experience of flavor is to use aesthetic forms that make possible other ways of sensing and recognizing the country. And this is not a minor detail for a highly diverse country like Colombia that has neglected its countryside. A meal at Mini-Mal can include *piangua* (a mollusk that grows among the mangroves of the Pacific coast and is collected mainly by Black women), *casabe* (an unleavened, crunchy, thin circular bread made from cassava flour made in the Caribbean and the Amazon regions), and *chicha* (a traditional fermented corn beverage from the Andes). These are flavors common to the particular communities where they have taken root but unfamiliar to the public at large. As such they serve multiple functions at once: they give pleasure, embody diversity while establishing a sensorial bond to another person or culture, and finally bring to the table a web of relationships.

Understanding the experience of flavor as an active process (something that can enlarge our perceptions and world), as members of Mini-Mal do, thus places the restaurant as an environment to "explore new horizons" (Rey 2019) and to "learn to be affected" (Latour 2004) by others. The recasting of the restaurant as an educational institution opens up possibilities for chefs and customers to perceive anew the edible and drinkable (Ulloa, Roca, and Vilaseca 2017). And in the case of Mini-Mal, this goes through a process of cultural awareness of that which is simultaneously strange and familiar. For instance, the use of familiar but stigmatized local staples such as *tomate de arbol* (tamarillo) *or cubios* (ancient tubers from the northern Andes) in unusual preparations contributes to the sense of wonder and estrangement sought after by the restaurant's team.[3] It is difficult for people to accept other aesthetics and culinary sensibilities, and even more so to ingest them. Sometimes, expectations can lead to frustrations. But it is through frustrations (that are intrinsic to experience) that we can learn to be affected by difference, entering into new forms of nondiscursive sensory awareness.

Lastly, in our conversation about the restaurant's gestures toward the valuation of the sensory attributes of local products, Eduardo considered there was another layer, perhaps more important, to this exercise. "The exercise of aesthetic valuation is an exercise that creates values in society," he argued. In the twenty years since the restaurant's founding the Mini-Mal staff have helped restore value and meaning to different types of products and their producers across various regions, and in doing so they have contributed to a widespread valuation of the knowledge and skills of traditional cooks, who are mostly women. These women are being called in their communities to become representatives and discuss local affairs. "I have just seen in Guaviare, for example, how women have really found in the kitchen a locus of power. And this is a tremendous change of role," Eduardo explained. Amid chefs' celebrity status internationally, this recognition, not of women's labor but of women's knowledge and sensory skills, is certainly a new avenue in the promotion of culinary sustainability.

Conclusion

Mini-Mal's efforts toward culinary sustainability over the twenty years since its founding include struggles over the valuation of lesser-known agricultural or culinary products from marginalized regions, not just as a matter of fair trade but as a more encompassing exercise of cultural, political, and sensory awareness over the power of food as transformative practice. Its pioneering work in this regard is part of an important expansion of cultural and political initiatives since the 1980s that promote the country's biodiversity and culinary heritage as stepping-stones to the development of Colombian cuisine, be it regarded as "traditional" or "new" (Duque-Maecha 2017, 92). Restaurants, governmental entities such as the Ministry of Culture and the Chamber of Commerce, private organizations, cooking schools, citizen groups, and other related actors have, from different vantage points, contributed to a discourse about sustainability through the revitalization of local food expressions.

As we confirmed through our research and interviews with Mini-Mal's staff, value is the result of a complex interaction among multiple agents, territories, and contexts, the outcome of a participatory network that ties otherwise fragmented experiences and communities together. At first sight it might seem odd to look at a restaurant for clues to new forms of solidarity, cultural awareness, and political action, but that is exactly what is happening, for example, at Mini-Mal, a site where the convergence of sustainability, aesthetic sensibility, fair economic practices, and an overall ethos of experimentation and expansion is nourishing and fostering demarginalization and democratization.

The relationship between cultural awareness and sustainability becomes manifest once we recognize the holistic nature of Mini-Mal's mission and operation, the way it has managed to tie together sensory sensitivization and the promotion of sustainability. Both are dimensions of a single effort, the attempt to expand our taste experience beyond the immediate, revealing connections otherwise hidden and often shunned in the fine-dining world. The taste of purple corn, for example, is inseparable from the story of its production by the families of San Miguel de Sotaviento, a realization that in turn is connected to agricultural practices that favor sustainability over profit. Thus, to taste this staple in one of Mini-Mal's dishes is to involve oneself in a two-tier learning process: on the one hand, expanding one's gustatory palette, and on the other, acquiring familiarity with the sustainable processes that are ultimately responsible for bringing ingredients to the table. Once again, to learn while we eat might sound like a concept foreign to our regular expectations when dining out, but that is just what happens when one visits Mini-Mal, where, as one is introduced to new flavors and preparations, one becomes an active participant in the network of practices that constitute sustainability.

As we tried the different dishes that Petronila and Miguel had brought out on that day of celebration at Mini-Mal, it became clear to us that culinary sustainability in a place such as Colombia is deeply connected to issues surrounding both cultural diversity and biodiversity. In addition, as Eduardo states and the work of Mini-Mal shows, the role of chefs and restaurants in promoting sustainability is based on the valuation of subtle differences, as found in seeds, flavors, aromas, culinary techniques, and quality artisan producers. This is why at Mini-Mal, its twentieth anniversary was marked by showcasing Zenú cultural practices that make feasible and desirable the cultivation of fourteen different types of yams (*ñame*), forty-two varieties of cassava, and eighteen varieties of beans.

In this case, there is culinary sustainability insofar as there is an interest from both the community and the restaurant in resignifying the importance of cultivating a variety of foods. In the words of Eduardo, "Restaurants can point to a different model of city-countryside articulation opting for products obtained from sustainable practices that promote an income for local communities and allow them to remain in their territories and live a dignified life. Furthermore, this should be a model that genuinely recognizes the value of local knowledge, that is, a sensitive model that understands the capacities of the environment and of cultural abilities in the promotion of regional diversity."

Notes

1. The most recent national agricultural census, carried out in 2014 by the DANE (Colombian government institute of statistics), signaled that of 36.7 million hectares suitable for agricultural use only 7.1 million were being used. See Delgado 2019. According to the FAO (United Nations Food and Agriculture Organization), 82 percent of productive land in Colombia is in the hands of 10 percent of landowners. This phenomenon is associated with large-scale agri-businesses (e.g., palm oil, sugarcane, cattle raising), and commercial speculation, violence, and territorial control.
2. This is an initiative that started in 1996 as a list of endangered foods (domestic species, wild species, or processed products) that are linked to the identity of a group and to local traditional knowledge.
3. These foods are stigmatized mainly because of their bitter or earthy overtones, but also for their association with an older generation and times of scarcity.

References

Blay-Palmer, Alison, Roberta Sonnino, and Julien Custot. 2016 "A Food Politics of the Possible? Growing Sustainable Food Systems through Networks of Knowledge." *Agriculture and Human Values* 33:27–43.

Camacho, Juana. 2017. "Una cocina exprés. Cómo se cocina una política pública de patrimonio culinario." In *El valor del patrimonio: Mercado, políticas culturales y agenciamientos sociales*, edited by Mauricio Montenegro, Margarita Chaves, and Marta Zambrano, 169–200. Bogotá: Editorial ICANH.

Counihan, Carole. 2019. *Italian Food Activism in Urban Sardinia: Place, Taste, and Community.* London: Bloomsbury Academic.

Delgado, Martha. 2019. "Uso potencial y efectivo de la tierra agrícola en Colombia: Resultados del Censo Nacional Agropecuario." Bogotá: Fedesarrollo. https://www.repository.fedesarrollo.org.co/bitstream/handle/11445/4079/Repor_Septiembre_2019_Delgado_05_05_2022.pdf?sequence=4&isAllowed=y.

Duque-Maecha, Juliana. 2017. "A New Culinary Culture in Colombia: Equality and Identity in the Interpretation of Traditional Cuisines." PhD diss., Cornell University.

De la Vega-Leinert, Cristina. 2018. "Ciudades y consumo de bienes agrícolas. Transformaciones del consumo alimentario en el contexto de cambios en el comercio agrícola y las cadenas comerciales." *Estudios Demográficos y Urbanos* 34 (1): 213–19. http://dx.doi.org/10.24201/edu.v34i1.1859.

Escobar, Arturo. 1998. "Whose Knowledge, Whose Nature? Biodiversity, Conservation, and the Political Ecology of Social Movements." *Journal of Political Ecology* 5 (1): 53–82.

Escobar, Arturo. 2008. *Territories of Difference: Place, Movements, Life, Redes.* Durham, NC: Duke University Press.

Food and Agriculture Organization of the United Nations (FAO). 2017. "Concentración y extranjerización de tierras productivas en Colombia. Marco conceptual, legal e institucional, contribución a la aplicación de las directrices voluntarias sobre la gobernanza responsable de la tenencia de la tierra." Bogotá: FAO.

Godart, Frédéric and Sorah Seong, and Damon J. Phillips. 2020. "The Sociology of Creativity: Elements, Structures, and Audiences." *Annual Review of Sociology* 46:489–510.

Goodman, David, and Melanie DuPuis. 2002 "Knowing Food and Growing Food: Beyond the Production–Consumption Debate in the Sociology of Agriculture." *Sociologia Ruralis* 42 (1): 5–22.

Glavič, Peter, and Rebeka Lukman. 2007. "Review of Sustainability Terms and Their Definitions." *Journal of Cleaner Production* 15 (18): 1875–85.

Helgesson, Claes-Fredrik, and Fabian Muniesa. 2013. "For What It's Worth: An Introduction to Valuation Studies." *Valuation Studies* 1 (1): 1–10.

Hernández, Amado. 2013. "Eduardo Martínez, el vigía de las riquezas autóctonas." *Revista Catering* 10 (59): 66–71.

Higgins-Desbiolles, Freya, Emily Moskwa, and Gayathri Wijesinghe. 2019. "How Sustainable Is Sustainable Hospitality Research? A Review of Sustainable Restaurant Literature from 1991 to 2015." *Current Issues in Tourism* 22 (13): 1551–80.

Hurtado-Bermúdez, Leidy Johanna, Irene Vélez-Torres, and Fabián Méndez. 2021. "No Land for Food: Prevalence of Food Insecurity in Ethnic Communities Enclosed by Sugarcane Monocrop in Colombia." *International Journal of Public Health* 65 (12): 1087–96.

Latour, Bruno. 2004. "How to Talk about the Body? The Normative Dimension of Science Studies." *Body and Society* 10 (2–3): 205–29.

Leon-Sicard, Tomás, Marina Sánchez de Prager, Leidy Johana Rojas, Juan Carlos Ortiz, Juan Adolfo Bermúdez, Alvaro Acevedo, and Arlex Angarita. 2015. "Hacia una historia de la agroecología en Colombia." *Revista de Agroecología* 10 (2): 39–53.

Martínez, Eduardo, Antounela Ariza, and Manuel Romero. 2021. *Mini-Mál: Sorprendentemente colombiano*. Bogotá: Hambre de cultura editorial.

Naredo, José Manuel. 2004. "Sobre el origen, el uso y el contenido del término sostenible." *Cuaderno de Investigación urbanística* 41:7–18.

RECAR. 2005. "Declaración del Resguardo Indígena Zenú, Córdoba y Sucre, como Territorio Libre de Transgénicos." *Semillas*, no. 26/27 (December): 8–10.

Rey, Santiago. 2019. "Hermeneutics of Flavor: Imagination and Solidarity." Lecture presented at the Association for the Study of Food and Society and the Agriculture, Food, and Human Values Society Conference, Anchorage, Alaska, June 28.

Ulloa, Ana María, Josep Roca, and Hèloïse Vilaseca. 2017. "From Sensory Capacities to Sensible Skills: Experimenting with El Celler de Can Roca." *Gastronomica. The Journal of Critical Food Studies* 17 (2): 26–38.

Wayne, Timothy. 2017. "Developing Paradise: Agricultural Science in the Conflicted Landscapes of Colombia's Cauca Valley, 1927–1967." PhD diss., Yale University.

Weiss, Brad. 2012. "Configuring the Authentic Value of Real Food: Farm-to-Fork, Snout-to-Tail, and Local Food Movements." *American Ethnologist* 39 (3): 614–26.

CHAPTER THREE

Strategies in Vegan Food Experience Design

The Case of Bellies Restaurant in Stavanger, Norway

JONATAN LEER

Introduction

Reducing meat consumption is often highlighted as a key issue in creating new food systems that are ecologically less burdensome (Dagevos and Voordouw 2013; Laakso et al. 2022). The sustainability argument for eating less meat seems to have sparked a rise in veganism over the last decade (Sexton, Garnett, and Lorimer 2022). During this period, the number of vegan restaurants has also risen significantly around the world, notably in major cities (Gvion 2021; Niederle and Schubert 2020).

The last five years have also seen some spectacular vegan makeovers of fine-dining restaurants that previously served meat. An example of this is Noma in Copenhagen—five times first on *Restaurant Magazine*'s World's 50 Best list—which introduced a totally plant-based menu for the 2018 summer season. Also in Copenhagen, Michelin three-star Geranium has been completely plant based since January 2022. In New York, the legendary Eleven Madison Park decided in 2021 to focus entirely on a plant-based menu.[1] The reasons for this shift were explained by head chef David Humm in his annual letter. He stressed that the decision was motivated by sustainability concerns and the ambition to "become better stewards of our planet." The chef also insisted that the shift, despite certain initial inquietudes, sparked "renewed energy in the kitchen," and finally, he asserted that "our guests have never been more diverse or enthusiastic."[2]

When you consider such testimonies and examples from three restaurants in the world's gastronomic elite, one might think that it would be straightforward for many other restaurants to do entirely plant-based menus, particularly as an increasing number of consumers are becoming more open to plant-based foods and flexitarian practices (Gheihman 2021). Some studies even talk about a kind of "mainstreaming" (Sexton, Garnett, and Lorimer 2022) or at least the "destigmatization" of vegan food (Lundahl 2020). However, the percentage of vegetarians and vegans is still relatively small in many Western societies: for instance, 3 percent of the population were vegans in the United States in 2019 (Gheihman 2021), and around 10 percent followed a meat-free diet in the United Kingdom in 2020 (McKeown and Dunn 2021), while the figure was 3 percent for Denmark in 2022 according to the Danish Vegetarian Society.[3]

Chefs can play a role as facilitators in the transition to a more sustainable plant-based diet, and it seems that there is a growing clientele for plant-based eating (Niederle and Schubert 2020). At the same time, chefs working exclusively with plant-based menus have to appeal to the meat-eating and flexitarian population as well in order to be able to run a successful business that is economically sustainable, given the relatively low percentage of vegans. On the basis of these reflections, this chapter explores the strategies used by chefs working with vegan cuisine to attract new omnivore consumers to their plant-based food. Previous studies have emphasized that "plant pushing" is more effective than "meat hating" (Crimarco et al. 2021), and that some restaurants combine discourses of health and environmentalism while toning down the vegan ideology of animal welfare (Gvion 2021; chapter 6 in this volume). Paolo Niederle and Maycon Noremberg Schubert (2020) argue that despite their sometimes loose ties to the vegan movement and ideology, vegan restaurants might still facilitate practices that can contribute to a more sustainable food system.

More specifically, this chapter explores the case of a plant-based restaurant that has opted for a rather different communication strategy compared to the outspoken tone of Humm's declaration, or to attempts to promote specific rational arguments for vegan food based on health issues or environmental discourses (Gvion 2021; this volume). The restaurant in question is Bellies in Stavanger in the southwestern part of Norway. The restaurant has decided not to use words such as "vegan" or "sustainability" on its website, menus, or other material despite being 100 percent vegan.

Rather, it focuses on giving its guests a varied and sophisticated sensory food experience. In short, it targets guests' bellies rather than their minds.

The case of Bellies was selected because it presents a novel strategy to attract omnivore consumers to vegan restaurants. Although the people behind the restaurant believe strongly in the vegan ideology and see vegan food as an essential part of creating more sustainable food systems, they refuse to communicate these strong opinions discursively. Instead they communicate via sensory (i.e., nondiscursive) statements. Hence Bellies's ambition is to "show" rather than "tell." This raises a series of questions concerning the different strategies adopted by chefs in promoting a new and more sustainable diet to the omnivore majority, notably questions about how chefs could and should balance ideology and sensory pleasure when they work as agents in the green transition. This case is discussed as an alternative way to promote plant-based fine dining. The chapter ends with a series of reflections on the complex role of the contemporary chef as a mediator of pleasure, activism, and sustainability in the age of the green transition. With this focus on restaurant strategies, the chapter builds on the generally accepted understanding of sustainability as encompassing environmental, social, and economic dimensions (Maxey 2006). The chapter has a particular focus on how chefs develop environmentally friendly vegan meals and try to embrace new social segments while maintaining an economically sustainable business.

Design and Ideology in Vegan Food Experiences

Previous research finds that vegan chefs differ in how they position themselves in relation to veganism, sustainability, animal rights, and other discourses associated with plant-based food and, furthermore, in how they design their dining experience to appeal to vegans and nonvegans alike (Crimarco et al. 2020; Fusté-Forné 2021; Gvion 2021 and this volume; Niederle and Schubert 2020). A major point of discordance among vegans is whether vegan food should include mock versions of meat-based dishes (e.g., vegan burgers, tofu bourguignon, beetroot tartare), or if these meat references should be eliminated to demarcate a distance from what they call the "carnist" ideology (Joy 2011). Fusté-Forné (2021) highlights that vegan tourists differ in their attitudes to this issue. Some find the vegan versions of burgers and hot dogs a way of making it easier to go vegan. Others have a profound disdain for this type of food and thus prefer to eliminate any allusions to meat.

Anthony Crimarco et al. (2020) explore vegan soul food restaurants, with a particular interest in how this kind of food can stimulate healthy eating among African Americans in the southern part of the United States. Their article includes various examples of how restaurant owners talk to nonvegan customers about changing to veganism, emphasizing the potential health benefits. Furthermore, they stress that tasting good and using high-quality products are crucial for vegan food to appeal to nonvegans.

Liora Gvion (2021; this volume) emphasizes that vegan restaurants in Tel Aviv, a city nominated as the vegan capital of the world, are rather discreet about their vegan profile. Instead of highlighting their adherence to the vegan movement and political issues such as animal welfare, these restaurants mask these aspects of veganism. Plant-based food is presented as the healthy or climate-friendly choice, but no controversial statements challenging meat-based food are offered, and the restaurants "do not contribute to representing veganism as an alternative food movement" (15). On the contrary, they have strong references to meat dishes and a frequent use of mock meat and vegan versions of meat dishes. Niederle and Schubert (2020) find a similar loose and downplayed connection between the restaurants and the vegan movement; however, their study nonetheless argues that the restaurants could still work to facilitate more sustainable food practices.

These studies involve casual eateries for everyday consumption. Bellies, the case discussed in this chapter, is positioned between these more casual eateries and the world-renowned restaurants mentioned in the opening paragraphs. An evening at Bellies with the full food and wine menu costs around two hundred euros per person, which is well above most everyday consumers' budgets but still only about a third of the price for a dinner at Noma or the other elite restaurants.

In this regard, there seems to be a clear distinction between the elite restaurants' manifest provegan and ideological declarations, as in the example of Humm, and the more "discreet" and "functionalist" veganism in the more common restaurants mentioned in Crimarco et al. (2020) and Gvion (2021; this volume). These differences should probably be explained by the nature of the competitive restaurant industry, as suggested by Gvion. The small vegan places need to be as attractive as possible to as many people as possible, while the restaurants mentioned in the opening paragraphs have such well-established brands that they can pretty much do what they like and still attract more than enough clients to be fully booked.

Bellies: A Vegan Restaurant

In this chapter, I focus on the restaurant Bellies because its strategy to promote vegan food differs from that of the restaurants described in the existing literature and focuses primarily on the sensory experience. The case of Bellies is also interesting because of the restaurant's market position between a casual vegan café and a world élite restaurant. This type of restaurant is accessible to a larger segment of the middle classes, but at this price, clients expect culinary innovation. This combination suggests that chefs can be understood as agents of the green transition by developing innovative plant-based food. Nevertheless, one should not forget that the customers for such restaurants are still mostly privileged individuals from the middle classes, and the impact is relatively small scale.

For this study, I collected data in three steps. First, I visited Bellies's website and social media accounts, making notes about the restaurant's online identity and aesthetic strategies. Second, I visited Stavanger and interviewed the owner and head chef of Bellies for one and a half hours in the restaurant. This interview focused on (1) their background, (2) their ambitions for the restaurant and local relations, (3) their ideals for vegan fine dining and sustainability, (4) how they balance ideology and pleasure in vegan fine dining, and (5) reflections on their work with the restaurant up to then and in the future. Third, as the sensory experience was central to Bellies, I used sensory ethnography (Pink 2015) to explore the experience design and the restaurant's strategy of showing rather than telling. I made two visits to the restaurant. The first was during the day to get an impression of the restaurant and its surroundings; this was on the same occasion as the interview. Later, I engaged in the full experience of Bellies and ate at the restaurant. I arrived at 8:30 p.m. and left around midnight. During this time, I ordered the full food and wine menu. I dictated observations on a smartphone recorder from the moment of leaving my hotel and throughout the meal. I commented on every aspect of the experience, and I had made a list of things to include in my observations beforehand. These included (1) the restaurant as a part of its neighborhood, (2) atmosphere and interior design, (3) interpersonal relations with staffers, (4) other guests, and (5) the food (taste, texture, visuals, odors). These observations were transcribed when I returned to the hotel.

Hence the dataset consisted of notes from the website and social media, a transcription of the interviews, and the written observations from the sensory ethnography. This methodological mix provided an understanding of the ideas behind the restaurant and an opportunity to dissect the sensory experience. The sensory ethnography data were an extremely important supplement to the interviews, as they allowed me to highlight the sensory strategies of the restaurant. In sensory ethnography (Pink 2015), it is important to situate the experience and describe the sensory dispositions of the researcher. I am a Danish, white, middle-class male in my forties. For this study, my being a meat-eater is particularly important, but I am one who tries, like so many other middle-class individuals, to reduce his meat intake for sustainability reasons (Leer 2018). Hence, I am very much in the target group for a restaurant such as Bellies and I go to gourmet restaurants in the Bellies price range a couple of times per year. I am also familiar with the cultural scripts of a fine-dining restaurant.

Bellies is located in Stavanger, a city with a population of 130,000 that is the center of the Norwegian oil industry. Stavanger is located in the Rogaland region, which is also considered the agricultural heartland of Norway. Much of Norway's long and expansive territory is mountainous and a large part of it is located north of the Arctic Circle. This renders agriculture difficult in many places. Rogaland is an exception. The coastal and southern territory of Rogaland has a mild climate and soil well suited to agriculture, notably production of carrots, potatoes, and leeks, for which it is still famous. Although the area has generally undergone a radical transformation from a farming and fishing community to an industrial area with the rise of oil production,[4] agriculture remains important and is a source of local pride, notably with the renewed interest in local food and Nordic food during the early 2000s (Jönsson 2013; Leer 2016a; Skårup 2013). As a culinary destination, Stavanger is known for the Norwegian Hotel Management School, which was established in 1912 as the second in the world. The GladMat Festival, the Stavanger food festival established in the early 2000s that is one of the most important in the Nordic countries, has also helped mark Stavanger as a place of culinary importance nationally and internationally (Einarsen and Mykletun 2009).

Bellies, the first fine-dining plant-based restaurant in the city, is located a few kilometers from the city center in an old part of the harbor. This neighborhood is undergoing a radical gentrification as the old industrial area is being turned into elegant modern apartment buildings. The restaurant is located on the first floor in a new building. Around it, there are still some old, deserted factory buildings. The area is thus still very heterogenous with small traditional houses, big modern residences with apartments, and old industrial buildings. An article in a Norwegian business magazine describing Pedersgata, a street that stretches from the outskirts of the city center and ends close to Bellies, compares it to Brooklyn, New York.[5] According to the article and my observations, the street is filled with entrepreneurs concerned with food, culture, and sustainability, with a strong focus on waste reduction.

The area could thus also be considered an example of what Fabio Parasecoli and Mateusz Halawa (2019) have dubbed "Global Brooklyn." This is a global trend in world cities where old industrial areas are transformed into gentrified hipster food areas with postindustrial design and a focus on craft products and a casual ambience, centered around carefully curated expressions of culinary connoisseurship that are antagonistic to mainstream food consumption and global chains. These spaces often embrace sustainable forms of food consumption and cater to an urban middle class with high cultural capital (Leer 2021; Parasecoli and Halawa 2021).

An Evening at Bellies

On a Wednesday evening in early November 2021, I set out for Bellies from my hotel in the city center of Stavanger. I had reserved a table at Bellies for the late seating at 8:30 p.m. It had already been dark for some hours and a light drizzle was falling. Bellies is situated on Pedersgata, which is a long street. I passed a number of restaurants where people were eating in cozy candlelit dining rooms. After a while, Pedersgata changed and the restaurants were replaced by private homes. A few minutes later, I passed a highway bridge and entered a more industrial zone. I arrived at Bellies, which is located next to an abandoned factory covered in graffiti. On the front, I noticed an inscription saying "Make the weather great again." I could not agree more. I was wet, hungry, starting to freeze, and very happy to arrive at my destination. Bellies stood out with its bright yellow façade among the grey residential buildings. Through the windows, I distinguished green plants, a warm light, and parties of guests in animated conversation.

Inside, I found myself face to face with a large, human-sized plant. It seemed to be greeting me. Then, I was met by a waiter who seated me in the corner of the restaurant closest to the open kitchen at a very nice table with an uninterrupted view of the head chef, Tony Martin, and his team.

They were working in a relatively big kitchen with a pizza oven as the centerpiece. I ordered the tasting menu and the accompanying wine menu. The first element was a glass of sparkling wine. All the wines were natural wines with light, fresh, and fruity expressions. As I enjoyed my glass, I sat back and admired the room with its mixture of natural elements in the new Nordic style and the "rough urban" look (exposed bricks and metal tubes), making me think of "Global Brooklyn" again. The tables were naked and I recognized the chairs from visits to classmates' homes in the 1980s, adding a slight retro element to the room, which was also present in the soundscape dominated by what I identified as the groovy music of the 1970s. The urban dimension was offset by a lot of green plants at floor level, along the walls, and rising to the ceiling—a feature that I have seen previously in various New Nordic restaurants.

The service was precise, and the waiters were very straightforward, almost understated when they served the food with a very short presentation and a smile. The menu started with a finger food: a crunchy miniature tart with flowers served on a plate decorated with leaves in autumn colors. This was followed by two more wet dishes—vegetable ravioli served in a broth topped with green and white mayonnaise, and a *bao*, a steamed bun with filling, topped with crushed pistachio nuts in an even more intense broth. The bao worked as a sponge absorbing all the broth. Then more filling servings followed such as freshly baked warm pita and variations on baba ghanoush. Like the bao dish, this was to be eaten with the fingers. Then came the vegetables of the season: a breadless celery "sandwich," a whole poached beetroot, and a beer-glazed parsley root. Although these three dishes all were based on root vegetables, they were quite distinct in taste and texture. The celery sandwich had a certain crunchiness in its texture, favoring the distinct flavor of the celery, whereas the beetroot was moist and had a round, warm taste. The parsley root had a distinct beer flavor and was topped with toasted grains to contrast its smooth texture with a crunchy one. Finally came fresh ice cream and a sweet dessert covered in what appeared to be very thin layers of meringue in dark green, red, and brown nuances. After three hours consuming this varied menu, I returned to the rainy street and reflected on the many impressions of this symphony of vegetables. It was evident that the chef's ambition was to showcase the diversity of vegan food in both taste and texture without clear references to well-known meat dishes in the standard repertoire of Western restaurants.

Local Vegetables Frame the Experience

The same week I had this multifaceted dinner, I interviewed the team behind the restaurant: manager Øystein Lunde Ohna and head chef Tony Martin. Ohna was relatively new to the restaurant industry. He had a background in the yoga and vegan community and previously worked in finance. He had tried to run a vegan café in the first decade of the 2000s, but it was very difficult at that time. Despite that difficulty, he was intrigued when the opportunity to run a restaurant in the new area of Pedersgata arose. Tony Martin was trained in the classic French tradition and had worked in various restaurants in Stavanger, increasingly focusing on vegetables. When he was asked to join the Bellies venture, he said yes right away, although he knew it would be a challenge to develop an entirely vegan menu.

The morning of the interview, Martin and Ohna had just had breakfast with the staff and seen the weekly selection of seasonal local vegetables that arrived from local farmers every week at this time. The restaurant is only open for lunch and dinner from Wednesday through Saturday. Each Tuesday is used to develop the week's menu on the basis of that week's vegetable selection. Ohna explained, "We say to the farmer, give me the best you have for as long as you have it." It is then Martin's job to create a menu on that basis. During the interview, Martin showed me his blank sheet of paper that, during the coming hours, he hoped to fill with a complete menu on the basis of the vegetables available that week. Often, calculations had to be made to ensure that there would be enough for all the guests during a regular week, which usually meant forty guests twice a day for lunch and dinner. Martin exemplified this kind of planning with the pumpkins that year. There were very few and they only lasted two weeks, so the kitchen staff had to cook very small pieces to allow all guests a tasting during the two weeks. They had to invent a recipe for roasted pumpkin that enhanced the taste of pumpkin to stretch the limited amount and ensure that all guests were given an intense experience of pumpkin.

Ohna stressed that they did not want to do an à la carte menu, because it was impossible to do a sustainable menu with local vegetables in this way. The ever-changing set menu was more sustainable, because it was designed on the basis of the ingredients offered by the local farmers in any particular week. This way, no dishes were prepared that guests might not order. Hence the food waste was minimal.

Nonetheless, this modus operandi challenged the traditional power relations in the restaurant. The guests must accept the plant-based concept of the restaurant and, furthermore, accept not knowing the menu in advance. In the kitchen, the chef must be very creative and innovative, week after week, and adapt to the produce available each week. Hence the food experience is not defined by the whims of guests, nor by the chef's signature dishes. It is shaped by the local material resources at hand. The farmer and the seasonal products frame the experience. In this sense, the experience is not client-centric ("the client is always right"), nor is it chef-centric ("the chef is a genius"); it is essentially defined by the farmer and the vegetables of the local terroir. The materiality of the food frames the experience and the human actors: the chef and the clients have to accept this particular dynamic of things and perform their role in respect to this hierarchy.

This concept is, of course, particularly challenging in the Nordic countries, where the vegetable growing season is short. There is, however, a long tradition of using large amounts of stored root vegetables in the winter (Marshall 2021) and recent innovations produce food throughout the year. When I was in Stavanger again in the summer of 2022, I visited one of Bellies's suppliers, the innovative mushroom company Topp Sopp, which has a sustainable year-round mushroom production using coffee grounds and other waste material in climate-controlled facilities.

Avoid Chewing and Talking

During my interview, I asked Martin how he composes his menus. He stressed that his guiding principle focused on what the plant-based food experience should *not* be: "You should not chew a lot." According to both Martin and Ohna, the stereotype of plant-based and vegan food is that you have to chew continuously, almost like a cud-chewing animal. To avoid reproducing this prejudice, their ambition was that the food experience should be anything but a general impression of chewing quantities of raw vegetables. The menus were thus composed to demonstrate the potential diversity of tastes and textures in plant-based food, which was also my experience.

Likewise, it was important to Ohna and Martin that the experience change according to the season—not just in relation to which kinds of vegetables are served, but also in terms of the "direction" of the meal and the "seasonal atmosphere," as Ohna pointed out. He elaborated by explaining that the spring menu was dominated by a "blooming" light feeling. In the summer, people often ate outside on the terrace and the menu consisted of small summer vegetables served in very simple compositions. In the autumn, the menu tended to be dominated by dishes that mix vegetables, often resembling a stew. In the winter, intensity was central, often in the form of concentrated bouillons. This, in turn, generated a longing for the lighter spring menu and completed the circle. Hence the menus reflected the materials accessible in any specific week, but also a cyclic form of seasonal transitions. This showed that sustainable vegetable-focused food is not a boring or uniform diet. It is a diverse and dynamic experience, and it meets the human need for stimulating foods and tastes. As Ohna concluded, "If you just eat raw carrots all year round, you go mad!"

Another aspect central to dining at Bellies was a focus on the sensuous and bodily aspects of the food experience. As Ohna explained, "We chose the name Bellies because we wanted to 'meet you [guests] in the belly.' When things get up here [pointing a finger to his head], we get strong ideas and express tough ideas, [but] things stay only in people's heads. That's why we don't talk about veganism or vegetarianism, it isn't written anywhere. That's why we don't talk about sustainability or local produce or such things. We only want to 'meet people in the belly.' " He then went on to say that he had an extended understanding of the belly as the center of the body and a kind of sensory reservoir. The focus at Bellies was on a bodily mode of experiencing rather than an intellectual, moral, or ideological one. I also noted this during my meal experience: the waiters talked very little about the food when they served the dishes compared to many other fine-dining restaurants I have visited, where waiters introduced a dish with a long description of its every element.

Making Meat-Eaters Feel Comfortable

Ohna estimated that at maximum 10 percent of the clients of Bellies are vegetarians or vegans. Both Martin and Ohna emphasized that they have fashioned the experience and the atmosphere of the restaurant to make it accessible and welcoming to nonvegetarians and nonvegans as well. To this end, it was important to have high standards and, at the same time, a relaxed atmosphere. Martin elaborated, "Standards are important. We must have an insanely high standard and guests must be met with comfort and functionality. We're a little removed from the city center, so people have to walk all the way up here and then everything is plant-based. It [the food] has to reach a standard they haven't seen before. And the space has to be a space they haven't seen before. And nice and comfortable to enter."

Ohna contrasted the restaurant experience at Bellies with that of more norm-breaking restaurants such as Alchemist in Copenhagen. Alchemist is transgressive because it challenges the guests with provocative eating designs and politicized statements. Ohna referred to its dish "Tongue Kiss," which guests have to lick from a silicone tongue. This is an example of what he sees as the "Alchemist fuck-off style" that puts guests on the spot. At Bellies, they have decided not to apply this kind of transgressive food design. As Martin mentioned, many meat-eaters already experience an element of transgression when entering a plant-based restaurant. The guests should be able to drop their guard when entering Bellies. They should feel welcome and comfortable.

Therefore, the comfortable and welcoming atmosphere seems to be created by toning down the transgressive element of plant-based food and also, as mentioned earlier, by avoiding too much talk, ensuring that guests do not feel lectured to. Hence the idea of "meeting guests in the belly" seems to imply that guests feel safe in a space that is not dominated by ideological or moral discourses but by varied and pleasant, sensuous impressions. So, the sensuousness of Bellies does not focus on dramatic changes in atmosphere or feelings, or on breaking boundaries as in Alchemist's theatrical meals. Rather, its sensuous ideal seems to rely on guests being relaxed and open to the plant-based food, which should be varied while remaining relatively pleasing and unchallenging for a meat-eater's palate. To avoid excessive chewing is thus not only about avoiding the cliché of the vegan cud-chewing character, but also about not challenging or demanding too much of guests, even in the design of meal textures. It seems that Bellies has been relatively successful, since the place is often fully booked. Ohna pointed out that, during the first three years it was open, it increased its prices by 10 percent twice without losing clientele.

The Mind and/or the Belly

As demonstrated in this chapter, chefs differ in how to design vegan food experiences and position themselves as facilitators of plant-based meals that appeal to nonvegan segments of the population. In this context, it is important to consider that while some claim that veganism has been through a kind of "destigmatization" (Lundahl 2020), Eva Haifa Giraud (2021) argues that vegans are still considered "killjoys" at the table of omnivores. Giraud builds on Sara Ahmed's concept of "feminist killjoy" (Ahmed 2017). A feminist killjoy is perceived by friends and family as killing the joy when calling out casual misogynistic and sexist jokes in a socializing situation. To Giraud (2021), the vegan is equally perceived as a killjoy by his or her mere presence at the table of omnivores, as if the existence of the vegan questions the legitimacy of an omnivore meat-based diet.

To some omnivores, the vegan diet and vegans might be inspiring. However, many omnivores still consider vegans and veganism "culinary killjoys," for instance, putting asceticism, ideology, and morals before good taste and culinary pleasures (Giraud 2021). It is in this context that it seems interesting to consider the strategies of vegan chefs and the case of Bellies. I think very few chefs would want to consider themselves killjoys; rather, they would strive for the opposite: being designers and producers of pleasurable and memorable experiences. Nevertheless, chefs are increasingly engaged in ideological and political activism and use it as part of their brand (Hollows 2022; Leer 2016b).

When it comes to balancing ideology and pleasure, these concerns seem to be fundamental differences between the casual eateries described by Gvion (2021; this volume) and the elite restaurants I mentioned in the opening paragraphs of this chapter. The latter advertise the fact that they are going plant based, hoping people will acknowledge the audacity of this ideological move as we saw with Humm. The vegan restaurateurs described by Gvion (2021; this volume) were very careful not to flag their vegan identity and, particularly, any form of radical vegan ideology. Some even tried to mask their vegan identity, hoping that their clients did not realize that they were at a vegan restaurant.

Bellies seems to take a different path with its ambition to "meet the client in the belly." All the other restaurants mentioned in this chapter focus, to a large extent, on the mind. They give people good, sensible arguments for eating vegan food, such as Humm's ambitions of "becoming better stewards of the planet" or the rational health and environmental arguments offered by the Israeli vegan restaurants discussed by Gvion (2021; this volume). This does not mean that they do not make exciting vegan food, but it comes with a clearly stated message. I understand Bellies's vision of "meeting the customer in the belly" as the ambition to put an innovative sensory experience at the center of vegan food and scrape off all moral issues and discourses. It downplayed the vegan ideology for very different reasons than those mentioned in Gvion (2021;

this volume). Bellies does not try to please meat-eaters by giving them a meat-like experience but rather by privileging the sensory qualities, diversity, and uniqueness of vegan food. The omnivore guest should forget all the killjoy aspects of veganism and be open to sensory arguments for veganism rather than intellectual ones.

Ohna acknowledges that this strategy also has its weaknesses. He highlights that the restaurant has not gotten the attention he had hoped for. He emphasizes that the media like the labels "vegan" and "sustainable" and that these are announced loudly in many other restaurants' branding. For instance, he mentions some Stavanger restaurants located not far from Bellies, which, although they serve meat and fish, have gotten much more credit for their sustainability efforts than Bellies because they use the word "sustainability" systematically in their image building. Hence the proprietors at Bellies are considering whether to articulate their position more explicitly going forward in relation to the buzz about sustainability.

This case also illuminates the dilemmas concerning vegan restaurants in this slow popularization of plant-based food among omnivores, and how their branding, food design, and positioning in the market are complicated and highly dependent on context. The situation is vastly different for a vegan café in Tel Aviv, Eleven Madison Park in New York, or a plant-based fine dining restaurant in Stavanger. Furthermore, the case also calls into question the role of the chef in relation to the green transition and which methods are most effective when a restaurant kitchen seeks to contribute to sustainable development. Should the sustainable chef focus on the mind or the belly? Or on a bit of both? And finally, how can a fine dining restaurant inspire sustainable solutions on a larger scale and not just please privileged middle-class clients? Ohna and Martin stressed that they were aware of the limited ability of fine-dining restaurants to effect change. However, they were confident that they had changed some people's views on vegan food, and they saw their kitchen as a lab where creative, tasty, and sustainable plant-based solutions were developed. Some of these could be used on a whole different scale someday.

Notes

1. Although it is often a matter of dispute, I use plant-based and vegan as synonymous in this chapter for diets that exclude all forms of animal products, while vegetarian diets exclude only meat, eggs, and dairy products. (See also Giraud 2021.)

2. Retrieved March 15, 2022, from https://www.elevenmadisonpark.com/.
3. Retrieved March 15, 2022, from https://vegetarisk.dk/statistik-om-danmark/.
4. The 2018 TV series *Lykkeland* narrates this radical transformation of the area around Stavanger.
5. Retrieved March 15, 2022, from https://ne.no/2021/04/13/et-lite-stykke-brooklyn/.

References

Ahmed, S. 2017. *Living a Feminist Life*. New York: Duke University Press.
Crimarco, A., G. M. Turner-McGrievy, M. Botchway, M. Macauda, S. A. Adams, C. E. Blake, and N. Younginer. 2020. "We're Not Meat Shamers. We're Plant Pushers." *Journal of Black Studies* 51 (2): 168–93. https://doi.org/10.1177/0021934719895575.
Dagevos, H., and J. Voordouw. 2013. "Sustainability and Meat Consumption: Is Reduction Realistic?" *Sustainability: Science, Practice and Policy* 9 (2): 60–69.
Einarsen, K., and R. J. Mykletun. 2009. "Exploring the Success of the Gladmatfestival (the Stavanger Food Festival)." *Scandinavian Journal of Hospitality and Tourism* 9 (2–3): 225–48.
Fusté-Forné, F. 2021. "Vegan Food Tourism." In *Routledge Handbook on Vegan Studies*, edited by L. Wright, 336–48. London: Routledge.
Giraud, E. H., 2021. *Veganism: Politics, Practice, and Theory*. London: Bloomsbury:
Gheihman, N. 2021. "Veganism as a Lifestyle Movement." *Sociology Compass* 15 (1): 1–14. https://doi.org/10.1111/soc4.12877.
Gvion, L. 2021. "Vegan Restaurants in Israel: Health, Environmentalism and Mainstreaming." *Food, Culture & Society* 26 (5): 1–18. https://doi.org/10.1080/15528014.2021.2015941.
Hollows, J. 2022. *Celebrity Chefs, Food Media and the Politics of Eating*. London: Bloomsbury.
Halawa, M., and F. Parasecoli. 2019. "Eating and Drinking in Global Brooklyn." *Food, Culture & Society* 22 (4): 387–406.
Joy, M. 2011. *Why We Love Dogs, Eat Pigs, and Wear Cows: An Introduction to Carnism*. New York: Red Wheel.
Jönsson, H. 2013. "The Road to the New Nordic Kitchen—Examples from Sweden." In *The Return of Traditional Food*. Lunds Studies in Arts and Cultural Sciences 1, edited by P. Lysaght, H. Jönsson, and A. Burstedt, 53–67. Lund, Sweden: Lund University.
Laakso, S., M. Niva, V. Eranti, and F. Aapio. 2022. "Reconfiguring Everyday Eating: Vegan Challenge Discussions in Social Media." *Food, Culture & Society* 25 (2): 268–89.
Leer, J. 2016a. "The Rise and Fall of the New Nordic Cuisine." *Journal of Aesthetics & Culture* 8 (1): 334–94.
———. 2016b. "What's Cooking, Man? Masculinity in European Cooking Shows After 'The Naked Chef.'" *Feminist Review* 114 (1): 72–90.
———. 2018. *Kød*. Aarhus: Aarhus Universitetsforlag.
———. 2021. "Porridge Bars, Nordic Craft Beer, and Hipster Families in the Welfare State." In *Global Brooklyn: Designing Food Experiences in World Cities*, edited by F. Parasecoli and M. Halawa, 81–95. London: Bloomsbury.

Lundahl, O. 2020. "Dynamics of Positive Deviance in Destigmatisation: Celebrities and the Media in the Rise of Veganism." *Consumption Markets & Culture* 23 (3): 241–71.

Marshall, M. 2021. "Prepared for a Crisis and the Unexpected: Managing Everyday Eventualities through Food Storage Practices." *Food, Culture & Society* 26 (2): 1–22. https://doi.org/10.1080/15528014.2021.1967643.

Maxey, L., 2006. "Can We Sustain Sustainable Agriculture? Learning From Small-Scale Producer-Suppliers in Canada and the UK." *Geographical Journal* 172 (3): 230–44.

McKeown, P., and R. A. Dunn. 2021. "A 'Life-style Choice' or a Philosophical Belief?" *Liverpool Law Review* 42 (2): 207–41.

Niederle, P., and M. N. Schubert. 2020. "How Does Veganism Contribute to Shape Sustainable Food Systems?" *Journal of Rural Studies* 78 (1): 304–13.

Parasecoli, F., and M. Halawa, eds. 2021. *Global Brooklyn: Designing Food Experiences in World Cities.* London: Bloomsbury.

Pink, S. 2015. *Doing Sensory Ethnography.* London: Sage.

Sexton, A. E., T. Garnett, and J. Lorimer. 2022. "Vegan Food Geographies and the Rise of Big Veganism." *Progress in Human Geography* 46 (2): 605–28.

Skårup, B. 2013. "The New Nordic Diet and Danish Food Culture." In *The Return of Traditional Food.* Lunds Studies in Arts and Cultural Sciences 1, edited by P. Lysaght, H. Jönsson, and A. Burstedt, 33–42. Lund, Sweden: Lund University.

CHAPTER FOUR

Umamification as a Culinary Means for Sustainable Eating at Home and at Restaurants

OLE G. MOURITSEN AND KLAVS STYRBÆK

Introduction

By accounting for at least 30 percent of the stressors on global climate and the use of land, water, and energy resources, the global food system is one of the main responsible factors for the current climate crisis (Foley, Defries, and Asner 2005; Steffen et al. 2015; Vermuelen, Campbell, and Ingram. 2012). It has become obvious that our current mode of food production, processing, and consumption is not sustainable in the most general sense of the word (Searchinger 2019). Actions are needed acutely to feed a growing global population, which is estimated to approach 9.8 billion people in 2050, a healthy, nutritious diet that is also sustainable. High-level reports, such as the EAT-Lancet Commission report (Willett et al. 2019), in alignment with the United Nations Sustainable Development Goals (United Nations 2019), point out that a dramatic change of our current eating behavior must take place, including a major decrease of food waste from production to consumption. The necessary change implies a shift toward a more plant-based

Acknowledgments: The authors' work was supported by the Nordea Foundation, through a grant to Taste for Life. OGM's work on sustainability and the green transition was supported by a grant from the Carlsberg Foundation. **Declaration of Competing Interests:** The authors declare that they have no known competing financial interests or personal relationships that could have appeared to influence the work reported in this paper.

diet, which is at the core of the so-called green transition in the food systems. The proposed planetary menu or diet includes 500 g of vegetables and fruit every day as well as whole grains, legumes, nuts, and unsaturated fats; small amounts of fish and poultry; and no or very little red meat, processed meat, added sugars, refined cereals, and starchy vegetables (Willett et al. 2019).

This change in eating behavior will have very different implications for different food cultures, and the picture becomes particularly complicated to evaluate as previously less affluent populations gain wealth and strive toward the living standards of more affluent countries. A few key numbers for animal-based food consumption (i.e., beef, pork, lamb, poultry, fish and shellfish, dairy, and eggs) put this in perspective. The 2050 target of yearly animal-based food consumption recommended in the EAT-Lancet Commission report is 125 kg per capita (Willett et al. 2019). The global yearly average consumption animal-based food was about 150 kg per capita as of the early 2020s (Klimarådet 2021). This may seem like a minor difference, but it is not so for many affluent regions of the world. For example, the European average was 340 kg per capita, and in Denmark, one of the most meat-consuming countries, the yearly average was 380 kg per capita, three times the target amount. An additional concern is that population-rich countries such as China currently are increasing their meat consumption (Zhu 2022).

The big question is, how can we change the eating behavior toward more plant consumption in food cultures that traditionally eat large quantities of meat? Can we do so by referring to the climate crisis? History tells us that it is likely to be difficult. We have known for a long time that we should eat more green food and less meat for the sake of our own personal health and for public health in general. The advice to consume 500 g of vegetables and fruit every day is part of the national dietary recommendations in many countries. However, the statistics clearly show that globally we have never been so ill due to dietary-related diseases (Global Burden of Disease Study 2017). Apparently, we do not listen to the advice, nor have we let ourselves be significantly affected by public campaigns. If there is any change toward a greener eating behavior it is extremely slow, less than one percentage point every year (Daverkosen, Ejlersen, and Mouritsen 2022; Smart Protein 2022).

As indicated above, the challenges in the green transition toward a more plant-based eating behavior are complex and very difficult to meet. In the present chapter we attack this challenge head on by focusing on one of the key barriers that persists in populations that really want to eat more plant-based foods (e.g., vegetables), but just do not do it even when there are no cultural, sociological, ethical, or religious circumstances prohibiting changes in eating behavior. It is the present authors' viewpoint that the real challenge is more a matter of innate basic physiological taste than learned taste preferences. We shall here argue that there are two fundamental reasons why human beings do not prefer the flavor of plants. One has to do with the biology of plants; the other has to do with key aspects of human evolution (Mouritsen and Styrbæk 2020; Schmidt and Mouritsen 2020). However, once these have been recognized, solutions immediately present themselves to overcome the challenges.

A Note on Sustainability

The United Nations' Brundtland Commission defined sustainability as "meet[ing] the needs of the present without compromising the ability of future generations to meet their own needs" (1987, 16). Sustainability has social, economic, and environmental dimensions. In the context of food and human eating behavior we here define culinary sustainability as a responsible mode of selecting ingredients, preparing dishes, consuming meals, and minimizing food waste without compromising flavor and culinary qualities. In our optics, culinary sustainability is about producing delicious food from food items that are as low in the food web as possible and treated with as few energy-consuming processes and as little waste as possible, with a simultaneous concern for health and nutritional requirements.

The present authors' take on this problem when working with culinary sustainability, not least when communicating to the general public and to children in particular, is based on the following pragmatic view of relative sustainability. From a scientific point of view (based on the second law of thermodynamics), no process in a closed system can be truly sustainable; there are always energy losses, and the task is to minimize these losses as much as possible. The Earth's biosphere is fueled by energy (light) from the sun, and this energy flows through the system and eventually ends up as "waste" (heat). The basis for all life, and hence our food, is formed by certain living organisms that can transform the sunlight, via photosynthesis, into large macromolecules such as proteins, carbohydrates, and fats, using only water and inorganic materials dissolved in the water or in soil. These large molecules constitute our food, and in this sense, we eat the Sun (Morton 2007).

Those organisms that in this way can form macromolecules from energy and simple constituents are at the bottom of the food web, and they include plants and algae. They do not need other organisms to survive (although many of them certainly live in some kind of symbiotic relationships with other organisms such as bacteria). All animals, small and large, need these photosynthetic organisms to produce food, and animals cannot sustain life without them. The whole food web is built on this primary production, and organisms in this web, so to speak, eat each other.

Two types of macromolecules are particularly important in the context of food sustainability. One is carbohydrates that become synthesized in plants and algae (small microalgae as well as the large marine macroalgae, the seaweeds). Carbohydrates are used by animals as an energy source, but animals cannot produce carbohydrates. The other important type of macromolecules is certain fatty acids, in particular the so-called superunsaturated fatty acids (some known as omega-3 and omega-6 fatty acids) that can only be produced by algae, in particular microalgae. We cannot get these essential fatty acids from plants, so animals need both plants and algae in the food web.

Turning now to sustainability, every time food molecules proceed from one (so-called trophic) level in the food web to the next, there are losses, in typical cases more than 90 percent. As an example, we lose more than 90 percent of the proteins by letting, for example, legumes pass through a domestic animal to produce meat rather than eating the legumes directly. Some organisms, such as insects, are better at limiting the losses when transforming plant proteins to animal proteins. But there is always a loss, and it can be safely stated that it is relatively more sustainable to eat lower down in the food web.

Other organisms apart from plants and algae are not at the bottom but are low-lying in the food web. Fungi are one example, and aqueous filter animals such as bivalves are another. It has recently been established that farmed bivalves, along with farmed seaweeds, are the most sustainable crops in the marine food chain (Gephart et al. 2021).

We would like to point out the obvious, but strangely enough often overlooked fact, that no food can be considered sustainable (or nutritious and healthy) before it is eaten. Hence a major challenge in the green transitions and change in eating behavior is simply the taste. Will we eat it or not?

The Green Challenge

Faced with the need for sustainable transitions toward eating more plant-based foods (including algae and fungi) and less meat, we are challenged by two fundamental conditions. Humans have universally a craving for food with sweet and umami tastes, and a natural disgust for food with a bitter taste (Dunn and Sanchez 2021). Sweet, umami, and bitter are so-called basic tastes and their perception is carried by physiological processes. The craving for sweetness has been genetically encoded in us over millions of years from the time when our ancestors lived off mature fruits. Sweetness signals calories, and calories are good for survival. The craving for umami is rooted in the fact that we and our ancestors have been meat eaters for more than two million years, and increasingly so after the advent of fire for cooking raw meat (Wrangham 2009). Umami signals the presence of free amino acids from proteins, in particular free glutamate, as well as free nucleotides, both of which are abundant in muscles. Umami hence signals accessible nutrients (as well as energy) that also are important for survival. Our sweet and umami receptors evolved to steer us toward important foodstuffs that gave us advantages over evolutionary time scales. Hence it is a universal trait with humans, independently of culture, ethnicity, traditions, and so on, to favor food that is sweet and/or has umami. In contrast, our receptors for bitter taste evolved to help us stay away from food that may be poisonous. No wonder that mother's milk is characterized by sweetness from lactose and umami from amino acids.

With this background, and now turning to the question as to which tastes (we are not talking about olfactory sensation or smell here) plant-based food can offer, it is generally the case that except for the ripe fruits, green plant foods often lack sweetness and umami. The sweet sugars are bound in carbohydrates in the plant tissues, and carbohydrates have no taste because the molecules are too large to bind to the taste receptors Similarly, umami-tasting amino acids are bound in proteins, of which there may be plenty in plants, but being large molecules, proteins also have no taste. Another reason why plants do not offer much in terms of umami taste is that they do not have muscles that are a key source of nucleotides from nucleic acids (the energy source ATP that fuels muscular motion). If we add that many plants (again disregarding the ripe fruits) often contain bitter compounds (to scare eaters away), it becomes obvious why it is difficult to eat 500–600 g of vegetables every day: we are up against our evolutionary heritage encoded in our genes and the fundamental biology of plants. Once this is said, two solutions to the challenge immediately present themselves: 1) to add the missing sweetness and umami to plant-based foods from other sources, or 2) release the plants' inbuilt potential to produce sweetness and umami themselves by liberating the sugars and the free amino acids from their carbohydrates and proteins, respectively. This is most easily done by fermentation.

Need for Interdisciplinary Collaboration

Having provided insight into why it is difficult for humans to eat plant-based foods and then proposed that the solution is to be found in cooking with a focus on taste, it is obvious to us that there is a call for collaboration between scientists who know about food composition, structure, and the effects of culinary transformations, and practitioners such as chefs and food innovators who can design and implement preparation techniques that focus on taste, texture, and gastronomic value (Mouritsen, Sörensen, and Flore 2019). In this context, the fields of neurogastronomy (Shepherd 2011), gastrophysics (Mouritsen 2016), and molecular gastronomy (Burke et al. 2021) have been proposed to furnish the basic quantitative scientific underpinnings of gastronomy.

The present authors, a physical scientist and a chef and food innovator, have for almost fifteen years worked together on combining gastronomy, science, and craft (i.e., cooking skills) along these lines. It has taken us from areas such as umami (Mouritsen and Styrbæk 2014), mouthfeel, food texture (Mouritsen and Styrbæk 2017), and cephalopod gastronomy (Mouritsen and Styrbæk 2018, 2021a), to vegetables and other green food (Styrbæk and Mouritsen 2020; Mouritsen and Styrbæk 2021b). A driving force has been to explore how an understanding of the science behind taste and texture can be used to produce delicious meals and dishes from a variety of sustainable and nutritious raw ingredients, in particular plants and marine products. Most recently this collaboration has manifested itself in books, articles, recipe collections, and outreach activities related to the green transition and a practical implementation of the national Danish dietary recommendations (Mouritsen and Styrbæk 2021c). About five years ago we realized that our many years of work on combining science and craft with a focus on umami taste and texture furnished a strong platform for working on joint projects related to culinary sustainability.

The collaboration between the authors of the present paper has for the last seven years been part of a large national Danish project and research center, Taste for Life (Smag for Livet) (Schneider et al. 2018), spanning research, craft, and communication. The center has engaged scholars and researchers from the humanities (pedagogical and didactical scientists), natural sciences (sensory scientists and gastrophysicists), and social sciences (anthropologists and media and cultural studies scholars), as well as educators, chefs, and food innovators. One of the bridging elements between sciences and crafts manifested itself in the development of the emerging field of gastrophysics (Mouritsen 2012; Pedersen, Hansen, and Clausen 2021) and the building of special kitchen labs, so-called gastrolabs, where scientists, chefs, apprentice chefs, and educators can work together on the taste of food (Christensen and Stuart 2019).

Communication-Driven Research

By engaging in public communication about culinary activities rooted in combining culinary crafts with scientific curiosity, the authors have discovered, identified, and stimulated novel research programs on topics that might otherwise not have been studied at all or studied only through more conventional approaches (Mouritsen 2021). This unconventional mode of operating, called communication-driven research, has led to new research questions about sustainability, for example, regarding novel uses of marine foodstuffs with umami potential that, as described below, can further a green transition. These research questions have then been addressed and results have been obtained that subsequently have appeared in the international scientific literature, often after popular accounts have been presented in other types of media. In parallel with the collaboration, the chef partner (KS) has used the results in his business as restaurateur, food innovator, and educator of apprentice chefs.

It is not likely that the same results would have been obtained if a more traditional approach had been adopted, for example, by a conventional research program set up to solve specific questions regarding culinary sustainability using a strategic research approach. We strongly believe that our solution to culinary sustainability through the umamification of green foodstuffs was fostered by and developed from a chef's and a physical scientist's commitment to do something together and tell others about it.

Fungi and Algae Are Special

Before we describe the two routes to umamification of plant-based foods as a driver for the green transition, it should be pointed out that there are two special types of food ingredients, algae and fungi, which should be considered together with plants in the green transition. Whereas algae perform photosynthesis, fungi such as mushrooms do not, and they need input from other organisms, typically plants, for their survival, although they often live on the debris from dead plant material and should hence be considered as relatively sustainable. Algae are a very heterogeneous and diverse group of organisms that do not constitute a single, well-defined kingdom. They are responsible for about 70 percent of the entire organic production on the planet and are key for capturing carbon dioxide and producing molecular oxygen in the atmosphere. The unicellular microalgae are less used for foods but are expected to increasingly be so used in the future. The multicellular, marine macroalgae, the so-called seaweeds, are on the other hand an important foodstuff around the world, and their popularity is increasing (Mouritsen 2013; Mouritsen et al. 2020). Seaweeds (Mouritsen, Pérez Llorens, and Rhatigan 2019) and mushrooms (Poojary et al. 2017) are specially interesting in the present context because some of them are extremely rich in compounds that elicit umami, and they are therefore instrumental for adding umami to vegetarian and vegan dishes.

Umami, Umami Synergy, and Kokumi

To use the full potential of umami to further a green transition and a change in people's eating behavior without compromising taste when cutting down on meat, it is helpful to understand the mechanism of umami and the particular synergistic relationship behind umami and how umami interacts with other basic tastes. The molecular mechanism and the receptor function behind umami are now known (Mouritsen and Khandelia 2012; Tracy 2018; Zhang et al. 2008). Umami is induced by binding free glutamate to the umami receptor (basal umami) and this binding, and hence the intensity of perceived umami, can be magnified many times by the simultaneous binding of free nucleotides to the receptor (synergistic umami). This synergy is possibly the most powerful instrument to umamify green foodstuffs, and it is exactly the same mechanism that renders the following food pairings delicious: egg and bacon, cheese and ham, tomatoes and meat, and tomatoes and mackerel (Schmidt and Mouritsen 2022). Some may find it amusing that the same principle has been proposed to be behind the taste pairing of oysters and champagne (Schmidt and Mouritsen 2020). Few raw ingredients can in themselves provide strong umami synergy; examples are sun-ripened tomatoes, nori seaweed (*Pyropia* spp.), and a variety of mollusks such as oysters and squid (Schmidt and Mouritsen 2022).

An important physiological aspect of umami taste is that umamification of food items can enhance both the perceived sweetness and saltiness without adding extra sugar or salt. At the same time umami tends to dampen the sensation of bitterness. These effects can obviously be very helpful to enhance the delectability of plant-based foods, such as cabbages, that often are bitter and carry no umami.

Finally, a word is needed about the concept of *kokumi*, which is a new term in gastronomical circles and still has not reached the general public, although it was proposed as a taste attribute already in 1990 (Ueda et al. 1990). Kokumi describes a certain sensation of mouthfulness, continuity, and lingering of the taste of certain food items such as garlic, onions, scallops, parmesan cheese, soy sauce, and fish sauce (Nishimura and Kuroda 2019). It is now known which molecular compounds elicit kokumi (certain di- and tripeptides), and it is interesting that these compounds have no taste in themselves but can act as taste enhancers. Specifically, they enhance sweetness, saltiness, and umami and at the same time suppress the sensation of bitterness. It is therefore obvious that kokumi, similarly to umami, can further green eating behavior.

Green Transition as a Matter of Taste: Umamification

As pointed out above, the lack of sweetness and umami in plant-based food ingredients can basically be mitigated in the kitchen via two routes: 1) adding sweetness and umami from other sources and 2) releasing the plants' own potential to produce sweetness and umami.

Concerning the first route, most food cultures use various sauces, soups, marinades, dressings, or extracts as condiments to add flavor to food, whether it is of animal or plant origin. Many of these condiments are very rich in umami, such as soup stocks, fonds, ketchup, soy sauce, miso, cheese powders, Worcestershire sauce, and fish sauce, and only small amounts are needed to accompany a green dish to enhance its deliciousness and make up for the missing umami in the plants. It is noteworthy that by far the richest sources of umami are from foodstuffs of animal origin.

The most famous umami condiment is the Japanese soup stock *dashi*, which consists of an aqueous extract of a brown seaweed species, konbu (*Saccharina japonica*), and a highly processed fish product, *katsuobushi* (San Gabriel, Ninomiya, and Uneyama 2018). Konbu contains large amounts of free glutamate and hence elicits basal umami. Katsuobushi is rich in a free nucleotide (inosinate) that, together with the free glutamate, enters a powerful umami synergy. A vegan version of dashi uses dried shiitake (mushrooms) instead of katsuobushi. Shiitake contains large amounts of another free nucleotide (guanylate) that is even more powerful in producing umami synergy. Marinating or steaming vegetables in dashi is a very simple way of imparting strong umami flavor to green preparations.

Concerning the second route, fermentation processes use microorganisms such as yeast, molds, and bacteria to break down carbohydrates into sugars, and proteins into free amino acids. Well-known examples include lactic bacteria (e.g., for producing cheeses or sourdough), yeast (to produce fermented drinks), and molds such as *koji* (*Aspergillus oryzae*) to produce soy sauce, miso, and various fermented vegetables, such as *tsukemono* (Mouritsen and Styrbæk 2021b). The fermented plant-based foods can constitute a meal or conveniently be used as condiments to umamify other green foods.

When Blue Is Green: Marine Food Sources for Umamification

The marine environment is one of the richest sources of umami from fish, shellfish, mollusks, and seaweed. Paradoxically, we are in many ways still hunters and gatherers when it comes to using the rich larder of the sea. We have over the years, with little insight into the ecological marine systems, overexploited the population of many wild species, not least fish, and consequently put enormous stresses on the marine environment (Golden et al. 2021). Global fisheries have fully exploited 60 percent of the wild stock, overfished another 30 percent, and endangered many wild populations, with the result that the global catch has declined in recent decades. The cost of this type of food production, mostly based on large-scale industrial fishing methods, has been a great loss in biodiversity, damage to whole ecosystems, and the emission of excess nutrients and greenhouse gasses (Willett et al. 2019).

We are only now learning how to set up sustainable aquaculture systems for production of farmed fish, shellfish, and seaweed. Aquaculture accounts for about half of the world's fisheries (FAO 2018), but due to problems with sustainability, pollution, and discharge of excess nutrients, it is difficult to scale up aquaculture further to meet world demand for fish and shellfish. Meanwhile we are harvesting large amounts of fish species that end up as feed for other fish or domestic land animals, such as pigs, wasting enormous quantities of high-quality protein by passing lower-level food sources from the food web through other species before they end up on our plates. Scrap fish and bycatch, although becoming more tightly regulated by international agencies, are either discarded or processed for feed. As an example, sprat are mostly caught commercially for feed and seldom directly reach the consumer before they have been turned into pork or farmed salmon, although sprat have high gastronomic and nutritional value. In Denmark, the commercial fisheries harvest an amount of sprat that could cover 30 percent of the Danes' need for protein. But we are just not accustomed to eating sprat, although the fish species is gastronomically similar to the anchovies and sardines that are so beloved in Southern Europe.

On this background, the present authors and our collaborators have worked on marine species that are little used in the Nordic countries, specifically seaweed, squid, and invasive oysters, and we are currently embarking on a study of marine roe from fish species for which the roe is little used or discarded. Our approach has been to start in the kitchen and learn about the gastronomical potential of the foodstuff in question, develop recipes, describe new preparation techniques, and then by scientific methods study the important aspects of the material, with respect to taste, texture, and consumers' preference. Examples include Nordic squid (Faxholm et al. 2018; Mouritsen and Styrbæk 2018, 2021; Smith et al. 2020,) and seaweed (Mouritsen et al. 2019; Mouritsen, Pérez Llorens, and Rhatigan 2019, with both research directions leading to new areas of gastronomy, cephalopod gastronomy, and phycogastronomy. We have proposed (Mouritsen and Schmidt 2020) that using marine foodstuffs, even in rather small quantities, can add the missing umami to plant-based foods and green dishes and thereby further a green transition (Schmidt and Mouritsen 2022). This principle is well known in many food cultures, such as Southeast Asian cuisines, where a drop of fish sauce, a bit of fermented shrimp paste, or some dried squid can impart deliciousness to a vegetable dish.

Table 1: The spice rack

Umami	Aioli, almonds, anchovy paste/sauce, asparagus, bacon, balsamic vinegar, black garlic, blue cheese, botargo, cured ham, chicken broth, corn, fungus/yeast powder, dashi, dried fish, egg, fish sauce, Gouda cheese, garum, hoisin sauce, katsuobushi, ketchup, koji, lees, Marmite, mirin, miso, mushrooms, nutritional yeast, oyster sauce, Parmesan cheese, ponzu, potatoes, rice vinegar (aged), sake, seaweeds (dulse, konbu), sesame seeds, shiitake, soy sauce, tahini, tomatoes, Worcestershire sauce, yeast/yeast flakes
Kokumi	Mature, hard cheeses (Parmesan, Gouda), beer, fish sauce, garlic, onions, scallops
Mouthfeel	*Crunchy:* almonds, croutons, nuts, roasted seaweed flakes, roasted sunflower/pumpkin seeds in soy sauce, pickles (tsukemono) *Creamy:* aioli, egg yolk, mayonnaise, miso, oil-water emulsions
Sweet	Carrots, cherry tomatoes, honey, mirin, sugar, sweet fruit, and fruit juices (e.g., apples, melons, pears)

The spice rack with items that contribute umami, kokumi, and crunch. For the sake of completeness, the rack also contains condiments that can contribute the sweetness that some green dishes also may need. Omnivores can freely use all items from the rack, whereas vegetarians and vegans have less choice.

The Taste and Texture Rack

In many food cultures one seasons the food by using a range of spices. Most spices are derived from fresh, dried, or fermented herbs or other plant-based materials. However, strictly speaking, items from the traditional battery of spices on the spice rack mostly contribute to aroma and smell and not taste proper. Other spices, such as black pepper, chili, wasabi, mustard, and gingerroot, impart a burning and irritating feeling, which is also not taste proper but a chemesthetic or trigeminal sensation. Some spices give a bitter note, but in terms of umami and kokumi the spice rack has little to offer. Similarly, spices do not contribute much to mouthfeel, for example, the crisp and crunchy sensation that could improve the texture of soft and mealy vegetables or legumes. It is interesting to note that many of the dressings that accompany traditional salad bars often have little umami if they are only prepared from sour milk products and oil-and-vinegar dressings seasoned with spices. Such dressings only serve the purpose of lubrication and mouthfeel.

To supplement the spice rack, we have therefore proposed the use of what is known as a "taste and texture rack" (Styrbæk and Mouritsen 2020; Mouritsen and Styrbæk 2020). In addition to covering the classical basic tastes such as sweet, sour, and salty (easily provided respectively by sugar, vinegar or lemon juice, and table salt), the taste rack contains items that specifically can elicit umami and kokumi. Some of these items can at the same time also be chosen to contribute to mouthfeel (e.g., crunchy or creamy).

An Example: Vegan Sauce Bolognese

Sauce Bolognese is the iconic Italian sauce that can make a tedious dish of pasta absolutely delicious. Pasta is an example of a staple food, along with, for example, cooked white rice, that provides a lot of nutrients in the form of carbohydrates but has no umami in itself. Unami has to be added, which in traditional Italian cuisine is furnished by a Sauce Bolognese for pasta, or a condiment such as soy sauce or miso in the Japanese cuisine for steamed white rice.

Traditional Sauce Bolognese is an example of perfect umami synergy in which the free glutamate comes from the tomatoes and free nucleotides (e.g., inosinate) from the minced beef. To maintain the culinary virtue of the sauce in a more sustainable way, it can be made completely without meat, and the trick is to conserve the umami synergy. The most concentrated umami taste from tomatoes comes from oven-roasting cooked whole tomatoes, vegetables, and herbs at low heat. If the tomatoes and vegetables are chopped coarsely, the resulting roasted tomato paste will end up with a texture that is similar to that of Sauce Bolognese, but without the meat. The oven-roasted vegetable-tomato sauce can easily be substituted for a meat sauce in a pasta dish. An even more powerful version of this sauce can be made with the addition of shiitake mushrooms, which add umami synergy via free nucleotides (e.g., guanylate) from the fungi. To add further umami as well as kokumi during serving, Parmesan cheese can be grated on top of the dish.

Slow-roasted sauce with tomatoes, root vegetables, and herbs

Recipe by Klavs Styrbæk (Styrbæk and Mouritsen 2020)
Serves 4

1 kg (2¼ lb) root vegetables, such as onions, celery, celeriac, parsley root (or parsnip), carrots, and leeks

2 kg (4½ lb) very ripe fresh tomatoes, skins removed, or high-quality canned ones without skins

4 cloves garlic

1 dl (⅖ cup) olive oil

A lot of fresh thyme

1 chili pepper

50 g (1¾ oz) tomato paste

4 or 5 bay leaves

Salt and freshly ground black pepper

Butter, for serving

Chopped fresh sage leaves, for serving

1. Put the root vegetables, chili pepper, tomatoes, and garlic through a meat grinder. Warm the olive oil in a large pot and stir in the vegetable-tomato mixture.

2. Remove the big stalks from the thyme, chop it, and add it to the pot together with the tomato paste and the bay leaves.

3. Cover the pot with parchment paper and a tight-fitting lid and simmer on the stove top for three to four hours. Alternatively, bake in the oven at 140°C (290°F). The longer this cooks, the better.

4. Season to taste, divide into portions as desired, and store in glass jars in the refrigerator or freezer.

5. When the tomato sauce is to be used, warm it up to the boiling point and whip some butter into it—the more butter you add, the fuller the taste will be. Season with a handful of chopped sage.

Conclusion

We have in this chapter given a personal account of some of our experiences from an almost twenty-year-long collaboration between a chef and a physical scientist who took the time to learn each other's language and mode of working in the kitchen and the university laboratory, respectively. The collaboration was driven by a joint curiosity regarding the wonders and magic of the kitchen, including raw materials, preparation methods, and concepts about taste/flavor and texture. The results of the work have over the years been communicated broadly via a wide range of channels, including books, recipe collections, scientific and popular articles, podcasts, social media, radio, and TV, as well as outreach in the form of talks, events, courses, food festivals, and so forth. A large part of the work has been performed as an integral part of a large national Danish communication and research center, Taste for Life. A common thread of all this work has been the sensory perception of food, in particular umami taste, and how scientific knowledge about the senses and foodstuffs can be used to make culinary exploration, innovation, and education, for instance, in the context of sustainability.

We have in our chapter demonstrated, from basic principles as well as with concrete examples, how a focus on taste (in particular umami and kokumi) and texture holds a key to promoting culinary sustainability, involving a transition to a more plant-based cuisine without compromising taste. We have pointed out that, in our optics, the most effective way to get many more people to eat much more green is a flexitarian approach by which we borrow a little from the animal kingdom, not least from organisms of marine origin, to supply the missing umami and kokumi to plant-based foods.

Declaration

Original manuscript submitted on April 20, 2022; revised on July 7 and October 2, 2022.

References

Burke, R., A. Kelly, C. Lavelle, and H. This, eds. 2021. *CRC Handbook of Molecular Gastronomy: Scientific Foundations and Culinary Applications.* Boca Raton, FL: CRC Press.

Christensen, M., and R. E. Stuart. 2019. "Teaching Science to Chefs: The Benefits, Challenges and Opportunities." *International Journal of Gastronomy and Food Science* 16:100133–37.

Daverkosen, S., S. Ejlersen, and O. G. Mouritsen. 2022. "Progression towards an 80:20 (Plant-Based: Animal-Based) Energy Balance via Specially Designed Meal Kits." *International Journal of Food Design* 7:143–57.

Doubleday, Z. A., T.A.A. Prowse, A. Arkhipkin, G. J. Pierce, J. Semmens, M. Steer, S. C. Leporati, S. Lourenço, A. Quetglas, W. Sauer, and B. M. Gillanders. 2016. "Global Proliferation of Cephalopods." *Current Biology* 26:R406–7.

Dunn, R., and M. Sanchez. 2021. *Delicious: The Evolution of Flavor and How It Made Us Human*. Princeton, NJ: Princeton University Press.

Faxholm, P. L., C. V. Schmidt, L. B. Brønnum, Y.-T. Sun, M. P. Clausen, R. Flore, K. Olsen, and O. G. Mouritsen. 2018. "Squids of the North: Gastronomy and Gastrophysics of Danish Squid." *International Journal of Gastronomy and Food Science* 14:66–76.

Foley, J. A., R. Defries, and G. P. Asner. 2005. "Global Consequences of Land Use." *Science* 309:570–74.

Food and Agriculture Organization of the United Nations (FAO). 2018. *The State of World Fisheries and Aquaculture 2018—Meeting the Sustainable Development Goals*. New York: FAO. https://doi.org/10.18356/8d6ea4b6-en.

Gephart, C. D., P.J.G. Henriksson, R.W.R. Parker, A. Shepon, K. D. Gorospe, K. Bergman, G. Eshel et al. 2021. "Environmental Performance of Blue Foods." *Nature* 597:360–66.

Global Burden of Disease Study 2017. "Health Effects of Dietary Risks in 195 Countries, 1990–2017: A Systematic Analysis for the Global Burden of Disease Study 2017." *Lancet* 393:1958–72.

Golden, C. D., J. Z. Koehn, A. Shepon, S. Passarelli, C. M. Free, D. F. Viana, H. Matthey et al. 2021. "Aquatic Foods to Nourish Nations." *Nature* 598:315–24.

Klimarådet. 2021. Klimavenlig mad og forbrugeradfærd. Copenhagen: Klimarådet. https://klimaraadet.dk/sites/default/files/imorted-file/klimavenlig_mad_og _forbrugeradfaerd_1.pdf.

Morton, O. 2007. *Eating the Sun*. London: Fourth Estate.

Mouritsen, O. G. 2012. "The Emerging Science of Gastrophysics and Its Application to the Algal Cuisine." *Flavour* 1:6.

———. 2013. *Seaweeds. Edible, Available & Sustainable*. Chicago: Chicago University Press.

———. 2016. "Gastrophysics of the Oral Cavity." *Current Pharmaceutical Design* 22:2195–2203.

———. 2021. "Culinary Sciences for the Enhancement of the Public Understanding of Science." In *CRC Handbook of Molecular Gastronomy: Scientific Foundations and Culinary Applications*, edited by R. Burke, A. Kelly, C. Lavelle, and H. This, 655–58. Boca Raton, FL: CRC Press.

Mouritsen, O. G., and H. Khandelia. 2012. "Molecular Mechanism of the Allosteric Enhancement of the Umami Taste Sensation." *FEBS Journal* 279:3112–20.

Mouritsen, O. G., L. Duelund, M. A. Petersen, A. L. Hartmann, and M. B. Frøst. 2019. "Umami Taste, Free Amino Acid Composition, and Volatile Compounds of Brown Seaweeds." *Journal of Applied Phycology* 31:1213–32.

Mouritsen, O. G., P. Rhatigan, M. L. Cornish, A. T. Critchley, and J. L. Perez-Llorens. 2020. "Saved by Seaweeds: Phyconomic Contributions in Times of Crisis." *Journal of Applied Phycology* 33:443–58.

Mouritsen, O. G., and C. V. Schmidt. 2020. "A Role for Macroalgae and Cephalopods in Sustainable Eating." *Frontiers in Psychology* 11:1402–7.

Mouritsen, O. G., and K. Styrbæk, K. 2014. *Umami: Unlocking the Secrets of the Fifth Taste.* New York: Columbia University Press.

———. 2017. *Mouthfeel: How Texture Makes Taste.* New York: Columbia University Press.

———. 2018. "Cephalopod Gastronomy—A Promise for the Future." *Frontiers in Communication Science* 3:38–49.

———. 2020. "Design and 'Umamification' of Vegetables for Sustainable Eating." *International Journal of Food Design* 5:9–42.

———. 2021a. *Octopuses, Squid & Cuttlefish: Seafood for Today and for the Future.* Springer Nature Switzerland AG.

———. 2021b. *Tsukemono: Decoding the Art and Science of Japanese Pickling.* Springer Nature Switzerland AG.

———. 2021c. "Tag smagen med på råd: om kostråd og den grønne omstilling" *SMAG* 13:1–152.

Mouritsen, O. G., J. L. Pérez Llorens, and P. Rhatigan. 2019. "The Rise of Seaweed Gastronomy: Phycogastronomy." *Botanica Marina* 62:195–209.

Mouritsen, O. G., P. M. Sörensen, and R. Flore, eds. 2019. "Chefs Meet Scientists: Gastro-Science-Chef-2018." *International Journal of Gastronomy and Food Science* 17:100162–63.

Nishimura, T., and M. Kuroda, eds. 2019. *Koku in Food Science and Physiology.* New York: Springer.

Pedersen, M. T., P. L. Hansen, and M. P. Clausen. 2021. "Gastronomy Unravelled by Physics: Gastrophysics." *International Journal of Gastronomy and Food Science* 6:153–80.

Poojary, M. M., V. Orlien, P. Passamonti, and K. Olsen. 2017. "Improved Extraction Methods for Simultaneous Recovery of Umami Compounds from Six Different Mushrooms." *Journal of Food Composition Analysis* 63:171–83.

San Gabriel, A., K. Ninomiya, and H. Uneyama. 2018. "The Role of the Japanese Traditional Diet in Healthy and Sustainable Dietary Patterns around the World." *Nutrients* 10:173–88.

Schmidt, C. V., and O. G. Mouritsen. 2020. "The Solution to Sustainable Eating Is Not a One-Way Street." *Frontiers in Psychology* 11:531–35.

———. 2022. "Umami Taste as a Driver for Sustainable Eating." *International Journal of Food Design* 7:187–203.

Schmidt, C. V., K. Olsen, and O. G. Mouritsen. 2020. "Umami Synergy as the Scientific Principle behind Taste-Pairing Champagne and Oysters." *Nature Scientific Reports* 10:2007–19.

Schmidt, C. V., M. M. Poojary, O. G. Mouritsen, and K. Olsen. 2020. "Umami Potential of Nordic Squid (*Loligo forbesii*)." *International Journal of Gastronomy and Food Science* 22:100275–85.

Schneider, M., A. Kamuk, K. Wistoft, M. B. Frøst, A. Olsen, L. Hedegaard, and O. G. Mouritsen. 2018. "Taste for Life: An Exemplary Case for Interdisciplinary

Collaboration between Scientists and Practitioners on Taste Research and Communication." *International Journal of Food Design* 3:164–65.

Searchinger, T. 2019. *World Resources Report: Creating a Sustainable Food Future. A Menu of Solutions to Feed Nearly 10 Billion People by 2050.* Washington, DC: World Resources Institute.

Shepherd, G. M. 2011. *Neurogastronomy: How the Brain Creates Flavor and Why It Matters.* New York: Columbia University Press.

Smart Protein. 2021. *What Consumers Want: A Survey on European Consumer Attitudes towards Plant-Based Foods with a Focus on Flexitarians.* https://smartproteinproject.eu.

Steffen, W., K. Richardson, J. Rockström, S. E. Cornell, I. Fetzer, E. M. Bennett, R. Biggs et al. 2015. "Planetary Boundaries: Guiding Human Development on a Changing Planet." *Science* 347:1259855–64.

Styrbæk, K., and O. G. Mouritsen. 2020. *Grønt med umami og velsmag: Håndværk, viden & opskrifter.* Copenhagen: Gyldendal.

Tracy, S. E. 2018. "Delicious Molecules: Big Food Science, the Chemosenses, and Umami." *The Senses and Society* 13:89–107.

Ueda, Y., M. Sakaguchi, K. Hirayama, R. Miyajima, and A. Kimizuka. 1990. "Characteristic Flavor Constituents in Water Extract of Garlic." *Agricultural Biological Chemistry* 54:163–69.

United Nations (UN). 2019. Sustainable Development Goals: Goal 12: Ensure Sustainable Consumption and Production Patterns. https://www.un.org/sustainabledevelopment/sustainable-consumption-production/.

Vermeulen, S. J., B. M. Campbell, and J.S.I. Ingram. 2012. "Climate Change and Food Systems." *Annual Reviews on Environmental Resources* 37:195–222.

Willett, W., J. Rockström, B. Loken, M. Springmann, T. Lang, S. Vermeulen, T. Garrett et al. 2019. "Food in the Anthropocene: the EAT–Lancet Commission on Healthy Diets from Sustainable Food Systems." *Lancet* 393:447–92.

Wrangham, R. 2009. *Catching Fire: How Cooking Made Us Human.* New York: Basic Books.

Zhang, F., B. Klebansky, R. M. Fine, H. Xu, A. Pronin, H. Liu, C. Tachdjian, and X. Li. 2008. "Molecular Mechanism for the Umami Taste Synergism." *Proceedings of the National Academy of Sciences* (USA) 105:20930–34.

Zhu, Y.-G. 2022. "Plant-Based Diet: Cook Up the Sustainable Future." *Soil Ecology Letters* 4:289–90.

PART II

Culinary Sustainability and Kitchen Practices

CHAPTER FIVE

Expanding "Ethical" Cooking
Parisian Chefs' Everyday Approaches to Culinary Sustainability

RAÚL MATTA

Introduction

Today, the word "chef" carries immediate associations with images of well-known culinary personalities, with considerable name recognition, piloting the busy kitchens of upscale, increasingly green-driven restaurants. Scholars and culinary commentators have written much on elite chefs as cultural and political intermediaries (Barnes 2017; Hollows and Jones 2010; Giousmpasoglou, Brown, and Cooper 2020; Johnston and Goodman 2015; Matta 2019; Rousseau 2012). In times when the realities and rhetoric of crisis shape public conversation over social, political, and environmental issues, the role of chefs as bridges between the food-related public and private spheres has emerged and risen to prominence. Mass exposure has endorsed chefs as food experts, trendsetters, and opinion leaders. Accustomed to working closely with the media, they excel at articulating principles and missions that exceed the social space of the restaurant, as well as at addressing social concerns in understandable, apparently "democratic" ways.

Acknowledgments: I would like to thank all my field consultants for their time and for sharing their knowledge. Also thanks to Jenny Herman for her invaluable feedback. This chapter benefited from a FIAS fellowship at the Paris Institute for Advanced Study (France). It has received funding from the European Union's Horizon 2020 research and innovation program under the Marie Skłodowska-Curie grant agreement No. 945408, and from the French State program "Investissements d'avenir," managed by the Agence Nationale de la Recherche (ANR-11-LABX-0027–01 Labex RFIEA+).

Some chefs are now also sustainability advocates. Several initiatives around the world, most of them funded by international organizations such as the United Nations, the European Commission, and Slow Food, have endorsed chefs as experts and opinion leaders who are capable of guiding both culinary workers and domestic cooks to actions that can contribute to sustainability. Examples of these, among many, are the Slow Food Cooks' Alliance in Kenya, described by Michele Filippo Fontefrancesco and Dauro Mattia Zocchi in their chapter in this volume; the "#Taste the Ocean" campaign by the European Commission, in which nine European chefs—from Michelin-starred restaurants to Top Chef winners—post online videos of recipes to encourage individuals to consume sustainable fish and seafood; and the Chefs' Manifesto by the SDG2 Advocacy Hub, which has built an online community of chefs who champion the United Nations' second sustainable development goal: Zero Hunger.[1]

Furthermore, some chefs have made sustainability the core of their "culinary persona" (Johnston, Rodney, and Chong 2014) by making explicit their individual engagements around food politics or by publicly addressing issues in health, poverty, agriculture, and the environment. Media, from magazines to television platforms such as Netflix, social networks such as Instagram, and video platforms such as YouTube, provide sites where chefs elaborate on their environmental values and knowledge to legitimize their new roles both in public life and in the industry (Mapes and Ross 2022; Matta and Panchapakesan 2021; Santos and Mansey 2022). Participation in media enables a potential win-win situation in which proclaimed environmentally conscious chefs obtain professional gains, and organizations aligned with sustainability ideals can achieve institutional goals. I use the adjective "potential" and the verb "can" because whereas scholarship has documented the rewards chefs obtain by mediatizing their work ethics, the capacity of chefs to inspire the transition of culinary workers and consumers toward sustainable practices remains to be proved in a consistent manner (Mrusek, Ottenbacher, and Harrington 2022; Pereira et al. 2019).

Media foster "intimacies" between chefs and consumers (Abbotts 2015). Chefs penetrate and reshape the domestic space, tastes, and bodies through the paraphernalia they bring into the marketplace and the home (cookbooks, social media, movies, kitchen equipment, and specialty ingredients). Yet, while the exposure to new cooking techniques and ingredients can be empowering and satisfactory for some consumers, it can also be alienating for others. People in more constrained economic circumstances are less able to participate fully in the cooking experiences or related lifestyles that chefs propose (Abbotts 2015). We can infer a similar situation when it comes to the promotion of sustainable culinary practices, as they generally rely on products and practices characterized by a sense of "right and good" that not only are unequally accessible, but also are "enlisted in claims to superior morality and taste" (Mapes 2018, 1; see also Shugart 2014).

Consider organic foods. As preference for these products has been shifting progressively from "an elitist behavior to widespread consumption" (D'Amico, Di Vita, and Monaco 2016, 64), policymakers and consumers look at organic foods as one of the main ways to promote sustainable food systems and healthy diets. However, although in most countries "organic food" is still a niche market with prices comparable to premium conventional foods, it is now well established within the "dominant ethical eating repertoire," which Josée Johnston and her colleagues define as a cultural discourse shaped by powerful economic actors which tends to normalize "privileged perspectives as universal standards that all citizens should live up to" (Johnston, Szabo, and Rodney 2011, 296). These perspectives are presented as "classless" despite the structural inequalities that make it difficult for low- and moderate-income groups to access foods credited with higher moral value such as those identified as (hyper-)local, fair, and pesticide- and cruelty-free. (AND International 2020; Johnston, Szabo, and Rodney 2011). This has led Daniela Spagnuolo (2022, 948) to investigate these discourses and conclude that dominant understandings of ethical eating "obscure and perpetuate issues of inequality, colonialism, and injustice within the broader food system."

As the ethical eating repertoire gives deference to the taste of elites (Alkon and Agyeman 2011; Guthman 2008), access to this mode of consumption is unequal and mediated by economic, cultural, and even geographic privilege. This does not mean, however, that moderate-income and marginalized peoples are unethical in their consumption in a general sense (Johnston, Szabo, and Rodney 2011). These groups may aspire to more sustainable diets that borrow from the dominant repertoire while showing particular orientations linked to their social positions. Beyond the price issue, cultural and contextual constraints limit the ability of certain groups to be receptive to and follow the recommendations of proponents of the dominant ethical eating repertoire (Brocard et al. 2022). Yet that does not make nonelite consumers necessarily less important when it comes to helping drive a shift to a system that favors fairer treatment of all the actors involved, enhances biodiversity through holistic sustainable practices, broadens farmers' access to financial resources, and incorporates the knowledge and opinions of multiple actors (Gliessman 2014; Lima, Mülling, and Gomes 2021). They simply have less economic and cultural capital and are not well aligned with the dominant discourse.

I contend that this pattern of food consumption parallels what occurs in the context of culinary professional work performed outside the world of celebrated chefs and high-end restaurants. Chefs in midscale restaurants and eateries may have a moral engagement with what they deliver to customers, but their engagement develops within limits set by resource conditions that make their initiatives appear as minimally relevant. The aim of this chapter is to show that there is a culture of culinary sustainability among chefs who feed people for a moderate price, a culture that builds both outside and within the dominant ethical eating repertoire. By culinary sustainability I refer to the approach that aims at minimizing, to the extent possible, the harming environmental and societal effects associated with the practices of cooking and eating, either in professional or domestic capacities. Culinary sustainability extends consideration to all the organic and inorganic matter and processes involved in bringing food and diners to the table. This holistic definition addresses sustainability in all its dimensions: social, economic, environmental, and cultural. For instance, a sound culinary sustainability endeavor would aim for fair working conditions for staff; appreciate the relationships not only within the social space of the restaurant but also with providers, producers, and diners; be sufficiently profitable to survive; and embrace ecological values and work ethics that see humans and nonhumans (animals, plants, water, bacteria, objects, etc.) as associates functioning in cooperation. A number of constraints make such an approach problematic for chefs of moderately priced restaurants. Therefore, I suggest that, to better contribute to a transformation toward more sustainable and fair food systems, it is important to recognize the efforts chefs make to balance the objectives outlined above, to situate these efforts in specific contexts, and to appraise their culinary sustainability not on the basis of what chefs do, but on the basis of what they do with the resources at their disposal.

To support my point, I draw upon semistructured interviews conducted between November 2021 and May 2022 in Paris, France, with chefs of venues where I had the occasion to visit and eat. This time frame coincided with my fellowship at the Paris Institute for Advanced Study. My stay in the city allowed me to renew contact with people dear to me from my student years. As I shared with them my research interests on food and sustainability, they put me in contact with members of their social circles, some of them cooks who are sensitive to the topic. The recruitment of participants was therefore done by snowball sampling. The interviews addressed the themes of professional training and experience, work ethics and values, types of ingredients and produce used, food sourcing and relationships with suppliers, cooking techniques, and food waste. I deliberately chose not to strictly frame the interviewees' experiences in terms of culinary sustainability, so they were free from concept-related constraints and welcome to bring up any thoughts as long as they considered them as related to the topic of cooking best practices and important to be mentioned. This inductive method corresponds to the objective of adding complexity and nuance to the dominant ethical eating repertoire by paying attention to contextualized and nonformalized knowledge and beliefs (or "naïve theories") expressed by culinary experts.

The individuals portrayed in the following vignettes share both a hope and a concern that can be linked to food sustainability issues. The hope is that there is still room to "do" food differently. The interviewees see their work as an attempt to oppose the resource inefficiency and highly profit-oriented models of the mainstream restaurant industry, which they perceive both as disconnected from notions of good taste and as environmentally damaging. The concern is that their efforts alone will not be sufficient, as they have little means of generating systemic changes. They realize that to make necessary changes, political mobilization for more sustainable food production is indispensable at local, national, and international levels. Their scarce capacity to bring about change in the wider food system does not prevent them, though, from taking action in contexts where the dominant ethical discourse has penetrated less fully.

Vignette 1: Christopher

The Paris Institute for Advanced Study (PIAS) is a prestigious research center located on the Île-Saint-Louis, one of the Seine's two natural islands. During several months of each academic year, the institute hosts an international cohort of research fellows who work in the fields of social sciences and the humanities. At the institute, the fellows are each given an office and a suitable environment to conduct research. The lunchtime is when the less formal, but not less important, exchanges take place. Unlike other similar institutions, the PIAS has its own canteen and indoor and outdoor seating areas in which to eat. The fellows can partake in lunch from Monday to Friday after registering their attendance previously on an Excel file shared on Google Drive. The buffet-style service includes a choice of salads, vegetables, animal protein, cheese, bread, and desserts for eight euros, a very fair price by Paris standards. As a fellow in 2021–22, I was able to conduct participant observation of the meals and interview the chef.

Christopher, thirty-five years old, is the chef and the manager for the canteen. He joined the institute in 2013 to take up responsibilities in logistics, but soon afterwards he was offered the opportunity to take the lead of the new canteen initiative, which meant placing the food orders, developing the rotating menu, and cooking for a daily average of twenty-five people. Christopher had worked previously for a French supermarket group, so he felt himself somewhat familiar with the food business. Yet, as he had never cooked professionally, he enrolled in several apprenticeships to learn the vocation, which he now enjoys very much. He describes the style of food served at the institute as "refined collective catering" (*restauration collective raffinée* in French). By identifying the cooking style as "refined," he clearly puts it in opposition to other forms of collective catering.

Christopher uses fresh products as much as possible and prepares all the dishes himself, with the support of one kitchen assistant. He contrasts fresh foods to canned and frozen preparations, which he says one might commonly find in refectories. With fresh products, he said, "One can see what one does." The only exceptions in which he uses frozen foods are the breaded fish and certain desserts. When he places orders, Christopher tries as much as possible to favor local products, which he views on a national scale (*origine France*). The meats, the tomatoes, and all the ingredients for green salads come from France. Christopher cannot source locally other produce, especially fruits and legumes such as green beans. He explained that the green bean season in France does not give high yields and therefore the price gets too expensive for his budget. He needs the imported foods because they allow him to achieve a balance that is beneficial for nutrition (*c'est bon pour la diététique*).

There is little red meat on the weekly menu, usually appearing only once a week. White meats are much more present: "White meats give you plenty of vitamins; red meat too, but if you eat too much red meat it's no good for the health," he explained. When he serves red meat, he aims for portions of 180 grams, which in his view is an average cut size for one person, unlikely to be damaging for the health and small enough to avoid waste ("Some restaurants put too much meat on the plate"). Due to dietary considerations, and also because an increasing number of fellows prefer to avoid red meat, Christopher serves fresh fish twice a week and frozen breaded fish once a week. Fish, which he sources from a wholesaler he trusts, makes it easier to "balance the meals" (*pour équilibrer les repas*).

The structure of the weekly menu at the canteen is also quite unique. On Mondays and Fridays fellows are offered what he calls the "salad bar," consisting of a large choice of cold salads and quiches. On these days, slices of serrano ham and smoked salmon are the only animal proteins. Serrano ham from Spain is the only meat that is not sourced from France. Christopher justified his choice through his knowledge of the fellows' preferences and his personal taste. The idea of the salad bar was introduced by a former general secretary of the institute, and it was adopted and implemented by Christopher. Salad-bar days are those on which fellows can satisfy their appetites with starchy foods, vegetables, and fibers. Each salad-bar day has a specific objective. On Fridays it is for the fellows to end the week in a lighter manner, without burdening their stomachs. On Monday, it is for them to have a more refreshing meal in case they have overeaten (or overdrunk) during the weekend, allowing them to start the workweek under more optimal conditions. Such a tactic takes into account the fact that the fellows are generally visitors in Paris for the duration of the fellowship and are therefore generally well positioned and motivated to explore the city's foodscapes. Unlike on salad-bar days, on Tuesday and Wednesday the vegetables are better adapted to complement the offer of meat and fish. Mondays or Fridays with no salad bar indicate that a special event with external guests is taking place on these days, forcing Christopher to change the menu. It also occurs that after an event on a Thursday, for instance, he repurposes the leftover foods on Friday. Christopher explained his broader approach to avoid waste as based on his precise knowledge of the portions fellows put on their plates. This and the registration system seem to him a good combination for the endeavor.

Christopher understands how the fellows and the institute staff eat. He explained that what they eat is quite homogenous, and that they do not generally eat much. Every year he learns and adapts his work to the fellows' food preferences, taboos, and habits. He also aims to please and accommodate vegan and vegetarian fellows. Any vegan individual would find suitable options for lunch, which is something not too common in

France. Fish is overrepresented because there are fellows he calls "fake vegetarians" (*faux végétariens*), pescatarians who do not eat meat but do consume fish. For their sake, for instance, he always makes the quiches vegetarian. Christopher's commitment to sustainability relies on a balance among the freshness and quality of the produce he can afford, his comprehension of the consumption practices in the canteen, and his concern for the fellows' health and enjoyment. There is a caring attitude in his work, which stems from adapting and calibrating the canteen as a living part of the institute's work environment.

Vignette 2: Raquel

Raquel, forty-two years old, arrived in Paris from San Luis Potosí, Mexico, in 2009. In France she worked for several years as a manager in the logistics department of an electronics retail company, a position not too different than the one she was occupying in her home country. In the long run she felt unhappy with the job and opted for leaving it to enroll in a one-year culinary specialization course. Such a decision was not without risks, as she was thirty-five years old at the time and had an infant child at home. Soon after obtaining her certificate of professional aptitude (CAP cuisine) she was offered a position in the kitchen of the Grand Central restaurant at the contemporary arts center the Centquatre Paris. She viewed the opportunity as a blessing as the Centquatre is just a few minutes' distance from her home in the nineteenth arrondissement of Paris, in the north of the city.

The Grand Central is a bistro-style restaurant, serving French cuisine and international dishes, with an emphasis on seasonal products. Raquel says she gained extensive knowledge and skills during the first years at the restaurant, but progressively suffered from mental exhaustion due to the hypermasculine and very hierarchical culture reigning in the kitchen. "In Mexico I was used to giving orders, not to receiving them," she explained. Noticing her distress, but also acknowledging her good work, the owner of Grand Central offered Raquel the command of the dine-in and takeout eatery under development to attract the permanent and temporary staff of the Centquatre arts center. The eatery, known as "the corner," is located within the premises of the restaurant, at one of the ends of the long bar counter that divides the restaurant room from the eatery room.

Raquel accepted the offer, aware that her decision implied a tradeoff between improving her professional skills and regaining her longed-for autonomy and mental well-being. Indeed, in her new position, she is expected to prepare sandwiches, wraps, salads, soups, and other simple dishes, not elaborate or necessarily sophisticated meals. Yet Raquel was enthusiastic about embarking on this project with the confidence gained after the apprenticeship and hands-on kitchen experience. Adding to this was the anticipation that in this new context she would have the opportunity to apply the culinary knowledge she had learned in Mexico from her mother and grandmother. At "the corner" Raquel cooks and runs the service independently, and she is in full control of the menu and work processes, which she develops in a very particular way.

Raquel works with less precise plans, instead intuiting a menu respecting the seasonality of each type of produce, which is in line with Grand Central's restaurant philosophy. At the start of every season, she makes a long list of salads, quiches, and soups that she finds appropriate to cook. However, that list serves merely as a reference, since Raquel has opted for operating on a daily basis approach. Indeed, she can only determine her menu on the morning of the same day, or the preceding day at the earliest, as she primarily works with the products that Grand Central has in excess. Although she always wakes up with an idea about what to prepare, it is only when she arrives at the restaurant, opens the refrigerator, and sees what is left (or in abundance) that she makes a final decision. "If I see that six out of thirty portions of the plat du jour are left, I will take them with me because it is a number too small to be put again on the restaurant menu." Raquel avoids as much as possible sourcing for the eatery directly, even though she is allowed to place specific orders for it. Her commitment is to create a menu in correspondence with the foods that Grand Central will not be able to reuse. The idea, she explained, is "to recompose and give a new life" to those products. If one morning she finds there are no significant leftover materials to work with, she will prepare some of the items from her seasonally inspired list.

Although Raquel does not precisely improvise, her working method involves a high degree of uncertainty and stress: "Sometimes it irritates me, as I make plans that most of the time I cannot follow. That makes me lose a lot of time. But what irritates me the most is to waste food," and restaurants often waste vast quantities of food. Aware of her cooking approach, her colleagues from Grand Central directly consult her when there are unsold portions so that she can rework them. As Raquel explained, that means that the colleagues have learned, thanks to her efforts, that good food products should not be thrown away.

Most of the clientele of "the corner" are employees at either the Centquatre or the surrounding area, attracted by the takeout offer at attractive prices (a meal can cost between nine and twelve euros). Raquel has come to know some of her clients personally and established cordial relationships. If that has, on the one hand, given her personal gratification, on the other hand it represents additional work, as she does her best to offer them a different menu every day. Yet that closeness is also a way for Raquel to communicate her views on food and her commitment against waste. The customers know that, even if "the corner's" food showcase is running low, Raquel will do a quick sprint to the restaurant's cold room to create something with what is available: "If there is nothing to eat I make them something to eat . . . I don't have this but I've got chicken . . . or, if you like ham I can make you a sandwich . . . should I put avocado in it?" In those cases, customers are willing to wait quietly until she has finished the job, a patience that is not typically associated with Parisian attitudes. Raquel, from her side, tries to convince them to bring along their own containers and cutlery to minimize the use of paperboard trays, packages, and wooden utensils as much as possible.

Raquel's work is based on an ethics of care for people (the people she feeds and initiates into environmentally sound practices) and care for the environment through her low-waste culinary recycling approach. Furthermore, she feels satisfaction to see that in her position she is able to serve those causes. " 'The corner' was not designed for that purpose; I was never asked to work the way I do. This is my choice and my initiative. . . . I am overwhelmed by the world we are leaving to my girls," she explained.

Vignette 3: Julien

After a woodworking apprenticeship that left him unsatisfied, Julien (thirty-three years old) realized that cooking could better suit his interests in finding a hands-on career. He arrived in Paris in 2011 from a small village in northern Île-de-France to enroll in culinary training in *alternance*, which is an educational system specific to France that basically means working part time and studying part time. Once he obtained his culinary certificate, Julien landed a series of short-term jobs in various restaurants until finally, arriving in his early thirties, he took on a more stable position as the chef of La Maison Montreuil, a restaurant that closed in 2024. I met him to discuss his experiences and views at his apartment in the city center of Paris. During our interview, along with breakfast cookies and coffee, we shared water kefir, a fizzy probiotic drink he fermented himself.

La Maison Montreuil was located, as its name indicates, in Montreuil, a neighborhood in the eastern suburbs of Paris. Since the turn of the twenty-first century, Montreuil has become the destination of choice for artists and young Parisians who look to escape city prices, buy property, and bring up families. It is now brimming with cultural venues and trendy cafés, bars, and restaurants. And it is perhaps no coincidence that La Maison Montreuil proposed "a rigorous and surprising cuisine that respects the seasons . . . a cuisine that changes almost every day, in motion and alive like Montreuil itself."[2] More particularly, the restaurant's website stated that it worked with fresh and local products, and that it offered a variety of natural wines and organic drinks, along with a convivial and relaxed atmosphere. The term "local," as used in the website, corresponded to products sourced within Europe's borders (an even more expansive view of the local than Christopher's geographical limit of France). Julien thinks La Maison Montreuil was a good place to work, as he appreciated the focus on fresh and seasonal produce and the freedom he was given to develop his creativity and skills. He considers the small size of the restaurant (twenty seats in the inside dining room and twenty seats in the terrace) and the kitchen (about eight square meters) as something positive: the lack of a cold chamber prevented him from using any frozen or preprocessed preparations as larger bistros often do.

This also explains why there was no printed menu, but instead a blackboard showing a menu that changed every day. As Julien commented on the restaurant's limited cooling facilities and rotating menu, our conversation evolved around the meaning of freshness. For Julien, freshness equals taste and, in his view, only agricultural workers who perform best practices are able to put on the market products that are "full of taste." Through this statement, he brings about a virtuous and productive dynamic where the moral connotations of "fresh," "good," and palatable entangle. For Julien, fresh food is not simply a measure of time, in correlation with how recently the food has been attached to its "roots," nor is it determined by how lovely it looks—actually, he mentioned he likes to work with "ugly" vegetables as long as they are seasonal.[3] We can infer then that for Julien fresh food is, above all, a gustatory experience. As he associates freshness with "quality" and "taste," he relates the act of eating fresh food to a total sensory act that creates meaning or a vision,[4] as we will see below.

Fresh products do not have to necessarily be organic. In fact, La Maison Montreuil could barely afford such foods: "As soon as you switch to organic, prices double, or almost double." Julien therefore placed the priority on seasonal ingredients and on what he calls "*produits raisonnés*" ("reasoned products" in English), which he could obtain at more affordable prices. "Reasoned products" are foods from small producers that have embraced environmental values but have not met the strict contractual specifications of organic-labeled production. Put simply, they are foods grown or raised with limited use of antibiotics for meat, poultry, and fish, and of pesticides for vegetables and fruits. Needless to say, Julien considers that these foods taste better than those one can find at Rungis in the south of Paris, the world's largest produce market, which sources food from intensive and small-scale French producers and supplies many Parisian restaurants: "[Rungis products] might be fresh, but have no taste," he said.

Julien affirmed that the sourcing of "reasoned products" could be particularly problematic: hard work and commitment are needed to contact and bring together small agricultural producers who "are alone in their worlds but seeking to get known." Julien's concern for other people's welfare and livelihoods was evident from his method of sourcing. He obtained "reasoned products" from initiatives supporting the autonomy of farmers within production and distribution channels, such as the Terroirs d'Avenir network, which connects small farmers with chefs of Parisian restaurants. His engagement also took place on his laptop and smartphone. Julien used digital platforms provided by food start-ups such as Ecotable and Choco to, respectively, be informed about the developments and trends in sustainable restaurant practices, and communicate on a regular basis with producers and suppliers who advised him on seasonal arrivals and "reasoned products."[5] These networking tools aimed at creating a local food ecosystem that is economically viable for all participants based on the use of ecologically sound production and distribution practices.

Toward the end of our meeting, Julien commented on the everyday lives of restaurant workers. That is a topic, he said, that people in France's restaurant industry have not spoken openly about until now. Working conditions in restaurants can be brutal, with kitchens being sites of hierarchy, arrogance, and domination that are exhausting and demoralizing for many (see Burrow, Scott, and Courpasson 2024), and that can occur even in venues that proclaim themselves as exemplars of sustainability (see McCarron 2022). If such attitudes were long accepted as normal outcomes of environments exposed to high pressure and multitasking, today they are more problematized. Julien feels satisfaction when culinary workers claim respect and dignity and stress the necessity of nurturing respectful and collaborative relationships in professional kitchens and beyond them. The pursuit of more livable working conditions complicates common understandings of food sustainability that posit it as primarily related to challenges with food production and consumption. The social dimension of sustainability includes establishing personal networks that generate the compatible cohabitation of diverse individuals and groups, with improvements in the quality of life for all involved. Conversing with Julien on this made me contemplate my unfinished glass of water kefir under a different light. I realized that it would be shortsighted to see that drink only as the result of human care toward the living organisms that compose it. Water kefir production can be better grasped as a reciprocal collaboration between the humans that help fungal organisms to reproduce themselves and the fungal organisms that act on humans' intestinal flora to improve their health and immunity. These different elements of fresh products, conscientious production circuits, healthy work environments, and even a healthy personal biome facilitated by what we consume, made me consider the work of Julien as a multifaceted approach to culinary sustainability.

Vignette 4: Jonathan

Up in the hills of Belleville, in the northeastern part of Paris's city center, Le Vieux Belleville restaurant seems frozen in time, like a memento of iconic French food culture: wooden interiors and furniture, checkered tablecloths, and dining tables situated inches apart. The menu is also typically French: *Confit de canard* (duck confit), *Mignon de porc à la moutarde* (pork tenderloin with mustard sauce), and *Magret de canard à l'orange* (duck breast with orange sauce) are among the dishes on offer, with relatively modest prices ranging from twelve to twenty euros. The restaurant fills up with regulars from the neighborhood for lunch, with a clientele of tourists arriving for dinner.

Jonathan has run the kitchen of Le Vieux Belleville since 2018. Although only in his midthirties, he has worked in several different styles of restaurants, from low end to high end, including a Michelin-starred venue. He is proud of being a cook from "the new generation" who has

been trained in the old way by chefs who champion classic French bour-
geois cuisine. He speaks of his instructors with respect and admiration:
people with over five decades of work experience deserve to be listened
to, he said. Jonathan longs for the decade of the 1980s, a time when, in
his view, the gastronomic business in France was at its apogee with big-
name chefs such as Michel Bras, Pierre Gagnaire, Alain Passard, and Marc
Veyrat. Yet this was a time he never experienced as a cook. Jonathan is
against veganism and against trends in high-end cuisine that privilege the
aesthetic of the plate rather than quality, comfort, and simplicity, which
he insists only "the real cuisine" (*la vraie cuisine*) can provide. Modern
gastronomy, he says, is "full of fuss" (*plein de chichi*). *Chichi* is a French
idiom that means affected, pretentious, or "made to impress." Its opposite
is *à la bonne franquette*, which means simple, unfussy, or, like this particular case, straightforward.

Jonathan welcomed me on a Friday morning in the restaurant's
minuscule kitchen—its alleged nine square meters looked much smaller
to me. For the interview I placed myself on the other side of the kitchen
door so we could speak through the service window without compromising his *mise en place*. My first exchanges with him reminded me of the
interview with Julien. Both have worked in kitchens whose dimensions
are too limited for installing a cold chamber or a big refrigerator, and both
have elaborated a positive argument regarding the impossibility of storing
significant amounts of food, as it forces them to work with fresh products only. Yet, unlike Julien, for whom freshness is a palatable attribute,
Jonathan sees a fresh product as a "neutral product" (*un produit neutre*),
meaning one that maintains its basic organoleptic qualities: "Fresh products are those that look the same as after harvest." To reinforce this explanation, he contrasted the fresh foods from the market with the packaged
and precut foods from professional wholesale shops. He called the latter
"scissor products" (*produits ciseaux*), which is a reference to the "cut here"
dashed-line-and-scissors image on the packaging of precut foods. For
him, only fresh products would permit a cook to produce truly "homemade cuisine" (*une cuisine faite maison*). Homemade involves manual
work in all the phases of preparation, from washing to peeling to cutting
to cooking ("I take my cutting board, my knife, I work, it is homemade").
Then Jonathan made a lively demonstration to illustrate that homemade
cooking does not apply to vegetables only: He took a duck leg that he had
precooked himself to prepare confit and brandished it in the air rapidly
and repeatedly. The leg remained intact after the shaking. He said that if

he would do the same with a precooked leg from a can or a plastic bag, pieces of meat would fall, and it would become a changed product. When I asked where this good-quality duck comes from, he answered that it is "local," meaning from France and, sometimes, from Spain. In the case that the meat comes from outside France, Jonathan indicates the origin on the menu "because customers want to know."

While Jonathan was portioning salmon, the kitchen help arrived with a box filled with potatoes. The box was labelled Metro, a professional wholesale supermarket. Potatoes are the main side dish at Le Vieux Belleville, as their versatility contributes to maintaining the moderate price points of the menu items. Potatoes also allow for unexpected adaptations. Since Russia's war in Ukraine starting in 2022 has driven sharp increases in the global cost of oil, Jonathan now replaces the French fries that usually accompany the confit duck with *gratin dauphinois*, a specialty that uses cream and is cooked in the oven, using less oil than frying. His vision of homemade cuisine seems then to be versatile and adaptable to variable conditions. Furthermore, it also seems apt to prevent food waste. For instance, Jonathan never puts potato purée on the menu because purée contains milk and thus cannot be kept for more than twenty-four hours. Instead, he prepares mashed potatoes with a small amount of butter and oil (*écrasé de pommes de terre*), which he can keep for forty-eight hours and therefore may be reused in case of need. That way, if a meat does not sell well on a particular day, he has the possibility to propose another protein with the mashed potatoes as a garnish.

Taste or, more precisely, the palate (*le palais*), to use Jonathan's words, plays an important role in discerning whether a dish is homemade: "Scissor products have high amounts of added sugars and preservatives that can be directly felt on the palate." Accordingly, to him, to differentiate a fresh product from one that is not is an easy task. This has led Jonathan to find a solution for his beef and poultry stocks, made of stock powder as the restaurant does not have a refrigerator with sufficient space to keep homemade stocks. To remove the "bad taste" of the industrial stock, Jonathan adds a small piece of ginger into the dissolving powder so that the ginger "absorbs all the chemicals in it." He said he learned that technique from one of his instructors.

Jonathan's representation of taste, based on basic and broad views on "freshness" and "the local," is challenged as he progressively transitions from chef to entrepreneur. Attracting a regular clientele that appreciates his work has given Jonathan the confidence and motivation to plan to open his own restaurant in the Reims region. There, he will ideally be sourcing vegetables from small local producers, whom he would visit personally because "one potato from the garden and one potato from Metro . . . they are not the same"—meaning that they do not have the same taste. Sourcing directly from producers would also allow him to obtain products at a better price than from intermediaries. By becoming a regular customer of small producers, he explains, he would be able to negotiate rates that permit both partners to make their money. "If you have a small agreement with [a small producer] there is a way to work it out." Jonathan's novel motivations should be acknowledged as renewed consideration of the environmental, social, and economic dimensions of sustainability.

Conclusion

The accounts of the culinary practices of chefs working in moderately priced restaurants are crucial to nuance, expand, and decenter conventional understandings of culinary sustainability. The latter are supported by discourses heavily inscribed within elite configurations composed of celebrated chefs, their research and educational ventures, international organizations, and consumption-driven initiatives that promote foods and culinary techniques belonging to the dominant ethical eating repertoire—organic, fair, hyperlocal, natural, whole, slow. These actors and strategies model a top-down educational approach that, although potentially valuable, may not reach beyond fairly affluent social groups and milieus from within which elite chefs are recognized as models to follow due to their accumulated cultural and social capital.

Alternatively, the kitchen life of the Parisian chefs portrayed above shows that cooking in a sustainable manner implies much more than the capacity to obtain, work with, and consume foods whose production allegedly causes little to no environmental damage. To consider their views (and those of other nonelite chefs) I have proposed a holistic definition of culinary sustainability that addresses the economic, environmental, cultural, and social dimensions of cooking as equally important: one that places attention on the specific contexts in which culinary practices are performed, with their constraints, (inter-)dependencies, and opportunities, as well as the broader effects these practices carry. This definition includes diverse professional voices, who, although not perceived as authoritative, have impactful perspectives to share. Surely, certain basic features seem to be fundamental and nonnegotiable to move toward a more sustainable food system, such as the respect for the seasonality of foods and the avoidance of food waste and ultraprocessed foods, as expressed by all of the interviewees.

Culinary sustainability implies dealing with different and sometimes ambivalent views on similar food attributes. "Freshness" can be a sensory experience involving the palate and perceptions (Julien) or a characteristic that can be primarily distinguished by the view of the observer (Jonathan). Similarly, "local" can either mean the nation (Christophe) or the whole European region (Julien). These different representations are contextual, relative to particular, constrained situations and, for this reason, are difficult to align with top-down agendas. There is therefore no single route to culinary sustainability but rather several. These vary according to the abilities of chefs and restaurant owners to navigate competing economic interests (e.g., baseline costs of produce versus sourcing it via local or organic growers; small-scale sustainable restaurants versus large-scale, less sustainable restaurants) and values (e.g., human oriented versus nature oriented), as well as individual beliefs (e.g., about origin and taste) and aspirations (e.g., obtaining benefits for themselves while making a positive impact on both the environment and society).

Yet, what is more salient in this study are the social and cultural dimensions of sustainability and their capacity to influence more immediate surroundings. Unlike the moralistic, potentially exclusionary messaging of chefs in the wider public eye, midrange restaurant chefs moderate, even disseminate (as in the case of Raquel), practical sustainable values, which resonate within their respective social and environmental spheres. This is manifested by the emphasis the interviewed chefs placed on culinary practices resulting from reciprocal human relationships and community involvement. Empathy and respect (healthy work conditions), compassion and trust (inclusive production circuits), commitment to serve what they consider to be "good food," and care and collaboration figure centrally in their conceptions of food sustainability.

Notes

1. See https://europa.eu/taste-the-ocean/index_en and https://sdg2advocacyhub.org/chefs-manifesto.
2. La Maison Montreuil closed permanently in 2024. The quotes are from 2022, from the now inaccessible restaurant website. Julien had already left his post as chef the year preceding its closure.

3. "Ugly" here refers to vegetables commonly known as "wonky." These are often rejected at the producing and selling stages for not meeting aesthetic standards (too big, too small, misshapen, wrong color, slightly cracked skin).
4. See Le Breton (2017), chap. 6.
5. See https://ecotable.fr/fr and https://choco.com/fr/.

References

Abbots, Emma-Jayne. 2015. "The Intimacies of Industry." *Food, Culture & Society* 18 (2): 223–43.

Alkon, Alison H., and Julian Agyeman, eds. 2011. *Cultivating Food Justice: Race, Class and Sustainability*. Cambridge, MA: MIT Press.

AND-International. 2020. *Le marché alimentaire bio en 2019. Estimation de la consommation des ménages en produits alimentaires biologiques en 2019*. Montreuil-sous-Bois: Agence Bio.

Barnes, Christine. 2017. "Mediating Good Food and Moments of Possibility with Jamie Oliver: Problematising Celebrity Chefs as Talking Labels." *Geoforum* 84 (August): 169–78. https://doi.org/10.1016/j.geoforum.2014.09.004.

Brocard, Charlie, Mathieu Saujot, Laura Brimont, and Sophie Dubuisson-Quellier. 2022. "Pratiques alimentaires durables: Un autre regard sur et avec les personnes modestes." *Décryptage* 1 (February). https://www.iddri.org/fr/publications-et-evenements/decryptage/pratiques-alimentaires-durables-un-autre-regard-sur-et-avec.

Burrow, Robin, Rebecca Scott, and David Courpasson. 2024. "Bloody Suffering and Durability: How Chefs Forge Embodied Identities in Elite Kitchens." *Human Relations* 77 (1): 111–39. https://doi.org/10.1177/00187267221132936.

D'Amico, Mario, Giuseppe Di Vita, and Luisa Monaco. 2016. "Exploring Environmental Consciousness and Consumer Preferences for Organic Wines without Sulfites." *Journal of Cleaner Production* 120 (May): 64–71. https://doi.org/10.1016/j.jclepro.2016.02.014.

Guthman, Julie. 2008. " 'If They Only Knew': Color Blindness and Universalism in California Alternative Food Institutions." *The Professional Geographer* 60 (3): 387–97.

Giousmpasoglou, Charalampos, Lorraine Brown, and John Cooper. "The Role of the Celebrity Chef." *International Journal of Hospitality Management* 85 (February): 102358. https://doi.org/10.1016/j.ijhm.2019.102358.

Gliessman, Stephen. 2014. *Agroecology: The Ecology of Sustainable Food Systems*. Boca Raton, FL: CRC Press.

Hollows, Joanne, and Steve Jones. 2010. " 'At Least He's Doing Something': Moral Entrepreneurship and Individual Responsibility in Jamie's Ministry of Food." *European Journal of Cultural Studies* 13 (3): 307–22.

Johnston, Josée, Alexandra Rodney, and Philippa Chong. 2014. "Making Change in the Kitchen? A Study of Celebrity Cookbooks, Culinary Personas, and Inequality." *Poetics* 47 (December): 1–22.

Johnston, Josée, and Michael Goodman. 2015. "Spectacular Foodscapes: Food Celebrities and the Politics of Lifestyle Mediation in an Age of Inequality." *Food, Culture & Society* 18 (2): 205–22.

Johnston, Josée, Michelle Szabo, and Alexandra Rodney. 2011. "Good Food, Good People: Understanding the Cultural Repertoire of Ethical Eating." *Journal of Consumer Culture* 11 (3): 293–318.

Le Breton, David. 2017. *Sensing the World. An Anthropology of the Senses.* London: Bloomsbury.

Lima, Felipe, Daiane Mülling, and Marcus Gomes. 2021. "Do Organic Standards Have a Real Taste of Sustainability?—A Critical Essay." *Journal of Rural Studies* 81 (January): 89–98. https://doi.org/10.1016/j.jrurstud.2020.08.035.

Mapes, Gwynne. 2018. "(De)constructing Distinction: Class Inequality and Elite Authenticity in Mediatized Food Discourse." *Journal of Sociolinguistics* 22 (3): 265–87.

Mapes, Gwynne, and Andrew Ross. 2022. "Making Privilege Palatable: Normative Sustainability in Chefs' Instagram Discourse." *Language in Society* 51 (2): 259–83.

Matta, Raúl. 2019. "Celebrity Chefs and the Limits of Playing Politics from the Kitchen." In *Globalized Eating Cultures: Mediation and Mediatization*, edited by Jörg Durrschmidt and York Kautt, 183–201. Cham: Palgrave Macmillan.

Matta, Raúl, and Padma Panchapakesan. 2021. "Deflated Michelin: An Exploration of the Changes in Values in the Culinary Profession and Industry." *Gastronomica* 21 (3): 45–55.

McCarron, Meghan. 2022. "Chef's Fable." *Eater*, July 6, 2022. https://www.eater.com/22996588/blue-hill-stone-barns-dan-barber-restaurant-work-environment-ingredients.

Mrusek, Natascha, Michael Ottenbacher, and Robert Harrington. 2022. "The Impact of Sustainability and Leadership on the Innovation Management of Michelin-Starred Chefs." *Sustainability* 14 (1): 330. https://doi.org/10.3390/su14010330.

Pereira, L., Rafael Calderón-Contreras, Albert V. Norström, Dulce Espinosa, Jenny Willis, Leonie Guerrero Lara, Zayaan Khan, Loubie Rusch, Eduardo Correa Palacios, and Ovidio Pérez Amaya. 2019. "Chefs as Change-Makers from the Kitchen: Indigenous Knowledge and Traditional Food as Sustainability Innovations." *Global Sustainability* 2:E16. https://doi.org/10.1017/S2059479819000139.

Rousseau, Signe. 2012. *Food Media: Celebrity Chefs and the Politics of Everyday Interference.* London: Bloomsbury.

Santos, Ana Rosa, and Carina Mansey. 2022. "Latin America in the Chef's Table." *Anthropology of Food*, S17. https://doi.org/10.4000/aof.13328.

Shugart, Helene. 2014. "Food Fixations: Reconfiguring Class in Contemporary US Food Discourse." *Food, Culture & Society* 17 (2): 261–81.

Spagnuolo, Daniela. 2022. "Problematizing Ethical Eating: The Role of Policy in an Ethical Food System." *Food, Culture & Society* 25 (5): 934–52.

CHAPTER SIX

"Vegan Cookery for Me Is …"

Israeli Vegan Chefs Negotiating Veganism and Sustainability

LIORA GVION

Introduction

Sustainability is a process that involves making decisions in which environmental, economic, and sociocultural endurance are satisfied. Key to this process is the construction of norms and agendas that bring the nonhuman world into thought and practice (Maxey 2006). This chapter explores how Israeli vegan restaurateurs interpret and account for sustainability in their establishments. It claims that in balancing the tension between economic viability and sustainability, Israeli vegan chefs equate the latter with health and trust in food, envisioning veganism as enabling them. Thus, they communicate the message that veganism, as a cuisine in progress, is also a responsible lifestyle that can potentially contribute to more sustainable eating because it renounces meat.

Restaurants are a good case study for examining the implications of sustainable practices and the meanings attached to them. On the one hand, they contribute some of the infrastructure supporting different or oppositional food movements, by providing spaces to engage customers into negotiating, practicing, and constructing new and sustainable foodways (Belasco 2005, 2007; Leer 2020; Sulek and Hensley 2004). Simultaneously, restaurateurs search for means to build a steady clientele and make a profit (Gupta, McLaughlin, and Gomez 2007; Harrington, Ottenbacher, and Kendall 2011; Parsa et al. 2005). For vegan restaurants in Israel this often requires abandoning sustainable practices that involve higher operational costs that might require an increase of the prices to a level that their clients, mostly millennials with limited means, would find difficult to pay. Additionally, some vegan cookery relies on industrially produced foods, a practice that undermines sustainability.

While Israeli vegan chefs and cooks interviewed for this chapter acknowledged the essentiality of sustainability, for example, refusing to support the meat and dairy industry and working toward minimizing the contamination of the environment, this issue was not high on their priority list. Instead, they often envisioned themselves as creating an alternative cuisine and rethinking the concept of the restaurant, interpreting their spaces as positioned between the public and domestic spheres. First, they deemphasized the essentiality of professional training, claiming it could be replaced by work experience in vegan domestic or restaurant cookery. Second, they envisioned their establishments as extensions of the dwelling, where homey, healthy dishes are served and customers are thought of as guests, entitled to receiving knowledge on vegan cookery. Third, although recognizing the importance of sustainable kitchens, vegan restaurateurs admitted to the low likelihood of them personally operating one. Rather, they approached sustainability by serving dishes made of local and mostly seasonal ingredients and minimizing the utilization of industrially produced foods, except when making vegan adaptations of animal-based dishes. Such dishes were claimed to be healthier and morally superior to meat dishes because they enabled the restaurateurs to engage in ethical consumption and minimize the damage to the environment.

The Social Actors: Methodology

Data were obtained from fifteen in-depth open-ended interviews with ten male and five female restaurateurs, the youngest being twenty-eight years old and the oldest forty-eight years old, who operated vegan restaurants in Israel. They had all worked in professional kitchens prior to opening a vegan restaurant. Only two of them were graduates of culinary institutes. They all downplayed the essentiality of professional training, claiming that culinary schools provide little knowledge of vegan cookery and that cumulative experience in domestic or restaurant cookery was sufficient for operating their businesses. Most of the interviews were conducted in the fall of 2019. Interviews lasted one to two hours and took place in their restaurants. We spoke about the circumstances that brought them to open a vegan restaurant, their considerations in planning the menu, the adjustments made to accommodate the needs of their clientele, and their thoughts on how to operate a sustainable business. Four of the restaurants closed permanently during the first and second COVID-19 lockdowns.

With one exception, all the interviewees had been practicing veganism for four to eight years. One identified as "practically vegan" because he had been eating all his meals in his own restaurant. Another identified as flexitarian. Only one of my interviewees claimed to be an ethical vegan. Three were environmental vegans and the rest were health vegans. One had intended to operate a farm-to-table restaurant where she could use the organic vegetables she had grown but realized it was unprofitable. Others claimed it was not essential to use organic vegetables because of the rich and high-quality produce in local markets.

Veganism and the Restaurant Industry

The increased awareness of consumers and businesses that consumption behaviors affect the environment has created a trend toward green and sustainable restaurants that adopt environmentally responsible strategies and rely on consumers' willingness to pay to support them (Hu, Parsa, and Self 2010; Namkung and Jung 2017). By providing food made of healthy, locally grown, or organic ingredients, restaurants gain a reputation for being green and protecting the environment (Namkung and Jung 2017; Tan and Yeap 2012). The more that consumers gain experiences in green restaurants and become aware of the benefits of green consumption, the more likely they are to be willing to pay more for green practices in restaurants (Namkung and Jung 2017). For example, American customers believe that restaurants can gain from their environmentally aimed efforts, provided they do not sacrifice quality and comfort. Indian customers are willing to pay higher prices for healthy food and Taiwanese consumers are willing to pay more at green restaurants if they understand sustainable practices and are concerned for the environment (Dutta et al. 2008; Hu, Parsa, and Self. 2010; Schubert et al. 2010).

Sustainability as a process, according to Larch Maxey (2006), allows an understanding of the negotiations and interactions that are continually being (re)made, stabilized, and undermined. Key to this process is the construction of norms and agendas for all involved. Jonatan Leer (2020), for example, tells the story of a Nordic restaurant that challenges the concept of eating out. Instead of passive consumers, visitors become participants in food preparation through foraging, cooking, and other hands-on activities before ultimately sitting down to their dinner. A visit to such a restaurant involves a physical interaction with the terrain where the food grows and an engagement in manual labor to earn the meal, defying the capitalist consumerist model. Restaurateurs differ in the extent to which their decisions involve and satisfy environmental, economic, and socio-cultural factors.

Generally, restaurateurs lag in providing their politically or environmentally conscientious customers with alternatives to the dominant food culture because of tensions between economic, social, and environmental goals (Chuck, Fernandes, and Hyers 2016; Greenbaum 2012). They acknowledge the benefits associated with sustainability, such as enhancing their public image, appealing to a niche tourist market, and showcasing their commitment to corporate social responsibility. However, they rank higher the short-term commercial profit to be gained from satisfying consumers' prioritization of value for money assessed through portion size, familiarity, variety of choice, and self-indulgence (Filimonau and Grant 2017).

Lifestyle movements often raise businesses' awareness of ethical consumerism and recruit them as active participants in their path from the margins to the mainstream, influencing ideas and altering practices in the service of a cause (Miller 2017). For instance, hip vegan restaurants and shops have helped veganism become trendy and mainstream. Vegan activists raise consciousness of the consequences of eating animal-based foods and of the unethical treatment of animals. Their actions cause people to consider the consequences of consumption on the environment and promote veganism as curbing climate change and alleviating world hunger (Cherry 2006; Cherry, Ellis, and DeSoucey 2011; Haenfler, Johnson, and Jones 2012; Twine 2018). Although vegan restaurateurs may wish to include environmentally sustainable practices, most entrepreneurs tend to be more passionate about their business sustainability, seeing the former as raising expenses and therefore unprofitable. Many also claim to have difficulty in implementing sustainable practices because they lack knowledge of effective methods and fear increased costs (Shubert et al. 2010). Moreover, given its fashionable, healthy image, persons who currently adopt a vegan diet or lifestyle may be doing so primarily for personal rather than environmental reasons and may not push for sustainable practices (Castricano and Simonsen 2016; Kalte 2020). This may hinder the motivation of vegan entrepreneurs to prioritize such practices.

Since the beginning of the twenty-first century, Israel has witnessed a growing popularity of veganism. The number of ethical vegan activists has risen, and they have received increasing support (Alloun 2018, 2020; Weiss 2016). This has led to a growing demand for vegan food, with restaurateurs having to decide how to transfer and reconfigure vegan cookery into their businesses. While they may be committed to promoting veganism as an ethical lifestyle movement, their dedication may conflict with attempts to earn a living off customers whose priority is good value for money (Gvion 2021).[1]

This chapter illustrates how Israeli vegan chefs envision themselves as instrumental in providing access to veganism while downplaying the essentiality of sustainable practices. They equate sustainable practices with serving simple, local, and seasonal food they see as healthy and ethical. Rather than investing in sustainable infrastructures, an investment they are not likely to get returns for, they promote sustainability by accessing and disseminating vegan food knowledge that helps keep the environment clean and expresses commitment to human health and animals' wellbeing—all in settings envisioned as expansions of the domestic space.

Israeli Vegan Restaurants

Most vegan restaurants I studied in Israel occupy small spaces with a counter, behind which vegetables are cut to make fresh salads, dishes are garnished, and large pots of stews or soups simmer. The spaces usually contain two or three tables, with another few on the sidewalk. The tables are bare, plates and utensils are inexpensive, and tap water is served upon request. Many of these restaurants attract regulars (both vegans and omnivores), mostly millennials with moderate financial means, who work nearby and come for their lunch. Owners deliberately serve large portions, claiming that lunch is the main meal of the day in Israel and that customers expect substantial and filling dishes.

Only three of the fifteen studied restaurants aimed to attract affluent middle-class professionals. One of them has wooden furniture and plates and utensils that vary in shape and size to match the food. It serves sophisticated high-end dishes, which include fermented ingredients, require intensive labor, involve complex compositions, and are about four to five times more expensive than dishes in other vegan restaurants. The second seats customers in a hyperdesigned indoor space, or in the back garden, where the vegetables and herbs used in preparing the salads grow in garden beds. The atmosphere connotes freshness and closeness to nature. The third place is in an area popular among middle-class professionals and members of the leisure class. It seats its visitors within a large glass-encased patio.

Most patrons claim to learn about the restaurants by word of mouth, and they recognize them as vegan by their appearance, the aroma of the dishes served, and the type of clientele. Menus vary. Some offer vegan adaptations of animal-based foods, such as lasagna, *haraime* (fish cooked in spicy tomato sauce), hamburgers, pasta Bolognese, or shawarma (thin slices of meat stacked in a cone-like shape and roasted on a slowly turning vertical rotisserie), using vegan adaptations such as tofu or mushrooms as meat substitutes. Several conform to a three-course meal structure, providing a familiar, "conventional" Israeli eating experience. Those restaurants operating in small spaces usually limit their menus to three to five soups or stews, two to three salads, and two to three dishes made of grains, legumes, and seasonal vegetables. Prices range from $15 to $25 for a meal, except for one upscale restaurant that offers a tasting menu of ten dishes for about $160 per couple, not including drinks.

Most of the cooking personnel have not been professionally trained. Lacking established vegan cookery knowledge to rely on, my interviewees regarded veganism as a cuisine whose foundations are in the process of being laid and saw themselves as engaged in forming its fundamental principles and providing the testing fields. Their restaurants were envisioned as extensions of their personal dwellings, where their time spent as domestic vegan cooks (along with their previous work experience in restaurants serving animal-based foods) qualified them to prepare what one chef named "real food"—simple, fresh seasonal dishes made of local ingredients. Customers were described as guests who substituted restaurant eating for home eating because they saw the former as an opportunity to learn how to follow a nutritionally balanced diet. This conferred upon the cooking personnel the responsibility to feed customers appropriately by serving healing dishes that repaired the damage caused by previous ingestion of animal-based foods.

None of my interviewees considered operating a sustainable establishment. Even though they could not estimate the costs involved in opening one, they all claimed it was beyond their financial means. Some claimed it was the government's responsibility to subsidize the means for operating sustainable establishments and that all that they, personally, could do to minimize the damage to the environment and the body was to serve local, seasonal, preferably organic and healthy dishes.

"There Is No Vegan Professional Cookery Yet"

Israeli vegan chefs and cooks experience a complex relationship with professional cookery and training. Unlike ethnic chefs, who encapsulate incongruities between professional proficiency and native cuisine (Ray 2016), my interviewees had neither native nor professional cookery knowledge to rely on. Rather, they claimed to be engaged in the foundation of vegan restaurant cookery and participating in its construction. Moreover, lacking opportunities for vegan professional training, the chefs and cooks admitted that they had to rely to some extent on "conventional cookery." On the one hand, they aimed to use veganism as a means to introduce into the culinary arena something more than just an abstention from animal-based dishes. On the other hand, in lieu of a shared body of culinary knowledge, they often referred to "conventional cookery" as the yardstick against which they defined their food preparation. Gabriella, a trained chef, admitted that she had difficulties differentiating her vegan from her animal-based cookery knowledge, saying:

> During my training I learned how to handle vegetables but not how to use them as the essentials of my cooking. It wasn't until a friend asked me to do the catering for a vegan dinner party that I started thinking about what it means to cook vegan. I still rely on all that I've learned to compose creative menus and plan the budget. I can't say that I'm a vegan chef the way people say they're trained as Japanese chefs.

Hannan, another trained chef, combined his acquired professional knowledge with his cumulative wisdom and experience as a domestic vegan cook. He considered his restaurant as an arena for experimenting with vegan cooking and contributing to its foundation as a distinctive cuisine:

> Professional vegan cookery is about something that we are still figuring out. I think that vegan cookery is about expressing care. We use food to care for our health, for animals, and for the environment. We are still figuring out ways to do it while eating high-quality, tasty food.

Whereas Gabriella still defined vegan cookery as stemming from and relying on "conventional cookery," for lack of a stock of knowledge to rely on, Hanan associated vegan cookery with social and environmental responsibility. My other interviewees, who neither had culinary school training nor had considered it, were relatively unconcerned with an elaborate rationale for veganism. Although, as Aviad said, "going vegan is about being part of a large-scale process that will change the way the world eats because it is about eating healthy in a manner that is environmentally and animal friendly," none of the chefs were motivated to cook for a vegan restaurant for environmental or ethical reasons. Some started cooking vegan after being complimented by their friends on their homemade dishes and took the opportunity to exhibit their culinary knowledge in the public sphere. Others entered the field for lack of other options. Previous experience in the restaurant business was perceived as potentially helpful. Eyal stated:

> I've been working in restaurants for over ten years. There's a lot of knowledge in my hands. I don't underestimate professional training when it comes to upscale restaurants. But vegan cooking is about cooking healthy without damaging the environment or killing innocent animals.

Alma thought in a similar vein:

> All I ever did as an adult was cook for restaurants. When I opened my own place, I knew I was going to serve only healthy dishes that I serve when I entertain because once you cook healthy, you can't go wrong.

The untrained respondents often relied on hired help to oversee the cooking. In most cases those hired were not professional cooks, but clinical nutritionists employed to plan balanced menus and train domestic cooks to prepare them. Alon hired Nadav, a domestic cook who consults his mother, a clinical nutritionist, whenever he plans menus. Gal insisted that he and the cook he employs follow the recipes planned by clinical nutritionists. Upon inheriting a store on one of Tel Aviv's busiest streets, Abraham, an engineer, engaged his father and uncle, who cook for a large hotel, to teach him how to prepare vegan dishes:

> They "veganized" five of their soups and took a week off from work to experiment with them, wrote detailed recipes for me to follow,

and for several weeks they worked the evening shift so they could help me out in the mornings.

Either due to a shortage of certified vegan cooks, or as part of the tendency to discredit professional knowledge, my interviewees chose to rely on alternative forms of knowledge in producing and assessing vegan restaurant food. Emphasizing healthy and simple eating, they articulated vegan restaurants as sustainable establishments because, as said by Gal, "when you serve healthy dishes and care for yourself you also care for the environment." They did not view dishes as resulting from creative processes aimed at producing unique compositions but rather as emerging from concerns and standards external to the field of gastronomy that enable relating healthy and ethical eating to caring for the environment by not consuming animals.

Operating vegan restaurants also requires chefs and cooks to acknowledge their complex relationship with animal-based foods. While wishing to be free of association with them, they acknowledge their reliance on adaptations of animal-based dishes. These dishes are meant to attract vegans who miss eating meat, as well as omnivores. Although these dishes are made of industrially produced ingredients such as tofu or seitan that challenge the restaurateurs' attempt to serve healthy and sustainable food, my interviewees claimed them to be healthier and morally superior for not involving the commodification or abuse of animals.

Alma's restaurant exemplifies the adjustments vegan cooks make to keep their regular diners who have gone vegan, as well as attempts to broaden their clientele. She explained:

> I must consider my customers' needs, or I'll go bankrupt. That's why my signature dishes, *haraime*, tuna salad, and hamburgers, taste like meat and fish. I respect [the customer's] need of meat and eggs, and there is nothing wrong with it. [My dishes] taste the same but are healthier.

The decision to serve vegan adaptations of animal-based foods requires cooks and chefs to decide whether they should use industrially produced ingredients. Alma, who claimed to be using "just enough tofu to produce the right taste," buys domestically prepared tofu. Hannan and Gabriella avoid using tofu and seitan because these ingredients are industrially produced. They consider vegan cookery as an opportunity to liberate themselves from an omnivore conception of food and meals.

Tofu and industrially produced vegan cheese make it possible for vegan junk food eateries to help young adults participate in a youthful urban lifestyle. These eateries are usually located in areas where young adults live or hang out and offer hamburgers, made either of tofu or mushrooms, served on buns, topped with fried onions, lettuce, and tomato, and served with French fries or shawarma made of mushrooms. Vegan pizzerias use "cheese" made of tofu or occasionally cashew nuts. Among the young vegans it is also common to meet parents with children who are sensitive to lactose or even celiac patients who claim to trust vegan establishments more than "regular" ones. Amos, trained as an economist and the oldest among my interviewees, owns two vegan junk food places he refers to as a small chain to be expanded when possible. One serves meat adaptations such as schnitzels, hamburgers, and shawarma and is located on one of the busiest streets of Tel Aviv. It mostly attracts soldiers on their lunch break, vegans, and omnivores who either work or live in the area. The other is a pizzeria operating in an up-and-coming and partly gentrified area not far from a neighborhood where many vegans live. The place attracts mostly inhabitants of the neighborhood who follow a vegan diet and vegans from all over Tel Aviv and the periphery who miss eating pizza. Amos told me:

> I know I'm substituting one industry for another, but a less damaging one. But my food makes people happy and enables them to eat out with their friends. I make shawarma from mushrooms because I don't want to use much tofu. Still, what does the government do for the environment? I know it is expensive but you can't expect me to invest my money to save the environment while the government isn't doing enough, anything to be exact.

Like vegan restaurants in France whose recipes consist of mock meat dishes that reinforce an eating culture marked by "carnism" (Veron 2016), in preparing vegan adaptations of animal-based foods, Israeli vegan chefs and cooks admit to the domination of animal-based foods in their modes of thought about meals. Not only does the preparation of mock animal-based foods testify to their prioritization of taste, shape, texture, and aroma, as well as appeal to a broad clientele. It is also indicative of their flexible definition of sustainability and its low priority in their considerations for operating a vegan restaurant. The decision to serve vegan adaptations of animal-based foods, even if made of industrially produced ingredients, is claimed to be justified within the framework of sustainable cookery, as vegan adaptations are overtly less damaging than meat and dairy products. The chefs' inability to make a living from dishes that differ substantially from conventional foods and dishes, coupled with the need to function in a small and compatible market with little profit margins, is used by the chefs to justify being less sustainable.

"I Wish I Could Operate a Sustainable Restaurant and Serve Only Healthy Dishes . . ."

Lacking an established vegan restaurant knowledge to rely on, my interviewees define their settings as differing from "conventional" restaurants, seeing them as an extension of the dwelling, where simple and healthy meals are served and customers are thought of as guests (Gvion 2020). Moreover, as previously shown, they apply a flexible definition of sustainability that enables them to position themselves as caring for the environment by choosing one or two principles they identify as sustainable and applying them in their restaurant. Among them are the avoidance of disposable dishware, the cooking of seasonal and mostly local ingredients, and the use of organic vegetables when possible.

In envisioning their restaurants as extensions of the dwelling and themselves as responsible for their customers' health, my interviewees introduce the concept of trust into the restaurant business. Trustworthiness is a condition that must be actively argued and demonstrated (Giddens 1994). Establishing the customers' trust in the food served to them has been claimed to enhance regular consumption patterns by those who patronize restaurants. Trust in the food to be healthy involves, for instance, familiarity with the people who make the food. Because my interviewees mostly rely on regulars who eat out daily, they seek to win their clients' trust by defining their cooking as substituting for home eating and themselves as committed to serving dishes they believe to be right for the body. Alon, for example, claimed that since the purpose of vegan restaurants is to provide healthy food, there should be no difference between restaurant and home cooking:

> Most of my customers are regulars who don't cook at home. They trust me to make dishes that I know for sure are good for the body, food that I prepare and eat at home. My job is to provide them with the food they need.

Eyal took a similar approach:

> I want to gain my customers' trust. I think about serving food that improves their well-being, the food that my girlfriend and I have every night.

Trust is not only constructed through the provision of healthy food. It is further communicated by revealing and disseminating self-acquired knowledge that my interviewees share with both regular and occasional customers, to enable them to maintain a healthy lifestyle. Alma admitted to relying on her own experience as a health vegan:

> Eating out shouldn't be a risky experience but like eating at home. I don't serve anything that I wouldn't eat or serve my family. You can't go wrong when you cook healthy, as vegan dishes are.

My attempts to have her identify the foundations of healthy cooking resulted in her equating it with home cooking made of good ingredients and preferably keeping a kosher kitchen, which embraces basic hygiene measures. Put differently, veganism, for her, is but one way among many of eating healthfully. Moreover, my interviewees see their food as capable of curing bodies of the damage caused by consuming animal-based food. Merav, who claimed to have recovered from her medical ailments by going vegan, saw her self-accumulated knowledge as a "truth" and felt compelled to share the information she possessed with others:

> I get lots of questions from people who eat here. I explain to them how to handle certain ingredients, I provide recipes, suggest they have a smooth transition [to veganism], and tell them to contact me should they need help. The more you explain, the more people are likely to recognize the benefits of veganism.

Ran agreed:

> I take my role as a guide very seriously because my clients see my recommendations as their key to a healthy life. I hired a clinical nutritionist who validated my knowledge, helped me with the menus, and made me feel confident that I was providing the right information.

Vegan chefs and cooks see veganism as a cure for a variety of maladies, one being eating disorders. According to Shira, going vegan enables people to "trad[e] one obsession for a healthier one." Having recovered from anorexia, she uses her position as a cook in a vegan eatery to help others:

> I recognize [anorexics] by the way they check our prepacked foods. I tell them that once you go vegan you can't gain weight, because you no longer need to concern yourself with calories but with getting enough proteins, even if that means eating carbs. I often teach them how to plan their meals, so they stop worrying about their weight.

The participants envision their customers' bodies as fields that their accumulated vegan food knowledge directly impacts, while being in constant need of care and repair. In engaging their customers to adopt alternative modes of thought about eating and to adjust their bodies to new food practices, my respondents promote nonscientific theories about achieving bodily health though nutrition. This corresponds to their disparaging the need for professional training in vegan cooking. They consider the knowledge they transmitted as a "truth" and provide their own experience as proof of its validity.

Unable or unwilling to invest in sustainable infrastructure, and yet recognizing and acknowledging the benefits of operating sustainable businesses, my interviewees chose one or two principles they identified as sustainable and applied them in their restaurants. For instance, they were preoccupied with the possibility of using organic vegetables, which they believed were beneficial to the body, but whose usage they considered unprofitable and impractical because of limited availability and high cost. Hannan explained as follows:

> I wish I could use organic vegetables, but I can't trust the growers to provide me regularly with all I need. It makes it impossible to plan a menu. My regulars come for particular dishes. I can't afford losing them. Organic vegetables are very expensive, and if I raise my prices some of my customers would not come as often as they do. I'm happy with the vegetables I use.

According to Omer:

> Israel is a paradise for vegans because of its rich supply of great vegetables all year round. I see no reason to use organic.

Miriam had been engaged in organic farming for over a decade before opening what she hoped to be a farm-to-table restaurant. However, soon after its opening, she realized the difficulties embedded in operating such an enterprise. She stated:

> We try to use as many organic vegetables as we can. But it isn't practical. Our customers won't go along with a changing menu that depends on whether we get certain vegetables. We can't take the risk. We buy our vegetables from credible suppliers.

My interviewees had difficulties linking organic farming and eating to either economic or social sustainability. They claimed, though, that organic farming does not exhaust the land and relies on natural fertilizers that are healthier for both the body and the environment, thus helping conserve it. None of them was concerned with the fact that much of the region's organic agriculture is taking place in the West Bank settlements relying on Palestinian labor, thus perpetuating the Israeli occupation. Only a small number of my interviewees considered the well-being of agricultural laborers. For instance, after watching a film on female workers in the cashew nut industry, Gabriella decided never to use or eat cashews:

> I learned that not only were these women making very little money, but they were also poisoned by the nut. I decided to stop buying, using, or eating these nuts. I won't contribute to abusing poor women. But I do use honey, although it implies abusing bees, because I don't want to deny my customers my best dessert.

Gabriella identified socially sustainable restaurant practices with her refusal to cooperate with workers' abuse. Lower on her priority list were measures promoting environmental conservation and economic sustainability. This was evident in her selective usage of ingredients. She was willing to give up items that brought little profit or could be easily substituted while continuing to use controversial ingredients, such as honey, that enabled her to produce dishes that won her customers' appreciation and guaranteed her income.

Merav was the only one among my interviewees who related ecological sustainability with restaurant work, stating restaurateurs should aim to produce less garbage. However, she too applied sustainable practices only if she could afford the financial consequences. For instance, she deliberately limited the usage of disposable dishes:

> I could raise my profit by 20 percent by providing takeout. But people produce too much garbage as it is. I encourage customers to bring their own receptacle so I can fill it with food for them to take home. But they forget to take a receptacle to work. Most Israelis would love their environment to be clean but would do little to make it happen.

To conclude, Israeli vegan chefs apply a flexible definition of sustainability. They view it as a spectrum that provides them with various possibilities to apply flexible measures and means that would improve their public image without risking their profit margins. Lacking the means to operate sustainable establishments and prioritizing health over other issues with which veganism concerns itself, they apply one or two principles they consider sustainable, provided they neither lower their profits nor raise operational costs and the wages of their workers. Thus, Israeli vegan chefs and cooks set their own yardsticks against which to measure the benefits of protecting the environment and balance them with other considerations.

Conclusions

This chapter focused on Israeli vegan chefs and cooks, examining the ways in which they interpret and account for sustainability in their restaurants and demonstrating that they view their establishments as a middle ground between the public and the domestic. Believing that veganism is more than just the private abstention from animal-based foods, my interviewees constructed settings where a distinctive cuisine was emerging and the relationships between the positions occupied by restaurant, customer, and chef were formed and reaffirmed. I demonstrated that Israeli vegan restaurateurs balanced the tension between economic viability and sustainability by equating the latter with health and claiming that food that is healthy for the body is also healthy for the environment.

This perception of the restaurant as a trusted setting, and of the restaurateur as a knowledgeable agent on matters of healthy dining, sheds light on sustainability as a complex process involving the construction of norms that translate into operational practices rather than a definitive end point. Israeli vegan chefs and cooks do not believe sustainability to consist necessarily of developing a progressive and heterogeneous network of human actors expressing care about the well-being of humans and animals. They understand sustainability as a multilayered and complex process in which norms and agendas, applying to all actors, are constructed and negotiated. While recognizing the essentiality of a sustainable kitchen to ensure the welfare of both human beings and animals within a protected environment, my interviewees admitted the low likelihood of operating such enterprises in a profitable manner.

Instead, they compromised by focusing on a particular aspect of sustainability, for instance limiting the inclusion of industrially produced ingredients in their dishes or featuring mostly local, seasonal, and fresh foods on their menus. They accordingly claimed their cooking to be morally superior, not only for involving neither the killing of animals nor the commodification of living creatures by exploiting their labor, but also for creating a bond with nature by changing seasonally and by curing the body of maladies caused by harmful modern food habits. Simultaneously, they did not advocate total abstention from industrially produced ingredients, but at most their minimization, acknowledging the trading of one industry for another that is more environmentally friendly and involves no animal abuse.

Notes

1. An exception to the abovementioned tendency is the African Hebrew Israelite community, which articulates veganism into its religious practices and history. Its members reject industrialized American foodways and elevate the soul food developed under slavery from its once lowly status by using products grown in the Holy Land (Avieli and Markowitz 2018). Their restaurants connect them to the tradition of vegan soul food establishments across the United States (Crimarco et al. 2019; Greenbaum 2018).

References

Alloun, Esther. 2018. " 'That's the Beauty of It, It's Very Simple!' Animal Rights and Settler Colonialism in Palestine-Israel." *Settler Colonial Studies* 8 (4): 559–74.

———. 2020. "Veganwashing Israel's Dirty Laundry?" *Journal of Intercultural Studies* 41 (1): 24–41.

Avieli, Nir. 2018. *Food and Power*. Berkeley: University of California Press.

Avieli, Nir, and Fran Markowitz. 2018. "Slavery Food, Soul Food, Salvation Food." *African and Black Diaspora: An International Journal* 11 (2): 205–20.

Belasco, Warren. 2005. "Food and the Counterculture." In *The Cultural Politics of Food and Eating*, edited by James L. Watson and Melissa L. Caldwell, 144–66. Berkeley: University of California Press.

Belasco, Warren J. 2007. *Appetite for Change*. Ithaca, NY: Cornell University Press.

Castricano, Jodey, and Rasmus R. Simonsen, eds. 2016. *Critical Perspectives on Veganism*. London: Palgrave Macmillan.

Cherry, Elizabeth. 2006. "Veganism as a Cultural Movement." *Social Movement Studies* 5 (20): 155–70.

Cherry, Elizabeth, Colter Ellis, and Michaela DeSoucey. 2011. "Food for Thought, Thought for Food." *Journal of Contemporary Ethnography* 40 (2): 231–58.

Chuck, Chelsea, Samantha Fernandes, and Lauri L. Hyers. 2016. "Awakening to the Politics of Food." *Appetite* 107: 425–36.

Crimarco, Anthony, Gabrielle M. Turner-McGrievy, Swann Adams, Mark Macauda, Christine Blake, and Nicholas Younginer. 2019. "Examining Demographic Characteristics and Food Access Indicators from the Location of Vegan Soul Food Restaurants in the South." *Ethnicity and Health* 27 (2): 483–98. https://doi.org/10.1080/13557858.2019.1682525.

Dutta, Kirti, Venkatesh Umashankar, Gunai Choi, and H. G. Parsa. 2008. "A Comparative Study of Consumers' Green Practice Orientation in India and the United States." *Journal of Foodservice Business Research* 11 (3): 269–85.

Filimonau, Viachaslau, and Michelle Grant. 2017. "Exploring the Concept of Dining Out Organically." *Anatolia* 28 (1): 80–92.

Giddens, Anthony. 1994. "Living in a Post-Traditional Society." In *Reflexive Modernization*, edited by Ulrich Beck, Anthony Giddens, and Scott Lash, 56–109. Cambridge: Polity Press.

Greenebaum, Jessica. 2012. "Veganism, Identity and the Quest for Authenticity." *Food, Culture & Society* 15 (1): 129–44.

———. 2018. "Vegans of Color." *Food, Culture and Society* 21 (5): 680–97.

Gupta, Sachin, Edward McLaughlin, and Miguel Gomez. 2007. "Guest Satisfaction and Restaurant Performance." *Cornell Hospitality Quarterly* 48 (3): 284–98.

Gvion, Liora. 2020. "Generation V." *Journal of Contemporary Ethnography* 49 (5): 564–86.

———. 2021. "Vegan Restaurants in Israel." *Food, Culture and Society* 26 (5): 996–1013. https://doi.org/10.1080/15528014.2021.2015941.

Haenfler, Ross, Brett Johnson, and Ellis Jones. 2012. "Lifestyle Movements." *Social Movement Studies* 11 (1): 1–20.

Harrington, Robert J., Michael C. Ottenbacher, and K. W. Kendall. 2011. "Fine-Dining Restaurant Selection." *Journal of Foodservice Business Research* 14 (3): 272–89.

Hu, Hsin-Hui, H. G. Parsa, and John Self. 2010. "The Dynamics of Green Restaurant Patronage." *Cornell Hospitality Quarterly* 51 (3): 344–62.

Kalte, Deborah. 2020. "Political Veganism." *Political Studies* 69 (4): 814–33. https://doi.org/10.1177/0032321720930179.

Leer, Jonatan. 2020. "Designing Sustainable Food Experiences." *International Journal of Food Design* 5 (1–2): 65–82.

Maxey, Larch. 2006. "Can We Sustain Sustainable Agriculture?" *The Geographical Journal* 172 (3): 230–44.

Miller, Laura J. 2017. *Building Nature's Market*. Chicago: University of Chicago Press.

Namkung, Young, and Soocheong (Shawn) Jang. 2017. "Are Consumers Willing to Pay More for Green Practices at Restaurants?" *Journal of Hospitality & Tourism Research* 41 (3): 329–56.

Parsa, H. G., John T. Self, David Njite, and Tiffany King. 2005. "Why Restaurants Fail."
  Cornell Hospitality Quarterly 46 (3): 304–23.

Ray, Krishnendu. 2016. *The Ethnic Restaurateur.* London: Bloomsbury.

Schubert, Franziska, Jay Kandampully, David Solnet, Kralj. 2010. "Exploring
  Consumer Perceptions of Green Restaurants in the US." *Tourism and Hospitality
  Research* 10 (4): 286–300.

Sulek, Joanne M., and Rhonda Hensley. 2004. "The Relative Importance of Food,
  Atmosphere, and Fairness of Wait." *Cornell Hotel and Restaurant Administration
  Quarterly* 45 (3): 235–47.

Tan, Booi-Chen, and Peik-Foong Yeap. 2012. "What Drives Green Restaurant
  Patronage Intentions?" *International Journal of Business and Management* 7 (2):
  215–23.

Twine, Richard. 2018. "Materially Constructing a Sustainable Food Transition."
  Sociology 52 (1): 166–81.

Veron, Ophelie. 2016. "From Seitan Bourguignon to Tofu Blanquette. *Critical
  Perspectives on Veganism,* edited by Jodey Castricano and Rasmus Simonsen,
  287–305. London: Palgrave Macmillan.

Weiss, Erica. 2016. "There Are No Chickens in Suicide Vests." *Journal of the Royal
  Anthropological Institute* 22: 688–706.

CHAPTER SEVEN

Sustainability as Craft
Introducing the Green Transition
at Danish Culinary Schools

SUSANNE HØJLUND AND
NANNA HAMMER BECH

Introduction: Sustainability Entering Danish Culinary Schools

"Vegetarians!—Oh they are such troublesome guests in the restaurants!"
In 2018 when our fieldwork at Danish gastronomy schools began, the
approach of the chef students to vegetarian customers was often like
this. Vegetarians were seen as eaters without the ability to enjoy what the
students defined as a normal restaurant meal, namely a plate designed
around a huge portion of meat. The teachers indirectly supported the
meat focus by teaching how to design meat-dominated plates, and
the cookbooks emphasized, and still do, meat supremacy by recom-
mending 225 grams (8 ounces) of beef per person on a plate serving
(Erhvervsskolernes Forlag 2008, 245). In 2021, three years later, when we
left the field, the criticism of vegetarians was muted, and vegetarianism
was to a higher degree seen as a foundation of sustainable consumption.
Students and their teachers were discussing how to make vegetables taste
delicious, how to diminish the amount of meat in a menu, and how to
use food resources better (including potato peels, seaweed, unfamiliar
fish, and so on).

We guessed that the silenced criticism of vegetarians had to do with
an increased focus on sustainability, both at the schools and in society.
In Denmark the "less-meat" strategy is often mentioned in discussions

about the current need to change food habits. In addition, new discussions on how to save energy in the kitchen, how to avoid food waste, and how to use local products have entered the public agenda. Sustainability is on the menu as never before. Perhaps as part of this development, at the culinary schools vegetarians are no longer a source of frustration but of inspiration. This rather sudden change during our fieldwork made us curious about how discourses on sustainability had entered the educational practices, and what it meant for learning to become a chef. Were we right that the introduction of vegetarian menus and a focus on food waste reflected a real change toward sustainability? Was it a change that not only reflected political awareness but could also lead to new practices? Can the life of these schools teach us new things about how chefs might define and work with sustainability?

These questions are the focus of this chapter. We ask how in culinary schools sustainability is defined in everyday practice, how the concept is communicated and given meaning by both teachers and students, and how it is practiced in the school kitchens. With this focus we highlight situations at the schools in which the concept of sustainability is made explicit in teaching and practice, but we also point to examples in which sustainability seems to be a goal, although it is not named. In vocational education, such as culinary schools, we assume that much knowledge is transferred through craftsmanship, the work of the hands. Our approach to sustainability is thus inspired by Molly Scott Cato (2014, 4),[1] who formulates a theory of "sustainability learning" that emphasizes the development of craft skills in relation to intellectual knowledge. Cato argues that sustainability is something you do, and that it has to be understood, learned, and trained in practice. To understand how craftsmanship and sustainability are connected is therefore central.

But food is not a neutral material. It cannot speak for itself, and it is ascribed symbolic meanings based on ideas and values: moral, political, philosophical, and so on (Barthes 1961). These meanings can be seen as communicative frames (Goffman 1974) or contexts (Bateson 1972) that make it possible to understand food as a cultural phenomenon. For example, meat and vegetables have changed in cultural value during recent years (i.e., "less meat, more vegetables")—even though it can be questioned whether this discourse has led to less meat consumption. This change of meaning is related to the emergence of sustainability as a new communicative frame during the three years we went in and out of the culinary schools. In contrast, "French cuisine" and "taste" have been strong and more long-lasting frames that have contributed to shaping the education on culinary craftsmanship.

Methodology

During the three years 2018–21, we visited four Danish vocational cooking schools (interrupted by coronavirus restrictions and lockdowns). We followed and interviewed the chef students in six different classes (each with twelve to fifteen students) and their eight teachers, we participated in both theoretical and practical classes and exam situations, we arranged a survey with fifty-four respondents, we held three focus groups, and we studied documents, internet links, film, and photos as supportive tools. We spent approximately twenty-five days at the schools, sometimes both of us at the same school, other times individually.

In Denmark it takes four years of schooling to become a chef (the Danish word is *gastronom*). The chef apprentices work at different restaurants, interrupted by three short periods at a school where they are trained in food production, cooking techniques, and kitchen language (in total twenty-seven weeks and an introductory course). At the culinary schools there are different educational paths; the one we followed was the traditional track toward becoming a chef. Other tracks educate people, for example, in "food, health and nutrition," and in "sandwiches (*smørrebrød*) and catering"; in addition, some of the schools educate bakers and butchers in separate tracks. The students are between seventeen and fifty years old and enter the schools with diverse educational backgrounds, from secondary school to full or partial university degrees. Many have worked in the restaurant sector beforehand, and most of the students are male: statistics for Danish vocational education from 2018 report 2,389 (66%) male *gastronom* students and 1,247 (34%) female *gastronom* students.[2] Vocational education to become a chef is gradually losing applicants, and Danish politicians are continuously trying to put this problem on the political agenda, advocating for more young people to choose a vocational rather than a university education. They see a need for reorganizing the work force in Denmark to avoid unemployment among academics and to meet a future need for more craftspeople in society (Regeringen 2022).

During interviews, and in the survey, we asked students about their motivations for wanting to become a chef. The answers stressed a passion for food and cooking, but at the same time expressed concern about the working conditions of the restaurant industry, the power and gender hierarchies, and the risk of negative atmospheres in the kitchen. In general, we met very engaged young people, burning with their interest in making food of high quality in a competitive Danish restaurant landscape enjoying public recognition as never before.

Cooking Pedagogy at the Schools

Before digging into the specific questions of how to teach and learn sustainable cooking, we will provide basic insight into everyday life at the schools. What was at stake when the chef students were there for only short periods between their apprenticeships at different restaurants?

A typical day at the school began early in the morning in a classroom with a teacher talking about a topic and facilitating group work or educational tests. It could be a lecture on food and the senses based on sensory studies, or one on the history of French cuisine. It could be a presentation on Auguste Escoffier and his ideas about a restaurant, or it could be a class where specific kitchen techniques were presented: for example, how to cut meat, how to cook vegetables, how to handle a fish. Also, the students had classes where the French kitchen and menu language were taught. Tradition and the French classic influence were also obvious in the language at the culinary schools during practical training. Students were encouraged to use the "right" expressions for techniques, dishes, and tools, which were often French words. When we asked one teacher why Escoffier and French cuisine were so dominant in all the schools we visited, he stared at us as if we were crazy. "The answer is simple: The French invented the restaurant," he stated, and then followed a long historical introduction to French gastronomy. The other half of the day was often dedicated to practical exercises in the kitchen, making food, and solving different tasks, such as producing classical Danish menus, experimenting with innovative dishes, exploring desserts, or learning to handle a piece of meat or fish. At some of the schools the competitive element was very visible, as talented students were often supported by several teachers, giving them space, extra teaching, and time to train for local or national cooking competitions.

As part of our fieldwork, we paid attention to how teachers and students framed their cooking, for example, by talking about taste,[3] tradition, innovation, sustainability, or French cuisine as important frames shaping their education. We thought in the beginning that "taste" would be the most important word we heard. Actually, we found only a few references to "taste" as a distinct word, among both teachers and students, except for the few lessons in which the basic tastes and their characteristics were taught. The students told us that taste was so obvious a concern that it was not necessary to mention it. And many teachers found taste difficult to put into words, as one very experienced teacher said: "Taste as a common reference does not exist. Everyone tastes differently. I cannot teach taste—I can only guide, and what I use is actually sensory science. It is the craftsmanship that counts." Another told us, "Taste is individual. We cannot judge it. But what we assess is how the students use their techniques."

We heard from the teachers again and again that kitchen techniques were the primary focus for their teaching and assessment of the students, here exemplified when talking about how students were taught to make ice cream: "His ice cream tasted really good, but anyway, I could not assess it, as he used the wrong techniques to produce it." Even though techniques were seen as essential, on the other hand, the teachers found it very important that the students could analyze and conceptualize their dishes. This was especially taught indirectly through a daily ritual of assessing the dishes produced in the kitchen by the students. Here we found an interesting combination of knowledge communicated to the students. And here we learned that *tasting* rather than the word *taste* was important to focus on.

Commenting on the techniques of the hand, adding conceptual meaning-making to the food, and ending with tasting it were elements that were combined every day in an important ritual that took a good deal of time, and that was respected and looked forward to by the students: the assessment. Every time a student made a dish in the kitchen the teacher would assess it by tasting and commenting on the food presented to him or her. Here is a typical example of this culinary evaluation:

> You should cut the carrots in julienne and brunoise . . . the potatoes
> need to be turned correctly . . . [naming the techniques] . . . but
> nevertheless it is a nice summery dish [adding a symbolic frame]
> . . . [tasting it, and nodding].

In another example the teacher told the student that the charred leeks did not belong with his presented dish, *Karbonader* (a traditional Danish dish of pork meatballs served with plain, not decorated, cooked vegetables), and he added:

"That is *not* how your grandma would have wanted it! Think about what the guests expect when you promise them this traditional dish! And I am sure your grandma would not eat it when it is so red inside."

Here the context and the reference were to the traditional trait of this dish, that the vegetables should be cooked and not decorated with burned leeks, as the student had chosen to do. Using burned leeks is part of a "novel cuisine"—not part of the traditional Danish cuisine. The metaphor used by the teacher, making reference to grandma's cooking, was necessary for understanding what kind of cooking, craftsmanship, and expectations should be the frame for making this particular dish. At the same time as he was talking about traditional Danish cuisine, the teacher was cutting into the meat, investigating it with a concentrated look, and commenting on the technique of frying. Again, the symbolic meaning of the food was accompanied by comments on techniques, here on how to fry a meatball in a pan. And the evaluation ended with a tasting, after which the teacher said, "Anyway, it tastes good."

These culinary evaluations at the schools bound words, skills, food, and tasting together into pedagogical tools revealing the values of the discipline. They provided a language for analyzing the contextual meaning of food and at the same time assessed the taste, techniques, and skills behind the dish. The evaluations were individual, given to each student with a varied and complex language expressed by dedicated and passionate experts: the teachers. We found these daily evaluations very central in communicating the learning philosophy at the schools, with their unique combination of techniques, meaning-making, and tasting. This practice was not described as an explicit activity in the curriculum but was built into the everyday practice of the teaching.

In this way, different frames (here "tradition" was a strong frame) allowed the students and teachers to make sense of the particular dishes prepared and served. The way language was utilized to describe, evaluate, and in some cases discuss these dishes within the particular frames prompted a certain culinary dialogue and understanding of the food. As Priscilla Ferguson argues, talking about food makes it possible to "share the un-shareable—that is our sensual, powerfully private experiences of eating" (2014, xxi).[4] She points to different genres of food talk and assigns the chef a specific role and responsibility as a food communicator. This was also expressed by the teachers: "They have to learn to reason," one teacher answered when asked why they used so much time every day on assessing and commenting verbally on the food that the students produced. "It's their job to communicate what food is," another said. A third explained to us that the task of the school's teaching is to make the students move away from their own personal taste preferences and learn to imagine the expectations and preferences of the guests, that is, to move beyond an individual framing to a collective institutionalized one. Learning how to construct dishes is thus also about learning to refer to the different frames accepted and used by the professional collective.

We noticed that sustainability was not yet built into these daily culinary assessments as an explicit frame. Given the importance that this ritual had on an everyday basis, it could be a sign of a still-vague consciousness about how to include sustainability as an educational frame, what it means to do sustainable cooking as both a technique and a message, and how to evaluate it through tasting.

Teaching Food Sustainability in a Danish Context

In Danish society there is a general commitment to sustainability. Denmark was the first country in the world (in 2021) to publish official national dietary guidelines that have sustainability built into them.[5] The dominant understanding of sustainability refers to the "three pillars" model of economic, environmental, and social sustainability, defined in the Brundtland Commission report from 1987 (*Our Common Future*), in which global sustainability was mentioned for the first time. The UN resolution on sustainability from 2015 and the seventeen Sustainable Development Goals that it presented are also widely recognized in Danish society and in schools and universities,[6] and these goals are used as by big companies to communicate how they commit themselves to one or several of the different goals, such as combatting poverty, working against hunger, striving for equality between men and women, ensuring sustainable energy, and promoting better health. These discourses serve as more or less visible background goals for the culinary schools. Regarding restaurant sustainability it is worth mentioning that Danish restaurants are highly engaged in the green transition: you can find ten Danish restaurants in the 360 Eat 2023 Guide's top thirty list of restaurants that prioritize sustainability.[7]

At a strategic level, in political documents describing the education at the culinary schools, it is also mentioned that the schools are obliged to teach about "sustainability," "ecology," and "energy use," but it is not specified how.[8] One path to learning about sustainability would be to increase education about vegetarian cuisine. However, as of the time of writing it is not possible for chef apprentices to take a full educational period in a vegetarian restaurant, as it is an obligation during their schooling to work with meat.

At the culinary schools, the United Nations Sustainable Development Goals were used as a reference, and sometimes in class the students were asked to analyze how their cooking practices referred to one or several of the goals. The schools had also included practices that were referred to as "sustainable" in different ways. Some schools had developed their own vegetable gardens to show the students how to be closer to local ingredients. One school had intensified the focus on vegetables and their taste characteristics. Others referred to the use of local and seasonal ingredients as a sustainable practice.

Although sustainability was not directly mentioned in the culinary evaluations we witnessed, during hands-on cooking classes in the kitchen, the students were sometimes reminded to avoid food waste, to save energy, to think about transportation, and to use local products in season. These reminders were tips and tricks mentioned here and there during processes of food preparation rather than part of a focused lecture or discussion. The teachers referred to the general societal demand for sustainability as something we all ought to remember, without defining what it was. It was presented as an obvious moral obligation rather than being brought into the professional language of a chef as something specific for the discipline. As noted before, these reflections were not part of the daily assessments of the dishes produced by the students during cooking classes.

But in the classroom, we heard teachers organizing dialogues on sustainability that were more explicit, making the students reflect on the concept itself, for instance, in a lesson in which the teacher asked all fifteen students to individually define what sustainability meant for them. Many different answers were formulated: To use everything from the animal, to avoid unnecessary packaging, to reuse plastic, to think about social inclusion, to use ecological food products, to collaborate with local farmers, to avoid long transportation of food, to learn to harvest plants directly from the surroundings, to save energy, and to think economically. It seemed that sustainability was a big box of possible actions, and that it was up to the individual to choose what to draw from it. Most of the proposals referred to environmental sustainability, while only a few were about the economic and social pillars.

The teachers at one of the schools arranged sustainability festivals where the students themselves were asked to develop dishes grounded in sustainable practices, and also to make a speech about how sustainability had inspired them. The examples of dishes were diverse and very creative: fried potato peels, a dish with a fish seldom eaten in Denmark, dishes made of food waste, menus using seaweed as an ingredient, tapenade with home-grown seeds, a sausage made of meat from a part of the animal that typically isn't used in Danish cooking, mussels used in innovative ways, old bread reused in new dishes, and so forth. The students talked about their dishes in relation to both environmental and economic sustainability, referring to upcycling principles, either rescuing food that would normally become waste or using food that is normally seen as inedible (Aschemann-Witzel et al. 2023).

We observed that sustainability at the schools had no single reference, and that sometimes teaching perhaps was about sustainability, but without framing it as such. For example, there was a continuous focus on the costs of cooking and preparing dishes for customers. All dialogues and exams with a student-produced dish had a component in them evaluating how the student had calculated the expenses and made a price for the customer. This focus was not framed as a sustainability focus, but it was actually central for learning how to sustain one's business financially as a manager of a restaurant.

Sustainability at the culinary schools is thus many things; it involves diverse practices and leaves endless possibilities for interpretation. At the present time it is not an explicit concept systematically taught in the curriculum at every school. It seems as if you can pick the version you want yourself and attach it to your practice. But if sustainability is not a coherent frame that informs your cooking, how do you then as a future chef choose to incorporate certain actions or strategies?

Students' Understanding of Sustainability

To understand better how the students thought about this, we arranged interviews focusing specifically on their ideas of sustainability. Several students pointed to the "brand effect" of sustainability: "Sustainability is about medals. The restaurants strive to get an award for their green profile." This skeptical approach, though, was not dominant. Most students supported ideas of a sustainable food system. Across the interviews we noted an interesting way of defining what sustainability is. Nearly all chef students picked their version of sustainability from their own life history and personal experiences in the food-making industry.

One male student said, "I have my sustainability approach from my parents. They taught me to avoid food waste and they use Too-Good-To-Go themselves."[9] A young man told us that his father always took him out fishing, and therefore he thinks that fish is the most sustainable product in the food chain. Another referred to his interest in the environment from his time as a scout: "I want to take care of the nature and environment . . . otherwise we do not have access to fish etc. anymore." Yet another connected his understanding of sustainability to his image of a good family and his visions for the future: "I have experienced enough stress around my choice of education before. I just want to be a chef with a good life, no stress, and a good family." Another said that sustainability to him was about having a good social environment, referring to his many years in a small local restaurant that always tried to create a good community atmosphere by producing staff food that everyone liked. A student who had worked many years as a ship's cook mentioned that traveling had formed his interpretation of sustainability. For him it was about using products from third world countries, helping them to be part of the worldwide food market. A man who in the class had mentioned that sustainability was about using everything from an animal, told us that his father was a butcher and that he had learned this from him. At the sustainability festival one of the students presented Japanese food with seaweed as an example of sustainable food, and he explained that he chose to present this dish due to his private long-term passion for Japanese cuisine. Drawing on his experiences in restaurants as an apprentice, a student told us that "his" restaurant had been working a lot on making sure that the packaging it used was made of recycled materials. Another chef student mentioned as an example of sustainability that she had worked at a restaurant abroad that only used local ingredients.

With these examples we want to point to how the meaning-making about sustainable cooking is constructed in quite another way than the traditional teaching and learning processes at the schools. Sustainability is not one frame, but many. In regard to the "three pillars" of sustainability, the environmental dimension dominates. The economic dimension is either grounded in skepticism (sustainability seen as part of a strong business brand) or muted (the economic calculations not connected to the concept of sustainability), whereas the social dimension seems to be a minor part of the dialogues. Thus, when choosing a sustainability frame, the students do not refer to authorities such as their teacher, sensory science, their cookbooks, Escoffier, or the French tradition. The frame is picked from their own life or "habitus," a set of practices that are learned over time as part of their history, lived life, and position in society (Bourdieu 1977). This is in opposition to the way they are expected to set aside their private taste preferences in order to learn to taste "as a chef."

When asked about when sustainability became a pedagogical topic, one of the teachers told us that the concept had only been part of the curriculum for a few years. But to him the topic of sustainability was adopted by the culinary schools in quite another way than other trends: "Chefs and restaurants are first movers when it comes to sustainability references, whereas former trends or headlines of organic and vegetarian food have not attracted attention for chefs in the same way," he said. There is an interesting contradiction between this expressed importance and the primacy of the sustainability agenda—and then the unstable position that it had on the schools' curricula during the period we were on fieldwork. Chefs are seen as first movers—but not because of a long-standing pedagogical engagement with sustainability by the schools. Perhaps these chef teachers are motivated by their own life histories, just as the students are?

Change takes time, and our study shows that there are many levels to work at to implement the green transition at the Danish culinary schools. If we look at the surrounding society and the larger structural forces, it is still not officially acknowledged that chefs need education in sustainability. As long as vegetarian restaurants have not been accepted as sites for official apprenticeships, the official study books have not been replaced by books with plant-based recipes,[10] the recommendations of meat portions in textbooks are still the same, sustainability is not a parameter in exams, and the French kitchen is still dominating without an explicit sustainability frame, sustainability has not really been anchored in the discipline yet. So, what could make it stronger?

Sustainability as Craft

The speculations in this chapter are built on the assumption that to become a chef is to learn to understand food, its potentials, its characteristics, its presentation, production, taste, and value, through craftsmanship and through contextual framing. This understanding makes a chef able to choose and use the right ingredients and techniques, be they chopping, grilling, boiling, stirring, freezing, blending, and so on, and thereby either create traditional dishes that satisfy a grandma or create an innovative plate for a gourmet restaurant or for a chef's competition. We have argued in this chapter that sustainability can be seen as a new frame chefs have to adapt to and make part of their professional practice. But it is not a simple frame, there is no one single authority to draw on, and overall, the gastronomy schools' engagement in sustainability is rather new. They are not alone, though.

The Michelin Guide published in 2020 a survey exploring how twenty-four Danish restaurants worked with sustainability (Michelin Guide 2020). The answers were just as diverse as those shown in this chapter. The restaurateurs answered that they worked for sustainability through concern for animal welfare, waste reduction, recycling, using wind as an energy source, composting, shopping with a cargo bike, reducing transportation expenditures, using sustainably sourced fish, working for biodiversity in both field and sea, fermenting, minimizing water use, reducing the use of glass bottles, using solar power, supporting local farmers, educating and mentoring staff, stressing seasonality, working with flavors and taste, caring for nature, nurturing a better work environment, and being carbon neutral. Perhaps because of this overwhelming diversity, the students turn to their own life experiences when they define what sustainability means in their cooking strategies (see also Mrusek, Ottenbacher, and Harrington 2022).

Nevertheless, there is a moment of societal awareness and a moral demand now that offer a new frame for the schools to include sustainability in their meaning-making. This happens at the same time as the role of the chef is changing toward being a prominent public figure in society—an authority that can interpret and communicate meanings of food (Matta 2019; McBride and Flore 2019). Therefore, there is a need for rethinking how to implement sustainability as a pedagogical topic.

At the gastronomy schools, central to pedagogical meaning production are the culinary evaluations. How can sustainability be included in them as a communicative frame? Can new language prioritizing sustainability "help produce the counter-hegemonic attitudes and behaviors fundamental to food system change?" (Counihan 2021). These questions touch upon a classical anthropological discussion about what people do and say, which are often not the same. As both the students and several scholars (and authors in this book) point to, sustainability can be an empty brand (Tsing 2017) with no actions behind it—something you speak about but do not actually put into practice, or something that has so many meanings that it is difficult to see it as one frame. The challenge is also how to include the personal frames that the students use from their own lives and to help forge these into a collective undertaking (Barr, Gilg, and Shaw 2011). As the theme is rather new in the culinary schools' curricula, it will probably take some time until it finds a legitimate place in texts, teaching, tasting, and kitchen techniques.

Sustainability is clearly a commitment that the culinary schools in Denmark have engaged in. The main idea or discourse is not questioned, but it is open for flexible definition in other ways than, for example, taste and cuisine definitions are. It is interesting that the students are expected to learn to set aside their private taste preferences in order to develop professional reflections on taste and food, whereas they, when it comes to sustainability, are encouraged to build on their private stories and life experiences, at least now in the formative phase. It is also interesting to learn how language, tasting, and techniques go hand in hand in the teaching practice of the schools. It shows how the craft of cooking is much more than the work of the hands.

Richard Sennet (2008, 9) put it like this: "Every good craftsman conducts a dialogue between concrete practices and thinking; this dialogue evolves into sustaining habits, and these habits establish a rhythm between problem solving and problem finding." To Sennet good craftmanship and thinking supplement each other. According to Cato, referring to Richard Sennet, craft learning *is* sustainability learning, both in mind and hands. She writes (2014, 23), "Perhaps the most important lesson of craft learning is that of the importance of relationship with your materials, and hence relationship with the natural world from which all those materials originate." This is the case whether you handle trees as a carpenter or food as a chef.

We should perhaps then talk not only about the craft of cooking but the craft of sustainable cooking. To the chef students this means that knowing how to cut a piece of meat or a carrot is dependent on their repertoire of thinking about the material or, in other words, on the different frames or contexts that they learn to draw on during their education. Cooking as a professional craft combines kitchen techniques, contextual understanding of the food, and a focus on the tasting experiences of the dish—in a complex interplay among all three elements. Therefore, for the schools to succeed in making sustainability a stable and specific competence of learning to become a chef, they must consider what sustainable cooking means to the sensory (taste) experience for the guest, how sustainability is related to cultural and other contexts, and what sustainability means for the kitchen techniques. It remains to be seen how these and other aspects of the green transition will continue to be incorporated in the schools' teaching practices.

Notes

1. Inspired by Richard Sennet's work on craftmanship: See Sennet 2008.
2. Dst.dk: Erhvervsuddannelser i Danmark 2019.
3. This project is part of the national research and dissemination project Taste for Life (Smag for Livet) funded by Nordeafonden. The overall aim was to explore the everyday life of chef students, and their motivations, learning strategies, interpretations of taste, and so on. See taste-for-life.org.
4. See also Fine (1996) for an analysis of the specific language chefs develop.
5. See dietary guidelines at https://altomkost.dk/raad-og-anbefalinger/de-officielle-kostraad-godt-for-sundhed-og-klima/.
6. https://sdgs.un.org.
7. https://360eatguide.com/nordic-2023/.
8. www.retsinformation.dk/eli/lta/2019/441.
9. Too-Good-To-Go is a Danish company that coordinates the selling of surplus food that would not be sold otherwise, from restaurants, supermarkets, and convenience stores.
10. As of the final editing of the manuscript of this book (2024), however, there are new initiatives on their way in the field, for example, more books and courses available for chefs on plant-based cooking.

References

Aschemann-Witzel, Jessica, Daniele Asioli, Marija Banovic, Maria Angela Perito, Anne Odile Peschel, and Violeta Stancu. 2023. "Defining Upcycled Food: The Dual Role of Upcycling in Reducing Food Loss and Waste." *Trends in Food Science & Technology* 132 (February): 132–37. https://www.sciencedirect.com/science/article/abs/pii/S0924224423000018?via%3Dihub.

Barthes, Roland. 1961. "Toward a Psychosociology of Contemporary Food Consumption." *Economies, Sociétés, and Civilisations* 5: 977–86.

Barr, Stewart, Andrew Gilg, and Gareth Shaw. 2011. "Citizens, Consumers and Sustainability: (Re)Framing Environmental Practice in an Age of Climate Change." *Global Environmental Change* 21: 1224–33.

Bateson, Gregory. 1972. *Steps to an Ecology of Mind.* New York: Ballantine Books.

Bourdieu, Pierre. 1977. *Outline of a Theory of Practice.* Cambridge: Cambridge University Press.

Cato, Molly Scott. 2014. "What the Willow Teaches. Sustainability Learning as Craft." *Learning and Teaching* 7 (2) (Summer): 4–27.

Counihan, Carole. 2021. "Food Activism and Language in a Slow Food Italy Restaurant Menu." *Gastronomica: The Journal for Food Studies* 21 (4): 76–87.

Erhvervsskolernes Forlag. 2008. *Kokkebogen.* Odense: Erhvervsskolernes Forlag.

Ferguson, Priscilla. 2014. *Word of Mouth: What We Talk About When We Talk About Food*. Berkeley: University of California Press.

Fine, Alan Gary. 1996. *Kitchens: The Culture of Restaurant Work*. Berkeley: University of California Press.

Goffman, Erving. 1974. *Frame Analysis: An Essay on the Organization of Experience*. Cambridge, MA: Harvard University Press.

Matta, Raul. 2019. "Celebrity Chefs and the Limits of Playing Politics from the Kitchen." In *Globalized Eating Cultures: Mediation and Mediatization*, edited by Jorg Dürrschmidt and York Kautt, 183–201. London: Palgrave Macmillan.

McBride, Anne E., and Roberto Flore. 2019. "The Changing Role of the Chef. A Dialogue." *International Journal of Gastronomy and Food Science* 17, article 100157. https://doi.org/10.1016/j.ijgfs.2019.100157.

Michelin Guide. 2020. "The New Sustainability Emblem: 27 Industry Role Models and 31 Worthy Initiatives are Highlighted in the Nordic Countries." https://guide.michelin.com/dk/en/article/news-and-views/michelin-guide-2020-the-new-sustainability-emblem.

Mrusek, Natascha, Michael C. Ottenbacher, and Robert J. Harrington. 2022. "The Impact of Sustainability and Leadership on the Innovation Management of Michelin-Starred Chefs." *Sustainability* 14 (1): 330. https://doi.org/10.3390/su14010330.

Regeringen. 2022. "Ansvar for Danmark: Det politiske grundlag for Danmarks regering." Statministeriet. https://www.stm.dk/statsministeriet/publikationer/regeringsgrundlag-2022/.

Sennet, Richard. 2008. *The Craftsman*. New Haven, CT: Yale University Press.

Tsing, Anna. 2017. "A Threat to Holocene Resurgence Is a Threat to Livability." In *The Anthropology of Sustainability. Beyond Development and Progress*, edited by Marc Brightmann, and Jerome Lewis, 51–65. London: Palgrave Macmillan.

United Nations. 1987. *Our Common Future: Report of the World Commission on Environment and Development*. Geneva: United Nations. https://sustainabledevelopment.un.org/content/documents/5987our-common-future.pdf.

Woodhouse, A. 2015. "Culinary Arts Pedagogy: A Critical Enquiry into Its Knowledge, Power and Identity Formation." Master's thesis, Otago Polytechnic.

CHAPTER EIGHT

Research Chefs in the United States and Scalable Opportunities for Sustainable Food Solutions

JONATHAN M. DEUTSCH

Introduction

In this study of research chefs and sustainability, I conducted informal and/or formal interviews with ten chefs working in the United States (though most work for companies that conduct business globally) who identify as research chefs or "Culinologists®." These chefs work with the food industry to develop and promote new food products in retail packages, for food-service buyers, or as ingredients used in the manufacture of other products. The emphasis of the interviews was on sustainability and the future food supply, as well as the research chef's role in shaping that food supply. I argue that the research chef is an underused and potentially powerful resource to improve the health of people and the planet. Sustainability is defined by the United Nations' Brundtland Commission as "meet[ing] the needs of the present without compromising the ability of future generations to meet their own needs" (1987, 16). While sustainability is often used as shorthand for ecoconsciousness, a triple-bottom-line approach to sustainability includes a focus not only on the environment but also on economic and social sustainability (Hagglund 2013, 12), which is the framing used in this paper.

When we speak of chefs as advocates for sustainable food and food systems, we are best served to be expansive and inclusive of who are these chefs and what are their roles. After introducing the study methods, the research chefs' role in history, and the establishment of the Research Chefs Association, the chapter explores how research chefs see themselves contributing to triple–bottom-line sustainability in multiple ways, but primarily through their role on interprofessional teams in selecting ingredients, making sustainable food more accessible, and advocating for a better food system more broadly. The paper concludes with examples in which the industrial food system and good culinary practice intersect on the benchtop of the research chef to promote more sustainable, health-promoting, and accessible food on the scale necessary to enact systemic change.

To many people the title "chef" means one or more management-level cooks at a restaurant, hotel, or other hospitality venue such as a country club or banquet hall. Some may be more expansive in their definition to consider chefs of other types of food-service establishments such as corporate cafeterias, hospitals, prisons, the military, or schools and colleges (Tsui et al. 2013, e14). However, our media, tourism, and consumer experiences focus on fine-dining restaurant chefs, looking to them for inspiration and guidance for what to eat and how to cook it (McBride and Flore 2019). These chefs win prestigious awards, appear on television and Internet cooking programs, and influence the public in matters of taste, both in the organoleptic sense of taste and in terms of what is fashionable (Black 2021; Contois 2020). As other chapters in this volume show, sustainability advocates can leverage the influential platforms of these restaurant chefs to influence consumers to make more sustainable food choices. For example, hearing a well-known chef such as Dan Barber draw attention to the negative climate impact of food waste and tasting a delicious meal he and his team made from food scraps that would otherwise be wasted might influence individuals to try to minimize their own food waste when cooking at home (Eckstein and Young 2018). Similarly, seeing chefs such as Rene Redzepi from Noma develop tasty dishes with insects as a sustainable alternative to more resource-intensive forms of animal protein may open consumers' minds and palates to the possibility that a proper restaurant entrée may include insect protein rather than a large center-of-plate serving of fish, poultry, or meat (Redzepi 2014).

Behind that very public type of commercial restaurant chef stands another group of chefs: research chefs, called Culinologists® by the Research Chefs Association (Cheng, Ogbeide, and Hamouz 2011). They work with food companies, from start-ups through multinationals, to develop the foods on supermarket shelves and in the freezers of food-service operations and chain restaurants that likely are filling the majority of US consumers' stomachs every day. While the chef-prepared elegantly served fine-dining meal we ate last weekend, or last month, may be top of mind when we think about the chefs who make the food we eat, for most of us, the bulk of calories we consume are much less remarkable— the energy bar in the car on the way to work, the pastry we share with a friend at the chain coffee shop, the bottled iced tea we select from the refreshment table at the conference hotel, the packaged salad we grab at the airport, or the meal kit that helps us make a quick home-cooked weeknight dinner. While we may not think of a chef as having had anything to do with the preparation of these foods, there is a vast roster of research chefs, sensory scientists, supply chain experts, food technologists, food engineers, packaging designers, and so on, who collaborate with one another and with suppliers to make this taken-for-granted food available, affordable, safe, tasty, and abundant. Most of the world's population will not have the privilege and opportunity to experience a meal helmed by Barber or Redzepi, but nearly everyone will have had the opportunity to taste many things daily developed by invisible research chefs at major food companies, from packaged snacks to fast food to airline meals (Research Chefs Association 2017). Given the ubiquity of food products developed by research chefs and their prominence in our diets, it is crucial to include the research chef in any consideration of chefs and their impact on sustainability.

Method

Using purposive sampling (Campbell et al. 2020, 653–54) via networking and snowball sampling (Parker, Scott, and Geddes 2019, 3) via referrals from study participants, I conducted interviews with ten active research chefs. Informal interviews were conducted via e-mail correspondence and in-person communications, with notes taken after the conversations and e-mail documents retained and used in analysis. Formal interviews were conducted via Zoom video meetings, which were recorded and transcribed via voice recognition software, followed by manual editing while I listened to the recording. All participants had informal interviews, with six consenting to additional formal interviews of thirty to sixty minutes. Following feedback on the initial draft of this paper, I conducted additional participant interviews with three previous respondents specifically about sustainability.

Data from informal and formal interviews were analyzed and coded using a manual method for naturalistic qualitative data analysis outlined by Margaret Anzul et al. (2003) in which categories and themes emerge from the participants' voices and are checked with the research team and participants. Also consistent with this method, the voices of the participants are presented verbatim so that the readers can follow the logic of the analysis and draw their own conclusions rather than having the researcher present obscured data in summary form. The goal, consistent with qualitative inquiry, is not to produce generalizable insights but rather to better understand phenomena.

All chefs in this study are identified by pseudonyms, and the names of their employers and specific projects are not disclosed. When necessary for explanation, the category of company was placed in brackets in the transcription and retained for subsequent uses. For example, "Since transitioning jobs from [a company known primarily for confectionery] to [a major poultry producer], sustainability has been top of mind." The data presented in this brief paper are drawn primarily from the formal interviews, with the informal interviews also used to generate the thematic analysis. The study was granted exempt status from the Human Subjects Protection Program of Drexel University.

Research Chefs

Research chefs work at the intersection of culinary arts and food science in the field of Culinology®, often called culinary science, which "blends the underlying principles of food science and technology with the chef's skilled art of culinary creativity and originality to satisfy public tastes in the marketplace" (Research Chefs Association 2017, viii). Prior to the mid-twentieth century, the domains of the chef and the food manufacturer had little overlap. Chefs trained primarily through apprenticeships in fine hotels and restaurants (Symons 2003), whereas food manufacturers engaged home economists and food technologists to develop industrial packaged food products and educate consumers (Elias 2008). The period of prosperity following each world war saw explosive growth in the packaged food industry as well as the democratization of American dining in the form of fast food and casual dining restaurants, tied inextricably to car culture and the emergence of a larger middle class (Belasco 1997).

The proliferation of restaurant chains such as Howard Johnson's, which started in 1925 and boasted over four hundred units by the mid-1950s, necessitated consistent offerings across their operations that contrasted with the traditional chef-helmed approach that might be used at an independent restaurant (Belasco 1979). Around the same time, packaged food became much more elaborate. Prior to the 1950s, consumer packaged goods were primarily branded commodities such as sugar, flour, baking powder, syrups, canned vegetables, crackers, canned meats, and so on. With the advent of home refrigerators and freezers and the birth of the large supermarket (also made possible due to the ubiquity of the automobile in the US), much more intricate foods such as pastries, sauces, ice cream, and salad dressings could be bought in packages. The intricacy of these new offerings was epitomized by a complete frozen dinner in a package, known colloquially as the TV dinner (Gust 2011, 50).

To meet its goals of providing good-tasting, consistent food of increasing intricacy on a large scale, beginning in the 1950s, the food industry made generous offers to prestigious chefs to leave their restaurant kitchens in favor of corporate chef positions that would later be known as research chefs. Famously, James Beard, one of the first television chefs, consulted for many well-known brands, including Omaha Steaks, French's Mustard, and Green Giant, to supplement his income as a cooking teacher and food media personality (Kamp 2009). Pierre Franey and Jacques Pépin, chefs at the country's premier French restaurant in the 1950s, New York City's Le Pavillon, were recruited by one of their restaurant's regulars, Howard Johnson, Sr., to be corporate chefs of Howard Johnson's in the 1960s (Pépin 2003). These chefs and many others were challenged to apply their culinary skills to attempt to capture restaurant-level flavors in a packaged food, develop recipes and standard operating procedures for dishes to be replicated across multiunit restaurant chains, or to demonstrate the virtues of various products and recipes to food-service buyers or home cooks, all tasks now identified as the domain of the research chef (Research Chefs Association 2017).

My own experience as a research chef intern (and later research chef and consultant) in the 1990s and 2000s was consistent with chefs making the restaurant–to–food company transition. At the time, none of us used the term "research chef," which was not yet in widespread use in the industry, but we rather identified as research and development (R&D) chefs. Our lab was run by four men, all accomplished European hotel and restaurant chefs who leveraged their Michelin stars to give their aching joints and intense restaurant schedules a rest by moving to a food company and working on packaged food products for home consumers and food service on an eight-to-five schedule. None of these chefs had any formal food science education, but they learned food technology and food processing principles such as food regulation, food analysis, and food engineering from colleagues and professional development seminars. Sustainability was not a large part of the conversation. Typical projects I engaged in included cost reduction exercises (such as switching one ingredient for a lower-priced alternative and testing to ensure that consumers could not tell the difference), fat reduction projects (such as reducing fat in a formulation and replacing it with water and gums, both to reduce cost and make a claim of "reduced fat"), or new product development.

The formal title of "research chef" was cemented in 1996 with the establishment of the Research Chefs Association, which spun out of an interest group meeting at the 1995 American Culinary Federation conference. "The Research Chefs Association (RCA) has grown to more than 2,000 members. Today, RCA is the premier source of global and inclusive culinary and technical information for the food industry, with a professionally diverse membership including chefs, food scientists and other industry professionals who are shaping the future of food research and development" (2023). The terms Culinology® and Culinologist® to describe the field of culinary science and the research chef respectively were trademarked by the Research Chefs Association in 2011.

Research chefs typically serve as part of a cross-functional product development team of professionals with expertise in project management, food technology, consumer insights, packaging, commercialization, sensory science, and regulatory compliance. They typically develop products for one of three markets: retail, to be sold as consumer packaged goods; food service, to be used in restaurants and institutions; or ingredients, to be used in the manufacture of other food products. An example of a retail product might be a packaged snack mix; an example of a food-service product would be a cheese sauce for restaurants or cafeterias to make nachos or cheesesteaks; and an ingredient might be caramel designed to be used as an inclusion in caramel swirl ice cream. Research chefs develop prototypes of new products, assist with sales by showing off a new product's capabilities (for example, leading a tasting of a new veggie burger for restaurant chefs, called a "cutting"), and develop new recipes and applications (for example, developing a menu item featuring a new barbecue sauce for a chain restaurant) (Crowell and Stuckey 2017).

At initial consideration, the role of the research chef may seem to have little to do with sustainability. And indeed, the term doesn't even appear in the index of the seminal text in the field, J. Jeffrey Cousminer's *Culinology* (2017). Our image of a sustainability-minded chef, such as those in the other chapters in this volume, may be a chef at a restaurant, school, or mutual aid organization who has chummy relationships with regional farmers and other local food producers. The chef buys seasonal products, prepares them efficiently, using all parts of the food products to minimize waste, and makes the products of the region accessible and delicious. In contrast, research chefs develop food products for major food companies that have mass appeal and accessible price points, using ingredients from large suppliers such as ADM and Cargill delivered in a truckload of 330-gallon pallet-sized totes rather than the farmer's bushel. But it is exactly that massive scale that makes it imperative to engage the research chef when discussing the chef's role in sustainability. And as you will see from the following pages, some research chefs very much want to be engaged in this conversation.

Sustainability and the Research Chefs' Role

Food service focuses on the triple bottom line of environmental, social, and financial sustainability of products and operations (Bui and Filimonau 2021). In professional cooking, key drivers of sustainable practices include water and energy use, food waste, sourcing (especially of meat, poultry, and seafood), and labor practices (Batat 2021). The triple-bottom-line framework was a familiar framing to all of the respondents and so will be used to present their responses in this paper.

Respondents emphasized their role in choosing or having input into ingredient selection as the primary driver for their sustainability influence. Because research chefs are working at mass scale, they emphasized that even incrementally more sustainable choices could have tremendous impact on the environment, the livelihoods of the people working in the supply chain, and consumer response to the product. They also emphasized the importance of using their knowledge of food science to make sustainable food accessible to the masses. Finally, they emphasized the challenges of advocating for positive sustainability improvements as part of a team that has a diverse set of other goals including supply chain consistency, regulatory compliance, consumer satisfaction, and profitability— all of which make a conventional supplier such as a large multinational food corporation the path of least resistance for many food companies. Research chefs I spoke with tended to take on the role of advocate for better, more sustainable ingredient choices, but they expressed frustration at their challenge of gaining traction within their employers.

Ingredient Selection and Sustainability

The public is often unaware that research chefs have shaped many global food products. Often the anonymity of the research chefs is a legal requirement of the companies they work for, protected under strict nondisclosure agreements designed to maintain the companies' competitiveness and protect their brands. As sustainability advocates, research chefs tend to advocate based on their personal commitments to wanting to see more sustainable products or a conviction that it is the best decision for the particular product on the benchtop and its associated brand. This stands in contrast with the sustainability work of other chefs, such as restaurant and institutional chefs, who may be front and center as the face of such advocacy. In lectures to my students, many of whom are aspiring research chefs, I tell the story of my thrill and frustration of being on an airplane and seeing a chocolate snack that I had worked on a couple of years prior in the basket of options distributed by the flight attendant for in-flight snacking. I wanted to elbow my sleeping seatmate awake and make an announcement to the entire plane on the PA system to share my pride that something I had worked on was now in their hands. Beyond how bizarre that behavior would be, it would have been strictly prohibited by my contract with the food company. I warn my students that if they wish to have a career in product development, they will be largely anonymous, despite the success and satisfaction of feeding millions of people their culinary creations. The anonymity of most research chefs is a challenge in that they cannot directly leverage the personality and visibility of the restaurant or media chef as role model or influencer of taste that is so common in present-day culinary culture (McBride and Flore 2019, 100157) to encourage sustainable practices among consumers.

Chef Allison (all names are pseudonyms), a chef at a major snack food and ingredients company, sees a big part of her role as a research chef as advocating for better (which she defines as more sustainable and ethical) ingredients in the products that her company makes, often over the objections of colleagues in supply chain management, finance, or marketing who might be more cost conscious or risk averse when it comes to sourcing. For example, using a conventional dried fruit from a major manufacturer is easier than sourcing dried fruit from smaller, more sustainably oriented producers that may involve inconsistencies, impurities, or shortages in supply. She asks,

> Where is our [research chefs'] responsibility and opportunity in this [sustainable] food conversation? For some reason the industrial food industry isn't leading that conversation because consumers don't know the true cost of the value chain and have not yet been inspired enough to pay for it. We, who are making the more expensive ingredient choice because it's better for the planet in the long run, doesn't mean that we can just add margin above that, right? . . . Research chefs tend to be the ones who get to drive those conversations internally, but it needs to be carried all the way to the consumer.

Allison contends that research chefs have been sources for bettering sustainability practices within food companies, but that these efforts are often obscured due to the lack of transparency in the supply chain and the lack of disclosures to the consumers about the sources of ingredients in their food (Belasco 2008). Further, in reality and at mass scale, environmental sustainability is often at odds with economic sustainability. The consumer of the raisin cookie may have no idea or concern about how the grapes were grown. And using an organic or regeneratively grown raisin would raise costs without necessarily allowing for a higher price in the marketplace.

Chef Allison suggests "upcycling" as a way to achieve sustainability without higher costs. Upcycled food is defined as "ingredients that otherwise would not have gone to human consumption, are procured and produced using verifiable supply chains, and have a positive impact on the environment" (Spratt, Suri, and Deutsch 2021). Allison commented, "When we are looking at ingredients to incorporate into formulations, I think we should look to the upcycling industry first and see what we can use, before going to the commodities." Allison continues,

> [We need to] understand the intent of the product and see if it's appropriate to fit certain more sustainable ingredients. It's on us as research chefs to create a product that's craveable . . . to work within the industry and within the ingredients . . . to continue using the

ingredients that are better for the world and to start dropping the ingredients that are not.

Bernard, a long-time research chef at sustainability-oriented start-ups, agrees.

> It's about really using the kitchen as a library for sustainable ingredients. I feel really strongly that chefs and food professionals can and should lead conversations about food and what we do with it, and how we source it and how we process it, and how we offer it to consumers. . . . From the very start that's where I think research chefs can be involved because we know what we are doing and what we are making and how to do that. From a sourcing perspective . . . understanding the supply chain and the farmer relationship and how that food is grown, how it's processed and how it gets to you. . . . Neither people nor food should ever go wasted.

Chef Charles, a consulting research chef, underscores the importance of educating consumers: "Most people don't know the extent of what's behind this . . . if you don't connect with people they're not going to appreciate and pay for sustainable products." Chef Davide, a restaurant chef who is new to a research chef role, a colleague of Chef Allison, reinforces the idea of having a big impact on sustainability with ingredient selection but takes a more data-driven focus.

> There are [sustainability analytics] tools now [e.g., Howgood.com] where you can plug in your formulation [recipe] and based on your individual ingredients, you can make your products more sustainable by changing the sourcing method and supplier and distribution of that product. [The idea] is to allow CPG [consumer packaged goods] owners to pull levers on one or two ingredients in the formulation, to make it more sustainable, and I think . . . the biggest opportunity from a development perspective is having that data and understanding. We can talk about sustainability as developers all day but, in my personal opinion, it has to be data driven, yeah without the data it's really just opinion. Around 30 percent of consumers care about sustainability. Consumers are expecting [it], and consumers are now becoming more focused [on it], so I think in the next five years we're going to see more third-party certifications or sustainability claims

and green packaging. What I'm optimistic about is that these companies are actually putting tools in my hand to say you can make this product, sell it for one dollar more, and it will be more sustainable according to these metrics, and I think that's very powerful.

Warren Belasco (2008) emphasizes the opacity of our food system. This lack of transparency hampers progress toward sustainability. Take any packaged food and you are faced with a slew of ingredients, each with a story, a supply chain, and many workers throughout that chain. A hidden force working for food companies, the research chef becomes key in advocating for ingredients that are incrementally more sustainable. Given the fast-paced production lines and global distribution of packaged foods, the impact of even marginal improvements to ingredients can be remarkable. For example, most people do not give much thought to the brownie chunks (called inclusions) in their favorite ice cream—who makes them, what are they made of, how much the bakers are paid, how they are hired, and so on. New York's Greyston Bakery specializes in the production of this ingredient and boasts an open hiring policy and inclusive workplace, welcoming people returning to the workforce after incarceration (Ben & Jerry's 2023). By featuring those particular inclusions, the research chef can promote social sustainability and family-wage jobs while appealing to consumers and meeting financial targets.

Making Food Accessible

Selecting an individual ingredient in a multicomponent food product shows how the research chef may have a real impact on typical, everyday consumers. They are looking for affordable and convenient food products and rely on the research chef, who is versed in fine-dining trends and sustainability, to bring it to them. Chef Allison says, "We in food manufacturing reach more people than all the organic farm stands, so we should be leading the change AND finding ways to bring back trust to our industry" (emphasis in original e-mail correspondence).

Chef Edwina says,

> I started in restaurants and quickly grew tired of how twee everything was. A perfectly cooked salmon being sent back for being undercooked. OK, I can send it to the dish pit and cook another one well done. But what's the point? Who am I helping here? What

impact am I having? I like what I can do [as a research chef] because even though I don't see or know the guests the way I would in a restaurant, I know I'm feeding real people, who are going to appreciate and benefit from my work. Their grocery bill is probably a bigger percentage of their paycheck than rich people's restaurant meals and I want to do what I can to give them a good product.

Chef Bernard says, "I believe that future of food is more than just, you know, plant-based [proteins] and food tech. The future of food should be equitable and diverse and inclusive. [Also equitable and inclusive] in its hiring and later employment practices for people of all economic statuses." Equitability and inclusion are essential to social sustainability.

Advocating for a Better System

The third theme that emerged from the data is that research chefs are often the ones on their team who advocate for a better food system—one that is more sustainable environmentally, socially, and economically. This was evidenced during the COVID-19 pandemic when research chefs were essential workers navigating supply chain problems, labor shortages, and other complexities of getting food to consumers. Producing food is not a job that easily transitions to remote work.

Chef Allison looks back to that time as a particularly vivid illustration of how fragmented and dysfunctional our conventional food system is. As the face of her company to many large retailers, she says she was the "punching bag" for supply chain problems, price hikes, and lack of consistency in products that resulted from COVID-19–related disruptions. She says, "We need to find ways to collaborate with each other, whether directly in manufacturing, in groceries, on the farms, or standing in the grocery aisles wondering what to have for dinner. Our economy is more circular than we know, and we need to deliberately close that loop." Far more than simply cooks, Chef Allison sees the research chefs as triple–bottom-line sustainable food system advocates whose work is much broader than making something taste good.

> Chefs really need to think about that intersection of food and community and activism. A chef needs to think about what kind of kitchen she wants, how it's going to work for the staffing, for the type of food, and everything like that . . . so from the very start that's

where I think research chefs can be involved. We can treat those farmers and processors appropriately as peers, not as populations and communities to be exploited. I think it's a call to action for research chefs to say find those brands and the product types that you are passionate about and go be in those conversations, find ways to get in.

For Chef Allison, the three pillars of sustainability, the triple bottom line—environmental, social, and financial—are inextricably linked.

Pay attention to food costs, it's one of the first things we learn in culinary school. And so upcyclers have a big role to play here. And research chefs have not been involved enough. Food rescue and conversion to usable product, those types of companies are the ones I look to first. The programs that have culinary/nutrition integrated together . . . should be leading this conversation because health, nutrition, food, those are all so interrelated.

Sustainability needs to be a holistic approach—integrating the people, the food and its production, and the finances.

Chef Bernard also highlights excessive food waste as emblematic of a broken food system.

The future of food is also about how to make vegetables—all parts of the vegetables—taste even more delicious. Using the whole roots of a plant, using the core of cauliflower, not just from like a philosophical perspective but from a business sense perspective, like you can put into a product and make money off of that? Chefs in a restaurant kitchen have to be sustainable and use all parts of a plant, all parts of an animal because they have to make the food costs work. We need to take the same approach [as research chefs in food manufacturing]. We need to utilize ingredients that already exist in our local, as well as global supply chains to establish a consistent supply chain, to work with a company that you know may be paying to dispose of their quote/unquote waste into something that is profitable for them. And growing for flavor because part of being flavorful I feel like is the ethos of where the product is coming from.

Chef Edwina identifies the research chef as grappling with issues most chefs don't need to.

If you are running a restaurant and you can't get product A, you either call other vendors to see if they have A, or you go with B or you eighty-six it from the menu. In the research chef world, you talk to the supplier or maybe visit the farm, work with procurement to contract out a year in advance to make sure product A is locked in. Most chefs have no clue how complicated this stuff is until they have experience with things like this.

Chef Davide's frustration is with what he sees as doublespeak in the food industry. Consumers, retailers, and manufacturers claim to want sustainable products, but are they actually prepared to pay for them?

The reality of cost is the deterrence in every case so far, I have seen. For example, you want to make something that has traceable ingredients. What we are trying to do now is establishing partnerships with data-driven companies who are producing platforms to help companies like us and CPG [consumer packaged goods brands] owners to make sustainability decisions, make better decisions with your sourcing and procurement practices and have that be data driven, so there are platforms [such as HowGood.com] that are allowing us to make better decisions that are backed by, you know, specific supply chain data. . . . You know, for a start-up brand to take a huge risk and create a, you know the highest-priced product on the market, because it is the most sustainable, I think it is a huge risk. . . . People often change their mind when they see things like cost or you know they change their sensibility around whether it's meant to be organic, conventional, domestic, [and so on].

While conscientious consumers may see the food industry as a key player in perpetuating a dysfunctional food system, research chefs see themselves as advocates for a better system—provided their employers and consumers together share a commitment to pay for more sustainable products and an improved system.

Conclusion

Numerous opportunities exist for research chefs, operating behind the scenes of major brands and food-service products, to inform conversations around sustainability. When a multinational food company has over a billion sales transactions daily, even small improvements to the health or sustainability of a product can have profound impacts on the health of people and the planet. Research chefs are knowledgeable and influential in the product development and marketing of the food that most of the world eats on a daily basis. But their role is largely unknown to the typical consumer. Leveraging their passion, knowledge, and commitment to improve the sustainability of packaged food and food-service products can be an important complement to the work of high-profile fine-dining restaurant chefs, who are often influential thought leaders in the sustainability conversation but who struggle to have sweeping impact among the majority of consumers.

A number of food products developed by research chefs epitomize the power of the research chef in building a more sustainable food system. Examples are products developed by the author's students and colleagues together with the author and private-sector commercialization partners. These include Matriark low-sodium broth made from fresh-cut vegetable scraps that would otherwise be composted; Reveal avocado seed brew, an antioxidant-rich ready-to-drink beverage made from avocado seeds; Happy Valley blended burgers made with roasted mushrooms to increase palatability, with the ratio of mushrooms as high as 35 percent; and spent grain tortillas that use dried high-protein and fiber-spent grains from beer brewing as a percentage of the flour and yield more nuanced flavor (Deutsch et al. 2019). These types of products add culinary interest to menus while capturing nutrients that would otherwise be wasted, improving sustainability.

As we seek to better the food system in all aspects of sustainability, social, environmental, and economic, it is important to be inclusive in our definition of what a chef is—to include not only restaurant and food-service chefs but also research chefs, who bring the scalability to the challenge of better food for all. Even incremental improvements to ingredient selection and sourcing, multiplied by millions of products produced every day globally, can have a profound and lasting impact on our food system.

References

Anzul, Margaret, Maryann Downing, Margot Ely, and Ruth Vinz. 2003. *On Writing Qualitative Research: Living by Words*. London: Routledge.
Aramouni, Fadi, and Kathryn Deschenes. 2014. *Methods for Developing New Food Products: An Instructional Guide*. Lancaster, PA: DEStech Publications.

Batat, Wided. 2021. "A Phenomenological Exploration into Sustainability in the Foodservice Industry in the MEA Region." *Journal of Services Marketing* 35 (7): 918–32.

Belasco, Warren. 2008. *Food: The Key Concepts.* New York: Berg.

Belasco, Warren J. 1979. "Toward a Culinary Common Denominator: The Rise of Howard Johnson's, 1925–1940." *Journal of American Culture* 2 (3): 503–18.

———. 1997. *Americans on the Road: From Autocamp to Motel, 1910–1945.* Baltimore: Johns Hopkins University Press.

Ben & Jerry's. 2023. "Brownies from Greyston Bakery." https://www.benjerry.com /greyston.

Black, Rachel E. 2021. *Cheffes de Cuisine: Women and Work in the Professional French Kitchen.* Champaign: University of Illinois Press.

Bui, Hien T., and Viachaslau Filimonau. 2021. "A Recipe for Sustainable Development: Assessing Transition of Commercial Foodservices towards the Goal of the Triple Bottom Line Sustainability." *International Journal of Contemporary Hospitality Management* 33 (10): 3535–63.

Campbell, Steve, Melanie Greenwood, Sarah Prior, Toniele Shearer, Kerrie Walkem, Sarah Young, Danielle Bywaters, and Kim Walker. 2020. "Purposive Sampling: Complex or Simple? Research Case Examples." *Journal of Research in Nursing* 25 (8): 652–61.

Cheng, Michael, Godwin-Charles A. Ogbeide, and Fayrene L. Hamouz. 2011. "The Development of Culinary Arts and Food Science into a New Academic Discipline— Culinology®." *Journal of Culinary Science & Technology* 9 (1): 17–26.

Contois, Emily J. H. 2020. *Diners, Dudes, and Diets: How Gender and Power Collide in Food Media and Culture.* Chapel Hill: The University of North Carolina Press.

Crowell, M., and B. Stuckey. 2017. "The Business of New Product Development and The Role of the Culinology® Professional." In *Culinology: The Intersection of Culinary Art and Food Science,* edited by J. Jeffrey Cousminer, 1–18. Hoboken, NJ: Wiley.

Deutsch, Jonathan, Alexandra Zeitz, Benjamin Fulton, Brandy-Joe Milliron, and Catherine Bartoli. 2019. "From Navigating the Regulatory Environment to Designing a Good Food Supply for Institutions: Cases from Philadelphia." In *Institutions as Conscious Food Consumers,* edited by Sapna E. Thottathil and Annelies M. Goger, 127–46. Cambridge: Academic Press.

Eckstein, Justin, and Anna M. Young. 2018. "wastED rhetoric." *Communication and Critical/Cultural Studies* 15 (4): 274–91. https://doi.org/10.1080/14791420.2018.1542502.

Elias, Megan J. 2008. *Stir It Up: Home Economics in American Culture.* Philadelphia: University of Pennsylvania Press.

Frøst, Michael B. 2019. "How to Create a Frame for Collaboration between Chefs and Scientists–Business as Unusual at Nordic Food Lab." *International Journal of Gastronomy and Food Science* 16 (July): 100132. https://doi.org/10.1016/j.ijgfs .2018.12.002.

Gust, Lauren. 2011. "Defrosting Dinner: The Evolution of Frozen Meals in America." *Intersect: The Stanford Journal of Science, Technology, and Society* 4 (1): 48–56.

Hagglund, Hans. 2013. "A Sustainability "Green" Certification Audit of Food Service Operations and the Development of a Restaurant Sustainability Instrument." PhD diss., University of Central Florida. https://stars.library.ucf.edu/etd/2538.

Kamp, David. 2019. *The United States of Arugula: The Sun Dried, Cold Pressed, Dark Roasted, Extra Virgin Story of the American Food Revolution.* New York: Crown.

McBride, Anne E, and Roberto Flore. 2019. "The Changing Role of the Chef: A Dialogue." *International Journal of Gastronomy and Food Science* 17 (October): 100157. https://doi.org/10.1016/j.ijgfs.2019.100157.

Parker, Charlie, Sam Scott, and Alistair Geddes. 2019. "Snowball Sampling." In *SAGE Research Methods Foundations,* edited by Paul Atkinson, Sara Delamont, Alexandru Cernat, Joseph W. Sakshaug, and Richard A. Williams. Los Angeles: Sage. https://doi.org/10.4135/9781526421036831710.

Pépin, Jacques. 2003. *The Apprentice: My Life in the Kitchen.* New York: Houghton Mifflin Harcourt.

Redzepi, René. 2014. "An Exploration of Deliciousness." In *The Insect Cookbook: Food for a Sustainable Planet,* by Arnold van Huis, Henk van Gurp, Marcel Dicke, Françoise Takken-Kaminker, and Diane Blumenfeld-Schaap, 132–37. New York: Columbia University Press. http://www.jstor.org/stable/10.7312/van-16684.37.

Research Chefs Association. 2017. *Culinology: The Intersection of Culinary Art and Food Science,* edited by J. Jeffrey Cousminer. Hoboken, NJ: Wiley.

Research Chefs Association. 2023. "Overview." https://www.culinology.org/about /overview.

Shnayder, Larissa, Frank J. van Rijnsoever, and Marko P. Hekkert. 2015. "Putting Your Money Where Your Mouth Is: Why Sustainability Reporting Based on the Triple Bottom Line Can Be Misleading." *PLoS ONE* 10 (3): e0119036. https://doi .org/10.1371/journal.pone.0119036.

Spratt, Olivia, Rajneesh Suri, and Jonathan Deutsch. 2021. "Defining Upcycled Food Products." *Journal of Culinary Science & Technology* 19 (6): 485–96. https://doi .org/10.1080/15428052.2020.1790074.

Symons, Michael. 2003. *A History of Cooks and Cooking.* Champaign: University of Illinois Press.

Tsui, Emma K., Jonathan Deutsch, Stefania Patinella, and Nicholas Freudenberg. 2013. "Missed Opportunities for Improving Nutrition through Institutional Food: The Case for Food Worker Training." *American Journal of Public Health* 103 (9): e14–e20. https://doi.org/10.2105%2FAJPH.2013.301293.

United Nations. 1987. *Our Common Future: Report of the World Commission on Environment and Development.* https://sustainabledevelopment.un.org/content /documents/5987our-common-future.pdf.

PART III

Culinary Sustainability and Social Relations

PART IV

Culinary Sustainability
and Social Relations

CHAPTER NINE

Sustainability through Social Commitments

Farm-to-Chef in the Era of COVID-19

SARRA TALIB AND AMY TRUBEK

> "We want to produce food in a new landscape.
> But we still want to feed the people."
>
> —Vermont chef-owner, December 2021

Introduction: Social Embeddedness in a Localized Food Value Chain

At a time when global food system dynamics are increasingly seen as major contributors to economic, social, and ecological degradation, there is evidence that localizing food systems is critical to transitioning toward sustainability (Lever and Sonnino 2022). Some of the advantages of localized food systems include the creation of trust via reciprocal relationships and shared values (Schreiber et al. 2022). Furthermore, the geographic proximity and personal relationships between actors in a localized system facilitate raising awareness and exchanging critical information about the various ecological, social, and economic impacts of food system dynamics. Thus, as feedback loops are tightened and communication between actors in the food system is enhanced, resources can be more effectively directed toward values-based goals (Brinkley 2017).

The farm-to-table movement is a vital component of a region's food culture, whereby localization of the food system is valued as a means of preserving the working landscape and promoting sustainable practices across the system (Pesci and Brinkley 2021). Thus, the farm-to-chef *value chain*, that is, a supply chain characterized by trust and commitment among its actors whereby the viability and success of all members in the system is the goal (Givens and Dunning 2019), is an integral part of the efforts to localize food systems as rooted in *socially embedded practices*. These efforts intersect with anthropological definitions of social sustainability, which, as Setha Low defines it, "includes the maintenance and preservation of social relations and meanings that reinforce cultural systems" (2001). In this chapter, we explore the commitments of Vermont chefs and restaurant owners toward the farmers (who provide the raw ingredients) and customers (who consume the finished meals) in the midst of the COVID-19 pandemic.

Making and serving food in restaurants easily reinforce Karl Polanyi's (1944, 47) powerful insight that "so-called economic motives spring from the context of social life." In this sense, restaurants are locations for the enactment of both "instrumental" and "relational" values (Jones and Tobin 2018). The instrumental values involved in the work of restaurants concern buying, transforming, and selling food; in this context, food is a commodity. However, the ingredients sourced and meals served require numerous decisions and actions that incorporate forms of social embeddedness in an otherwise seemingly commodity-based transaction. For most restaurant businesses, each decision—what to procure, what menu to create, how to provide a conducive eating environment, and more—emerges from an intersecting set of values driving decisions and behaviors. These relational values often emerge from specific contexts, and they often are explicitly articulated by restaurant chefs and owners, who are shaping and responding to the demands and desires of their community. For the chefs and owners we interviewed, social sustainability, which involves fostering and continuing relationships with producers and consumers based on shared values, helped to create a culture of support in their communities that ultimately impacted the sustainability of their businesses *and* the sustainability of the local food system.

The empirical focus of our study is twenty qualitative interviews with chefs and owners of independently operated restaurants in the small state of Vermont, a part of the northeastern region of the United States called New England.[1] The interviews capture the reflections of chefs and owners on their experiences from March 2020 to November 2021, focusing on the intertwined instrumental and relational practices of purchasing ingredients from local farmers, an important set of transactions that are part of the farm-to-table culinary movement animating many small restaurants in this region for over twenty years (Trubek 2008). These transactions, although fundamentally economic in nature, rely on robust social relations; everyone participating in the value chain needs to be committed to one another for its success. This was made even more clear during the COVID-19 pandemic, when the global food system was disrupted and its vulnerability and inflexibility were exposed.

The COVID-19 pandemic was a world-historical event, a universal experience of disruption, risk, and transformation. The initial uncertainty as to the mode of transmission through social interactions, combined with the stunning stresses on global supply chains due to shutdowns, illnesses, politics, and other problems small and large, meant that restaurants—food purveyors but also centers of hospitality and sociability—existed at the epicenter of such disruptions, risks, and transformations (Chenarides, Manfredo, and Richards 2020). While the global food supply chain was being tested by an unprecedented shock, the resilience and sustainability of the farm-to-chef value chain was simultaneously being tested. As the future of restaurants was suddenly upended by COVID-19 (Madeira, Palrão, and Mendes 2021), standard operating procedures that shaped everything from how food was ordered to how tables were set had to be abandoned, and decisions needed to be made quickly.

In the case of the chefs and owners that we interviewed, their connections to farmers, their commitments to local purchasing, and their embeddedness in the community immediately *informed* how they responded to a situation over which they had very little control. One chef-owner described the comfort he felt from the immediate exchanges he had with his local suppliers about the way forward at the start of the shutdowns in March 2020: "Our farmer friends and us . . . we're texting now, 'this is what's gonna happen.' Or, 'we don't know what's gonna happen, but let's just keep in touch.' And I don't know, to me, it's a beautiful thing . . . because I don't think a Sysco rep or whatever would be calling me, some little rinky small restaurant in Vermont." Being able to communicate directly with a local producer because of a personal relationship and geographic proximity allowed for true adaptiveness and responsiveness within the local food system (Marusak et al. 2021). Thus, relationally informed exchanges (considered here as the building blocks of social sustainability) became crucial to the long-term viability of these individual businesses and ultimately supported the resilience and sustainability of the local food system. This is the story we will tell in this chapter.

The Shutdown and Then . . .

Three broad questions concerning the shared values intrinsic to the farm-to-chef purchasing model drove the design of this research project. First, do localized supply chains that are based in direct connections and commitments between farmers and chefs serve as a model for more sustainable food systems? Second, what happens to these commitments in the face of a large disruption? Finally, do explicit values toward direct purchasing connections mediate the resilience of a restaurant (or other similar food-service) operation? The interview questions sought to uncover the general experiences of chefs and owners with a focus on their procurement practices and menu (re)design during the pandemic.

As of November 2022, we had conducted twenty short semistructured interviews with chefs and/or restaurant owners about their experiences. Initially, participants were recruited due to their membership in the Vermont Fresh Network (VFN), a small nonprofit organization that facilitates farmer and chef relationships by building networks and promoting the farm-to-table movement to consumers. However, the use of purposive snowball sampling meant that many but not all participants were current or previous members of VFN. All interviewees owned or worked in individually owned food-service businesses (not corporate franchises) across ten different counties of Vermont.[2] The interview scripts were formulated in advance.[3] Due to the restrictions of the pandemic, the interview format varied from online to by phone to in person. The lead author conducted all the interviews. The interviews were transcribed and coded multiple times by both authors (with the help of NVivo, a qualitative and mixed-methods data analysis software package used across the social sciences) for emergent themes related to the following topics in the context of their impact on local food system sustainability: social embeddedness, commitment to values-based sourcing, and operational innovations due to COVID-19.

Our questions focused on general responses to COVID-19 between March 2020 and November 2021. Interestingly, many interviewees chose to start the interview with a narrative about what happened in March 2020 as the United States shut down. The intensity and immediacy of that experience—from some version of business as usual to a full stop—meant that before-and-after stories emerged in response to questions that were designed for what might be called a simple summary response. Also, the reliance on the before-and-after narrative reveals the dramatic changes to standard business practices across the board. One owner recalled the powerful impetus to resume business operations as quickly as possible once Vermont's "Stay Home, Stay Safe" orders were issued.[4]

> We tried to get open as soon as we could. As soon as we could do curbside, we did curbside. As soon as we could let people in the store, we did that. As soon as we could have people in the restaurant, we did that. Some businesses opted not to open at all until they were in the clear. But not us, we said, "No, we're going to forge ahead. We're going to keep things going forward." . . . And it was interesting, during that time in 2020, it was very slow coming back. April was terrible. May was awful.

This owner was primarily driven by the sense of responsibility in service to the entire social network of the restaurant, including customers, employees, and farmers—the decision to open as soon as allowed, to continue the social interactions and transactions required to make and sell food to others. Thus, as Polanyi suggests, the instrumental and relational values of the business were entangled.

Reckoning with Systems Failures and Engaging with Embeddedness

Each interviewee had a different "before" story to share, and each devised, multiple times, various strategies to deal with what eventually happened after the initial government shutdowns. But everyone shared the same temporal pivot point: mid-March 2020. Anyone trying to sell food that was prepared in some manner had to respond to the many pronouncements and protocols around social engagements that dominated everyone's life during the spring of 2020. One chef-owner recalled the frequency with which they were required to make significant changes to how they ran their business: "It was literally a pivot every couple of weeks as a new governor's order came down . . . it was constant in terms of the pivoting and what our staffing level allowed." During this first period of the pandemic in Vermont, the rules and regulations in terms of operating any business, especially one that relied on close interaction and contact with other persons, were in constant disarray. Any shared systems of practice—from what and when to purchase ingredients to whether and how to serve customers—had to be reinvented, time and again.

The intensity of the disruption forced chefs and owners to fully engage with the social embeddedness of their businesses—to identify that, at the end of the day, their choices about business practices operated within a larger social framework that they depended upon but also that depended on them. A chef-owner shared how service to their community guided their decision making: "I think community is the only reason we did as well as we did. Emotionally and from the business perspective, we looked at the staying open part as not exactly just strict community service, but we wanted to be there for our community. And it was a time when so much was unknown about how [COVID-19] worked and there was fear about going to the grocery store and fear about everything." Another chef-owner explained the feeling of urgent responsibility as a business owner in a small community: "I felt responsible to come up with a plan to make sure that people had food. I mean, I literally was thinking, 'Should I start warehousing dry goods and order in beans and rice?' because it was unknown what was gonna happen." After all, as Ethan Schoolman (2020) points out, localized food systems engender values among its actors who understand themselves as embedded in a place, and thus feel responsible for the people and things in that place.

When those interviewed stepped back from telling the stories of what happened due to the singular disruptions in March 2020, another theme emerged: transformations. These occurred as part and parcel of being forced into a before-and-after situation that was unanticipated, and that dictated the very nature of the social relationships and thus the structure of restaurants and other food operations. One chef-owner mused, "You know, when the pandemic hit, it was like ok, people can't worry about risks—it's either do something, or die. You have to survive. And so, in some ways, the pandemic was a boon to those of us who may have already been entrepreneurially minded, but perhaps maybe slightly reluctant on the heavier risk side—the pandemic pushed people like me to say, 'No, no, you've got to [take a risk]'. . . and it paid off, right?" Pivoting to a completely different business model, such as shifting from full-service dining to preparing meal kits for customers to cook at home, for example, was a risk that took creativity, flexibility, and the ability to navigate and leverage social relationships. While the risks taken and pivots made by chefs and owners helped keep their individual businesses afloat, they also helped keep their employees employed, supported local farmers by making consistent purchases, and provided meals to consumers, which contributed to the resilience and sustainability of the local food system.

Another theme that emerged after, as some said, "the before times," involved maintaining principles and practices while responding to structural disruptions in sourcing and serving food amid intense labor issues. One owner recalled trying to remain conscious of waste despite restrictions that made it very difficult to do so:

> It's also been hard for us because of the stop-and-go nature of the way COVID has made doing food. It's really hard to know how much to order. At first, we were like, we'll just order like we've always ordered for prep and everything. And then, we were throwing away so much food, which is a terrible feeling because you get to the end of the day and you're like, maybe we will make some extra and hand it out—but how will we hand it out because people aren't anywhere?

This owner's continued consciousness about minimizing waste during the pandemic speaks to the evolving yet enduring set of practices of chefs that are reinforced by "normative anchoring," whereby they are ultimately motivated to remain committed to those practices (Nelson, Beckie, and Krogman 2017).

Finally, a persistent theme involved the failures of the larger supply chains upon which everyone we interviewed relied for at least some aspects of their business. From encountering difficulties when sourcing a staple kitchen product due to national and global shortages (e.g., fryer oil) to struggling to get the attention of a large distributor to source any ingredients, interviewees noted the challenges of trying to navigate their needs within the larger food supply chains. Many of the chefs and owners we spoke with confirmed Hiran Roy and Paul W. Ballantine's (2020) observations about the perceived barriers by restaurant operators as to working with wholesale distributors, such as having a limited range of products (due to nationwide shortages), inability of the distributor to effectively communicate product shortages, and in some cases being ignored by the distributor. One chef-owner expressed exasperation with national distributors: "It's insane. We had to look at things and say, 'All right, do we really need this product, or if we don't, what can we replace it with? And if we do need the product, where can we source it [so] that it's not gonna put us out of business, but also not support something like Jeff Bezos and his mission to send himself to the moon?' " Another chef-owner recalled the challenges of sourcing ingredients from the larger distributors they worked with: "We definitely noticed . . . price increases with lettuce and tomatoes and things like that. Chicken wings—the most bizarre thing. They were like nonexistent for weeks. Cream cheese—you can't get it from the distributor [these days]. There were many, many weeks where there were just things [on the menu] we couldn't put out because they weren't available." One chef highlighted the difference between working with distributors and local suppliers: "Definitely the larger distributors is where we saw the most disruptions—and still a little bit continuing today. With whether or not it was just [bulk commodity] products not being available for weeks at a time, or orders not getting picked properly because there [weren't] enough people in the warehouse, or deliveries being late, that kind of thing. As far as local purveyors, farmers, producers . . . we saw very little disruption from that side."

These shared experiences created the context for a series of operational pivots. Not every business made the same decisions about such matters as when and how to reopen, the organization of ingredient purchases, the relationship to customers, and so forth. Yet, for all those interviewed, the farmer-chef relationships remained. And in some cases, they were strengthened and enhanced. Why? Because they became more relevant. Ultimately, the disruptions to the organization of the food supply at the global and national level meant that relational exchange systems were easier to enact than instrumental ones. As one chef recalls, "They [farmers] were able to supply us with what we needed, when we needed it." More anonymous commodity exchanges across long distances lost their reliability and convenience. The result, the easing up of the transactional exchanges, ultimately created spaces for novel organization of business practices that supported the resilience and sustainability of both the businesses and the local food system.

Local Sourcing as an "Innovation"

The pandemic exacerbated a number of already pressing food system fissures. As product shortages drove up prices across the national and global supply chains, ingredients that were previously sourced based on price and convenience were no longer more competitive than those produced locally. In some product categories, such as fresh vegetables, wholesale food prices were up by over 50 percent during the height of the pandemic (National Restaurant Association 2022). As one chef recalled, "We've talked a lot about trying to get our potatoes locally since the beginning of the business—it just wasn't financially viable back at the beginning.

And now that potato prices have gone up so much, it's become more of a realistic possibility, because if the price difference isn't going to really be the deciding factor, it's really only 'Can they supply enough potatoes to meet what we're trying to do' "?

Many of the chefs and owners we interviewed were prompted to look more deeply into their sourcing and to explore purchasing more of their ingredients closer to home. One chef-owner gushed about new local products that they began to source due to connections they had with local producers and purveyors: "I got some amazing squash and apples . . . [fresh] pasta . . . and some beef—like prime rib and brisket and just really high-quality cuts of meat." Another chef-owner recalled, "Before COVID, I was probably able to slip up from time to time. 'Oh, I can get it a little cheaper from this place, so I'm gonna do it because I'm feeding 120 people and that makes a huge difference in profit.' [Post-COVID], it actually became even more important for me to focus on the locality than what I had [done] before." Some saw the frustration they experienced with the larger distributors that they had been working with as an opportunity to increase the number of partnerships with local producers. An owner recalled, "Well, of course when COVID hit, all the major distributors had a collective meltdown—if you look at it one way, it's an opportunity because we had to go seek out either new providers or new products, and we did that. In most cases, we've never gone back to the big supplier for those things." For this owner, new relationships were established with local producers for sourcing ingredients such as flour, eggs, dairy, and fresh produce. In fact, an emergent theme from our conversations was that the COVID-19 pandemic had jump-started a transition to a business innovation that was already on the horizon for chefs and owners who had a strong commitment to sourcing a percentage of their ingredients locally.

Drawing on Everett Roger's diffusion of innovation framework to understand how, why, and at what rate chefs and restaurants adopt local food, Shoshanah M. Inwood et al. (2009) noted that chefs value the flexibility and transparency of sourcing ingredients from farmers rather than distributors, citing closer and stronger relationships with farmers that allowed farmers to communicate anticipated harvest dates and enabled chefs to plan their menus more effectively. For those we interviewed, the disruption provided an opportunity to leverage established relationships with local producers to pivot to a more fully informed and sustainable local purchasing model: "We have the real business conversations [with our local producers]. E.g., 'It's been a wet growing season and our crop yields weren't what we thought,' or 'The door on our chicken coop somehow managed to be opened on a -20°F night . . . we're gonna be out for six months.' " Having clear and direct communication with producers may allow chefs and owners to make timely alternative plans in the case of expected supply shortages, supporting more efficient and sustainable purchasing practices.

Labor and the Customer Experience

Challenges to the economic sustainability of the individual businesses also emerged due to preexisting structural issues that are part and parcel of running a contemporary restaurant. One such challenge involved labor. With COVID-19, the number of people who were willing and/or available to work was significantly reduced, especially in service work. As demand and pressure to find labor rose, it became increasingly clear that the prevailing assumptions as to wages and working conditions were now obsolete. The often below-minimum wages that once propped up the food-service industry were no longer acceptable. As one owner recalled, "Because of the lack of workforce, we had to raise the wages of our employees. We were paying our employees well [before], but now we're paying them very well, which is great, it spreads the wealth out." Those interviewed thus wanted to keep this system-level change required for a more resilient and sustainable local food system, but at the moment, the ability to pay higher hourly rates for servers, line cooks, and dishwashers was dependent upon a sense of crisis. It was not, for example, because the businesses were generating more revenue to be able to pay higher wages.

Furthermore, the traditional model of restaurant operating hours that often absorbed the cost of being open during less profitable hours of the day was no longer viable. A chef explained, "There were certain hours of the day that we served prepandemic that never made money—just [staying] open to serve people whenever they would want to come—that would be the lunchtime hours or the late-night hours between ten o'clock and twelve o'clock. We don't serve those [times] anymore, and it's helped us because of the labor shortage; we haven't had to fill those hours of the day which has helped a lot. And yeah, just operating at a loss during certain hours doesn't make sense." Another chef-owner noted the financial trade-off between a higher volume of food sales and having less staff: "Because of the staffing issues, I had to reduce my offerings. [However],

I'm finding that there's a trade-off . . . maybe even from a business perspective because of the cost of having, retaining, and maintaining employees, it just doesn't pay."

Being able to provide a consistent experience for customers was another pressure that chefs and owners faced—the sudden shock to the food-service industry necessitated a reimagination of the chef-customer relationship. Flexibility was necessary in cases where it was no longer feasible to provide a certain menu item because the ingredients could not be sourced, food had to be served in a different way because the original packaging was unavailable, or the price of a dish had increased substantially due to the rising costs of its components (for example, certain cuts of meat were difficult to acquire due to vastly reduced processing capacity during the height of the pandemic, and thus were more expensive). One chef-owner recalled, "[There] was almost a disconnect between what regulations I was supposed to be following versus what I could get my hands on. There were times, in all honesty, where I was like, I can't even get the bottom half of the container I need to serve in, but also trying to meet Vermont's guidelines for compostable products." In the case of this chef-owner, sourcing takeout containers that were available *and* environmentally friendly was a challenge. Another chef-owner felt that it was their job to communicate the need for flexibility—about everything from reduced hours to limited menus—during a time of constant flux and uncertainty: "I think that we have to train our customers how to be, in some sense . . . flexible. There was a period in 2020 where people understood. They're like, oh yeah, it's COVID. We get it. But by 2021 it was no longer [just] COVID and people didn't understand it, so there was a lot of frustration." One chef-owner expressed gratitude for customers' flexibility: "I think that the general public realized we were all kind of in the same boat, so they were willing to say, 'Okay, we're fine with it [limited menus].' [It was] more embarrassing I think as a restaurant trying to say, 'Well, let me tell you what I do have on my menu versus what I don't because that's an easier list.'"

Looking Forward: Relational Values and Social Sustainability

While everyone scrambled to quickly manage what was an unprecedented disruption to their operations, many also found themselves taking the time to reflect on the future. As one owner put it, "The shutdown allowed us to reexamine what we were trying to do with the business." Another chef mused, "It was an opportunity to reassess." It was also a time to innovate—and take risks. Quoting an old proverb with a cheeky smile, one owner said, "Necessity is the mother of invention." Another owner recalled the important role of creativity in moving forward:

> It was pretty clear to me, pretty early, that we were given a blank slate at that point. Never in a million years did I expect to ever shut down and then reopen, lose 99 percent of my staff, and [then] rehire everybody. And so, at the time, I just remember being like, "All right, well we just need to come back better than we were before," which is what we did. And we had to kind of choose what areas we felt needed the most improvement first. And so, doing that, yeah, led to having to be pretty creative.

One chef told us that creativity was about flexibility: "It was really just about, how do you stay fluid? With all of the ever-changing rules, it's like okay, I can't have people in. I'm not supposed to interact with them, but maybe I can do deliveries. No, the delivery thing cost too much money. It was a lot of on-the-spot trying to figure out how to make that work." Another chef described creativity as letting go: "We've always wanted to be as creative as we can and do things that work and let go of things that don't. I think that's the important part; not holding on to the things that obviously aren't going to work." In speaking with these chefs and owners, it was evident that their geographic and especially their *social* proximity to producers played an important role in their ability to be flexible and fluid while adapting to unprecedented changes.

Being creative also meant reconsidering and then recommitting to relational values. As one owner told us, "We sort of had to stop and relook at everything and see where we could save money but also support local businesses [local farms, mills, breweries, etc.] as much as possible because I personally feel that supporting businesses that are based in Vermont, it's not only supporting their employees, but the people who own [local businesses] are pumping their proceeds back into the Vermont economy." Many chefs and owners stressed their commitment to working with more Vermont-based producers and suppliers moving forward as they acknowledged how it contributed to building the resilience and sustainability of the local food system. As one chef-owner recalled, "I definitely was becoming very creative at finding [local] products . . . like bread. I found a local baker that was willing [to supply bread], so, we connected.

That was actually one of my best discoveries and relationships." Another chef-owner enthusiastically shared, "Whatever we can get from local farms that is seasonal and fun and different we're gonna do. The summer veggies, when those are available and then [we'll] move on to the fall harvest and then come winter, it's more a lot of root veggies and things that can store and last through the winter." This also extended beyond the direct purchasing relationships with farmers to the availability of locally produced foods provided through distributors. Recognizing the critical role regional distributors played in supporting the sustainability of the local food system, one owner stated, "We're gonna decide if we're gonna continue to work with you [distributors] based on you bringing us products that are local, and when we say local, we mean Vermont, not Eastern Seaboard, not—New England, maybe. Northern New England, you're a little warmer. Vermont? We'll talk."

As Hiran Roy, C. Michael Hall, and Paul W. Ballantine (2018) concluded in their analysis of the farm-to-chef supply chain, social networks were necessary for local food systems across Vermont to thrive, and personal connections between restaurants and producers were especially important. Being able to reach out to a producer directly to find out if an order could be fulfilled or to speak to a fellow restaurateur to gripe about staffing challenges allowed the chefs and owners we spoke with to move more nimbly forward as they navigated a new reality. When national and global supply chains were disrupted, local suppliers were able to slot almost seamlessly into an already existing structure, facilitated in large part by the established relationships between restaurants and producers. This meant that the framework for organization and action was reconsidered, which was a process of innovation within the broader crisis that put forward an alternative model for food system sustainability and resilience—that is, a more localized food value chain.

The Postpandemic Restaurant, Meals, and More

The shutdowns and pivots related to the COVID-19 pandemic forced an explicit reconsideration of many of the underlying assumptions of what defines a restaurant meal. Many ideas about the appropriate way to serve a meal, what consumers expect and want when it comes to purchasing rather than making a meal, or how businesses making prepared food should operate, were upended. As one chef-owner reflected, "We feel like a lot of our colleagues who experienced [insurmountable] challenges were weighed down by the legacy model of full service." Many were also taking stock of all the innovations that were forced upon them due to the restrictions and failures during the most intense periods of the COVID-19 pandemic, and were wondering if the assumed structures underpinning their values and practices made sense anymore. From creating contactless menus to brand new "to-go" infrastructure (e.g., pickup windows, integration with delivery platforms), and from reimagined kitchen and dining spaces to reduced hours of operation, the time had come to let go of certain "standard operating procedures" in order to create more viable businesses for both the producers and consumers. Another chef-owner provided a sober reflection: "Moving forward, I just believe that things [will] continue to get weird for a little while. I have this thought that maybe the to-go-out-to-dinner, out-to-lunch industry may be dying a little bit. And so, how do we redefine what that looks like?"

The disruptions to the order of things—the possible end of the American full-service restaurant that relies on long supply chains, large menus, and cheap labor—disentangle the structure of these meals and the associated values from a notion of standard practice. As one chef-owner who ultimately shifted away from a classic full-service restaurant to what is now a prepared meals market put it, "Our approach culinarily has just shifted to be, this can go into a quart container or a pan that you can then put into your oven. So, it's a shift in our approach. But it's funny. The same product is just being delivered in a radically different way." The need for the meal continues, but the contexts for its sourcing, preparation, and service, in what remains a commodified transaction, have been transformed.

Conclusion: A Localized Approach for a More Sustainable Food System?

For the chefs and owners we spoke with, it appeared that relational values took precedence in their response to the shock of the pandemic, while the instrumental nature of their business operations was less central. The ability of chefs and owners to leverage their social networks to weather the pandemic—and in many cases, to thrive—was due in part to the nature of the connections among the local food system stakeholders (Thilmany et al. 2020). The proximity of farmer and chef relationships also allowed for greater proactivity and risk-taking. Recognizing that returning to "normal" was no longer an option, chefs and owners focused their energies on adaptation and on the sustainability of their businesses and communities.

While very little was certain for these chefs and restaurant owners during the height of the pandemic, it is clear that creativity and flexibility were essential for the continuation of operations, and that strong social networks facilitated the innovation necessary to respond to such a drastic shock. This reinforces other research about food supply chains during the COVID-19 pandemic; a restaurant had little chance of surviving if it did not attempt to adapt (Norris, Taylor, and Taylor 2021). Though this is a story about what happened in Vermont, the evidence of resilience along the farm-to-chef value chain during a period of crisis underscores the role of relational values and social commitments as critical components of a sustainable and resilient food system anywhere. Furthermore, the fact that principles and practices driven by shared values persisted among actors despite the extreme disruption that the pandemic caused is further evidence of the potential for a localized approach to food systems to be a more resilient and sustainable one.

Perhaps the shock to the system has finally made space for a mindful redesign—a food system that is more resilient because of its emphasis on social commitments and values, as per Polanyi's compelling logic; a food system that is economically and socially sustainable; and a food system that is ecologically sustainable too, as strong social relationships are expected to positively affect environmental practices (Hedberg and Zimmerer 2020). In discussing the way forward for restaurants postpandemic, one chef-owner mused about relocalizing food systems through strengthening social connections: "I do think our best and maybe only solution to all this is to shrink our footprints." That is, as another chef-owner put it, "I think being able to have those open lines of communication directly with the vendors, just having those kinds of local relationships . . . having those lines of communication and relationships in place just made [surviving the pandemic] possible."

Notes

1. Most interviewees were both chefs and owners.
2. Study participants (and their food businesses) were located in ten Vermont counties: Chittenden, Washington, Addison, Windsor, Lamoille, Caledonia, Rutland, Windham, Bennington, and Orange.
3. The interview questions were: How have your purchasing decisions changed because of COVID-19? Was the change in purchasing from local farmers/suppliers noticeably different than purchasing from distributors? (If so, in what ways?) Did the changes you had to make due to the pandemic create any new opportunities/relationships with farmers or any other local or regional

food-related businesses? Were menu design changes made as a result of changes in your relationships with farmers? If so, to what extent were local farm products incorporated into the new menus? How did your established relationships with local farmers or other food-related businesses play a role in any decisions you did make to pivot or innovate your business?

4. On March 24, 2020, Vermont governor Phil Scott issued a "Stay Home, Stay Safe" order in consultation with the Commissioner of the Vermont Department of Health to "minimize all unnecessary activities outside the home to slow the spread of this virus and protect the public." See https://governor.vermont.gov /press-release/governor-phil-scott-issues-%E2%80%9Cstay-home-stay -safe%E2%80%9D-order-directs-additional-closures.

References

Brinkley, Catherine. 2017. "Visualizing the Social and Geographical Embeddedness of Local Food Systems." *Journal of Rural Studies* 54 (August): 314–25. https://doi .org/10.1016/j.jrurstud.2017.06.023.

Chenarides, Lauren, Mark Manfredo, and Timothy J. Richards. 2020. "COVID-19 and Food Supply Chains." *Applied Economic Perspectives and Policy* 43 (1): 270–79. https://doi.org/10.1002/aepp.13085.

Givens, Graham, and Rebecca Dunning. 2019. "Distributor Intermediation in the Farm to Food Service Value Chain." *Renewable Agriculture and Food Systems* 34 (3): 268–70. https://doi.org/10.1017/S1742170517000746.

Hedberg, Russell C., and Karl S. Zimmerer. 2020. "What's the Market Got to Do with It? Social-Ecological Embeddedness and Environmental Practices in a Local Food System Initiative." *Geoforum* 110 (March): 35–45. https://doi.org /10.1016/j.geoforum.2020.01.022.

Inwood, Shoshanah M, Jeff S. Sharp, Richard H. Moore, and Deborah H. Stinner. 2009. "Restaurants, Chefs and Local Foods: Insights Drawn from Application of a Diffusion of Innovation Framework." *Agriculture and Human Values* 26 (3): 177–91. https://doi.org/10.1007/s10460-008-9165-6.

Jones, Kristal, and Daniel Tobin. 2018. "Reciprocity, Redistribution and Relational Values: Organizing and Motivating Sustainable Agriculture." *Current Opinion in Environmental Sustainability* 35 (December): 69–74. https://doi.org/10.1016 /J.COSUST.2018.11.001.

Lever, John, and Roberta Sonnino. 2022. "Food System Transformation for Sustainable City-Regions: Exploring the Potential of Circular Economies." *Regional Studies* 56 (12): 2019–31. https://doi.org/10.1080/00343404.2021.2021168.

Low, Setha M. 2001. "Social Sustainability: People, History, and Values." In *Managing Change: Sustainable Approaches to the Conservation of the Built Environment*, edited by Frank Matero and Jeanne Teutonico, 47–64. Getty Conservation Institute Proceedings Series. Los Angeles: Getty Conservation Institute.

Madeira, Arlindo, Teresa Palrão, and Alexandra Sofia Mendes. 2021. "The Impact of Pandemic Crisis on the Restaurant Business." *Sustainability* 13 (1): 40–53. https:// doi.org/10.3390/su13010040.

Marusak, Amy, Narjes Sadeghiamirshahidi, Caroline C. Krejci, Anuj Mittal, Sue Beckwith, Jaime Cantu, Mike Morris, and Jason Grimm. 2021. "Resilient Regional Food Supply Chains and Rethinking the Way Forward: Key Takeaways from the COVID-19 Pandemic." *Agricultural Systems* 190 (May): 103101. https://doi.org/10.1016/j.agsy.2021.103101.

National Restaurant Association. 2022. "Food Costs." Accessed September 9, 2022. https://restaurant.org/research-and-media/research/economists-notebook /economic-indicators/food-costs/.

Nelson, Paul, Mary A. Beckie, and Naomi T. Krogman. 2017. "The 'Locavore' Chef in Alberta: A Situated Social Practice Analysis." *Food, Culture and Society* 20 (3): 503–24. https://doi.org/10.1080/15528014.2017.1288798.

Norris, Cortney L, Scott Taylor, and D. Christopher Taylor. 2021. "Pivot! How the Restaurant Industry Adapted during COVID-19 Restrictions." *International Hospitality Review* 35 (2): 132–55. https://doi.org/10.1108/IHR-09-2020-0052.

Pesci, Sasha, and Catherine Brinkley. 2021. "Can a Farm-to-Table Restaurant Bring about Change in the Food System? A Case Study of Chez Panisse." *Food, Culture and Society* 25 (5): 997–1018. https://doi.org/10.1080/15528014.2021.1948754.

Polanyi, Karl. 1944. *The Great Transformation: The Political and Economic Origins of Our Time*. Boston: Beacon Press.

Roy, Hiran, and Paul W. Ballantine. 2020. "Preferences and Attitudes toward Locally Produced Food Sourcing in Wholesale Distributors: Restaurant and Chef Perspectives." *Journal of Hospitality and Tourism Management* 45 (December): 544–58. https://doi.org/10.1016/j.jhtm.2020.10.011.

Roy, Hiran, C. Michael Hall, and Paul W. Ballantine. 2018. "Supply Chain Analysis of Farm-to-Restaurant Sales: A Comparative Study in Vancouver and Christchurch." In *Case Studies in Food Retailing and Distribution*, edited by John Byrom and Dominic Medway, 87–104. Amsterdam: Elsevier. https://doi.org/10.1016 /B978-0-08-102037-1.00007-4.

Schoolman, Ethan D. 2020. "Local Food and Civic Engagement: Do Farmers Who Market Local Food Feel More Responsible for Their Communities?" *Rural Sociology* 85 (3): 806–39. https://doi.org/10.1111/ruso.12326.

Schreiber, Kerstin, Bernard Soubry, Carley Dove-Mcfalls, and Graham K. Macdonald. 2022. "Untangling the Role of Social Relationships for Overcoming Challenges in Local Food Systems: A Case Study of Farmers in Québec, Canada." *Agriculture and Human Values* 40 (1): 141–56. https://doi.org/10.1007/s10460-022-10343-0.

Thilmany, Dawn, Elizabeth Canales, Sarah A. Low, and Kathryn Boys. 2020. "Local Food Supply Chain Dynamics and Resilience during COVID-19." *Applied Economic Perspectives and Policy* 43 (1): 86–104. https://doi.org/10.1002/aepp.13121.

Trubek, Amy B. 2008. *The Taste of Place: A Cultural Journey into Terroir*. Berkeley: University of California Press.

CHAPTER TEN

Sustainability, Race, and Culture in New Orleans Restaurants in the Wake of the Pandemic

DAVID BERISS AND LAUREN DARNELL

Introduction

Is New Orleans seafood—and with it, New Orleans culinary culture—sustainable? Restaurants are the public face of New Orleans food, and locals and visitors alike consider the presence of locally sourced seafood on menus a reassuring sign of authenticity. Yet the survival of the restaurants and their ability to access seafood from the Gulf of Mexico seem increasingly problematic. At least twice in this century, all the restaurants in the city have been forced to close in the face of disaster, first after the 2005 hurricane and floods and again during the COVID-19 pandemic. Threats to fisheries in the Gulf of Mexico, ranging from industrial hazards such as the 2010 BP oil spill to the annual development of a vast "dead zone" extending for thousands of square miles from the mouth of the Mississippi River in which there is too little oxygen to sustain life, have rendered access to affordable seafood uncertain (Schleifstein 2022). Thousands of square miles of land along the coast have been lost, both because of the rising sea and because of subsidence caused by a century of river management that has deprived vast areas of south Louisiana of land-building sediment from the river (Anderson 2014).

In early December 2022, the authors of this chapter joined two New Orleans chefs on a boat tour of the wetlands in lower Plaquemines Parish. The trip started in Empire, Louisiana, about sixty miles south of the city, near the end of the river. The land is reduced to a narrow strip that far south, with the Mississippi delta fanning out into surrounding bays and sounds and, eventually, into the Gulf of Mexico. The tour was organized by "Chefs on Boats," a group that aims to connect New Orleans restaurant personnel with the people and places that make up the core of the south Louisiana seafood industry. Our guides, Captain Richie Blink and Chef April Bellow, showed us acres of oyster leases and crab traps. They discussed the challenging mixture of oil industry and fishing and explained restoration efforts meant to help rebuild the land. Seeing people dredging oysters, along with the boats of shrimpers and other fishers, helped make the connection between chefs, seafood, and the people who harvest it. We saw evidence of the challenges—oil spills, land loss, low-cost imported seafood, hurricanes, and more—faced by people in the fishing industry. We returned to New Orleans with questions about how sustainable the seafood industry can be.

In New Orleans, as in much of south Louisiana, the concept of "sustainability" can refer to a lot of different things. The land loss and the threats to fisheries that we witnessed in Plaquemines Parish are only some of what people have in mind when they use the concept of sustainability in south Louisiana. The list of things threatened with being "unsustainable" is quite long, including the coastal environment, the fisheries and fishing industry, the oil and gas industry, and the towns and communities that support them. The public cultures that make New Orleans and the region famous, including food, music, and architecture, are also among the things people refer to when they list the challenges to sustainability in the region. This chapter focuses on the ways people use the concept of sustainability in relation to the culinary culture of New Orleans. What people mean by "sustainability" and what they think needs sustaining reveals, we argue, a set of distinct and divided ideas about the city's identity and culture.

Sustainability is often defined through the intersection of environmental, economic, and social issues (Alkon and Vang 2016; Cauvain 2018; Davenport and Mishtal 2019; Higgins-Desbiolles, Moskwa, and Wijesinghe 2019, 1553). This model points to the need to think about the ways that efforts to preserve environmental resources for the future necessarily impact economic and social relations. Given that a majority of people in the world—and particularly in the United States—live in cities, this tripartite model helps raise questions about what "urban sustainability" might mean (Cauvain 2018; Checker, McDonogh, and Isenhour 2015; Lorr 2012; McDonogh 2011). Along with many other coastal (or near-coastal) cities, New Orleans finds itself confronted by a changing natural environment, which in turn raises questions about the ability of the city's economic life and social relations to survive into the future. Any attempt to make sense of the impact of changing natural environments in the city must necessarily deal with the different ways those changes impact different groups. In New Orleans, for example, wealthier and whiter people tend to live on higher ground and are thus less impacted by flooding (Campanella 2008). Analyses that focus on urban sustainability must attend to the differential impacts of changing climate and policies meant to promote sustainable cities.

Thus, the idea that sustainability is more than just an environmental concept is widely accepted. Sustainability has been particularly notable in recent research on restaurants and hospitality (Bertoldo et al. 2021; Higgins-Desbiolles, Moskwa, and Wijesinghe 2019; Higgins-Desbiolles and Wijesinghe 2019). As a key part of the food system, restaurants are often called upon to exhibit exemplary behavior, through control of waste, use of environmentally sustainable resources, and more (Dai, Cui, and Xu 2018; Fabinyi and Liu 2014; Hyde 2020). In addition, chefs and restaurant owners have increasingly made their commitment to the environment an explicit part of how they market their restaurants (Higgins-Desbiolles and Wijesinghe 2019).

In this chapter, we want to turn this debate around, asking what discussions, practices, and policies around sustainability can tell us about the city and its culture. We began this research in 2019, when the state of Louisiana enacted a law requiring that restaurants indicate the origins of shrimp and crawfish on their menus. Drawing on newspaper and legislative accounts of how the law came about, along with interviews with environmental and seafood industry activists, we began to examine the intersection of symbolic and substantive issues in efforts to create policies that support the seafood and restaurant industries. We began to look more closely at coverage of these policies in the local media and quickly noticed a surprising divide. When reporters in New Orleans want to talk to chefs about seafood and sustainability, they speak almost exclusively to white chefs. When they want to speak about the survival of New Orleans culinary culture, they are more likely to interview Black chefs, a phenomenon that became even more pronounced during the pandemic and the 2020 social justice movement. This division prompted us to ask why some restaurateurs are thought to have insights into environmental sustainability, while others are sought out as experts in the "cultural slot." What does this division suggest about the meaning of sustainability, race, and culture in New Orleans? We pursued this question with a series of in-depth interviews with about a dozen chefs, focusing on their perceptions of sustainability and seafood in Louisiana. Interestingly, the same divides we had observed in the media were reproduced in our conversations with white and Black chefs. If everyone agrees that sustainability is important, there are sharp disagreements over what, exactly, needs to be sustained.

In what follows, we will show how sustainability has become central to debates about how to think about cuisine and culture in New Orleans. We begin with seafood, because it ties the coastal environment to the city's chefs, but also because, as we will show below, it seems to stand as the key symbol through which many people think about the local culinary culture. We will then turn to the efforts to make sustainable seafood central to the "mission" of a certain number of New Orleans restaurants. These efforts rely, we will show, on ways of thinking about the city's culture and social structure that avoid historic questions of how race and class have shaped the city. Finally, we will focus on what sustainability means to chefs of color in New Orleans. In contrast to the mission-driven chefs, Black chefs raise questions about the recognition of the contributions of Black people to the city's culinary culture. They argue that the culinary culture can only be sustained through recognition and promotion of Black-owned and Black-operated restaurants.

Labeling Seafood

As already noted, sustainability is both a frequent topic of public debate and an object of public policy in south Louisiana. Coastal land loss, rising seas, pollution, disaster, and climate change all contribute to discussions about how to preserve both the industries and the communities that rely on access to coastal resources. State policies ranging from regulation of fisheries and restoring lost land to moving whole communities away from the coast are frequently debated in the media and among activists (Honn 2021; Restore the Mississippi River Delta, n.d.; Tolliver 2022). We begin with an effort by the state of Louisiana that initially appeared designed to use restaurants to help sustain Louisiana fisheries and the seafood industry. While the legislation ultimately had a rather narrow focus and impact on the fisheries, it did place restaurants at the center of the pursuit of sustainability.

While chefs all over the United States have emphasized eating locally and seasonally, New Orleans's culinary identity has been linked to regional resources before that was fashionable elsewhere (Collin 1973; Tucker et al. 2009). The city is surrounded by the Mississippi River and Lake Pontchartrain (itself an estuary of the Gulf of Mexico), two bodies of water that remind residents of the ever-present threat posed by nature, but also of the seafood resources available nearby. It is, therefore, perhaps shocking to discover that the seafood found in local grocery stores and restaurants is often not local. Finding shrimp, crab, or crawfish from other countries is surprisingly easy in New Orleans. Although they are labeled as such, their origins are often obscured by their presentation. Shrimp might be laid out on a pile of ice in a small pirogue (a style of canoe common in Louisiana) or crawfish might be branded with a Cajun-sounding name. At least in some of the bigger chain stores, those presentations may distract consumers from the label indicating that the shrimp came from Ecuador and the crawfish were farmed in Vietnam.

Environmentalists and fishers in Louisiana have long objected to the dominant position of imported seafood both locally and nationally (Harrison 2012; Lallo 2019; Tooker 2009). They assert that imported seafood comes from countries with poorly regulated fisheries and environmentally harmful aquaculture practices. They claim that imported seafood can carry health risks and argue that the US government is only able to inspect a small percentage of imports for those threats (Severson 2014). In addition to health hazards, imported seafood is generally cheaper than domestic, so it is increasingly difficult for American fishers to successfully compete. Imported seafood, then, is thought to be both an environmental and health hazard and a threat to the sustainability of the domestic seafood industry (Lallo 2019; Smith et al. 2020, xl).

There is, however, an additional problem that the local seafood industry must confront. Louisiana seafood is itself often maligned in the rest of the country as either environmentally tainted or dangerous for consumers. While Louisiana supplies a large percentage of the oysters used in restaurant dishes around the United States, oysters from the Gulf coast are infrequently listed on the raw bar menus in trendy restaurants outside the region, where diners find them "unwieldy and bland," according to one analysis (Anderson 2019). The 2010 BP oil spill called attention to the persistence of pollution in the Gulf and probably harmed the reputation of the region's seafood. When asked, during the spill, when seafood from the Gulf would again be safe to eat, one local food critic suggested that in less than a year "we will be wondering what we were so worried about" (Fitzmorris 2010). For locals, this sort of comment can be seen as both reassuring and a sign of the region's cavalier attitude toward the environment. After all, nearby Morgan City, a center for both the commercial seafood industry and for oil, has had an annual Shrimp and Petroleum Festival for many decades (Priest 2016). However, people elsewhere do not necessarily appreciate the combination and Louisiana's seafood brand suffers accordingly. A variety of efforts have been pursued to try and restore the reputation of Gulf seafood, including trying to build a national brand for quality, advertising innovative fishing methods, and promoting Louisiana seafood to restaurants around the country (Severson 2014; Tooker 2009).

Until 2019 Louisiana restaurants were not required to indicate where they sourced their seafood. Environmentalists, food activists, and fishers had long favored creating a policy that would require indicating the origins of all seafood served in restaurants. Diners, as noted above, already expected the seafood served in restaurants to be local, but by calling attention to its origins, environmentalists hoped to increase support for policies that would protect the Gulf, as Kendall Dix, then a campaign organizer at Healthy Gulf, told us in an interview. Fishers hoped to improve the reputation of their products and to increase their ability to compete with imports. Dix also noted that many in the restaurant industry, most notably the Louisiana Restaurant Association (LRA), opposed the measure. For the LRA, requiring seafood origin information on menus would be a difficult burden for many neighborhood restaurants.

In 2019, the state legislature successfully enacted a law that required restaurants to indicate where they sourced their seafood. The legislation was lauded as a victory by environmentalists and fishers, but it also reflected a much narrower set of objectives than originally sought (Mosbrucker, McNulty, and Boone 2019). At first, it was framed as an effort to protect the public from potentially tainted seafood from other countries (Davis 2019). Rather than finding ways to inspect seafood for such threats, the law required that restaurants indicate, either on menus or via signage, only whether they served imported shrimp or crawfish. No other kinds of seafood were mentioned in the law.

Despite this, the significance of the law would appear to lie less with health or economics than with the impact it has on calling attention to two of the most culturally significant seafood harvests in the state. By focusing specifically on restaurants, the law puts them at the center of efforts to sustain the seafood industry. Although the law only requires labeling imported shrimp and crawfish, many restaurateurs suggested that they would take the new law as an opportunity to emphasize their use of all kinds of local seafood on their menus (Mosbrucker, McNulty, and Boone 2019). The law is part of a broader effort by the state, as well as by seafood producers and state promoters in the region, to assert the Louisiana and Gulf seafood brand as distinctively better in quality than imports (Lallo 2019). As we will show next, this branding fits nicely with the strategies used by at least some restaurants to assert their own public commitment to sustainable seafood.

Sustainable Restaurants and Sustainable Relationships

Even before the 2019 labeling law, there were many New Orleans restaurants whose reputations were built on serving local seafood. Visitors arriving at the New Orleans airport were greeted with an advertisement for the Red Fish Grill with the slogan "Friends don't let friends eat frozen fish," indicating its commitment to fresh local fish. As early as 1973, restaurant critic Richard Collin asserted the centrality of Gulf seafood to New Orleans restaurant menus (1973, 18), something that other critics have frequently reaffirmed since then (Fitzmorris 1996, 5; Johnson 2005, 4; Murphy 2014, 23). Certainly, seafood is frequently on the menus of New Orleans restaurants. However, committing to local seafood requires, as we found out in our interviews, particular knowledge, strategies, and relationships.

Early in 2022, David sat down for a discussion with Chef Ryan Prewitt, chef and co-owner of Pêche Seafood Grill. As the restaurant's name indicates, seafood is at the core of the menu. According to Prewitt, however, the restaurant's objective is to "shine a light" on products from the Gulf of Mexico. "If it grows here or swims here, we eat it," he said. When it comes to seafood, Prewitt says that figuring out which local seafood is sustainable is not a simple matter. Prewitt is active in Audubon Nature Institute's GULF Chef Council (Gulf United for Lasting Fisheries, https://audubonnatureinstitute.org/gulf), an organization that advocates for sustainability in local fisheries and provides information to restaurateurs. Prewitt remarked that "a sustainable fishery must be populated by people who can support themselves." At that time, Pêche had worked with the same shrimpers for seventeen years, and it has long-established relationships with fishers who can provide it with a wide range of fish.

Dana Honn is another chef committed to using sustainable seafood in his restaurant, Carmo, which he co-owns with Chef Christina do Carmo Honn. Over the course of a couple of interviews Honn outlined Carmo's commitment to sustainability. In terms of seafood, this means working long term with the same fishers so that they can maintain stability in their businesses. It also means learning about the fisheries and expanding the species he and the restaurant can use. He has assembled a database of at least eighty species, along with methods to prepare them, that he can acquire from fishers in the Gulf. Like Prewitt, Honn is committed to persuading his customers to eat species they will not find in other restaurants, sponsoring "bycatch happy hours" to introduce them to species that are not regularly on local menus. He also puts unusual fish on the menu, such as lionfish, an invasive species that must be spearfished.

For chefs such as Prewitt and Honn, their relationships with fishers are a key part of making their restaurants sustainable. Through their supply chains, which they sometimes refer to as "value chains" (Beriss 2016), they emphasize knowing who is involved in every step between fisher and chef. Journalists have noted an increase in efforts by shrimpers to sell directly to restaurateurs as a way of competing with imports (Mosbrucker 2019). One local fisher, Lance Nacio, and his Anna Marie Shrimp Company have received extensive coverage in local media because of the way they have expanded from shrimping into providing unusual species to restaurants. Rather than toss back his bycatch, Nacio reaches out directly to a network of chefs in New Orleans who are often happy to feature rarer fish on their menus (McNulty 2019). Nacio is part of a broader community of fishers on Louisiana's Gulf coast who are working to find ways to sustain their way of life in the context of climate change and competition from imported seafood. Working with chefs in New Orleans, along with farmers' markets and other alternative forms of distribution, has become an increasingly important strategy for them (Tolliver 2022).

One of the chefs who works with Nacio is Marcus Jacobs, co-owner of Marjie's Grill and Seafood Sally's in New Orleans, both of which feature seafood from the Gulf. Lauren interviewed him in early 2022. Like Prewitt and Honn, Jacobs is involved with the Audubon GULF Chef Council. He invoked a range of people who he works with, including specific Gulf oyster farmers, fishers, shrimpers, and others, eschewing larger seafood houses in the area. Jacobs noted that the 2019 law requiring that restaurants indicate foreign origin of shrimp or crawfish is rarely enforced.

For Jacobs, as for Prewitt and Honn, indicating the origin of seafood on their menus is a central part of their brand, which means that they go far beyond the law's requirements on their menus.

This is not a commitment shared by all the chefs in New Orleans. Some of the chefs we spoke with pointed out that developing the knowledge and relationships necessary to keep sustainable seafood on their menus was difficult. Chef Michael Gulotta, whom David spoke with in the spring of 2022, pointed out that a commitment to sustainability could end up making his menu too expensive for his customers. Gulotta owns two restaurants in New Orleans, MoPho and Maypop. Gulotta strives to balance his efforts to source seafood locally with keeping his menus affordable and his restaurants profitable. This means, he noted, working to maintain close relationships with particular purveyors, but it also means recognizing that some items cannot make it to his menus, simply because they are unaffordable.

As noted in the introduction to this chapter, the organization Chefs on Boats works to help chefs learn more about local seafood. Chefs on Boats is part of a broader coalition of local chefs and activists, Chefs Brigade (https://www.chefsbrigade.org/), which was established early in the pandemic to help build ties between New Orleans restaurants and farmers, fishers, and environmental activists. Their work, from tours such as the one we took to bringing aid to communities impacted by disaster, plays a role in helping establish relationships between chefs and the people who harvest seafood locally (McNulty 2022). Between the state's efforts to legally create a sustainable environment for at least some local seafood and the work of New Orleans restaurateurs to build social relationships with fishers, there is clearly a movement to address the environmental, economic, and social aspects of sustainable fisheries in the region. This leaves unaddressed the question, fundamental to many New Orleans chefs and residents, of the sustainability of the city's culinary culture.

Sustainable Culture

When Lauren sat down with Chef Byron Bradley to talk about sustainability, he did not want to talk about fisheries or the coast. Instead, the discussion focused on the creative culture of New Orleans. Bradley wanted to talk about how to sustain New Orleans culture by acknowledging who has contributed to it. He discussed the importance of ownership of one's work as a means to ensure the future. His comments recalled the work of the New Orleans artist Phlegm, who designed a T-shirt to address the city's ongoing conversations surrounding displacement, cultural ownership, and belonging. The T-shirt is white with a black typeface that says, "Everything You Love About New Orleans is Because of Black People."[1] The slogan has helped popularize the idea that Black people should be acknowledged as "culture bearers" in New Orleans, including musicians, artists, and, of course, chefs who represent the city's culinary culture. For the chefs and restaurateurs of color we spoke with, the importance of acknowledging the contributions of Black cooks and chefs is central to what they do.

The white chefs we interviewed, including the chefs mentioned in the previous section of this chapter, all declined to discuss the relationship of their sustainability work—or their cooking—to the city's culinary culture. When we interviewed Black chefs, however, sustaining culture was at the core of what they wanted to discuss. Each interview highlighted that sustainability is only possible through giving back to the community, supporting neighbors and the next generation, and acknowledging the contributions of others.

Vance Vaucresson, a third-generation Creole New Orleans sausage maker, told us that it is common knowledge among Black chefs and cooks in New Orleans that "the menus of historic restaurants are designed by Black cooks." Recipes, he noted, have long been taken from line cooks and used on menus without acknowledgment or credit. There have been attempts, both scholarly and popular, to develop public acknowledgment for the contributions of Black cooks in New Orleans (Burton and Lombard 1978; Harris 2011). Vaucresson argued that these have not been sufficient. Recognizing the significance of race in shaping restaurants and food in New Orleans is, he argued, still not legitimate. And until it is, the culinary culture will remain in danger of erasure.

Byron Bradley—a Black chef and a New Orleans native—similarly noted that Black people are at the core of the city's culinary mix. "We have general references that it's Black only but as much as we celebrate it, Black is the most oppressed. There is no recognition that it all came from us and that is still part of what we call our culture." Bradley has a resume that reflects extensive experience with and knowledge of the city's cuisine, having trained under Leah Chase, the "Queen of Creole Cuisine"; served as a chef instructor for the Mardi Gras School of Cooking, where he offered classes on traditional Creole dishes; and worked as the executive chef in fine-dining restaurants. Despite his experience and reputation (he also competed on the Food Network's show *Chopped*), when he was interviewed on the *PBS News Hour*, he pointed out that being Black had put a brake on his career (Chavez and Lincoln Estes 2022).

Prince Lobo, co-owner of the Ethiopian restaurant Addis NOLA, spoke of his heightened awareness of how his management today can equip the next generation and how significant that is to everything he and his family are building. When asked about sustainability, he said that "I think about one thing pouring into another and a community that is able to take care of itself. Feeding the community and everything that flows together is the most important part . . . because children will all be the benefactors." Sustainability, he added, includes thinking about everyone in his community with an emphasis on his legacy and his contribution to helping strengthen the community as a whole. For Lobo, making and maintaining relationships—with purveyors, workers, and community members—was central to his idea of sustainability. He centered the idea of culture in his very comprehensive view of sustainability.

Lauren interviewed Chef Amarys Herndon, a New Orleans transplant and white female chef who is co-owner and operator of Palm & Pine Restaurant in New Orleans's French Quarter. Herndon sees sustainability in terms of how she can support everyone on her team and in their community. Arriving in New Orleans in 2008 via Texas, Amarys and Jordan Herndon learned about the diversity of the workforce in New Orleans. They encountered Hondurans who had come to help rebuild the city after Hurricane Katrina and they learned about Honduran food. While working at a restaurant, Amarys and Jordan were taught by a Vietnamese coworker in their spare time how to make the Vietnamese dish Nuoc Cham, which inspired one of their most popular dishes, "Corner Store Crudo." From her perspective, "It is a privilege to think about the environment. You can't do that when you're hungry." For Amarys, since the pandemic, sustainability has come to include what is sustainable for her team, focusing on a sustainable work environment, from a nutritious family meal for the staff to a tipping policy that attempts to ensure a livable wage. Amarys and Jordan prioritize feeding their community; during the pandemic they offered free meals to feed artists, musicians, performers, and fellow service industry staff who had been laid off (Ranjbar 2020). Their business model on every level is focused on sustainability as a practice for the community, considering all people and how they fit into New Orleans hospitality.

In the beginning of this chapter, we mentioned two chefs who joined us on the Chefs on Boats tour. The two chefs were Chef Byron Bradley and Chef Chris Okorie, both Black New Orleanians who have made their living creating and cooking New Orleans cuisine. Chefs Brigade, which sponsors the tours, wants to educate chefs and other food-service workers about the people and places their key ingredients come from, showing them what it will take to ensure the sustainability of Louisiana seafood and the livelihoods of the people who harvest it. April Bellow, program manager for the Chefs on Boats Tour, said, "You can't have sustainability if no one is here to do the work. Sustainability is a lot more than environmental." That observation applies, of course, to both the people who work on the coast and those who work in the city's restaurants. For New Orleans Black chefs such as Bradley, Okorie, and others we interviewed, acknowledging their role as bearers of the city's culinary culture is central to the idea of making sure their community is itself sustainable.

Conclusion

If there is a consensus in New Orleans, it is that many aspects of life in and around the city may be unsustainable. As we have noted, threats to fisheries in the Gulf of Mexico, including industrial pollution, coastal erosion and subsidence, cheap imports, and more, make access to seafood, a key ingredient in the city's cuisine, increasingly uncertain. The state of Louisiana, along with the federal government, is engaged in a variety of efforts to restore the coastal land. The 2019 law requiring the labeling of imported shrimp and crawfish on restaurant menus may be more symbolic than substantive, but it did succeed in raising awareness of the role of restaurants in helping sustain local fisheries. Some chefs, mostly white and mostly in relatively expensive fine-dining restaurants, go further than required by the state. They have diversified the kinds of seafood they serve, developing ties to specialized purveyors on the coast and educating themselves and their customers about more sustainable seafood.

On August 29, 2021, Hurricane Ida made landfall just to the southwest of New Orleans as a devastating category 4 storm. Damage from Ida was especially significant in the fishing communities south of New Orleans. In the city, restaurants, which were still struggling with restrictions related to the pandemic, were mostly forced to close due to power outages and wind damage. In the sweltering August heat, unrelieved by air conditioning, a lot of people began to wonder out loud about whether it made sense to continue to live in New Orleans. Despite doubts about the long-run sustainability of the city and region, people in the restaurant community sprang into action, as they often do after disasters, to prepare and bring food to some of the most devastated areas around the city. Faced with the long power outages and dangerous heat, two local activist groups joined forces to propose turning restaurants into solar-powered cooling, feeding, and recharging centers for future disasters. The new project, "Get Lit, Stay Lit," would raise funds to install solar panels and battery walls in restaurants around the city, allowing them to keep their refrigeration going and to provide cooling and recharging stations for their neighborhoods in the next extended power outage. At $60,000–$90,000 per restaurant, this was a substantial effort, but a year later, the first two restaurants were equipped and ready to go. Both are Black-owned restaurants in predominantly Black neighborhoods.[2]

For most residents of New Orleans, disaster is an expected condition of life in the city and region. Although the city celebrated its tricentennial in 2017, the question of its ongoing survival is never far from residents' minds. And the question of sustainability is especially fraught when it comes to the city's culinary culture. New Orleans cuisine has long been tied to local products, especially seafood. For chefs, the sustainability of local fisheries plays a key role in their success. The fisheries, along with the hospitality industry, are similarly fundamental to the regional economy and to the social relations that initiatives such as "Get Lit, Stay Lit" are meant to make sustainable, despite the constant threat of disaster.

As we have noted, New Orleans food culture—especially in professional kitchens—has long been shaped by people of color. If the public face of New Orleans cuisine has often been that of white men, the workers in the kitchens, including many of those who have created the city's most celebrated dishes, such as gumbo, have come from African roots. In the context of the 2020 racial justice movement, public attention started to shift toward recognizing the contributions of Black workers and the existence of Black-owned restaurants. A wide range of questions comes with this shift, ranging from an examination of racial equity within restaurants across the city to recognition for the accomplishments of workers from a variety of backgrounds within professional kitchens. These questions are not, of course, unique to New Orleans and have been raised across the United States.

What is perhaps distinct in New Orleans is an insistence that any serious debate about sustainability must include culture. The threat to the city is not only from hurricanes and rising seas, but also from an historic failure to recognize the contributions of Black people to the making of the city in general, and to its culinary culture in particular. Although we have not touched on it in this chapter, the same issue occurs among fishers, so that the face of commercial fishing is white, leaving Vietnamese, Native, and Black fishing families and communities unacknowledged. For chefs and cooks, as well as fishers, of color, the recognition of the centrality of their place in making the local culture distinct is a key part of what must be addressed in discussions of sustainability. That recognition is at least as important as noting the origin of shrimp and crawfish on local menus.

Notes

1. See https://mynameisphlegm.com/.
2. For more details on this effort, visit https://www.feedthesecondline.org/programs/getlitstaylit.

References

Alkon, Alison Hope, and Dena Vang. 2016. "The Stockton Farmers' Market: Racialization and Sustainable Food Systems." *Food, Culture & Society* 19 (2): 389–411.

Anderson, Brett. 2014. "Louisiana Loses Its Boot." *Medium*, September 8. https://medium.com/matter/louisiana-loses-its-boot-b55b3bd52d1e.

———. 2019. "Gulf Oysters Are Dying, Putting a Southern Tradition at Risk." *New York Times*, November 12. https://www.nytimes.com/2019/11/12/dining/gulf-oysters.html.

Beriss, David. 2016. "Slow Fish Report: On Value Chains, the Privatization of the Seas, and the Food Movement." *FoodAnthropology,* March 28. https://foodanthro.com/2016/03/28/slow-fish-report-on-value-chains-the-privatization-of-the-seas-and-the-food-movement/.

Bertoldo, Jaclyn, Robert Hsu, Taylor Reid, Allison Righter, and Julia A. Wolfson. 2021. "Attitudes and Beliefs about How Chefs Can Promote Nutrition and Sustainable Food Systems among Students at a US Culinary School." *Public Health Nutrition* 25 (2): 498–510.

Burton, Nathaniel, and Rudy Lombard. 1978. *Creole Feast: Fifteen Master Chefs of New Orleans Reveal Their Secrets.* New York: Random House.

Campanella, Richard. 2008. *Bienville's Dilemma: A Historical Geography of New Orleans.* Lafayette: Center for Louisiana Studies, University of Louisiana at Lafayette.

Cauvain, Jenni. 2018. "Social Sustainability as a Challenge for Urban Scholars." *City* 22 (4): 595–603.

Chavez, Roby, and Diane Lincoln Estes. 2022. "Black and Creole People Defined New Orleans Cuisine, but Black Chefs Don't Get Top Jobs." *PBS News Hour.* May 24. https://www.pbs.org/newshour/show/new-orleans-nonprofit-works-to-counter-the-restaurant-industrys-racial-imbalance.

Checker, Melissa, Gary McDonogh, and Cindy Isenhour. 2015. "Introduction: Urban Sustainability as Myth and Practice." In *Sustainability in the Global City: Myth and Practice,* edited by Cindy Isenhour, Gary McDonogh, and Melissa Checker, 1–25. Cambridge: Cambridge University Press.

Collin, Richard H. 1973. *The New Orleans Underground Gourmet*. New York: Simon and Schuster.

Dai, Shanshan, Qingming Cui, and Honggang Xu. 2018. "The Resilience Capabilities of Yumcha Restaurants in Shaping the Sustainability of Yumcha Culture." *Sustainability* 10 (9): 1–17.

Davenport, Sarah Grace, and Joanna Mishtal. 2019. "Whose Sustainability? An Analysis of a Community Farming Program's Food Justice and Environmental Sustainability Agenda." *Culture, Agriculture, Food and Environment* 41 (1): 56–65.

Davis, Leslie. 2019. "Fact Sheet on Act 372: Restaurant Notice of Foreign Seafood. Louisiana Fisheries Forward." https://www.lafisheriesforward.org/fact-sheet-on-act-372-restaurant-notice-of-foreign-seafood/.

Fabinyi, Michael, and Neng Liu. 2014. "Seafood Banquets in Beijing: Consumer Perspectives and Implications for Environmental Sustainability." *Conservation and Society* 12 (2): 218–28.

Fitzmorris, Tom. 1996. *The Eclectic Gourmet Guide to New Orleans*. Birmingham, AL: Menasha Ridge Press.

———. 2010. "Dining Diary: Saturday, May 22, 2010. The Oil Thing. Maple Street Books. Ciro's Cote Sud For Mussels." https://nomenu.com/posts/saturday-may-22-2010-the-oil-thing-maple-street-books-ciro-s-cote-sud-for-mussels.

Habans, Robert, and Allison Plyer. 2018. "Benchmarking New Orleans' Tourism Economy: Hotel and Full-Service Restaurant Jobs." The Data Center. https://www.datacenterresearch.org/reports_analysis/benchmarking-new-orleans-tourism-economy-hotel-and-full-service-restaurant-jobs/.

Harris, Jessica B. 2011. *High on the Hog: A Culinary Journey from Africa to America*. New York: Bloomsbury USA.

Harrison, Jill Ann. 2020. " 'Down Here We Rely on Fishing and Oil': Work Identity and Fishers' Responses to the BP Oil Spill Disaster." *Sociological Perspectives* 63 (2): 333–50.

———. 2012. *Buoyancy on the Bayou: Shrimpers Face the Rising Tide of Globalization*. Ithaca, NY: Cornell University Press.

Higgins-Desbiolles, Freya, Emily Moskwa, and Gayathri Wijesinghe. 2019. "How Sustainable Is Sustainable Hospitality Research? A Review of Sustainable Restaurant Literature from 1991 to 2015." *Current Issues in Tourism* 22 (13): 1551–80.

Higgins-Desbiolles, Freya, and Gayathri Wijesinghe. 2019. "The Critical Capacities of Restaurants as Facilitators for Transformations to Sustainability." *Journal of Sustainable Tourism* 27 (7): 1080–1105.

Honn, Dana. 2021. "Op-ed: New Orleans Chefs Can Help the Gulf Coast Brace for Extreme Weather." *Civil Eats*, June 25. https://civileats.com/2021/06/25/op-ed-new-orleans-chefs-can-help-the-gulf-coast-brace-for-extreme-weather/.

Hyde, Zachary. 2020. " 'Ethical' Gentrification as a Preemptive Strategy: Social Enterprise, Restaurants, and Resistance in Vancouver's Downtown Eastside." In *A Recipe for Gentrification: Food, Power, and Resistance in the City*, edited by Alison Hope Alkon, Yuki Kato, and Joshua Sbicca, 202–22. New York: New York University Press.

Johnson, Pableaux. 2005. *Eating New Orleans*. Woodstock, VT: The Countryman Press.

Lallo, Ed. 2019. "Gulf Seafood Seeks New Approach to Compete with Imports." *Gulf Seafood News*, June 23. https://gulfseafoodnews.com/2019/06/23/gulf-seafood-seeks-new-approach-to-compete-with-imports/.

Lorr, Michael J. 2012. "Defining Urban Sustainability in the Context of North American Cities." *Nature and Culture* 7 (1): 16–30.

McAuley, Anthony. 2019. "Even $10m Black-Owned Businesses Hit Lending Roadblocks; A New Program Seeks to Help." *Nola.com*, July 1. https://www.nola.com /news/business/even-10m-black-owned-businesses-hit-lending-roadblocks-a-new -program-seeks-to-help/article_926db3c6-9c12-11e9-bfb8-d75033176d3f.html.

McDonogh, Gary W. 2011. "Learning from Barcelona: Discourse, Power and Praxis in the Sustainable City." *City & Society* 23 (2): 135–53.

McNulty, Ian. 2019. "From Boat to New Orleans Table—and Fast: How Fishermen, Chefs Chart a New Seafood Path." *Nola.com*, July 3. https://www.nola.com /entertainment_life/eat-drink/from-boat-to-new-orleans-table----and-fast-how -fishermen-chefs-chart/article_874aa17e-9925-11e9-b6c3-1b2441e8cb6b.html.

———. 2021. "At a Haitian Restaurant in New Orleans, Deep Creole Flavor, a Glimpse of Something More." *Nola.com*, June 9. https://www.nola.com/entertainment_life /eat-drink/at-a-haitian-restaurant-in-new-orleans-deep-creole-flavor-a-glimpse -of-something-more/article_12c77e34-c47b-11eb-a439-87af9523ff87.html.

———. 2022. "Seeking Allies for a Changing Coast, New Orleans Chefs, Fishermen Connect on the Water." *Nola.com*, April 11. https://www.nola.com/entertainment _life/eat-drink/seeking-allies-for-a-changing-coast-new-orleans-chefs-fishermen -connect-on-the-water/article_c81277e0-b6af-11ec-89f8-1f40dc33cb1c.html.

Mosbrucker, Kristen. 2019. "Louisiana Fishermen Sell Directly to Survive, Hoping for Boost from Restaurant Menu Labeling Law." *Advocate* (Baton Rouge, Louisiana), August 11. https://www.theadvocate.com/baton_rouge/news/business/louisiana -fishermen-sell-directly-to-survive-hoping-for-boost-from-restaurant-menu -labeling-law/article_26a17980-a409-11e9-83ea-9f8e4b3ebf94.html.

Mosbrucker, Kristen, Ian McNulty, and Timothy Boone. 2019. "Now It's the Law: Here's How Shrimp, Crawfish Will Be Labeled in Louisiana." *Advocate*, September 2. https://www.theadvocate.com/baton_rouge/news/business /now-its-the-law-heres-how-shrimp-crawfish-will-be-labeled-in-louisiana /article_805cec8e-c9b6-11e9-9bb3-3b4fa8b15cce.html.

Murphy, Michael. 2014. *Eat Dat New Orleans*. Woodstock, VT: The Countryman Press.

Priest, Tyler. 2016. "Shrimp and Petroleum: The Social Ecology of Louisiana's Offshore Industries." *Environmental History* 21 (3): 488–515.

Ranjbar, Kim. 2020. "Palm & Pine Pivots and Perseveres." *French Quarter Journal*. July 7. https://www.frenchquarterjournal.com/archives/palm-pine-pivots-and -perseveres.

Restore the Mississippi River Delta. n.d. *A Community Guide to Coastal Restoration*. https://mississippiriverdelta.org.

Schleifstein, Mark. 2022. "Gulf of Mexico 'Dead Zone' Again Expected To Be Larger than Connecticut." *Nola.com*, June 2. https://www.nola.com/news/environment /gulf-of-mexico-dead-zone-again-expected-to-be-larger-than-connecticut /article_bfc1ba32-e2ac-11ec-9909-5fd0e4edb56b.html.

Severson, Kim. 2014. "Cooking with the Locals." *New York Times*, August 6.

Smith, Madelyn, Geoffrey T. Stewart, Meghan Massaua, Doborah Atwood, Michael Lesnick, and Thomas Humel. 2020. *An Economic Development Strategy for Louisiana's Coastal Seafood Industry*. Lafayette: University of Louisiana Meridian Institute.

Theriot, Jason P. 2021. "Oil and Gas Industry in Louisiana." *64 Parishes*. https:// 64parishes.org/entry/oil-and-gas-industry-in-louisiana.

Tolliver, Domonique. 2022. "Fishing for Solutions: The Race to Protect Coastal Louisiana's Cultures and Way of Life." *Gambit*, August 13. https://www.nola .com/gambit/news/the_latest/fishing-for-solutions-the-race-to-protect-coastal -louisianas-cultures-and-way-of-life/article_37474b6a-1991-11ed-9cf4 -d397d48159ab.html.

Tooker, Poppy. 2009. "NOLA Heroes: The White Boot Brigade." *Civil Eats*, November 5. https://civileats.com/2009/11/05/nola-heros-the-white-boot -brigade/.

Truong, Thanh. 2021. "Worker Shortage May Be a Reckoning for New Orleans' Service Industry." WWLTV.com, June 11. https://www.wwltv.com/article/news /local/orleans/worker-shortage-may-be-a-reckoning-for-new-orleans-service -industry/289-8b94b22c-fe7d-47c9-9f60-8614c6cf37cc.

Tucker, Susan, with Cynthia LeJeune Nobles, Karen Trahan Leathem, and Sharon Stallworth Nossiter. 2009. "Setting the Table in New Orleans." In *New Orleans Cuisine: Fourteen Signature Dishes and Their Histories*, edited by Susan Tucker, 3–27. Jackson: University of Mississippi Press.

CHAPTER ELEVEN

"To Sustain the People"
Native Chefs and the Food Sovereignty Movement

ELIZABETH HOOVER

Tocabe: Eating with Tradition

There are currently only a handful of Native American–owned restaurants serving Native American food in the United States. One of the most well-known examples currently in operation is Tocabe in Denver, Colorado, founded in 2008 by Ben Jacobs (Osage) and his friend Matt Chandra (with an additional location in Greenwood Village added in 2015). In 1989, when Ben was six, his parents opened Denver's first Native American restaurant—Gray Horse American Eatery, a small walk-up establishment in a food court—in an effort to make Native foods available to the broader community.[1] A few decades later, Ben sought to build on this idea through Tocabe (which means "blue" in Osage, Ben's mother's favorite color), a "Native based fast casual restaurant" that draws from the foods his Osage relatives were preparing in Oklahoma (Jacobs 2017). As Ben described to the audience at the 2015 Great Lakes Intertribal Food Sovereignty Summit, food is important to the Osage community, but this type of food was not generally available outside of the annual dances, powwows, or special occasions at grandma's house. "Some of my fondest memories are my aunt's backyard in our village in Oklahoma and the smell of the fire, the burning of the wood, the pots sitting and cast iron and pulling those off and sitting at the picnic table and eating right there. Those are some of my fondest memories. And so that's how I feel like the food is designed to be in a casual, comfortable, welcoming environment."

In order to bring this food to a wider audience, Ben went to his mother, aunts, and uncles to learn more about his grandma's recipes, and then gave them his own style.

When you enter the restaurant, the menu is printed on the wall behind a long counter, offering the opportunity to assemble your own meal by pointing to ingredients behind the glass partition (sort of like an Indigenous version of Chipotle). Ben felt that it was important that people could see the food as they were ordering it because "when you talk about our foods outside of Native communities, people don't know what you're talking about. So for them to visually see that is very important. Also, to build up the ingredients along the line, to see the quality the freshness, is very important" (2015).

Upon approaching the counter, customers choose a base for their meal, selecting from fry bread–based foods such as an Indian Taco or Stuffed Fry Bread, or they can also go with the Medicine Wheel Nachos or Posu Bowl (a grain bowl with a choice of wild rice or quinoa and wheat berries). Then they select a protein—beef, chicken, ground bison, shredded bison, or veggies—and then add toppings, such as the restaurant's signature Osage Hominy Salsa.[2] Whenever possible, Tocabe supports local food producers by buying local ingredients. But the restaurant prioritizes buying from Native food producers first—even if that means wild rice, beans, and corn may have to travel across the country. Ben noted that the restaurant is developing its own unique food system, connecting tribal food producers from around the nation, in order to efficiently source products such as blue and white corn from Bow and Arrow, Ute Mountain Ute tribe; olive oil and elderberry vinegar from Seka Hills, run by the Yocha Dehe tribe; tepary beans and wheat berries from Ramona Farms on the Gila River reservation; and wild rice and maple syrup from Red Lake Nation foods in Minnesota. Ben noted that when Tocabe first opened, they didn't have this ability—he didn't know Native producers with enough quantity available, and Tocabe couldn't afford to pay extra for ingredients. But now the restaurant, and the number and size of Native food producers, have grown together.[3]

My first time to the restaurant, Ben was kind enough to assemble his favorite version of each of the dishes for me to try. There was a salad with mixed greens, red quinoa, hominy, and purple potatoes, dressed in a maple vinaigrette. Next, a rice bowl with wild rice, ground buffalo, green chili, lettuce, and Osage Hominy Salsa (made from hominy corn, cranberry, red onion, and cilantro). Then a plate-sized fluffy fry bread, topped with seasoned ground buffalo meat, beans, lettuce, cubes of butternut squash, cheese, sour cream, hominy corn, peppers, and onions. (I would note, more vegetables than one often expects to see on an Indian Taco). Then savory and sweet slow-cooked buffalo ribs smothered in a blackberry sauce. This was followed by a hearty spicy pozole soup with ground buffalo, hominy, and green chili. For dessert, we had little round fry bread bites dusted in powdered sugar, dipped in blueberry sauce.

Ben's focus for Tocabe is not just procuring the best ingredients from Native producers, but also providing an environment and an ethos for patrons. In describing his restaurant to the audience at a 2015 Food Summit at Oneida, Ben stated,

> We have a mantra that we go by and it's called eat with tradition. And
> that's not just the ingredients. That's the whole concept of what we do.
> So that's going back and eating with family. It's going back and eating
> at home. It's going back and using ingredients. That's eating grandma's
> food. The whole idea of eating with tradition is all-encompassing of
> who we are and what we do. So that's how we carry ourselves now. The
> goal behind that is to, again, define what Native food is. (Jacobs 2015)

Part of the goal of eating with tradition is supporting the local Denver Indian community. Ben works to hire mostly Native staff in his restaurants and encourages them, where they are comfortable to do so, to talk to patrons about their tribal backgrounds (Jacobs 2017).[4] He also encourages employees to bring in recipes from their own families or communities if they are interested, building the menu in a collaborative fashion. Ben built Tocabe in the hopes that it could create a space for community. He cites his community as the source of his cooking knowledge and recipes, declaring honestly, "I have no training. I learned from grandmas and aunties and moms and uncles, and I learned from people in our communities." He describes the restaurant as an institution that works not just to make money, "but we also do development—people development, community development. So it's not just a restaurant." But at the same time the importance of being a restaurant and not just a community center is that it gives Native people an opportunity to "have a larger voice in the culinary world as a restaurant" (Jacobs 2017). Ben has noted that in Denver, patrons can find cuisines from all over the world. And now, finally, they can also try foods local to the Indigenous people of the region. Through all of these efforts, Tocabe is supporting sustainability in myriad ways—socially, culturally, environmentally, and economically—as well as providing an important example for other Native American chefs seeking to establish their own restaurants.

Introduction and Methods

I open with this long description of Tocabe as an example of many of the layers of sustainability that Native chefs are seeking to support and achieve through their work—supporting Native and environmentally responsible food producers, sustaining the surrounding Native community, and working to sustain broader Native food culture through making this food readily available to not only Native customers, but a broader group of patrons who may have never had the opportunity to learn about this cuisine before. This chapter is based on the work of a group of Native American chefs who are focused on not only environmental but also social, cultural, and, out of necessity, economic sustainability for their work.

This chapter is based on a broader project for which I included the voices of twenty-eight different Native American chefs and notes from at least forty-five different Native American food sovereignty summits and conferences between 2011 and 2020, as well as over three dozen dinners and cooking events that I attended outside of these conferences during that same time period. I first became aware of the Indigenous chef movement as a significant wing of the food sovereignty movement in 2013 when I attended the Native American Culinary Association (NACA) conference at the Sonoran Desert Museum in Tucson, coordinated by Apache/Navajo chef Nephi Craig as an opportunity for Indigenous chefs, and those aspiring to become so, to come together and share their experiences. Since then, I have been continuously attending food summits and dinners, during which, in addition to enjoying the food and helping out in the kitchen where I could, I recorded presentations, conversations, and interviews that were later transcribed. The information presented here draws from all of that work but specifically features the words of ten of these Native American chefs, some working catering businesses out of their home kitchens, others working in their own restaurants, who explicitly address some angle of sustainability in their presentations or interviews. My goal here is to present but a few of the broader themes specific to the topic of sustainability that have arisen in these conversations over the past several years that I have been participating in as an enthusiastic eater and listener.

Defining Sustainability

A standard definition of sustainability might focus on the ability of a system to be maintained at a certain rate or level over time. Most often, sustainability is utilized in environmental contexts: working to avoid overdepleting natural resources in order to maintain an ecological balance in the present, and for the future. However, as Melissa Nelson and Dan Shilling have noted in their recent edited volume (2018), the term "sustainability" has been so widely applied across a varying number of industries that has almost lost all meaning. They point to the need to look to Indigenous land-based cultures and philosophies to guide practices and development that are truly sustainable. Along this vein, Indigenous legal scholar Rebecca Tsosie (2020, 235) notes that "for most Indigenous peoples, sustainability is the result of conscious and intentional strategies designed to secure a balance between human beings and the natural world and to preserve that balance for the benefit of future generations." Some of these strategies include the ecocultural restoration of traditional land care practices that are based in what Dennis Martinez (2018) calls kincentric ecology, practices that are governed by five key principles: responsibility, restraint, biodiversity enhancement, adherence to natural law, and wealth distribution.

It is essential values such as these that Anishinaabe scholar Deborah McGregor, Steven Whitaker, and Mahisha Sritharan (2020, 36) point to as necessary to support a sustainable future, and the absence of these values on the part of many government leaders and policymakers that has led to the continued deterioration of the planet and oppression of Indigenous peoples and other-than-human relations. "Indigenous peoples assert that a just path to a sustainable future must consider all relations, an approach best expressed through Indigenous knowledge systems, legal orders, governance and conceptions of justice. These systems offer a diagnosis and path forward that answers the call for the 'transformative change' needed to alter global society's current trajectory." Working toward environmental justice for Native communities will entail supporting Indigenous sustainable food systems, a topic Potawatomi philosopher Kyle Whyte has written extensively about. He notes that "settler-industrial state institutions are arranged to bolster their own adaptivity at the expense of Indigenous adaptivity" and in doing so permanently alter landscapes on which Indigenous food systems are based while also enabling unsustainable settler adaptation (Whyte 2015, 20–21).

Food justice scholars have also taken up the issue of sustainability in the context of food systems for marginalized communities more broadly. Julian Agyeman (2011) describes the world of food justice as a bridge between social justice and just sustainability, which he and his colleagues argue needs to "ensure a better quality of life for all, now, and into the future, in a just and equitable manner, while living within the limits of supporting ecosystems" (Agyeman, Bullard, and Evans 2003, 2). Agyeman and Alison Alkon note that the future sustainable food system envisioned by food justice advocates goes beyond the "vote with your fork" campaigns of green capitalism in favor of a system in which all communities regardless of income or race "can have both increased access to healthy food and the power to influence a food system that prioritizes environmental and human needs over agribusiness profits. This vision clearly weaves together justice and sustainability" (2011, 6). They note that food justice scholars have established a relationship among food, social status and cultural identity that has a lot to offer the environmental justice and just sustainability literatures, as well as the field of food studies.

Some food studies scholars, such as those featured in this edited volume, have begun to look to the role of cooks and chefs in working toward a sustainable food system. Laura Pereira and colleagues describe kitchens as "sites of transformative innovation in the food system where cooks and chefs can leverage traditional food knowledge about local food species to create delicious and nutritious dishes. Achieving a sustainable food system is a grand challenge, one where cooks in particular are stepping forward as innovators to find solutions." (Pereira et al. 2019, 1). In some cases, cooks and chefs are doing this by applying their own sense of place and heritage and making innovative use of a diversity of tastes, textures, and visual arrangements in order to promote the consumption of underutilized species. The hope is that this will support biodiversity while promoting and preserving traditional knowledge and improving health (Pereira et al. 2019, 2–3). They note that promoting traditional food cultures in commercial kitchens can support Indigenous farming practices that are essential to safeguard agrobiodiversity (Johns et al. 2013; Nazarea 2006) and to enable dietary diversity (Fischer et al. 2017), contributing to human and planetary health (Allen et al. 2014; Perreira et al. 2019, 3).

In conclusion, as Dan Shilling (2018, 4) points out, "Sustainability is foremost a moral, not technological, undertaking, beginning with how our species relates to its surroundings." For many of the Native chefs I spoke with, being part of a sustainable operation included supporting sustainable Indigenous food producers; learning about and serving culturally important "sustainer" foods; being sustained emotionally, mentally, and financially by this work; and sustaining community through their restaurants and other food businesses.

Supporting Indigenous Food Producers

Part of creating a culinary operation that supports broader environmental and community sustainability entails sourcing from Indigenous food producers. As described above, Ben Jacobs's restaurant Tocabe espouses a "Native first" buying policy in order to ensure that he is supporting the broader Native community first and foremost. As Ben stated to an audience of Native food producers at the 2015 Great Lakes Intertribal Food Sovereignty Summit, "As one boat rises, we all are rising. Everyone is growing together. So we're able to now start sourcing not only native products, but native products from a Native source." Ben sees it as important for his restaurant to patronize Native food producers in order "to get the voice out, to get the ingredients out to the larger communities. It's a way for us to expose others to what our foods are, what we do, what we create." He described his restaurant as a resource to support these food systems: "It's a community of people, it's a web of things that all support this growth" (Jacobs 2015). In showing a photo of one of his salads to an assembled crowd, he described the number of people involved in getting all of those ingredients to the plate: "Someone cleaning it, someone processing it, and someone packaging it, getting it to us before we cook it, cut and prepared [and] put it on the plate. So, it's a whole level of people that go into making a salad. I think that's very important. That is who we are as people, to be very community focused and then to make something of the highest quality" (Jacobs 2015).

Ho-Chunk chef Elena Terry created the program Wild Bearies, which works to help community members who have suffered from substance abuse issues or emotional trauma to learn gardening, food preservation, and culinary skills with the ultimate goal of helping them gain employment in kitchens. Elena notes that while many people who like to cook might call themselves a chef, what she works to teach are the logistical skills a chef actually requires, such as how to "make a menu, cost it out effectively, source everything in a proper way and then, you know, cooking is like the fun part." One of the important aspects of sourcing is "who to go to for sustainability that is a responsible forager or producer and that are in line with our goals" (Terry 2020). In her eyes, to be a proper community-based Native chef requires not just sourcing from the most affordable distributor but instead applying cultural values and supporting producers who are growing and harvesting in a sustainable manner.

Sean Sherman (Lakota) is another Native chef who has worked hard to source specifically from local Native food producers as part of the ethos of his operations. In 2014 he started The Sioux Chef in Minneapolis, a catering company that focuses exclusively on what he describes as "precontact pre–European-style foods, trying to really showcase what healthy foods were here before, and the flavors that were here" (Sherman 2014). This includes a combination of foods produced through Native agriculture, foods that were foraged from the forests, and wild game and fish. The Sioux Chef also works to incorporate traditional food preservation and cooking techniques (such as smoking foods and cooking over fire) as a means of capturing those flavors. In 2021 he cofounded Owamni, a restaurant dedicated exclusively to Native foods, on the banks of the Mississippi River in Minneapolis. In addition, he codirects the nonprofit NATIFS (North American Traditional Indigenous Food Systems), which seeks to educate up-and-coming Native chefs and help them develop a plan to start food businesses in their home communities. The Indigenous Food Lab was started through NATIFS, and it is currently housed in the Midtown Global Market in Minneapolis, along-side eateries representing cuisines from around the world. Each of these operations works to support local Native food producers, highlighting on the menu not just the ingredients but who produced them and how. This is a practice that Sean employs during meals that he produces while serving as a featured chef in other locations—he works to ensure that the foods of local Native producers in each of the places he works are featured on the menu (Hoover and Sherman 2019).

Dan Cornelius (Oneida) and the Intertribal Agriculture Council (IAC) have also worked to help connect tribal food producers with home chefs and culinary businesses. Dan created the Mobile Farmers Market, through which he embarked on a "Reconnecting the Tribal Trade Routes Roadtrip" in 2014 that collected, purchased, and exchanged food-stuffs from tribal communities across the United States (Hoover 2017). The market later morphed into a brick-and-mortar store in Madison, Wisconsin, stocked with food products and other nonfood items traded for food from across Indian country. The IAC runs the American Indian Foods (AIF) program to help Native American food producers find mar-kets. Through Native Food Connection, the AIF program works to create domestic market opportunities for Native products and services, have Native food products featured at Native organization–sponsored conferences and events, provide support for more effective branding and trademarking of products, and partner events with Native chefs and menus (IAC, n.d. a). To help with branding, the "Made/Produced by American Indians" trademark program distributes gold logo stickers to affix to qualifying products, allowing consumers to easily identify authentic American Indian–produced goods (IAC, n.d. b).

Find Your Sustainers

In addition to the importance of which food producers are being sustained is the focus on which ingredients are being utilized. Anishinaabe scholar Melissa Nelson (2018, 265) has asserted that "if sustainability is to mean anything relevant for us, our more-than-human relatives, and future generations, then we must put our environmental ethics into action and get back in our tracks by re-rooting to specific landscapes." Part of this re-rooting necessitates getting to know the specific plants and animals that have sustained Indigenous people for eons. Potawatomi botanist Robin Wall Kimmerer (2018, 27) writes that "we inhabit a landscape of gifts peopled by nonhuman relatives, the sovereign beings who sustain us, including the plants." Living in "cultures of reciprocity," as she describes it, entails an acknowledgement that "our human lives are utterly dependent on the lives of other beings and thus our first responsibility is for gratitude," as well as engaging Indigenous values of kinship and responsibility to express a reciprocal relationship with the plant world (35). Getting to know these "sovereignty beings who sustain us" is seen as an important distinction that sets Native chefs who are part of the Native food sovereignty movement apart from other culinarians. As Potawatomi chef Loretta Barrett Oden has described, "Corn is a staple crop, nurtured in many Indigenous communities, often by women, to sustain and strengthen their families," and as such plays an important role in her cooking (2017). But while corn is one of the most well known, there are also other important sustainers. In reflecting on advice that he has for Native people who are interested in becoming chefs like himself, Oneida chef Arlie Doxtator (2015) advised that they look deep into their own cultures and

> Find out who your sustainers are. Not everybody has the three sisters. Out west you have the salmon people. Not everybody has corn.

You have Ojibway neighbors that the wild rice was their sustainers. Find out your foods, find out who your relatives are. Put it that way. Find your relatives, find your food relatives. Who are they? In the best way you can—without sounding mystical or anything—get in contact with them. Find out who they are, talk to them. And by communicating with them, I mean cook with them and listen to them.

On a panel of chefs at the 2015 Great Lakes Intertribal Food Sovereignty Summit, Arlie described how elders he had learned from instructed him to "view not only food as just food, but . . . [as] our medicine. It's there to give us sustenance, but it's also so many other things. They are our relatives. And when we do our opening address, we thank the creator for all those relatives in creation that we say are continuing the responsibilities. The responsibilities to us as the human beings" (Doxtator 2015).

But while corn and salmon and wild rice are seen as traditionally held sustainers, other, more recently introduced foods have also come to been seen in this role, but not without controversy. When it comes to foods made entirely from introduced ingredients that have been adopted by communities and come to be considered "traditional food" by some, the most controversial and widespread is fry bread. Made from white flour fashioned into dough and fried in lard or vegetable oil, fry bread is calorically dense, containing 700 calories and 27 grams of fat in an average serving according to the USDA (Wagner 2015), and delicious, but it is lacking in nutritional value and is everything a person with diabetes should not be consuming. Native American people suffer from higher rates of diabetes and metabolic disorders than any other ethnic group in the United States,[5] and a great deal of effort is being applied to improve upon these numbers.

Fry bread is described in popular media and around kitchen tables as a survival food—a symbol of the ingenuity of Native women and families who were given the bare minimum of foreign ingredients to prevent starvation, and who then turned these ingredients into something filling and tasty. Native communities around the country cite stories of forced relocations and land theft that left them unable to feed themselves, and so they turned to fry bread as a means of creatively working with government rations (Lewis 2018). For many of these communities, the nineteenth century began a time of rapidly changing diets during which people had to make do with what they had in order to survive. And even now, after most families have become more food secure, people continue to cook fry bread for myriad reasons—because of poverty, because they think it tastes good, or because they want to honor those women cooks who helped their ancestors survive. Fry bread has also developed its own social capital, and its ubiquitous presence at Native functions across the country attests to its unifying function (Lewis 2018).

Despite its colonial history and nutritional issues, some people still see fry bread as a culturally important food because it represents a history of resiliency. At a panel at the Great Lakes Food Sovereignty Summit, when the room became embroiled in a debate about whether people should continue serving fry bread, Ben Jacobs described how, while he agrees it is not the healthiest food, he works to serve it in a healthier way. At his restaurant, cooks don't use lard. He studied oil absorption into the bread and found that it was less than one tablespoon—which is less than that in a serving of French fries. He sees serving fry bread as important because it's "respecting what the women in our lives have done to sustain us. It was something done to sustain the people, to give us the opportunity to stand here" (2015). He elaborated on this during a conversation with me a year later, describing with gratitude the way that he was able to connect with his grandmother through her fry bread recipe, and the opportunity that it provided for him and his family: "One recipe has given me so much opportunity in my life" (2016). He recognizes that fry bread is not a healthy food but feels that it is the daily doses of soda and other refined-sugar–laden processed foods that are the greater contributors to the epic rates of diabetes—foods that people do not have a cultural connection to the way he feels they do to fry bread. "We have cultural connection to fry bread. I haven't felt my grandma in years—this makes me feel like I'm sitting in her kitchen. It reminds me of my sister when I was little. I'm going to keep doing it, I won't apologize." But Ben has also not limited his business to fry bread, recognizing that it gave him "the opportunity to do new and better things . . . I know we're doing something when people don't order fry bread" (Jacobs 2016). Ben is now expanding the range of dishes available in his restaurant through traveling to and learning from other Indigenous communities around the country.

> We are moving beyond the idea of just fry bread. Fry bread was the doorway into the idea of Indian cuisine, and now we're evolving, truly trying to become what we see as real American Indian people using all these products and other ideas in our food. Our idea behind

this food is to develop it and learn from firsthand accounts. So, we don't just go online and find recipes and then use it, we actually go to communities. So last week we were in Cherokee Country working on some things with Cherokee. We've been to Flathead. We've gone to Houma, we learned—a lot of people understand that Houma Nation of Louisiana were the originators of jambalaya and gumbo and things like that, that then became what you know as Cajun or Creole. Or clam chowder is a Wampanoag recipe, it is Native tradition. So, in many ways, we're trying to help reestablish what the real beginnings of these foods are and then venturing into evolving upon them. We, as we want to say, change that image of what people expect the food to be. (Jacobs 2015)

While fry bread is the quintessential food that will get patrons in the door, Ben and his staff are working hard to give them the option to eat and learn about other Indigenous foods as well.

Sustaining Self, Community, and Culture

In addition to celebrating the sustainers, the Native chefs I have visited with have described how taking part in this work sustains them as well, emotionally, financially, and culturally. Loretta Barrett Oden (Citizen Band Potawatomi), who opened one of the first well-known Native restaurants in the country in 1993, the Corn Dance Café in Santa Fe, New Mexico, is described by Chef Arlie as "the grand dame of Native American cuisine" and by younger chefs as "the OG of Native chefs," and she has made it her life's work to ensure that people understand Native food.[6] She also works to pass this knowledge on to the next generation of Native chefs through mentoring people at numerous food sovereignty summits and other events, and she describes how this work sustains her:

> All of these endeavors speak to an intergenerational transfer of knowledge that truly sustains me. Even when I am exhausted after traveling, presenting and cooking, the satisfaction of knowing that I have inspired the next generation of Native chefs, food producers, and eaters sustains me in my work. . . . I seek to inspire Indigenous youth, and especially other Indigenous women, to find their passion and pursue it whole heartedly, as I have sought to do over these past many decades. (2017)

In addition to being sustained emotionally, the chefs also recognize the need for their culinary projects to be financially sustainable. Mohawk chef Tawnya Brant (2020), who opened the restaurant Yaweko in Six Nations, Ontario, described how it's much easier for chefs to talk about the emotionally gratifying parts of this art and profession than the challenging financial issues: "How do I take this hobby and how do I make it a sustainable business that I can raise my family on right? And there's definitely not enough talk in any conference that I've really seen because it's hard and a hard issue to address right?" She has worked with cooks in her community to encourage people not to undersell their services—underselling may benefit the customer in the immediate present but hurts the industry overall.

In some cases these culinary businesses were also utilized as a means of reviving and sustaining tribal food culture. Café Ohlone was originally nestled on the back patio of the quirky University Press bookstore on Bancroft Way in Berkeley, California. Founded by partners in life and cooking Vincent Medina (Muwekma Ohlone) and Louis Trevino (Rumsen Ohlone), who first established the ma-'kamham (Ohlone for "our food") catering business, Café Ohlone is a labor of love that serves as a community gathering space, as well as a bougie little pop-up restaurant, whose main focus is the revival of Ohlone cuisine—to nourish community members and educate visitors. Vincent describes their goal not just as preserving culture for present community members, but for his food revitalization projects to have these traditions "come back in meaningful ways that are going to be sustained so that they touch the next generation and the next and the next. And it's almost like they never left us because now they're back" (2018). In working with his community, "We're all nurturing each other and we're supporting each other to bring back these things collectively and meaningfully so that they're sustained and that's why it's important to respect all of this because it's for our people and it's going to be centered on our people and our people deserve respect" (2018). Vincent continued this thread two years later, speaking to a crowd assembled for brunch at the café. He described his and Louis's efforts "to make sure that these foods grow stronger. So, they're sustained into our future and that they're passed on to a younger generation of our community and that our elders who love the flavors of these foods get to have them. Make them accessible again so that they are a sustained part of our culture. Louis and myself started this café space Café Ohlone in September of 2018 because we wanted to teach people directly with our community about who we are as the first people of this space" (2020). In a city known for its food connoisseurs and promoters of the local food movement, it was important to Café Ohlone's proprietors to revive and share the original cuisine of the area—to educate the broader public about it as well as to sustain it into the future for their own people.

Conclusion

The Native American chefs who are featured here are working to sustain Native cuisine through creating a web of producers, preparers, and consumers. Speaking at the 2015 Great Lakes Intertribal Food Sovereignty Summit, Ben Jacobs described how he sees the role of Native restaurants in particular:

> In terms of food, the way that I see, not only our restaurant and restaurants like ours are the way to be a resource to get the voice out, to get the ingredients out to the larger communities. It's a way for us to expose others to what our foods are, what we do, what we create. So I see our establishment as very much a resource to support systems. It's a community of people, it's a web of things that all support this growth. (2015)

On the supply end, there is a whole community of food producers that these chefs support through their businesses. One of Martinez's (2018) principles of kincentric ecology cited earlier in this chapter is wealth distribution, and as Ben has noted, as Native chef enterprises have thrived, so too have Native food producers: "We all are rising," as he describes it.

Sustainability advocates cited above have also described ecocultural restoration and biodiversity enhancement as elements that are both promoting and resulting from the transformative changes that McGregor, Whitaker, and Sritharan (2020) are calling for. Revitalizing Native American cuisines provides a market for Native-produced crops that might be outside of what is ordinarily purchased and cooked by more conventional restaurants, and providing this market gives Native producers the resources to plant and harvest more of these varieties.

Another aspect of sustainability often focuses on the benefit to future generations of the work that is being done. As is described here, many of these Native chefs are working to revitalize and preserve ancestral food culture for the benefit of elders and present generations, and to ensure that these food cultures will be more accessible for future generations—so that they will be able to eat this cuisine more regularly and also open these types of businesses more easily themselves.

These businesses center not only on food justice—making this food more accessible—but also culinary justice, defined by African American chef Michael Twitty (2016) as "the idea that oppressed peoples have the right to not only be recognized for their gastronomic contributions, but they have the right to their inherent value, to derive from them uplift and empowerment." Through revitalizing Native food traditions, supporting Indigenous food producers, finding and connecting with their "sustainers," and providing for their communities through facilitating intergenerational transfer of food culture, these chefs featured here are working toward a sustainable food future for Native people.

Notes

1. Ben described at a Wisconsin food summit in March of 2017 that his parents named their restaurant Grey Horse "because it was our family name and my grandmother when she was little used to watch the horses run and she always liked the gray horse. And so that's why my mother named it Gray Horse American Indian Eatery."
2. Check out its full menu at https://www.tocabe.com/menu.
3. For an up-to-date list of food products and their sources, see https://shoptocabe.com.
4. At a food summit in Wisconsin in March of 2017, an audience member at the chef panel that Ben was participating in asked if he had hired many Native employees. Ben replied, "So my first store is about 80 percent, my second store we're about fifty-fifty, and the food truck crew is 100 percent. It's three people (laughs)" (2017).
5. According to the United States Department of Health and Human Services Office of Minority Health's "Diabetes and American Indians/Alaska Natives" report, American Indian/Alaska Native adults are almost three times more likely than non-Hispanic white adults to be diagnosed with diabetes and two and a half times more likely than non-Hispanic whites to die from diabetes.
6. OG, borrowed from hip-hop culture, is short for "original gangster" and is a slang term for someone who is old-school, exceptionally authentic, or a highly respected originator.

References

Agyeman, Julian. 2011. "Preface." In *Cultivating Food Justice: Race, Class, and Sustainability*, edited by Alison Hope Alkon and Julian Agyeman, xi–xiv. Cambridge, MA: MIT Press.

Agyeman, Julian, Robert Bullard, and Bob Evans. 2003. *Just Sustainabilities: Development in an Unequal World*. Cambridge, MA: MIT Press.

Alkon, Alison Hope, and Julian Agyeman. 2011. "Introduction: The Food Movement as Polyculture." In *Cultivating Food Justice: Race, Class, and Sustainability*, edited by Alison Hope Alkon and Julian Agyeman, 1–20. Cambridge, MA: MIT Press.

Allen, Thomas, Paolo Prosperi, Bruce Cogill, and Guillermo Flichman. 2014. "Agricultural Biodiversity, Social-Ecological Systems and Sustainable Diets." *Proceedings of the Nutrition Society* 73 (4): 498–508.

Brant, Tawnya. 2020. Phone interview with author, March 26.

Doxtator, Arlie. 2015. Interview with author, Green Bay, Wisconsin, April 15.

Fischer, Joern, David J. Abson, Arvid Bergsten, Neil French Collier, Ine Dorresteijn, Jan Hanspach, Kristoffer Hylander, Jannik Schultner, and Feyera Senbeta. 2017. "Reframing the Food-Biodiversity Challenge." *Trends in Ecology & Evolution* 32 (5): 335–45.

Hoover, Elizabeth. 2017. " 'You Can't Say You're Sovereign if You Can't Feed Yourself': Defining and Enacting Food Sovereignty in American Indian Community Gardening." *American Indian Culture and Research Journal* 41 (3): 31–70.

Hoover, Elizabeth, and Sean Sherman. 2019. " 'The Answers to Our Ancestors' Prayers': Seeding a Movement for Health and Culture." In *Seeds: Proceedings of the Oxford Symposium on Food & Cookery 2018*, edited by Mark McWilliams, 198–211. Blackwaton, UK: Prospect Books.

Intertribal Agriculture Council (IAC). n.d. a. "American Indian Foods." https://www.indianag.org/americanindianfoods.

———. n.d. b. "American Indian Trademark." https://www.indianag.org/trademark.

Jacobs, Ben. 2015. Chef panel at Great Lakes Intertribal Food Summit, Oneida, Wisconsin, April 15.

———. 2016. Phone interview with author, October 29.

———. 2017. Chef panel at the Food Sovereignty Symposium and Festival, University of Wisconsin, Madison, March 12.

Johns, Timoth, Bronwen Powell, Patrick Maundu, and Pablo B. Eyzaguirre. 2013. "Agricultural Biodiversity as a Link between Traditional Food Systems and Contemporary Development, Social Integrity and Ecological Health." *Journal of the Science of Food and Agriculture* 93 (14): 3433–42.

Kimmerer, Robin. 2018. "*Mishkos Kenomagwen*, the Lessons of Grass: Restoring Reciprocity with the Good Green Earth." In *Traditional Ecological Knowledge: Learning from Indigenous Practices for Environmental Sustainability*, edited by Melissa Nelson and Dan Shilling, 27–56. Cambridge: Cambridge University Press.

Lewis, Courtney. 2018. "Frybread Wars: Biopolitics and the Consequences of Selective United States Healthcare Practices for American Indians." *Food, Culture & Society* 21 (4): 427–48.

Martinez, Dennis. 2018. "Redefining Sustainability through Kincentric Ecology: Reclaiming Indigenous Lands, Knowledge, and Ethics." In *Traditional Ecological Knowledge: Learning from Indigenous Practices for Environmental Sustainability*, edited by Melissa Nelson and Dan Shilling, 139–74. Cambridge: Cambridge University Press.

McGregor, Deborah, Steven Whitaker, and Mahisha Sritharan. 2020. "Indigenous Environmental Justice and Sustainability." *Current Opinion in Environmental Sustainability* 43:35–40.

Medina, Vincent. 2018. Interview with author, Berkeley, CA, October 14.

———. 2020. Speech at Café Ohlone brunch, Berkeley, CA, January 12.

Nazarea, Virginia D. 2006. "Local Knowledge and Memory in Biodiversity Conservation." *Annual Review of Anthropology* 35 (1): 317–35.

Nelson, Melissa. 2018. "Back in Our Tracks—Embodying Kinship as If the Future Mattered." In *Traditional Ecological Knowledge: Learning from Indigenous Practices for Environmental Sustainability*, edited by Melissa Nelson and Dan Shilling, 250–66. Cambridge: Cambridge University Press.

Nelson, Melissa, and Dan Shilling, eds. 2018. *Traditional Ecological Knowledge: Learning from Indigenous Practices for Environmental Sustainability*. Cambridge: Cambridge University Press.

Oden, Loretta Barrett. 2017. Personal communication with author, July 20.

Pereira, Laura M, Rafael Calderón-Contreras, Albert V. Norström, Dulce Espinosa, Jenny Willis, Leonie Guerrero Lara, Zayaan Khan, Loubie Rusch, Eduardo Correa Palacios, and Ovidio Pérez Amaya. 2019. "Chefs as Change-Makers from the Kitchen: Indigenous Knowledge and Traditional Food as Sustainability Innovations." *Global Sustainability* 2 (e16): 1–9. https://doi.org/10.1017/S2059479819000139.

Sherman, Sean. 2014. Interview with author at the All My Relations Gallery, Minneapolis, Minnesota, August 30.

Shilling, Dan. 2018. "Introduction: The Soul of Sustainability." In *Traditional Ecological Knowledge: Learning from Indigenous Practices for Environmental Sustainability*, edited by Melissa Nelson and Dan Shilling, 3–14. Cambridge: Cambridge University Press.

Terry, Elena. 2020. Interview with author at the Indigenous Farming Conference, White Earth, MN, March 7.

Tsosie, Rebecca. 2020. "Indigenous Peoples and 'Cultural Sustainability': The Role of Law and Traditional Knowledge." In *Traditional Ecological Knowledge: Learning from Indigenous Practices for Environmental Sustainability*, edited by Melissa Nelson and Dan Shilling, 229–49. Cambridge: Cambridge University Press.

Twitty, Michael. 2016. "Gastronomy and the Social Justice Reality of Food." TED archive. https://www.youtube.com/watch?v=8MElzoJ2L6U.

United States Department of Health and Human Services Office of Minority Health. "Diabetes and American Indians/Alaska Natives." Last modified March 1, 2021. https://minorityhealth.hhs.gov/omh/browse.aspx?lvl=4&lvlid=33.

Wagner, Angie. 2015. "Icon or Hazard? The Great Debate over Fry Bread." NBC News, August 21. https://www.nbcnews.com/id/wbna9022063.

Whyte, Kyle Powys. 2015. "Indigenous Food Systems, Environmental Justice, and Settler-Industrial States." In *Global Food, Global Justice: Essays on Eating under Globalization*, edited by M. Rawlinson and C. Ward, 143–56. Newcastle upon Tyne: Cambridge Scholars Publishing.

Culinary Sustainability and Diversity, Equity, and Activism

CHAPTER TWELVE

Black Chefs and Just Sustainability

Affirming Systems of Food and Racial Justice

MARILISA NAVARRO

Introduction

In late spring 2020, the premier Philadelphia-based daily newspaper, the *Philadelphia Inquirer*, began publishing a series of six articles highlighting Black chefs and Black-owned restaurants in the Philadelphia and greater Philadelphia-metropolitan area. The articles showcase restaurants, chefs, and images of Philadelphia-area black and African-diasporic restaurants. These articles came on the heels of the very public murder of forty-four-year-old George Floyd, a Black man killed by police officer Derek Chauvin, in the middle of the afternoon on May 25, 2020, in Minneapolis, Minnesota. George Floyd's killing incited a public outcry for greater attention to systemic racism in the United States—and anti-Black racism in particular—including police violence, exclusionary institutional policies and practices, issues of representation, and historic and contemporary inequities. In addition to the public outcry to bring attention to inequities, there came a push to highlight the skills, expertise, and knowledge of Black communities. As a result, a series of articles were printed in the *Philadelphia Inquirer* from spring 2020 through spring 2022 highlighting

Thanks go to editors Carole Counihan and Susanne Højlund for their thoughtful and constructive feedback. I would also like to thank my family for their continuous support of my work.

the work of Black chefs and restaurateurs in Black communities in the food and restaurant industry in the greater Philadelphia area. The articles represent the chefs' and restaurateurs' work as promoting well-being, attention to local needs and resources, and social justice.

This manuscript analyzes six articles published in the *Inquirer*, which focus on the efforts of Black chefs, restaurateurs, and restaurants. Those articles include the following:

"He's Fed Thousands of Philly Kids and Taught Hundreds How to Cook, but Setbacks Are Keeping Him from What He Loves" by Stephanie Farr (January 19, 2022);

"Vittles Food Hall Provides a Home to Everybody Eats and Support to the Chester Community" by Michael Klein (January 31, 2022);

"Chefs Lead a Food Giveaway to Help West Philly, and Beyond" by Michael Klein (June 4, 2020);

"KeVen Parker Laid the Groundwork for a New Generation of Black Chefs and Restaurateurs" by Craig LaBan (January 22, 2021);

"Two Philly Chefs and a Ceramics Artist Are Collaborating for a New York Restaurant Series" by Craig LaBan (February 26, 2021); and

"Philadelphia Didn't Become America's Poorest Big City by Chance. Here's How We Fix It" by Inga Saffron (October 13, 2020).

I argue that the articles represent the Black chefs as producing just sustainability through collective agency and community resilience. In particular, I analyze three strategies followed by Black chefs: food security; entrepreneurship; and collaboration, mutual aid, and mentorship. The *Philadelphia Inquirer* articles communicate a narrative of communal care in which Black chefs are central to the improvement of the health and well-being of working-class Black communities through food-related efforts.

American poor and working-class Black communities suffer food apartheid; they have limited access to healthy foods and experience diet-related illness as a result. Food apartheid refers to the way in which food inequity is systemic and structural and working-class communities of color have disproportionately less access to nutritious foods than do their white middle-class counterparts (Brones 2018). However, the chefs featured in these articles intervene in that narrative and make changes in the material conditions that produce food insecurity. Additionally, they center Blackness, community, and philanthropic efforts in their understanding of what makes them chefs. Finally, the articles demonstrate the chefs as collaborators who view working with others as meaningful forms of mutual aid.

Through emphasizing the pillars of food security, entrepreneurship, and collaboration, mutual aid and mentorship, the *Philadelphia Inquirer* articles produce a unique representation of Black chefs and restaurateurs in the greater Philadelphia region. The chefs engage in varied forms of just sustainability to meet the needs of those around them who are suffering, by improving the well-being of community members and engaging local resources to do so. They demonstrate their commitment to improving the lives of Black communities.

Addressing Inequities through Just Sustainability and Collective Agency and Community Resilience

I use Julian Agyeman's (2012) understanding of "just sustainability," a concept that emphasizes the importance of social justice and equity to discussions of sustainability, which have tended to focus primarily on ecology/the environment and/or science. Agyeman, Robert Bullard, and Bob Evans define "just sustainability" as "The need to ensure a better quality of life for all, now and into the future, in a just and equitable manner, whilst living within the limits of supporting ecosystems" (2003, 2). While Agyeman argues that ecology and the environment are important aspects, there must simultaneously be a central focus on issues of social welfare and social well-being for all.

Studies demonstrate that countries and regions with greater social equity also have better environmental standards ("measured in lower concentrations of air and water pollutants, access to clean water and sanitation") as well as stricter environmental policies, less environmental stress, lower infant mortality, and fewer premature deaths (Agyeman, Bullard, and Evans 2003, 1). People of color tend to live in areas that are more environmentally unsafe and experience greater environmental inequities, resulting in health disparities and premature death. In 2021, a report published by the American Lung Association ranked the Philadelphia area as one of the top twenty-five most air-polluted places in the United States. Black children have higher rates of asthma in the region than their white counterparts, and Black communities in Philadelphia suffer worse pollution than white areas (Hill 2021).

Just sustainability considers equity and social justice to be as important as ecological well-being. In his discussion of just sustainability, Agyeman suggests that living within ecosystem limits might also include promoting poverty alleviation, food security, infrastructural developments, and public health (2012). The *Inquirer* articles feature chefs and restaurateurs whose efforts in food security, alternative entrepreneurship, and collaboration and mutual aid emphasize the importance of social welfare while using the resources readily available in local environments. The chefs produce events such as food drives and work with area social and community services to meet the needs of community members.

Additionally, I argue that the method through which the chefs participate in just sustainability is through collective agency and community resilience (CACR). Sociologist and environmental and food studies scholar Monica White defines collective agency and community resilience as practices engaged in by community members to produce self-reliance and self-sufficiency (2018, 8). These methods contest social inequities and counter the lack of state support and funding to meet the needs of community members. I argue that the descriptions of the chefs in the *Philadelphia Inquirer* articles represent a form of collective agency and community resilience, in which Philadelphia-based chefs use resources available to them and work with other local chefs to produce just sustainability through food-related efforts.

In the articles spotlighted, the chefs and restaurateurs engage in social change efforts because they recognize a failure on the part of larger political and economic systems to meet the needs of everyday community members, such as food security and community-based programming. Like the Black Panther Party's Free Breakfast Program, the chefs and restaurateurs represent themselves as social actors who build upon their skills, knowledge, resources, and one another to address racial and economic inequities that produce violence, food insecurity, and limited social resources. In the *Philadelphia Inquirer* articles, chefs raise consciousness about injustices in the greater Philadelphia area through community-based food-related efforts, including local food programming and food giveaways.

The Philadelphia Inquirer: Cultural Studies and Representation

The method I use is a cultural studies analysis, deeply shaped by the Birmingham School of Cultural Studies (Turner 2002). British cultural studies analyzes popular culture (loosely defined) to understand how meanings are shaped for the purpose of analyzing power dynamics, who benefits from those power relations, and who suffers. The goal is also to analyze the experiences of the working class not only to understand their significance, but also to understand popular culture as a site to contest inequities and injustices. I focus on representations in order to develop the meanings that are produced and to understand them within a broader context of power, inequity, justice, and contestation. In this chapter, I analyze how the *Philadelphia Inquirer* represents Black chefs and entrepreneurs at a crucial historical moment when discussions of a "racial reckoning" are in mainstream discourse, which is highly unusual and provides a unique opportunity to bring attention to Black struggles. These articles demonstrate how these social actors build upon this moment of national racial dialogue about systemic racism to produce an account of themselves as building sustainable networks, fighting food insecurity, emphasizing Blackness, and participating in community, philanthropy, and collaborative efforts. By being represented in Philadelphia's premier newspaper, they are potentially able to reach a wide audience and contest the narrative that Black lives are (solely or exclusively) marked by food-related proximity to death. They produce a counternarrative that imagines Black lives as central to and productive of a sustainable future. While they do not use the language of sustainability, I argue that their efforts are a form of just sustainability, as their representation focuses on futurity, food security, creating and strengthening infrastructural development, and enhancing public health.

The *Philadelphia Inquirer* is the premier newspaper for the Philadelphia metropolitan area, reaching an audience of 193,497 on weekdays and 265,181 on Sundays. Founded in 1847 as the *Pennsylvania Inquirer* (Britannica, n.d.), the newspaper covers wide-ranging issues, events, and people in the Philadelphia metropolitan area, also known as the Delaware Valley, which encompasses over six million people (Wilmington Office of Economic Development 2023). The city of Philadelphia itself is the sixth largest city in the United States, in which over one and a half million people reside. Significantly, as of July 2021, 43.6 percent of Philadelphia's population was Black or African American, according to the US Census (US Census 2021a).

Between spring 2020 and spring 2022, the *Inquirer* published a number of articles spotlighting the work of Black Philadelphia-area chefs and restaurateurs. I focus on the aforementioned six articles in particular because they highlight a variety of chefs, community-based efforts, and the specific needs of community members. The article authors are diverse in the types of reporting they do, and therefore they include columnists, food and restaurant writers, and writers on urban design. While they are neither chefs nor African American, I bring attention to their articles because of the way in which they use their platforms to bring attention to the work of regional Black chefs and restauranters. They allow us to examine how the *Philadelphia Inquirer* represents these social actors and their understandings of social justice through the work they do. The *Inquirer* has published numerous articles on Black chefs that address a number of different topics, including restaurant openings, menu tastings, and more. I selected these six articles because they best represent practices of just sustainability of Black chefs in the Philadelphia area. Representations matter not for their truth-value, but significantly for the ways in which they contest unequal distributions of power. The Black chefs and restaurateurs featured here narrate their experiences through the stories they tell to journalists in the *Inquirer* and through their actions. They use the resources at their disposal to make changes in their communities to improve the lives of those around them.

Black Businesses, COVID-19, and Economic Inequities

The COVID-19 pandemic exacerbated inequities for Black business owners and entrepreneurs working in the food industry. In a survey completed at the end of April and early May 2020, soon after the declaration of the pandemic in March 2020, reported by the *New York Times*, only 12 percent of Black and Latinx business owners who applied for federal support postpandemic, most through the Paycheck Protection Program, received the full amount of aid requested. The rest received a partial amount or no monies at all. The federal Paycheck Protection Program had the goal to help small businesses recover from the economic impacts of COVID-19. Almost half of those interviewed thought they would need to permanently close their businesses. According to the *New York Times*, "Two-thirds of respondents sought loans of less than $50,000 through the government's aid program. Nearly half said they had to lay off some employees" (Flitter 2020). Additionally, many business owners had difficulty accessing loans through private banks.

According to *Forbes*, "Between February and April of 2020, black business ownership declined more than 40%, the largest drop across any ethnic group," according to a report by the US House of Representatives Committee on Small Business (Washington 2021). Black businesses were less likely to handle mandated closure due to lack of access to financial relief. Even before the COVID-19 pandemic outbreak, Black people faced many financial inequities and roadblocks. Some of those roadblocks include the racial wealth gap, lack of access to bank loans, and lack of other financial capital. Additionally, many Black communities faced disparities in health care, wealth, employment, and poverty (Brooks 2020). During the pandemic, businesses had to shut down for both the short term and long term, lay off employees, and in many cases forgo an income for months on end. In addition, Black business owners were still growing their businesses back from the 2008 Great Recession (Brooks 2020). Additionally, as one Black business owner said, "Blacks receive business loans at about half the rate of their white counterparts, and when we [Black business owners] do receive loans, it's at higher interest rates." Even before the pandemic, while only 27 percent of white businesses were considered "at risk for financial distress," that percentage was much larger for Black businesses: 58 percent (Washington 2021). During the pandemic, Black businesses came under even greater financial strain with limited funding and staff.

Therefore, Black chefs and restaurateurs in the Philadelphia region have faced significant challenges with opening and maintaining businesses and employment before and during the pandemic. Black chefs who had previously had employment, owned a restaurant, or worked as a high-profile chef in a restaurant found themselves out of work. Nonetheless, many Black chefs in the Philadelphia area chose to invest their time, energy, and money into engaging their vocational skills in or near the city. Though a major metropolitan city, historically Philadelphia has not garnered the same attention for its restaurants and ability to attract high-profile chefs as other East Coast cities, including New York, Boston, and Washington, DC. Yet the *Philadelphia Inquirer* articles demonstrate that Black chefs have indeed been drawn to Philadelphia, particularly in recent years, with a desire to improve social conditions (food-related and otherwise) for Black community members. The police murders of Ahmaud Arbery, Breonna Taylor, and George Floyd, among others, resulted in wide-ranging and urgent calls for investments in Black communities, creating an opportunity for Black chefs and restaurateurs to showcase their skills, knowledge, and efforts in a way they had previously not been able to.

Food Security

The chefs and restaurateurs contest structural racism that produces food insecurity for Black communities. As I have stated elsewhere, "Dietary food and health inequities are forms of structural racism built upon legacies of racial violence, oppression, and marginalization. Racism is the differential access to health, resources, power, and life itself that is normalized into society, privileging whites over communities of color" (Navarro 2021, 285). Black Philadelphians experience a high amount of food insecurity in their communities. Two-thirds of those who are poor in Philadelphia are either Black or Latino (Saffron 2020). Philadelphia has been designated the poorest big city in the United States by news sources (Moselle 2016). Prior to the pandemic, one in five adults in Philadelphia experienced food insecurity (de Groot 2021). As Elizabeth Adams et al. argue, "Food insecurity is defined as limited or uncertain availability of nutritionally adequate food and safe food or ability to acquire adequate foods in socially acceptable ways" (2020, 2056). Within the first few months of the start of COVID-19, there was a 20 percent increase in the number of food-insecure families across the United States who increased purchase and consumption of low-quality, nonperishable foods, desserts and sweets, high-calorie foods, and processed foods (Adams et al. 2020). According to Philabundance, the Philadelphia-based non-profit food justice organization, by March 2021, families of color had been deeply impacted by COVID-19, which produced greater hunger, a greater need for emergency foods, and lack of access to nutritious foods (Philabundance 2021). Research from the food justice nonprofit Feeding America shows that Philadelphia County had a 14.4 percent rate of food insecurity while contiguous Chester County had 6.3 percent food insecurity in October 2021 (6ABC 2021).

The *Philadelphia Inquirer* articles highlight Black chefs who use food security as a strategy for just sustainability, collective agency, and community resilience. They work to ensure that those who do not have safe and enduring food access have nutritious options available. For example, on June 4, 2020, the *Inquirer* published an article titled "Chefs Lead a Food Giveaway to Help West Philly, and Beyond" (Klein 2020). The article showcases a group of Black chefs who promote food security by supporting food giveaways for dried goods, toiletries, and basic needs. The chefs include Elijah Milligan, Stephanie Willis, Aziza Young, Kurt Evans, and

Omar Tate. According to the article, "Between the coronavirus and the protests, 'there's essentially a war going on outside,' said Milligan. 'We're chefs. We want to give back to the community. We wanted to do something. We all know people who can't find groceries or medicine in their neighborhoods.' . . . 'We don't condone violence,' said Milligan. 'We also understand the anger, too.' " Milligan argues that the chefs' goal is to use resources available to them to produce both food security and a sense of community resilience to the police killings of Black people. The group's giveaways fed more than six hundred families during their first food drive or "food activation" in June 2020 (Cooper 2022).

A later *Inquirer* article dated January 31, 2022, "Vittles Food Hall Provides a Home to Everybody Eats and Support to the Chester Community," announced the February 5, 2022, opening of Vittles Food Hall in Chester, Pennsylvania (Klein 2022). As of July 1, 2021, the city of Chester was 70.9 percent African American, with a median income of $32,867, and 30.4 percent of the population was living in poverty (US Census 2021b). According to the Chester County Food Bank, more than 40,000 Chester County residents are food insecure, and it seems very likely that this percentage is much higher for the city of Chester itself, which is primarily working class (Chester County Food Bank 2023). Vittles Hall is run by Everybody Eats Philly, a Philadelphia-based nonprofit group run by Black chefs focused on ending hunger in community-based settings. Located approximately eighteen miles outside of Philadelphia, Vittles Food Hall builds on the work Everybody Eats first started in West Philadelphia. According to the *Inquirer* article, "Vittles will serve two purposes: It will provide low-cost food to people in an underserved community and become a home base for Everybody Eats Philly." Now open, Vittles offers soul food, Mexican food, salads, seafood, and breakfast food at low cost. Everybody Eats Philly is run by renowned Black chefs, including Stephanie Willis, Kurt Evans, Aziza Young, Gregory Headen, and Malik Ali. Everybody Eats' primary goal is to reduce hunger in the greater Philadelphia area. Chef Kurt Evans states, "[Vittles Hall] helps us be able to give communities access to healthy food that they deserve. That's a basic human right. We believe that everyone should have access to this type of food." Building on Agyeman's concept of just sustainability, Everybody Eats is an organization that promotes poverty alleviation through increased food access and infrastructural development (Vittles Hall), two central components of just sustainability. These efforts promote food security and work to improve the public health of those in Philadelphia and Chester through community and collaborative efforts.

Another *Inquirer* article, "He's Fed Thousands of Philly Kids and Taught Hundreds How to Cook, but Setbacks Are Keeping Him from What He Loves" by Stephanie Farr (2022), spotlights a Black Philadelphia chef focusing on food security named Ariq Barrett. Barrett created and sponsored several child-centered food security programs. Like Everybody Eats Philly, Barrett saw a need for food distribution, particularly for children. Barrett's work is showcased in the January 19 article (Barrett had become ill and was no longer able to participate in the activities with which he'd previously been involved). According to the article, Barrett, who lived in the Kensington neighborhood of Philadelphia in March 2020 when COVID-19 struck, stated, "Kids were out there asking for money . . . I was like, 'Kids should not have to be doing this to eat!' " He soon began making boxed lunches for children from his home and driving all over the city distributing them. Ultimately, needing help and space, he found a partner in Laura Lacy, who offered space in her brewery, Attic Brewing Company in the Germantown neighborhood of Philadelphia, for him to create his boxed lunches. Ultimately, Barrett called the enterprise Kidz Meals on Wheels, and it was comprised dozens of volunteers who made and delivered more than twelve thousand boxed lunches between March and July 2020 (Farr 2022).

For these chefs, food security is an integral component to producing equitable and sustainable communities, which they use their agency and resources to promote. They recognize the importance of food security as a means of social justice, particularly for Black communities that have been subjugated by police violence and other forms of systemic racism. In the following section, I analyze how Black chefs and restaurateurs engage in entrepreneurship by defining the construction of "chef" as racialized, community oriented, and socially conscious. In doing so, they underscore improving quality of life, justice, and equity—thus, promoting core elements of just sustainability.

Entrepreneurship and Just Sustainability: Defining Being a Chef through Blackness, Community Development, and Philanthropy

The writers of the *Philadelphia Inquirer* articles narrate the chefs as social actors. The chefs define their roles through their relationships to Black communities, community-based projects, and raising political and social awareness. In other words, the articles describe how the chefs find a great deal of value in using their craft to benefit others and meeting the needs of their community members. In the discussion below, chefs communicate the importance of addressing community needs and improving representation of African American and West African communities in Philadelphia.

Chefs draw attention to Black experiences in particular, engaging food to broaden conversations about inequity, justice, and racialized violence. For example, chef Kurt Evans, who owns Down North Pizza, a restaurant in the North Philadelphia neighborhood of Strawberry Mansion, is an outspoken advocate of abolishing prisons, drawing attention to the disproportionate number of Black people incarcerated. Evans employs people who were previously incarcerated as a means to promote greater equity and reduce recidivism (LaBan 2021a). Additionally, Chef Omar Tate argues that Philadelphia communities of color need better and more resources for community support: "'What really needs to happen is that city, state, and federal governments need to pinpoint black and brown organizations doing the groundwork and invest in those,'" he said. 'The thing people are not asking these communities is: What do you need?' . . . 'It's about bringing change to the neighborhoods,' says Tate" (LaBan 2021a). Tate's comment emphasizes the importance of meeting the needs of community members and promoting a greater sense of equity. In addition to Tate's commitment to community service, he worked in an upscale restaurant with the same goal of bringing attention to the experiences of Black community members. As chef in residence at the distinguished New York restaurant Blue Hill at Stone Barns in 2021, he served a nine-course meal on "black existence" for $250 per person. He did this in part to bring attention to police violence against Black bodies (LaBan 2021b). Tate understands food as activism: the culinary is a form of knowledge production about Black experiences. Additionally, Tate and his wife, Cybille St. Aude-Tate, are seeking sufficient funding to open a community center, named after their pop-up dinner in West Philadelphia, Honeysuckle, which was recognized as Pop-Up of the Year in 2020 by *Esquire* (Stone Barns Center for Food and Agriculture, n.d.).

I argue that these chefs emphasize their roles as "chefs" through Blackness as not only African American experiences, but African-diasporic experiences as well. Shola Olunloyo was the very first chef in residence at Blue Hill at Stone Barns, who highlighted Yoruba Nigerian foods. Currently based in Philadelphia, Olunloyo has worked as a private chef and consultant. Recently, conversations around cultural appropriation and recognition of African foods have become mainstream through Chef Adjepong, one of the three finalists on Bravo's *Top Chef* in 2019, who introduced viewers to Ghanaian cuisine. It was the first time in *Top Chef*'s sixteen-season run that West African food was featured on the show, and many commented on the lack of awareness of the other chefs and judges about West African foods (Williams 2021). A *Philadelphia Inquirer* article titled "In Search of Jollof Rice with Chef Shola Olunloyo as West African Flavors Surge in Philly and Beyond," published on December 3, 2021, demonstrates the attention now being brought to West African foods as a significant part of the Philadelphia experience (LaBan 2021c). This increased representation of West African foods enhances just sustainability by giving value to diverse cuisines and their Black purveyors.

Ariq Barrett expands the definition of chef by focusing on the needs of children in the Philadelphia area. As previously mentioned, Barrett created Kidz Meals on Wheels to distribute food to hungry children in Philadelphia. Barrett, trained through Le Cordon Bleu, also originated Black Kidz Can Cook in 2015 (initially Black Boyz Can Cook), a summer camp for children to learn about nutrition, cooking, and community service, which has served over three hundred children (Farr 2022). Chef Barrett's emphasis on meeting the needs of children of color through philanthropic efforts enhances just sustainability's cornerstones of improving quality of life and public health for disadvantaged local residents.

In each of the examples described above, the chefs understand their work as focusing on the needs and representation of local Black communities, both African American and West African, through community-based efforts and/or through philanthropic pursuits to improve the daily lives of community members. In doing so, they work to impact the long-term outcome of those they serve as well as how the *Philadelphia Inquirer*'s readership understands what it means to be a "chef." In the following section, I highlight the collaborative and mutual aid efforts of Black chefs and restaurateurs in the greater Philadelphia region.

Just Sustainability through Collaboration, Mutual Aid, and Mentorship

The *Philadelphia Inquirer* articles emphasize that the Black chefs featured in their stories focus on working together to meet the needs of community members. Additionally, mutual aid efforts are rooted upon the principle that everyday people are responsible for and accountable to one another. Mutual aid efforts point to systemic inequities and the limits in federal or state support in meeting the needs of everyday people. As Monica White points out, collective agency, community resilience, and mutual aid produce a better and more vibrant future (2018).

As previously mentioned, chefs have engaged in various collaborations with local chefs, artisans, business owners, and city services. The June 4, 2020, *Inquirer* article, "Chefs Lead a Food Giveaway to Help West Philly, and Beyond," describes chefs who not only worked together for the pop-up dinner series, Cooks for the Culture, but also for food giveaways; they included Elijah Milligan, Stephanie Willis, Aziza Young, Kurt Evans, and Omar Tate (Klein 2020). Several chefs from Cooks for the Culture are members of the previously discussed organization Everybody Eats, which seeks to promote food security in the greater Chester region and created Vittles Food Hall in Chester. In both examples, the chefs' efforts to produce greater food security are represented as communal responsibility and as shared benefit for residents of Chester and Philadelphia.

As previously discussed, Chefs Olunloyo and Omar Tate both collaborated, independently, with Blue Hill at Stone Barns restaurant in New York to raise awareness of Black experiences and Black foods. They build on the concept of just sustainability through collaboration and the use of local ingredients. Owner Dan Barber wanted to use the chef in residence program at the Stone Barns Center for Food and Agriculture in Pocantino Hills, New York, to provide informative and educational experiences that showcase a variety of lived experiences, particularly non-Eurocentric experiences. As the first chef in residence in January–February 2021, Olunloyo collaborated with a ceramic artist named Greg Moore from Glenside, Pennsylvania, a suburb just outside of the northwestern section of the city. By hiring a Philadelphia-area artist, Dan Barber utilized local labor and resources, emphasizing just sustainability's focus on localism as well as social justice. Moore created a large black bowl to present one course of Olunloyo's Nigerian tasting menu for $125 per person in January 2020, which included "carrot soup, akara bean fritters, and suya-spiced beef tartare on a rice cracker with crumbled kuli-kuli peanut cake" (LaBan 2021b). (The current average cost for dinner at Blue Hill is $348–$398 per person.) Focusing on locally sourced foods, Olunloyo replaced West African ingredients that were not readily available in the Hudson Valley with local ingredients for spices, baking, and roasting. As the second chef in residence at Blue Hill at Stone Barns from February to March 2020, Tate also collaborated with Glenside ceramic artist Gregg Moore to turn a piece of concrete from in front of his mother's house in West Philadelphia into a plate for the first portion of a seven-course dinner series Tate called Black Lung, to bring attention to police violence against black bodies. The first course of the seven-course meal was "the physical representation of 'a terrarium of black breath,'" a salad called Black Lung: "Its contrast of heat against the delicacy of greens and hard materials imprinted from Tate's home is intended to create tension—a 'visceral and empathetic response, an acknowledgment of life . . . to really bring people onto the ground that I walk every day'" (LaBan 2021b). I argue that just sustainability is present in the work of both of these chefs. Olunloyo's use of local foods and ingredients in his dishes builds on just sustainability by emphasizing the need to improve well-being for those who experience suffering or oppression while living within the limits of the local environmental resources. Tate, on the other hand, focuses on uplifting Black communities through his food activism and work with a local Philadelphia-area ceramic artist.

I build on Agyeman's concept by arguing that among these chefs, mentoring is a key component of just sustainability. It enables chefs to share knowledge, promote improved social welfare, and meet local needs. Mentoring is represented as a significant part of the collaborative experience for several chefs. The January 19, 2022, *Inquirer* article on Chef Ariq Barrett describes his mentoring of Philadelphia-area children, which empowers them to learn self-sufficiency, cooperation, and healthy food practices (Farr 2022). In addition to his collaborative work with Laura Lacy on Kidz Meals on Wheels, Chef Barrett volunteered with the Philadelphia Public School District and Education Works to teach children to prepare food at home in the event that their parents became ill or were not available. Barrett also worked with Forget Me Knot Youth Services, which offers transitional housing and programs for kids. In working with local community services to meet the needs of Philadelphia-area children, Barrett improves well-being for community members through food-based programming and utilizing local support services. Mentoring is also discussed in the *Inquirer* article on KeVen Parker published January 22, 2021 (LaBan 2021a). Parker, who owned Ms. Tootsie's, a highly respected soul food restaurant on Philadelphia's famous South Street, mentored other regional Black chefs, including Hannah Ahzai, Kurt Evans, Joy Parham, and Aaliyah Al-Amin. He provided advice as these chefs considered expanding their businesses, he served as a role model for the possibilities of what a Black chef could accomplish in Philadelphia, and he was a well-respected example of Black excellence in the culinary field. His famed Ms. Tootsie drew well-known celebrities, including Patti LaBelle. Chef Kurt Evans states of Parker's influence on him, "If you were going downtown and you were black in the 2000s, Ms. Tootsie's was the spot," says Evans. "You could get dressed up and go down to South Street and eat soul food. And for the black community that was huge . . . because representation is really important . . . I can have a restaurant downtown one day, because I've seen it" (LaBan 2021a). This quotation demonstrates the importance of seeing oneself in the work of others who share a similar background. Chef's Parker's mentoring of other chefs produced an exchange of knowledge and improved equity in business ownership by demonstrating to other Black chefs that they, too, could one day own their own restaurants.

The Black chefs and restaurateurs represented here focus on the unique needs of people and communities in an effort to care for others. They produce a sense of collectivity, collaboration, and mentorship as mutual aid efforts that help meet the needs of children, adults, and other chefs. It is through uniting their varied skills and knowledge that the chefs are able to improve the lives of Philadelphia-area community members.

Conclusion

The Black chefs and restaurateurs in the *Philadelphia Inquirer* series emphasize food security, entrepreneurship, collaboration, mutual aid, and mentorship as significant strategies in their food efforts in Philadelphia and greater Philadelphia area. Philadelphia has experienced crucial negative impacts to Black food security and Black food businesses since the start of the COVID-19 pandemic. The three themes that emerge from the *Philadelphia Inquirer* articles communicate that Black chefs and restaurateurs continue to use their resources, skills, and knowledge to meet the needs of community members, redefine the meaning of "chef," and work in collaboration with one another.

In doing so, the *Philadelphia Inquirer* articles represent the chefs and restaurateurs as participating in just sustainability through collective agency and community resilience. Just sustainability considers the importance of social justice alongside environmental needs. Food security is one means of producing an improved environment for community members. Defining entrepreneurship through Blackness, community development, and philanthropy is a method of improving quality of life for others through community-based efforts. Lastly, through collaboration, mutual aid, and mentorship, the chefs work to meet the needs of present and future generations while seeking to better social welfare. Food justice is one effort in a larger effort toward social justice. The narratives in the *Inquirer* articles exemplify how the chefs and restaurateurs improve social well-being for those most marginalized. The chefs and restaurateurs use the resources readily available to them to ensure that community members, now and into the future, are well cared for. This form of collective agency and community resilience illuminates how Black communities come together in solidarity and community-based efforts in moments of struggle.

Analyzing representations in this study allows us to see how Black chefs and restaurateurs are narrated, particularly at this time of greater attention to racial violence, racial inequities, and racial justice. Often, studies of representations in newspapers demonstrate the ways in which newspapers frame oppressed communities in problematic, demeaning, and one-dimensional ways. It is difficult to know why the six authors of the articles discussed in this paper chose to write about the Black chefs they center. It is possible that they have a genuine interest in highlighting the experiences of Black chefs as they relate to just sustainability, out of a sense of equity and justice. It is equally possible that they (and the *Inquirer* in general) recognize this critical moment of racial dialogue as one in which they need to represent the contributions, experiences, and excellence of Black communities in the hopes of gaining a larger readership. My interest lies less in the motivations of the individual chefs and more in the possibilities that are presented when representations focus on the collaborative, community-oriented, and racially conscious work of the chefs they discuss. These representations demonstrate that Philadelphia-area chefs and restaurateurs engage just sustainability through their meaningful and continuous food-related efforts.

References

Adams, Elizabeth L., Laura J. Caccavale, Danyel Smith, and Melanie K. Bean. 2020. "Food Insecurity, the Home Environment, and Parent Feeding Practices in the Era of COVID-19." *Obesity: A Research Journal* 28 (11): 2056–63.

Agyeman, Julian, Robert Bullard, and Bob Evans, eds. 2003. *Just Sustainabilities: Development in an Unequal World*. Cambridge, MA: MIT Press.

Agyeman, Julian. 2012. "Just Sustainabilities." https://julianagyeman.com/2012/09/21 /just-sustainabilities/.

Brittanica. n.d. "The Philadelphia Inquirer." https://www.britannica.com/topic /The-Philadelphia-Inquirer.

Brones, Anna. 2018. "Food Apartheid: The Root of the Problem with America's Groceries." *Guardian* [Manchester], May 15. https://www.theguardian.com /society/2018/may/15/food-apartheid-food-deserts-racism-inequality-america -karen-washington-interview.

Brooks, Rodney A. 2020. "More than Half of Black-Owned Businesses May Not Survive COVID-19." *National Geographic*, July 17. https://www.nationalgeographic .com/history/article/black-owned-businesses-may-not-survive-covid-19.

Chester County Food Bank. 2023. "A Look at Food Security in Chester County." Accessed June 10, 2024. https://chestercountyfoodbank.org/a-look-at-food -insecurity-in-chester-county/.

Cooper, Kenny. 2022. "Everybody Eats Philly Opens Its First Location, in Chester. The Mission to Fight Food Insecurity Is the Same." WHYY, February 18. https:// whyy.org/articles/everybody-eats-philly-opens-its-first-location-in-chester-the -mission-to-fight-food-insecurity-is-the-same/.

de Groot, Kristen. 2021. "Fighting Food Insecurity." *Penn Today*, December 20. https://penntoday.upenn.edu/news/fighting-food-insecurity-fox-leadership -program-penn.

Farr, Stephanie. 2022. "He's Fed Thousands of Philly Kids and Taught Hundreds How to Cook, but Setbacks Are Keeping Him from What He Loves." *Philadelphia Inquirer*, January 19. https://www.inquirer.com/life/ariq-barrett-black-kidz-can -cook-20220119.html.

Flitter, Emily. 2020. "Few Minority-Owned Businesses Got the Relief they Asked For." *New York Times*, May 18. https://www.nytimes.com/2020/05/18/business /minority-businesses-coronavirus-loans.html.

Hill, Grant. 2021. "Why the Air Quality in Philly Might Be Worse than We Know." WHYY, May 2, 2021. https://whyy.org/articles/why-the-air-quality-in-philly -might-be-worse-than-we-know/.

Klein, Michael. 2020. "Chefs Lead a Food Giveaway to Help West Philly, and Beyond." *Philadelphia Inquirer*, June 4. https://www.inquirer.com/food/philadelphia-chefs -give-away-food-west-philadelphia-elijah-milligan-20200604.html.

——. 2022. "Vittles Food Hall Provides a Home to Everybody Eat and Support to the Chester Community." *Philadelphia Inquirer*, January 31. https://www .inquirer.com/food/vittles-food-hall-everybody-eats-chester-20220131.html.

LaBan, Craig. 2021a. "KeVen Parker Laid the Groundwork for a New Generation of Black Chefs and Restaurateurs." *Philadelphia Inquirer*, January 22. https://www .inquirer.com/food/craig-laban/keven-parker-philly-black-owned-restaurants -chefs-20210122.html.

——. 2021b. "Two Philly Chefs and a Ceramics Artist are Collaborating for a New York Restaurant Series." *Philadelphia Inquirer*, February 26. https://www .inquirer.com/food/craig-laban/chefs-omar-tate-shola-olunloyo-collaborate -with-philly-ceramics-artist-stone-barn-restaurant-series-20210226.html.

——. 2021c. "In Search of Jollof Rice with Chef Shola Olunloyo as West African Flavors Surge in Philly and Beyond." *Philadelphia Inquirer*, December 3.

Moselle, Aaron. 2016. "How Philadelphia Became the Poorest Big City in the United States." WBUR, July 29. https://www.wbur.org/hereandnow/2016/07 /29/philadelphia-poorest-big-city.

Navarro, Marilisa. 2021. "Radical Recipe: Veganism as Anti-Racism." In *The Routledge Handbook of Vegan Studies*, edited by Laura Wright, 282–94. New York: Routledge.

Odoms-Young, Angela, and Marino A. Bruce. 2018. "Examining the Impact of Structural Racism on Food Insecurity." *Family and Community Health* 41 (2): S3–S6.

Philabundance. 2021. "Impact of COVID-19 on Communities of Color," March 26. https://www.philabundance.org/impact-of-covid-19-on-communities-of-color/.

Saffron, I. 2020. "Philadelphia Didn't Become America's Poorest Big City by Chance. Here's How We Fix It." *Philadelphia Inquirer*, October 13. https://www.inquirer .com/business/philadelphia-poverty-unemployment-racism-education-upskilling -20201013.html&outputType=app-web-view.

Stone Barns Center for Food and Agriculture. n.d. "The Chefs." Accessed May 18, 2022. https://www.stonebarnscenter.org/chef-in-residence-at-stone-barns/.

6ABC. 2021. "Local Nonprofit Speaks on Difficulty to Keep Up with Food Demand Increase amid the Pandemic," October 15. https://6abc.com/philabundance -nonprofit-organization-food-insecurity-covid-19-pandemic/11084778/.

Turner, Graeme. 2002. *British Cultural Studies: An Introduction*. 3rd ed. Oxfordshire, UK: Routledge.

United States Census. 2021a. "Quick Facts Philadelphia County, Pennsylvania." Accessed May 18, 2022. https://www.census.gov/quickfacts/philadelphiacountypennsylvania.

———. 2021b. "Quick Facts Chester City, Pennsylvania." Accessed May 18, 2022. https://www.census.gov/quickfacts/chestercitypennsylvania.

Washington, Kemberly. 2021. "Covid-19 Has Had a Disproportionate Financial Impact on Black Small Businesses." *Forbes*, January 3. https://www.forbes.com /advisor/personal-finance/covid19-financial-impact-on-black-businesses/.

White, Monica. 2018. *Freedom Farmers: Agricultural Resistance and the Black Freedom Movement*. Chapel Hill, NC: University of North Carolina Press.

Williams, Vonnie. 2019. "Why Some 'Top Chef' Viewers Want the Show to Expand Its Palate." *Food and Wine*, March 18. https://www.foodandwine.com/news/top -chef-judges-diversity-representation-reaction-eric-adjepong.

Wilmington Office of Economic Development. 2023. "Delaware Valley." Accessed June 10, 2024. https://www.choosewilmingtonde.org/site-selection/regional -profile/p/v/data/item/915/delaware-valley.

CHAPTER THIRTEEN

A Cooks' Alliance

Building Food Awareness and Cultural
Sustainability in Kenya

MICHELE FILIPPO FONTEFRANCESCO
AND DAURO MATTIA ZOCCHI

Introduction

The achievement of sustainability, and specifically cultural sustainability—
the protection and maintenance of cultural values, practices, and knowledge,
and their transmission to future generations (Throsby 1997)—and environmental sustainability—a condition that allows human society to satisfy its
needs while neither exceeding the capacity of its supporting ecosystems
nor diminishing biological diversity (Morelli 2011)—is an open challenge
for the Ho.Re.Ca. (hotel, restaurant, and café) sector worldwide (Zocchi et
al. 2021). Chefs play a crucial role in this process as actors of change. Since
the second half of the twentieth century, the role of the chef has undergone
great transformations. While in the past these professionals were almost
exclusively relegated to the kitchen, they have progressively gained visibility
in the public sphere and become potentially crucial actors in supporting a
transition toward more sustainable food systems (Pereira et al. 2019). In
other words, chefs have been key stakeholders in promoting "social and economic justice by transforming food habits" (Counihan 2019, 1) and pursuing
"the vision of an ecologically sound, economically viable, and socially just
system of food and agriculture" (Hassanein 2003, 84).

Chefs with an international following and reputation, such as Jamie
Oliver, Alice Waters, and Gastón Acurio, are central actors in this evolution. Better known as "celebrity chefs," they have revolutionized views
of cooks and cookery and have contributed to the improvement of the
profession's status (Johnston and Goodman 2015). Moving from being

business operators to opinion leaders and sociocultural mediators, chefs have brought the restaurant sector closer to the world of social entrepreneurship (Navarro-Dols and González-Pernía 2020). In several regional and national contexts, they have championed relevant campaigns aimed at fostering biodiversity conservation and food sustainability. For instance, celebrity chefs belonging to the so-called Peruvian Gastronomic Revolution, including Gastón Acurio, have played a pivotal role in contributing to the rediscovery of neglected and marginalized foods and the promotion of local culinary heritage, by introducing formerly disregarded Andean and Amazonian products and ingredients in global gastronomic settings (Matta 2013, 36). Similarly, Freya Higgins-Desbiolles, Emily Moskwa, and Stuart Gifford (2014) emphasized the impact of initiatives, such as healthy school meals campaigns in the United Kingdom promoted by Jamie Oliver and Alice Waters's Edible Schoolyard project in the United States, in shaping the eating habits of consumers toward more environmentally friendly and ethical choices.

In recent years, scholars have extensively discussed the role of these professionals, their ethical contradictions (Garcia 2013; Markowitz 2012; McDonell 2019; Sammells 2019), and their controversial role in the rescue and promotion of indigenous food cultures that risks triggering new forms of culinary colonialism (Cox Hall 2020; Cusack 2000; Grey and Newman 2018). In so doing, they have opened a space for inquiry concerning the role that chefs outside the mediasphere (e.g., those working in school canteens as well as traditional and street-food cooks) can have in building a more resilient and effective approach to sustainability and promotion of local gastronomies, especially in the Global South.

While scholars have particularly explored the trends in South America (e.g., Matta 2019), scarce attention has been devoted to the African continent (Pereira et al. 2019). In this respect, the chapter offers its contribution focusing on Kenya, where initial research has concentrated on the role of the catering sector (schools, canteens, and restaurants) in promoting agricultural change (Mwema and Crewett 2019). Here, we examine its role in fostering cultural and environmental sustainability.

In 2020, according to the International Monetary Fund, Kenya had a population of about fifty-five million people and a national GDP of roughly $110 billion. The country has been a forerunner in the development of tourism in Eastern Africa (Dieke 1991; Sindiga 1999). However, little attention has been given to its culinary traditions and the development of the restaurant sector, until very recently (e.g., KBC 2022). The panorama of the Kenyan catering sector in the 2020s still presented a gastronomic offer deeply rooted in the Western, Franco-British tradition (Zocchi and Fontefrancesco 2020). It continued a colonial legacy that has been clear since the early years after independence when the first Kenyan cookbooks were published, and the ideal Kenyan cuisine was represented through dishes such as horseradish sauce, dandy pudding, potato salad, and lemon cake (Members of St. Andrew's Church Women's Guild 1987). However, in the past decade, the sector as a whole has discovered the importance of local food heritage as a resource for economic development (Zocchi and Fontefrancesco 2020). Despite that, little attention is given to the interplay between the daily activities of "less highly regarded" actors (Ayora-Diaz 2012) in the culinary fields and their potentially crucial role in fostering more sustainable food systems.

This chapter aims at shedding light on this crucial aspect by exploring the link between cooks and the Slow Food movement, focusing on the Slow Food Cooks' Alliance and its role in terms of conceptions, practices, and the communication of social and cultural sustainability. Overall, the chapter presents the Slow Food movement and the Slow Food Cooks' Alliance in Kenya, based on ethnographic work conducted between 2018 and 2021. Exploring the life stories of the cooks, it points out how these gastronomic actors are able to activate bottom-up processes of culinary change aimed at promoting a culture of sustainability, thus providing a contribution to the decolonization of the local foodscape by reintroducing products and foodways marginalized after the colonial period.

The Research

The present chapter is based on ethnographic work conducted in Kenya by the authors between 2018 and 2021. Specifically, the study was conducted through desk research, fieldwork activities (February 2019 and January–February 2020), and remote interviews (June–August 2021). The research took place within the framework of the Sustainable Agri-Food System Strategies (SASS) project, which was funded by the Italian Ministry of University and Research. The project explored the promotion of traditional food products, and specifically African leafy vegetables, among local communities with a specific focus on Nakuru County, a multiethnic region situated in the former Rift Valley Province and an emerging Kenyan agricultural and tourist hub (Rampa et al. 2021). The authors were directly involved in this project, conducting field research aimed at documenting Kenyan food heritage (Barstow and Zocchi 2018), investigating the dynamics underpinning the commercialization of traditional foods (Fontefrancesco and Zocchi 2020) and exploring the role covered by Kenyan cuisine in the regional catering sector (Zocchi and Fontefrancesco 2020). The ethnographic gaze also explored those grassroots initiatives that supported the production, transformation, and commercialization of traditional foods. Particular attention was given to the case study of Slow Food Kenya, the national branch of the international Slow Food movement, which was established in the country in the early 2000s.

Slow Food is a grassroots global organization. It was founded in 1989 in Italy to counteract the negative impact of the industrialization and standardization of food systems on regional food cultures and traditions (Petrini 2003). From its beginnings as a national movement, Slow Food has expanded its reach to become a global player in the safeguarding and promotion of food and biocultural heritage, tackling issues such as food sovereignty and the civil rights of rural and Indigenous communities. In over thirty years of activity, it has spread worldwide, with over one hundred thousand members and 1,500 local chapters in 160 countries. By 2017, the Slow Food network was present in thirty-five African countries, among which the Kenyan chapter is one of the most active and widespread (Slow Food 2017).

Slow Food supports local small-scale production through a combination of interconnected initiatives, involving consumers, farmers, chefs, and sellers. The most relevant initiatives include the Ark of Taste (Barstow and Zocchi 2018, 14), a project aimed at documenting and cataloging endangered food products and associated heritage, and the Presidium, an initiative targeted at rescuing and promoting marginalized food products and endangered foodscapes and assisting producers in the creation of local associations/cooperatives, as well as with the establishment of production protocols, capacity-building activities, and alternative marketing channels (Siniscalchi 2013). Moreover, since its inception, Slow Food has been working to enhance the relationships between food producers and actors in the Ho.Re.Ca. sector. It is within this framework that the Slow Food Cooks' Alliance was created. The project consists of a network of cooks promoting a new form of catering, the "Osteria Nuova" (Capatti 2000), which wants "the restaurant to be an affordable place of conviviality and community life, and an interface between the consumer and the local terroir that promotes a gastronomic encounter, based mainly on local products and traditional recipes" (Fontefrancesco and Corvo 2020, 771).

Kenya is the seat of one of the four Slow Food Cooks' Alliance branches active in Africa. For this reason, the research was intended to explore this initiative and its actors. With this goal, the fieldwork involved the completion in 2020 of an interview campaign based on the life history method (Bertaux and Kohli 1984) aimed at documenting the life, works, and expectations of the Slow Food Cooks' Alliance members. The interviews shed light on the principles that drive their (daily) working activities, the reasons and expectations behind their involvement in the Slow Food Cooks' Alliance, and the potential contribution of the project to issues connected to the sustainability and inclusion of the local foodscape. In addition, at the end of 2021, we conducted follow-up phone interviews with representatives of the Slow Food Kenya network to further explore the evolution of the Kenyan Slow Food Cooks' Alliance and the future trajectories of this initiative.

The Slow Food Cooks' Alliance in Kenya

Founded in 2004, Slow Food Kenya brings together sixty food communities from different areas across the country, with Nakuru County as the main center of the movement. The initiatives of the association have focused on the defense of food biodiversity, sustainable agriculture, and the promotion of local and traditional food. Through this, several traditional products were documented for the first time (seventy-five included in the Ark of Taste database; see Barstow and Zocchi 2018) and, for some of them, Slow Food supported their commercialization through the Presidium project. Following the establishment of the Presidium project in Kenya, the commercial distribution of lambs from the Molo area (an heirloom sheep breed), Mau Forest dried nettles (a powder made from dry leaves of *Urtica massaica*), Lare pumpkin (fresh fruits and flour made from a local ecotype of pumpkin cultivated in the Njoro district), and Ogiek honey (from the Mau Forest) has progressively expanded. Some restaurants and school canteens (both local and regional ones) have introduced these products in their menus and meals. At the same time, different activities were launched in order to support food education in rural communities and in schools. Specifically, through the 10,000 Gardens in Africa project, 480 community and school gardens were opened across the country (Slow Food 2022a). On this bedrock, the Slow Food Cooks' Alliance initiative was launched, adapting the international model to the local milieu.

On a global level, the Slow Food Cooks' Alliance focuses on the restaurant sector and consists of a network of cooks promoting local, sustainable, and "good, clean, and fair food." The path toward the development of this network started in 2006, during the second edition of Terra Madre (a biennial conference of food producers, chefs, and activists held in Turin), when the key role of chefs in the safeguarding of food biodiversity and promotion of gastronomic heritage was highlighted. In 2009, the Slow Food Cooks' Alliance was officially launched in Italy. Over the course of 2012, the initiative started in the Netherlands and Morocco and, as of 2022, it existed in twenty-five countries, with over one thousand cooks involved (Slow Food 2022b).

According to the Slow Food Cooks' Alliance manifesto (Slow Food 2015), members of the Alliance should develop direct relationships with food producers, providing visibility to small-scale farmers and artisanal food producers and their efforts to preserve traditional dishes, knowledge, and techniques. To this end, in their menus, they should include products linked to the Slow Food network through Presidia, Ark of Taste products, food communities, and Earth Markets; and buy local ingredients that are produced with respect for the environment, landscape, and animal welfare. Moreover, they should promote local gastronomic practices and their associated heritage, cooking traditional recipes but also interpreting the tradition according to their creativity. In so doing, they should aim at fostering more sustainable production and consumption choices among their customers, workers, and suppliers (minimizing the environmental impact of their activities and reducing food waste). Overall, members of the Slow Food Cooks' Alliance should contribute, concretely and with everyday actions, to the support of Slow Food international campaigns regarding food biodiversity and the activities of the Terra Madre network.

The Slow Food Cooks' Alliance is organized on a national level and generally involves cooks with heterogeneous backgrounds active in different restaurant facilities (from simple street-food stalls to more sophisticated bistros and hotels). In the case of Kenya, however, the organization of the Slow Food Cooks' Alliance took a slightly different and more inclusive direction. "Everyone should enjoy local, nutritious food. It is not just about restaurants," explained John Kariuki, president of Slow Food Kenya. "For this reason, we wanted to involve not just chefs who work in restaurants but also cooks that work in school canteens and with community restaurants. Moreover, we wanted to make stronger the link with the local producers." The attempt to strengthen the relations between small-scale producers and actors in the catering sector has been one of the main reasons underpinning the establishment of the Slow Food Cooks' Alliance in Kenya.

The initiative was launched in 2016 by the national Slow Food association headquarters, and by 2021 it involved eleven restaurants and similar facilities from Nakuru, Kiambu, and Nairobi counties (see Table 2 and Figure 1). The network comprises chefs and cooks, who

Table 2: List of the Slow Food Kenya Cooks' Alliance chefs in 2021

Chef	Location	Type of restaurant	Name of the restaurant
Nicholas Kariuki	Molo, Nakuru County	Canteen	Baraka Agricultural College
Hezekiah Mwene Magitu	Naivasha, Nakuru County	Canteen	Naivasha Basin Sustainability Initiative
Ezekiel Mwathi Manyara	Nakuru, Nakuru County	Restaurant	Emboita Hotel
Martin Muhia Nyambura	Nairobi	Canteen	European Union Embassy Restaurant
Paul Njenga	Nakuru, Nakuru County	Restaurant	Hillcourt Resort and Spa Nakuru
Mary Chepkemoi Ondolo	Mariashoni, Nakuru County	Restaurant	Mariashoni Guest House
Beatrice Kanini Njeru	Embu, Embu County	Canteen	Ministry of Agriculture Embu County
Charles Mundia Waweru	Gatukuyu, Kiambu County	Restaurant	Organic Slow Food Restaurant
Francis Maina Wachira	Nakuru, Nakuru County	Canteen	Rift Valley Institute of Business Studies
Nellym Maritim	Eldoret, Uasin Gishu County	Canteen	University of Eldoret
Lesiamon Ole Sempele	Nairobi	Restaurant	Nyama Mama

The table indicates the names of the chefs, as well as the locations, typologies, and names of their businesses. *Credit: Dauro Mattia Zocchi.*

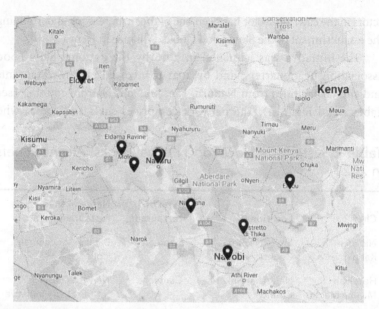

Figure 1. Location of the businesses associated with Kenya Slow Food Cooks' Alliance (File credits: Google Maps CC BY- SA 3.0)

have heterogeneous ethnic and professional backgrounds. While some members (45%) currently worked in "conventional" restaurant facilities (e.g., restaurants, hotels, and lodges), other members were employed in canteens (schools, universities, and offices) located in national and international institutions focused on issues connected to agriculture, rural development, and the sustainable management of environmental resources (55%). Despite the different employment areas, all the cooks of the Slow Food Cooks' Alliance in Kenya are directly involved in the promotion of traditional food through the introduction of dishes such as millet *ugali* (polenta made with millet flour), *matoke* (plantain stew), and *mursik* (fermented cow, sheep, or goat milk), as well as heirloom ingredients (especially traditional leafy vegetables such as black nightshade, amaranth, spider plant, and slender leaf) in their menus, creating a new interface between consumers and producers and an entry point for the customers to experience traditional dishes tied to the food cultures of the different tribes and regions of Kenya.

Two examples may clarify the path undertaken by the Slow Food Cooks' Alliance members. Lesiamon Ole Sempele, head chef of Nyama Mama restaurant in Nairobi, combines home-style dishes made with traditional ingredients with a modern eclectic twist. Drawing from the traditional food cultures of the inner and coastal regions of Kenya, he designed a menu that combines traditional dishes, such as *tumbukiza* (lamb stew), *kuku mhogo* (chicken stew), Maasai *muteta* beef broth, and traditional ugali, with the so-called Mama's signature burgers, made with traditional Kenyan ingredients and sauces (e.g., African nightshade, amaranth leaves, *kachumbari* [a fresh tomato, chili pepper, and onion salad], and Molo lamb meat patties). Conversely, Mary Chepkemoi Ondolo, the owner of an organic farm and the chef of Mariashoni Guest House, offers to her customers traditional dishes and beverages tied to the Kalenjin food culture (the ethnic group she belongs to), such as *mursik* and *isageek* (a traditional leafy vegetable stewed with milk and vegetables) served with brown ugali and mashed arrowroot. Both highlight traditional dishes made from local ingredients produced by Kenyan farmers.

The Actions of the Alliance

With few exceptions, such as the Slow Food Cooks' Alliance members, the Kenyan foodscape is still deeply influenced by Western cuisine. This configuration was the result of concurrent factors. On the one hand, the cultural impact of British domination established Western cuisine as a point of reference for the new middle and upper classes (Cusack 2000). On the other hand, the erosion of traditional practices accelerated with the migrations from rural to urban areas and the consequent increasing urbanization that led to deep changes in everyday eating and culinary practices among the local population. This resulted in increased consumption of food products processed and packaged by Western-owned corporations, as well as in the replacement of traditional grains (e.g., millet and sorghum) with wheat, maize, and rice (Raschke and Cheema 2008). Overall, the phenomenon led to a substantial homogenization of the food habits of the Kenyan ethnic tribes (Maundu and Imbumi 2003).

Another factor influencing modern Kenyan foodways was the training of professional chefs. "When I was at school, I was taught to cook like in Paris," remembers Ezekiel Mwathi Manyara, one of the chefs of the Kenyan Slow Food Cooks' Alliance who trained at the Rift Valley Institute of Science and Technology in Nakuru in the early 2000s and undertook a career in the restaurant industry that took him across the country. "I cooked that way for years. It was the way it was," the chef commented, pointing out how he was used to offering Sunday roasts, fish and chips, or coq au vin for his clients, including the Kenyan ones since this was considered the proper gastronomic standard at the time. "Only in the past decade, more and more Kenyans started asking for traditional food." For this reason, Ezekiel began using heirloom ingredients from his home community and introducing traditional dishes tied to the food culture of people from the western part of Kenya, such as *ugali wimbi* (millet ugali) and *saget* (spider plant). "[The customers] order [Kenyan cuisine] because it is healthier and tastier. So I cook it as I learnt from my grandmother. And the Slow Food Cooks' Alliance helped me in this because I discovered I was not alone."

The mid-2010s marked a turning point in the Ho.Re.Ca sector, the chefs pointed out. Several food scandals linked with food poisoning and adulteration raised awareness of the risks of food mass production (e.g., Biehl 2021). At the same time, awareness campaigns promoted by the Kenyan government, in collaboration with international agencies, showed the public the beneficial health proprieties of traditional products such as African leafy vegetables, legitimating traditional practices among the urban elites (Gido et al. 2017) and supporting a process of the retrieval of indigenous cuisine, as the UNESCO report titled "Success Story of Promoting Traditional Foods and Safeguarding Traditional Foodways in Kenya" testified (2022). This trend has reverberated in the catering sector, resulting in the rise of restaurants, specialized in traditional Kenyan cuisine, that target local patrons but also national and international customers (Zocchi and Fontefrancesco 2020). In major cities and tourist areas, several restaurants started offering dishes and beverages tied to the traditional food cultures of the emerging urban middle classes such as *mukimo* (starchy side dish made with potato, maize, and greens), *githeri* (a stew made with beans and maize), *uji* (fermented porridge), and *mursik* (Zocchi and Fontefrancesco 2020), and it is nowadays common to find restaurants and hotels offering dishes made with traditional ingredients such as African leafy vegetables (Cernansky 2015).

The institution of the Kenyan Slow Food Cooks' Alliance should be read in this context as a plural response to the new, emerging needs of the chefs and the public. On the one hand, the Kenyan Slow Food Cooks' Alliance answers the chefs' needs by offering an ideal space for discussion and training, through the sharing of best practices and personal experiences. On the other hand, the Kenyan Slow Food Cooks' Alliance aims at raising the awareness of the public, through the organization of workshops, public events, and tastings. These include at the national level the Disco Soup event organized every year, the Shaping the Future of Food of in Africa festival organized in December 2019, and the "Agroecology and Indigenous Foods Symposium" hosted in Nakuru in November 2021. On the international level these include the Karibu-Kilifair event held in Arusha in 2019 and the show cooking events held in Chengdu in 2017 for the Slow Food International Convention in Turin in 2018 during the Terra Madre–Salone del Gusto fair. These events create visibility for the members, promoting and legitimating their work and role in the local food system, and they reinforce cultural sustainability by promoting Kenyan food heritage and raising awareness about its value.

"The Slow Food Cooks' Alliance should be helpful to its members," explains Samson Kiiru, Slow Food Kenya officer and campaigner. "We support them [Slow Food Cooks' Alliance chefs] with training and information so that they can continue their work promoting local food, the fruits of our farmers and our land. . . . We organize events with them to explain to the people the role and importance of traditional products and cuisine. They are recreating the memory of our food."

Differently from what has happened in other social and cultural contexts (Matta 2013; Sammells 2019), the food advocacy of Kenyan Slow Food Cooks' Alliance cooks does not follow the model of celebrity chefs based on the extensive use of mass and social media. Rather, their actions follow a bottom-up approach, linked to their presence in the communities and the insertion of products and preparations within the daily experience of broad social sectors. This explains the involvement of professional cooks working outside of restaurants. "Their presence is crucial," explains Kariuki, "because they can reach every day hundreds of kids and people otherwise outside our reach."

Six of the Kenyan Slow Food Cooks' Alliance chefs (see Table 2) work in canteens and community restaurants aimed at providing quotidian food to hundreds of people, especially to the young generations. In these contexts, the food advocacy of the Slow Food Cooks' Alliance chefs is linked not to particular events, but rather to the daily choice of offering traditional food to the consumers, promoting traditional gastronomy and ingredients, and communicating the stories and values linked to these products. "Every day I prepare food for all the students of our school," states Nicholas Kariuki, a professional with over twenty years of experience who works as chief cook at the Baraka Agricultural College.

> I serve the breakfast, lunch, and dinner. Always, here, they find our food. The very dishes I have learned from my mother and my

community. This is important because it is nutritious, healthy, and it is ours. No fast food. No industry. Genuine, organic food the students grow in the school, in our garden. This is the best food they can have. They learn how to make it, how to grow it, and they will continue to make it at their home, for their children. This is good and I am proud of being a member of the Slow Food Cooks' Alliance because they think the same.

Together with the dietary aspects, the work of Nicolas has a strong impact in terms of creating awareness about local culinary heritage among the younger generations. For many students of the college, who come from across eastern Africa, every meal turns into an opportunity for tasting and appreciating traditional dishes of the Rift Valley and for learning how to prepare them. In this respect, a piece of culture otherwise jeopardized by the process of gastronomic standardization is preserved and passed on to new generations.

Similarly to Nicholas, other members of the Kenyan Slow Food Cooks' Alliance have been at the forefront of the rescue and popularization of traditional ingredients and dishes. For instance, two food products included in the Ark of Taste, *njahi* (a traditional legume variety tied to the culinary culture of the Kikuyu community) and *muhatato* banana, have been promoted by Martin Muhia Nyambura, a member of the Kenyan Slow Food Cooks' Alliance and chef at the European Union Embassy restaurant in Nairobi, who has won awards for his innovative recipe *mukimo* and *njahi* with *mbuzi choma* (roasted goat served with a mixture of maize, beans, green leaves, bananas, and potatoes that are mashed together). Moreover, in 2019, some members of the Kenyan Slow Food Cooks' Alliance participated in the Kilifair Tourism Fair in Arusha, Tanzania, and on that occasion, chef Martin Muhia Nyambura, the No Food Waste ambassador for Slow Food, prepared a dish known as *muhimo*, made from fresh Lare pumpkin leaves, Muibaì sweet potatoes, and Githigo maize, all products belonging to the Ark of Taste of Kenya. While these examples pertain mostly to chefs of the urban areas working in the fine dining sector, those who work in community restaurants, mostly in rural areas, see their advocacy as tied to their daily gastronomic choices rather than the organization of specific events or media appearances. Also, in this case, their contribution is strong in terms of cultural sustainability.

"This guest house was built by the Ogiek people [the local community]," remarks Mary Chepkemoi Ondolo, the owner of an organic farm and the chef of Mariashoni Guest House. "Yes, tourists come and for them, I cook our dishes so that they know who we are and what our land produces. But here I cook the same dishes for the community members, and I want this place to be a place where everyone feels at home. This I believe is the meaning of my being part of the Alliance and the reason I am proud of it."

Applied Gastronomic Reformism

Overall, the Kenyan Slow Food Cooks' Alliance is an association aimed at improving the sustainability of the local and national foodscapes. Sustainability in particular is epitomized by the Slow Food principles of "good, clean, and fair," indicating that "food should be pleasant and safe for consumers (good), its production should protect the environment and promote biodiversity (clean), and it should be sold in a way that guarantees a just profit for the producers and an accessible price for consumers (fair)" (Fontefrancesco 2022, 5). Together with this ethos that promotes cultural (good), environmental (clean), and socioeconomic (fair) sustainability, the Kenyan Slow Food Cooks' Alliance aims at reactivating local food production and foodways by reintroducing traditional products, making them available in restaurants and other catering facilities.

In their activities, the Kenyan Slow Food Cooks' Alliance chefs do not follow a top-down approach based on the extensive use of mass media, in which the chef turns into a social actor detached from society and enshrined in the mediasphere (Johnston and Goodman 2015). Rather, they are actors embedded in their communities who concentrate their actions on transforming food in its vernacular spaces, as exemplified by the cases of Mary Chepkemoi Ondolo, Ezekiel Mwathi Manyara, and Nicholas Kariuki presented above. Their actions are configured as a form of incremental change aimed at creating a new interface between consumers and traditional foods. In this way, cultural sustainability is achieved through acculturation, education, and knowledge transfer, exposing a larger segment of the population to information and dishes.

This approach takes away an authorial aura from the role of the chef. Roland Barthes (1967) points out that the character of the author is a modern Western cultural creation that, through the celebration of the individuality and individual genius of the artist, makes his identity and public persona the final explanation and justification of the artwork. In regard to literary criticism, Barthes recommends against considering these aspects, instead focusing only on the text. In contemporary celebrity chef culture, one can find the very absolute relevance and great attention given to the individual culinary practitioner that Barthes discussed in literature. In this context, through awareness campaigns promoted globally by celebrity chefs in order to foster traditional and national cuisines (e.g., Cox Hall 2020), the very figure of the chef hides with his personality the aura of the product, imposing a hegemonic cultural and gastronomic transformation on the community propelled by the charisma of the practitioner. On the contrary, in the case of the Kenyan Slow Food Cooks' Alliance, the chefs, especially those professionals working in canteens and community restaurants, such as Nicholas Kariuki, Martin Muhia Nyambura, and Beatrice Kanini Njeru, have a quieter role, facilitating a quotidian culinary encounter and focusing attention on the products, as well as their stories and properties.

While the Kenyan foodscape of the Ho.Re.Ca. sector still appears to be deeply influenced by international culinary traditions and forms, the approach of the Kenyan Slow Food Cooks' Alliance chefs represents an example of gastronomic reformism. Reformism is a political doctrine that advocates the improvement of an institutional system through specific and targeted changes, rather than its overthrow. It has been associated with the food sector in order to describe gradual political approaches to the achievement of key objectives such as food security, food sovereignty, and food justice (e.g., Holt-Giménez and Wang 2011). The actions of the Kenyan Slow Food Cooks' Alliance chefs represent a form of applied gastronomic reformism since they are generating change within the system. The cooks open up fresh spaces and repopulate them with Indigenous and traditional foods thus promoting cultural and environmental sustainability. In so doing, they complete the suggestion made by Ngugi Wa Thiong'o (1987) in relation to language and literature. Whereas the Kenyan intellectual pointed out that to decolonize the mind of Africa one needs to repopulate it with the sound of its native languages, the Kenyan Slow Food Cooks' Alliance chefs are decolonizing the table of the country by repopulating it with the tastes of its Indigenous cuisines in a context of growing demand for traditional products and rising attention from domestic travelers in their journeys, as well as workers and professionals in their daily lives (Fontefrancesco and Zocchi 2020).

Conclusions

The chapter illustrates the case study of the Kenyan Slow Food Cooks' Alliance. In doing so, it shows how cooks can contribute to the sustainability and the promotion of traditional foods. Specifically, this case study suggests an alternative path to the authorial model represented by celebrity chefs, one in which the chefs play a role as grassroots agents that through quotidian culinary practice conducted outside the spotlight of the media can create new gastronomic opportunities for their communities to learn and reinforce their awareness, knowledge, and skills. In this regard, the case study suggests a way forward that does not require the spectacularization of food heritage, reducing the risks of the commodification of cultures and products. This way appears particularly promising, especially in a context in which the recent international recognition awarded to traditional foods and foodways suggests a growing recognition of the specificities of this country that adds further resources for the development of tourism and the Kenyan economy as a whole. Thus, the Kenyan Slow Food Cooks' Alliance offers a model for supporting the transition toward more sustainable food systems in both developed and developing countries.

References

Ayora-Diaz, Steffan Igor. 2012. *Foodscapes, Foodfields, and Identities in the Yucatan.* New York: Berghahn Books.

Barstow, Charles, and Dauro M. Zocchi. 2018. *The Ark of Taste in Kenya: Food, Knowledge and History of the Gastronomic Heritage.* Bra: Slow Food Editore.

Barthes, Roland. 1967. "The Death of the Author." Aspen. Accessed May 1, 2022. http://www.ubu.com/aspen/aspen5and6/threeEssays.html.

Bertaux, Daniel, and Martin Kohli. 1984. "The Life Story Approach: A Continental View." *Annual Review of Sociology* 10 (August): 215–37. https://doi.org/10.1146/annurev.so.10.080184.001243.

Biehl, Konstantin. 2021. "Maize as a Nightmare: Food Safety and Toxicity in Rural Kenya." *Anthropology Today,* 37 (August): 11–14.

Capatti, Alberto. 2000. *L'osteria Nuova: Una Storia Del XX Secolo.* Bra: Slow Food Editore.

Cernansky, Rachel. 2015. "The Rise of Africa's Super Vegetables." *Nature* 522 (June): 146–48. https://doi.org/10.1038/522146a.

Comaroff, John L., and Jean Comaroff. 2009. *Ethnicity, Inc.* Chicago: University of Chicago Press.

Counihan, Carole. 2019. *Italian Food Activism in Urban Sardinia: Taste, Place and Community.* Oxford: Bloomsbury.

Cox Hall, Amy. 2020. "Cooking Up Heritage: Culinary Adventures of Peru's Past." *Bulletin of Spanish Studies* 97 (January): 593–613. https://doi.org/10.1080/14753820.2020.1699364.

Cusack, Igor. 2000. "African Cuisines: Recipes for Nation-Building?" *Journal of African Cultural Studies* 13 (December): 207–25. https://doi.org/10.1080/713674313.

Dieke, Peter U. C. 1991. "Policies for Tourism Development in Kenya." *Annals of Tourism Research* 18 (2): 269–94. https://doi.org/10.1016/0160-7383(91)90009-Z.

Fontefrancesco, Michele F. 2022. "Good, Fair and Clean Food for All." In *The Palgrave Handbook of Global Sustainability*, edited by Robert Brinkman, 1–9. New York: Springer.

Fontefrancesco, Michele F., and Paolo Corvo. 2020. "Slow Food: History and Activity of a Global Food Movement toward SDG2." In *Zero Hunger. Encyclopedia of the UN Sustainable Development Goals*, edited by Walter Leal Filho, Anabela Marisa Azul, Luciana Brandli, Pinar Özuyar, and Tony Wall, 766–74. New York: Springer.

Fontefrancesco, Michele F., and Dauro M. Zocchi. 2020. "Indigenous Crops and Cultural Dynamics in the Markets of Nakuru County, Kenya." *International Journal of Gastronomy and Food Science* 22 (October): 100269. https://doi.org/10.1016/j.ijgfs.2020.100269.

García, María. 2013. "The Taste of Conquest: Colonialism, Cosmopolitics, and the Dark Side of Peru's Gastronomic Boom." *Journal of Latin American and Caribbean Anthropology* 18 (November): 505–24. https://doi.org/10.1111/jlca.12044.

Gido, Eric O., Oscar Ingasia Ayuya, George Owuor, and Wolfgang Bokelmann. 2017. "Consumption Intensity of Leafy African Indigenous Vegetables: Towards Enhancing Nutritional Security in Rural and Urban Dwellers in Kenya." *Agricultural and Food Economics* 5 (July): 14. https://doi.org/10.1186/s40100-017-0082-0.

Grey, Sam, and Lenore Newman. 2018. "Beyond Culinary Colonialism: Indigenous Food Sovereignty, Liberal Multiculturalism, and the Control of Gastronomic Capital." *Agriculture and Human Values* 35 (September): 717–30. https://doi.org/10.1007/s10460-018-9868-2.

Hassanein, Neva. 2003. "Practicing Food Democracy: A Pragmatic Politics of Transformation." *Journal of Rural Studies* 19 (January): 77–86. https://doi.org/10.1016/S0743-0167(02)00041-4.

Higgins-Desbiolles, Freya, Emily Moskwa, and Stuart Gifford. 2014. "The Restaurateur as a Sustainability Pedagogue: The Case of Stuart Gifford and Sarah's Sister's Sustainable Café." *Annals of Leisure Research* 17 (July): 267–80. https://doi.org/10.1080/11745398.2014.937346.

Holt-Giménez, Eric, and Yi Wang. 2011. "Reform or Transformation? The Pivotal Role of Food Justice in the U.S. Food Movement." *Race/Ethnicity: Multidisciplinary Global Contexts* 5 (1): 83–102. https://doi.org/10.2979/racethmulglocon.5.1.83.

Johnston, Josée, and Michael K. Goodman. 2015. "Spectacular Foodscapes: Food Celebrities and the Politics of Lifestyle Mediation in an Age of Inequality." *Food, Culture and Society* 18 (May): 205–22. https://doi.org/10.2752/175174415X14180391604369.

KBC. 2022. "Kenya Attempts to Set New Standard for Tourism through Gastronomy – KBC." Accessed May 1, 2022.

Markowitz, Lisa. 2012. "Highland Haute Cuisine: The Transformation of Alpaca Meat." In *Reimagining Marginalized Foods: Global Processes, Local Places*, edited by Elizabeth Finnis, 34–48. Tucson: University of Arizona Press.

Matta, Raúl. 2013. "Valuing Native Eating: The Modern Roots of Peruvian Food Heritage." *Anthropology of Food* S8 (August): 1–16. https://doi.org/10.4000 /aof.7361.

———. 2019. "Mexico's Ethnic Culinary Heritage and Cocineras Tradicionales (Traditional Female Cooks)." *Food and Foodways* 27 (August): 211–31. https:// doi.org/10.1080/07409710.2019.1646481.

Maundu, Patrick, and Maryam Imbumi. 2003. "The Food and Food Culture of the Peoples of East Africa (Kenya, Uganda, Tanzania, Rwanda, Burundi, Sudan, Ethiopia, Eritrea, and Somalia)." In *Encyclopedia of Foods and Culture*, edited by Solomon H. Katz, 27–34. New York: Charles and Scribner's Sons.

McDonell, Emma. 2019. "Creating the Culinary Frontier: A Critical Examination of Peruvian Chefs' Narratives of Lost/Discovered Foods." *Anthropology of Food* 14 (June): 1–22. https://doi.org/10.4000/aof.10183.

Members of St. Andrew's Church Women's Guild. 1987. *The Kenya Cookery Book and Household Guide*. Nairobi: Heinemann Kenya.

Morelli, John. 2011. "Environmental Sustainability: A Definition for Environmental Professionals." *Journal of Environmental Sustainability* 1 (November): 1–9. https:// doi.org/10.14448/jes.01.0002.

Mwema, Catherine, and Wibke Crewett. 2019. "Institutional Analysis of Rules Governing Trade in African Leafy Vegetables and Implications for Smallholder Inclusion: Case of Schools and Restaurants in Rural Kenya." *Journal of Rural Studies* 67 (March): 142–51. https://doi.org/10.1016/j.jrurstud.2019.02.004.

Navarro-Dols, Jorge, and José Luis González-Pernía. 2020. "Gastronomy as a Real Agent of Social Change." *International Journal of Gastronomy and Food Science* 21 (October): 100240. https://doi.org/10.1016/j.ijgfs.2020.100240.

Pereira, Laura M., Rafael Calderón-Contreras, Albert V. Norström, Dulce Espinosa, Jenny Willis, Leonie Guerrero Lara, Zayaan Khan, Loubie Rusch, Eduardo Correa Palacios, and Ovidio Pérez Amaya. 2019. "Chefs as Change-Makers from the Kitchen: Indigenous Knowledge and Traditional Food as Sustainability Innovations." *Global Sustainability* 2 (September): e16. https://doi.org/10.1017 /S2059479819000139.

Petrini, Carlo. 2003. *Slow Food: The Case for Taste*. New York: Columbia University Press.

Rampa, Francesco, Massimo Labra, Nunzia Borrelli, Hellas Cena, Enrico Chiappero Martinetti, Palo Corvo, Michele F. Frontefrancesco et al., 2021. *SASS: Sustainable Food System and Indigenous Vegetables. Final Report*. Milan: Fondazione Feltrinelli.

Raschke, Verena, and Bobby Cheema. 2008. "Colonisation, the New World Order, and the Eradication of Traditional Food Habits in East Africa: Historical Perspective on the Nutrition Transition." *Public Health Nutrition* 11 7 (July): 662–74. https://doi.org/10.1017/S1368980007001140.

Sammells, Clare A. 2019. "Reimagining Bolivian Cuisine: Haute Traditional Food and Its Discontents." *Food and Foodways* 27 (October): 338–52. https://doi.org /10.1080/07409710.2019.1677396.

Sindiga, Isaac. 1999. *Tourism and African Development: Change and Challenge of Tourism in Kenya*. London: Routledge.

Siniscalchi, Valeria. 2013. "Environment, Regulation and the Moral Economy of Food in the Slow Food Movement." *Journal of Political Ecology* 20 (November): 295–305. https://doi.org/10.2458/v20i1.21768.

Slow Food. 2015. "Slow Food Chefs' Alliance. Manifesto and International Regulations." https://www.fondazioneslowfood.com/wp-content/uploads/2015/04/ING _regolamento_alleanza.pdf.

——. 2017. *Slow Food in Africa 2012–2017 Report*. Bra: Slow Food.

——. 2022a. "10.000 Gardens in Africa." Accessed May 1, 2022.

——. 2022b. "Slow Food Cooks' Alliance." Accessed May 1, 2022. https://www .fondazioneslowfood.com/en/what-we-do/slow-food-chefs-alliance/.

Slow Food Foundation for Biodiversity. 2022. "Chefs' Alliance in Kenya." Accessed August 22, 2022. https://www.fondazioneslowfood.com/en/nazioni-alleanza /kenya-en.

Throsby, David. 1997. "Sustainability and Culture Some Theoretical Issues." *International Journal of Cultural Policy* 4 (1): 7–19. https://doi.org/10.1080 /10286639709358060.

UNESCO. 2022. "Success Story of Promoting Traditional Foods and Safeguarding Traditional Foodways in Kenya." https://f5vip11.unesco.org/en/BSP/success -story-of-promoting-traditional-foods-and-safeguarding-traditional-foodways -in-kenya-01409?Art18=01409.

Wa Thiong'o, Ngugi. 1987. *Decolonising the Mind. The Politics of Language in African Literature*. Harare: Zimbabwe Publishing House.

Zocchi, Dauro M., and Michele F. Fontefrancesco. 2020. "Traditional Products and New Developments in the Restaurant Sector in East Africa. The Case Study of Nakuru County, Kenya." *Frontiers in Sustainable Food Systems* 4 (November): 599138. https://doi.org/10.3389/fsufs.2020.599138.

Zocchi, Dauro M., Michele F. Fontefrancesco, Paolo Corvo, and Andrea Pieroni. 2021. "Recognising, Safeguarding, and Promoting Food Heritage: Challenges and Prospects for the Future of Sustainable Food Systems." *Sustainability* 13 (August): 9510. https://doi.org/10.3390/su13179510.

CHAPTER FOURTEEN

From New York's Silverbird to Santa Fe's Corn Dance Café

Sustaining Indigenous Restaurants

L. SASHA GORA

Introduction

"Maple red corn pudding with nixtamalized red corn, hickory, crispy corn silk, burnt maple sugar, and corn shoots." This dish—*Chuskënàpòna*—ended Oglala Lakota chef Sean Sherman's October 2017 six-course dinner at New York City's James Beard House. Each course toured Manhattan's Indigenous foods. A trio of hors d'oeuvres spotlighted the three sisters: corn, beans, and squash: "Duck livers with blue corn crisps and apples," "Potato bean spread with smoked scallops and dried ramps," and "Pumpkin-sunflower fritters with wild plum and sorrel." Entrees starred precontact ingredients, pairing *qhahog*—hard clams—with sea lettuce, smoked venison leg with dried strawberry, and dried rabbit with toasted hickory nut (The Sioux Chef 2017).

That same month Sherman published *The Sioux Chef's Indigenous Kitchen*, which the James Beard Foundation crowned Best American Cookbook of 2017. But his dinner in one of the United States' gastronomic capitals pointed to an important absence. There are 573 federally recognized tribes, and New York City has the country's highest urban Indigenous population (Skinner, Pratley, and Burnett 2016, 1).[1] Yet as of 2024 there are no Indigenous restaurants in New York. This had not always been the case. Three decades earlier, in 1986, Reuben Silverbird opened his namesake restaurant—the city's first "American Indian" eatery—but it closed two years later.

Restaurants must be economically viable, culinarily palatable, and ecologically grounded to be sustainable. This chapter aims to explain the dearth of Indigenous restaurants in the United States by narrating Silverbird's history in tandem with a second example—Santa Fe's Corn Dance Café—to discuss what I call Indigenous culinary sustainability. It also aims to recuperate the work of early restaurants in spreading awareness of Indigenous culinary cultures.[2] This chapter demonstrates the key characteristics of Indigenous sustainability: reciprocity, an awareness of human relationships to the plants and animals that become food, the continuation of cultural heritage, and Indigenous food sovereignty.

This chapter builds on my research about Indigenous restaurants in the lands now called Canada.[3] I am a fourth-generation settler from Tkaronto (Toronto)—the traditional land of the Huron-Wendat, Seneca, and Mississaugas of the Credit. Positionality, as Cree-Métis scholar Deanne Reder emphasizes, involves recognition "that all knowledge is generated from particular positions, that there is no unbiased, neutral position possible" (Reder 2016, 7). I inherit the "place-based responsibilities" of North America (Hargreaves 2016, 109), which many Haudenosaunee and Ojibwe nations call Turtle Island. Drawing from newspaper archives, I employ narrative analysis to detail how critics have represented Indigenous restaurants and engaged with sustainability. I consider a broad sample—from local to national papers—to construct how the mainstream media has viewed and "othered" these eateries. To counter this imbalance, I draw from Indigenous resurgence scholarship to center Indigenous voices.

Silverbird's: New York City's First Indigenous Restaurant

On November 24, 1985, the *New York Times* reported "that long-overdue credit is being given to American Indian food." Journalist B. Blake Levitt described such food as "so esoteric that one has to forage for the ingredients of cattail pollen cake" yet also "so mainstream that we consume clam and corn chowders, baked beans, steamed lobsters and barbecues without considering their origins" (Levitt 1985, CN11). This other-yet-ordinary paradox previewed Silverbird's, "an American Indian restaurant scheduled to open soon in New York City," and profiled its consultant E. Barrie Kavasch—the author of *Native Harvest: On Recipes and Botanicals of the American Indian*.[4] The article highlighted Silverbird's all-Native staff and its sourcing from reservations, exemplifying its commitment to supporting Indigenous communities. Although it does not mention sustainability, it does hint at Indigenous cultural survival by noting forced relocations and the loss of food knowledge and oral traditions, creating "cultural amnesia" (Levitt 1985, CN11).

In summer 1986 Silverbird opened at 505 Columbus Avenue, between Eighty-Fourth and Eighty-Fifth streets—then a "trendy" location (Sones 1986, FD).[5] The *New York Times* wrote that "Reuben Silverbird had long dreamed of establishing a restaurant devoted to American Indian cuisine" (Yarrow 1986, C1). Managed by Silverbird in partnership with his German wife Inge, the restaurant was "part business venture and partly a desire to expose people to AmMerican [*sic*] Indian heritage and culture." Silverbird is Nedhni/Apache and Cherokee and, as he detailed, "Too many people know too little about native Americans beyond stereotypes presented in films and on television" (Parisi 1986, NJ11). His method for countering this was to appeal first to the palate and second to social consciousness (Miller 1986).

As soon as Silverbird opened, business was booming (Rosenthal 1986, F1). One review called its dining room "winsome"—decked out "in a Southwestern theme with colorful Indian art and artifacts" (Miller 1986). Another compared it to "a stage set for a play about the Southwest. Walls are orange stucco; columns, ersatz tree trunks. Papier-mâché cactuses crowd the room, and kachinas line the bar" (Sones 1986, FD). Artist Melody Lightfeather, a Pima-Pueblo married to chef Jim Gallegos of "the Mexico-Jemez tribe from the Southwest," painted its watercolors and murals (Sones 1986, FD).

The menu covered much geographical ground, from "Gulf shrimp in green chili sauce" to "salmon jerky," and many dishes were new to customers and critics alike. Reporter Melissa Sones called Silverbird's blue corn chips and soup and "Navajo fry bread" "the latest and strangest culinary attraction to hit New York in years." With a few exceptions, she characterized "Indian food" as "not spicy" and underlined its medicinal powers and high meat content. "Native American entrees are macho pieces of lamb, venison, beef or buffalo," she chronicled, "that are broiled and served plain with simple sauces or garnishes like butter, mint or cranberry sauce" (Sones 1986, FD). Silverbird used only fresh herbs and spices, which led one review to mention its "back-to-nature aspect" (Rosenthal 1986, F1).

Press coverage also pointed out bison's "return to the table" and its starring role in dishes such as "Buffalo tartare," "Buffalo meatballs," and "Buffaloburgers" (Dullea 1986, B1; Evans 1987, C3; Sones 1986, FD). The

Buffaloburger was plump and tasty, reviews exclaimed, barely distinguishable from beef except a tad leaner. Silverbird considered diners ready to embrace bison. "'They're tired of hormone-injected livestock and recognize the need to lower cholesterol and fat,' he said. 'Buffalo is 25 percent lower than beef and it was here before cattle'" (Preuss 1986, 99). Silverbird grew up eating lamb, not bison, yet recognized its importance for the Plains Indians and ordered a shipment from South Dakota every two months (Sones 1986, FD).

Reviews chronicled a growing interest in Indigenous foods. "With so many cooks now exploring the cultural beginnings of this country," summarized one critic, "our oldest cuisine is becoming the newest source of culinary inspiration" (Preuss 1986, 99). Another wrote, "The hottest restaurants in Manhattan right now are those that feature American food—be it nouvelle American or regional American, Tex-Mex, or Mexican. But until now, no one has tried dishing out native American food—the exotic cuisine that American Indians call their own" (Rosenthal 1986, F1). This critic recommended Silverbird's South Dakota buffalo, Pennsylvania boar, and Colorado rattlesnake to "those with adventurous palates." His choice of words exoticized the restaurant, as did his comparison of Silverbird's menu to Chinese and Mexican cuisines. "A Papoose Platter, sort of an Indian version of a Chinese PuPu Platter (complete with open flames and skewers)," he explained, "offers a sampling of buffalo, venison, lamb, and sunflower seeds" (Rosenthal 1986, F1). He described the "Navajo jojo" as "sort of like a Mexican chimichanga: meat and refried beans wrapped in fried dough" (Rosenthal 1986, F1).

But not all reviews were positive. A couple of months after its debut, the *Daily News* published one titled "Please Fly Away, Silverbird." "Given the economics of opening a business on Columbus Ave.," begins critic Arthur Schwartz, "I think we can immediately discount the theory that Silverbird, New York's first Native American restaurant, was opened solely to take revenge on the white man. But the hypothesis does come to mind when you taste the food" (Schwartz 1986, 20). He hesitates "to say 'eat'" because his table hardly ate. "We were hungry enough to finish the dry buffalo burger . . . and I think we did some shrimp in green chili sauce more than the justice they were due. But I can say unequivocally that this was among the most dishonestly conceived and badly cooked meals of my entire restaurant-going life." He then softens his tone: "I say this with some sadness. I mean, think of how culturally and gastronomically fascinating an American Indian (sorry, Native American) restaurant might be if it was done with any integrity and skill." His tone is clearly patronizing and hostile. Surprisingly, however, he does not dismiss Indigenous fare per se, concluding that "there is plenty of delicious Native American food to be explored . . . But something went haywire—or rather, typically upper West Side—at Silverbird" (1986, 20).

In addition to critics, Silverbird attracted celebrities, including Robert Redford, Donny Osmond, and Goldie Hawn. Some, such as June Carter Cash and Buffy Sainte-Marie, even promised to gift it recipes (Rosenthal 1986, F1). But, more importantly, it attracted Indigenous peoples living in the tri-state area and became a gathering place for civic groups engaged in Indigenous affairs (Parisi 1986, NJ11) and contributing to sustaining Indigenous communities and cultures. Yet this gathering was short lived. On July 29, 1988, the *New York Times* announced Silverbird had closed, providing no further details (Miller 1988). Decades later, a 2014 *Food Republic* headline remembered it: "New York's First Native American Restaurant Was Run by an Indian-American Chef." Rahul Akerhkar's name did not appear in earlier press coverage, but he worked at Silverbird while studying for a Columbia University master's degree in biomedical engineering.[6] He recounted, "We'd cook buffalo and possum, rattlesnake, rabbit, gator, all in the traditional way. We didn't use black pepper, we used spices that were indigenous to the U.S., like pollen and sage" (Kapadia 2014). This decolonial approach would later define other Indigenous eateries. Silverbird's sojourn in New York City was short, but important. The visibility it gave to Indigenous foodways also drew attention to their colonial erasure and how imperial appetites rewrote the history of ingredients such as corn and potatoes without their Native pasts. Loretta Barrett Oden then set out to correct this history.

The Corn Dance Café's Impact in Santa Fe and Beyond

Loretta Barrett Oden, a member of the Citizen Potawatomi Nation, opened the Corn Dance Café in Santa Fe, New Mexico, in 1993. She grew up in Shawnee, Oklahoma, where she picked wild possum grapes and learned about the "three sisters": corn, beans, and squash (Dowell 1998, 2).[7] "Oden savored the cuisines of close to 50 American Indian tribes uprooted from their ancestral lands and marched to Oklahoma, a state aptly nicknamed 'the melting pot of Indian Country,'" narrated the *Santa Fe New Mexican* (Lim 2002, C-2). At the age of forty-eight, she set out on "the grand adventure" of the second half of her life—opening the cafe (Dowell 1998, 2).

"Before we opened," she explains, "I spent three years traveling around the country learning more about Native American foods." The diversity stunned her: Smoked salmon and seafood in the Northwest; chiles and sassafras in the Southeast; the clam bake and "*original* Boston baked beans, which the Native Americans made with maple syrup" in the Northeast (*Santa Fe Reporter* 1994). Oden's culinary education sparked the idea of opening a restaurant. "I wanted to heighten people's aware-ness of Native American culture and the diversity of it through foods," she expressed (Dowell 1998, 2). *The Santa Fe Reporter* described her as a "woman with a mission—to reintroduce Native foods and culture to every person in the land" (*Santa Fe Reporter* 1994).

In 1993, Oden settled in Los Angeles, "determined to set up her dream, 'a little Native American food stand' along Venice Beach. But Californians didn't understand her version of the food she wanted to sell" (Dowell 2003a, 2-D). Her focus shifted to New Mexico. "'People come to Santa Fe for a Native American experience. But where are they going to get the food?' she asked" (Silverman 1994, 92). On January 12, 1994, the *Santa Fe New Mexican* provided the answer by welcoming the Corn Dance Café, which had opened in 1993. It called its menu "spectacular," writing, "Portions are plentiful and beautifully presented and desserts are delicious—don't miss the Little Big Pie. Dinner prices range from $14 to $18—not cheap—but you are paying for and receiving a high quality, pleasant experience" (*Santa Fe New Mexican* 1994, C-3). One review spelled out her multiple aims: "While serving healthy food is one of the objectives of the Corn Dance, Oden also sees the restaurant as a way to reclaim American Indian tradition both through the serving of food and the hiring of American Indians" (Silverman 1994, 92). By combining cultural, social, and economic concerns, Oden promoted Indigenous culinary sustainability.

Corn Dance Café was an instant "smash hit" that sparked ideas "to open a chain of Native American restaurants across the country" (*Santa Fe Reporter* 1994). Critics called the food "well-prepared and creative" and entrees "simply stunning,"—applauding dishes such as barbecued buffalo showered in chives, sage, and ribbons of crème fraîche (Gabin 1994, E11). Although Oden spotlighted Indigenous foods, the use of crème fraîche exemplified that she did not exclude postcontact ingredients.

The *New York Times* described its "rustic" Water Street location: "Raw pine walls, reed flute music, the scent of searing buffalo meat—they could all be found on a visit to an American Indian's home. But they're also part of the ambiance at the Corn Dance Café, where simple foods are served with flourish." The restaurant seated fifty-eight "beneath a turquoise ceiling painted with cirrus clouds" and "surrounded by warm adobe and rough sawed pine walls and by paintings of charging bison." The patio offered room for another eighty guests among "beds of corn, beans, squash and edible flowers like nasturtiums" (King 1995, C4). "Plates are arranged to take natural advantage of each food's color, shape and texture; and best of all, the food looks like food," proclaimed the *Albuquerque Journal* (Gabin 1994, E11).

Some dishes, however, landed better than others. One review in the *Albuquerque Journal* pronounced the "Smoked quail with house-made mustard" as "just ordinary"—stating that "it seemed a lot of bother to find the two very small pieces of tough (but tasty) bird amid the greenery." The "Tlingit grilled salmon" was a consistent hit, reputed to be "one of the best salmon dishes in town." Pecan wood infused the fish and "Refreshing rose-hip purée heightened with orange zest was robust enough to hold its own with the salmon." While the *Journal* reviewer, Vickie Gabin, considered dinner at the Corn Dance Café "a treat," she remained puzzled: "It's an attractive, comfortable spot and serves some wonderful food, but why does every meal come with what reads like a lecture?" Her question refers to a letter detailing "Native American contributions to what was an undeniably mediocre European diet" and with which each place was set. She continued, "I'll willingly agree that plants first cultivated on this continent are now a welcome and major part of our modern diet. But it's hard to swallow both a paean to basic Native American foodstuffs and a call to celebrate a 'reverence for the gifts of Mother Earth' in a restaurant with entree prices guaranteed to exclude most Native Americans and other working joes and janes" (Gabin 1994, E11). In contrast, reporter Kate Ferlic confessed that she had an appetite for such a lecture and noted that the restaurant "rebels against the grain by offering healthy, savory fare that tantalizes the tongue and refreshes the body" and "leads guests back to Native American agricultural roots through what you could call nouveau Native American cuisine" (2000, 45).

After two and a half years on Water Street, the Corn Dance moved to Hotel Santa Fe in 1996. Run by the Picuris Pueblo, it was the city's "Only Native American Owned Hotel" (Dowell 1998, 2; *Albuquerque Journal* 1997, C2). Oden became its consulting chef and was no longer its owner (*Albuquerque Journal* 1996, 13). In its new space, which once again was seating fifty-eight, as critic Michelle Pentz detailed in the *Albuquerque Journal*, "The central mood-setter is the larger kiva fireplace which warms guests"

(Pentz 2001, 4). A tepee offered outdoor seating. "Although the idea seems novel, the tepee is a hook and sinker for many tourists," complained Ferlic in the *Santa Fe New Mexican*. "Corn Dance Cafe is not a place where many Santa Feans eat, but they should," she concluded (2000, 45).

At its new location, the "Tlingit Salmon" was once again a hit, and Pentz called it "outstanding." The "spice-rubbed American bison tenderloin" was too. She was, however, disappointed with the "Indian Triad Salad" of heirloom beans, corn relish, squash, and greens with piñon sage vinaigrette (2001, 4). News of the Corn Dance Café even traveled to Canada. In 1997, *The Edmonton Journal* promised that you won't forget its "kick-ass buffalo chili in a jalapeño bread bowl" (1997, G1). In 2001, Toronto's *National Post* called its menu "innovative" (2001, G4).

The theme of expansion arose again and again. Already in 1994, Oden shared, "I want to open a chain of fast-food restaurants featuring Little Big Pies, which are made of traditional fry bread dough which is *not* fried, but baked. . . . My dream, my vision, is a tipi-like Little Big Pie restaurant planted next to every McDonald's in the world. I want to lure children away from McDonald's with wonderful Native food and wonderful stories about Native culture" (*Santa Fe Reporter* 1994). This dream combined culinary and cultural aims to promote Indigenous culinary sustainability. A 1998 *Daily Oklahoman* article announced her plans to open a Corn Dance Café in Los Angeles (Dowell 1998, 2). And a 2004 article mentioned that she was working as a consultant for a Tokyo-based restaurant company that "hope[d] to open a Corn Dance Café in San Francisco within a year" (Herzog 2004, 10A). None of these eateries ever opened.

The word "sustainability" did not appear in reviews of the Corn Dance Café, but sustainable practices did. For example, Oden "saves corn cobs, then makes a corn stock that's used in a variety of dishes, including an unusual corn ice cream served with raspberry sauce" (Dowell 1998, 2). As the *Santa Fe New Mexican* recounted, "Oden's vision quest led her to research and share with the world the diverse foods of the Americas, suggesting she use food as a vehicle to showcase the history, ecologically correct agriculture and culturally rich heritage of Native peoples." Furthermore, Oden procured organic ingredients from Indigenous producers (Lim 2002, C-2).

The Corn Dance Café fed the city for nine years. Hotel Santa Fe continues to be Indigenous-run; however, one newspaper reported that in 2001 it decided to switch "from an American Indian theme" to a European one, and so Oden decided to close the restaurant and return to Oklahoma

(Dowell 2003a, 2-D). In April 2003, she opened the Corn Dance Café in Shawnee to serve "creative native cuisine" on the reservation (*Daily Oklahoman* 2003, 3-D). Old dishes accompanied its new location, including "cedar plank salmon with wild huckleberry sauce and smoked oyster potato cake on sauteed spinach" (Dowell 2003b, 2-D). But the new Corn Dance Café "didn't last long, she said, because of 'tribal politics' " (Herzog 2004, 10A). What these politics were, the review leaves out. However, in 2021 Oden became the consultant at Thirty Nine Restaurant, hosted by the First Americans Museum in Oklahoma City, and in 2024, at the age of eighty-one, she published her first cookbook commemorating the Corn Dance Café's culinary contributions (Oden and Dooley 2024).

In 2004, a *Miami Herald* headline asked about "The Next Craze in Exotic Cuisine?" only to answer "Native American." A similar proclamation accompanied Silverbird in the 1980s, yet nearly two decades later American media continued to "other" Indigenous cuisines by labeling them "exotic." The *Herald* then narrated the movement underway "to return to such healthy foods of their heritage, and to teach non-Indians about their little-understood cuisine." The newspaper also mentioned sustainability. "Whenever she [Oden] talks about American Indian cuisine, she tells the legends of the foods and stories about where the recipe came from," it reported. "She also promotes a link with traditional farming methods that make these crops sustainable for future generations" (Herzog 2004, 10A), fostering Indigenous culinary sustainability.

Ten years later the *Taos News* mistakenly called the Corn Dance Café "the first restaurant in the country that showcased the indigenous foods of America" (Dovalpage 2014, C1), revealing the sense of novelty with which the press continued to narrate Indigenous restaurants. A 2000 review claimed that "Corn Dance Cafe carves a niche taking a chance on the barely charted territory of Native American cuisine" (Ferlic 2000, 45). But another acknowledged the debts world cuisines owe to Indigenous ingredients, writing that "Native American restaurants haven't swept this nation the way that Italian, French and Spanish eateries have. But without Native contributions, we'd barely recognize those other cuisines" (Van Buskirk 1998, 30).

Toward an Indigenous Restaurantscape

Oden also set an example for other chefs. Oakland-based Crystal Wahpepah, a member of the Kickapoo tribe, realized at a young age that "we didn't have our food in restaurants" (Wahpepah 2019). Then as a teenager she ate at the Corn Dance Café, which she remembers as "an elegant restaurant with precolonial foods. I had never seen this food in a nice restaurant." This is one reason why Indigenous restaurants matter. They inspire younger generations to represent their culinary points of view and claim a contemporary cultural presence. In 2012 Wahpepah launched a catering company and in November 2021 she opened a restaurant: Wahpepah's Kitchen. While translating her catering business into a restaurant plan, she traveled to Minneapolis to consult with Sean Sherman—whom she met at a 2015 workshop and who had just opened his restaurant: Owamni (Kormann 2022).

In 2019 the *New York Times* published "Sean Sherman's 10 Essential Native American Recipes." Sherman recounted his childhood on Pine Ridge Reservation in the 1970s. He grew up hunting pheasants, jackrabbits, antelope, and grouse, and learning to harvest chokecherries, juniper berries, and *timpsula* (a wild prairie turnip). He contrasted these wild foods with government commodity foods, such as powdered milk and canned meat, that weighed down kitchen cupboards. There was one grocery store and a couple of gas stations—no restaurants (Sherman 2019b).[8]

Sherman's first job was at a steakhouse at age thirteen. He became fluent in the cuisines of Italy and Spain. "But it wasn't until I spent time in Mexico, observing how closely Indigenous people live to their culinary traditions, that I realized I had very little idea of what my own ancestors ate before colonization," he recounts (2019b). He spoke with Elders and ethnobotanists, chefs and academics. "In piecing together so much of the story that has been lost, I learned that the original North American food system was based on harvesting wild plants for food and medicine, employing sophisticated agricultural practices, and on preserving seed diversity," Sherman wrote. "My ancestors used all parts of the animals and plants with respect, viewing themselves as part of our environment, not above it" (2019b). In 2014 he started the catering company The Sioux Chef with Dana Thompson. In 2021 in Minneapolis they opened Owamni on the bank of the Mississippi River, on land that was once the Dakota village Owamniyomni—a place of falling water. As Carolyn Kormann wrote in the *New Yorker*, "Nearly overnight, it became the most prominent example of Indigenous American cuisine in the United States" (Kormann 2022).

Kormann did not mention sustainability. Nor did Tejal Rao's (2016) *New York Times* article "The Movement to Define Native American Cuisine," which quoted food historian Lois Ellen Frank, who described

Sherman as the second generation doing this work. From the Kiowa Nation, Frank became curious about Indigenous cuisines in the 1980s. In 2002 she published *Foods of the Southwest Indian Nations*, which became the first Indigenous cookbook to win a James Beard Award. In June 2021, Owamni won the James Beard Award for best new restaurant in the United States. Kormann tweeted, "There should be a restaurant like Owamni in New York. And in every city in the U.S" (@carolynkor, September 13, 2022). And yet the American restaurantscape continues to underrepresent Indigenous cuisines.

Sustainability and Human-Animal-Plant Reciprocity

The United Nations defines sustainability as "meet[ing] the needs of the present without compromising the ability of future generations to meet their own needs" (1987). In 1994 business author John Elkington extended this concept by adding the "triple bottom line" to encompass society, economics, and the environment. In their study of how farm-to-table restaurants spark food system change, Sasha Pesci and Catherine Brinkley use "sustainable" to refer to practices defined by "lack of synthetic fertilizers or pesticides, humane raising of animals, avoiding the use of antibiotics for animals, a less-is-more approach, sustainable growing practices, biodynamic practices, natural composting, and diverse crop production" (2021, 17). However, this movement is predominantly Euro-American (Crawford O'Brien and Wogahn 2021, 145). It largely concentrates on individuals as agents of change—the vote-with-your-fork model—whereas Indigenous culinary sustainability advocates for structural change promoting food sovereignty.

Advocates of culinary sustainability must consider how environmental, social, and food justice intersect, which is where Indigenous chefs lead by example. Sustainable restaurants serve their communities—including their ecological ones—in addition to their customers. Teresa M. Mares and Devon G. Peña propose the term "AlterNative": "the deeply rooted practices of Native peoples that *alter* and challenge the dominant food system" (2011, 201). As they make clear, "There can be no sustainable agriculture without cultural survival and political autonomy," no culinary sustainability without cultural sustainability (2011, 203; Peña 2002, 24), and no Indigenous food sovereignty without Indigenous sovereignty. This requires looking beyond food to the relationships with the plants and animals that become food and the lands and waters they come from.

Robin Wall Kimmerer, an environmental scientist and member of the Citizen Potawatomi Nation, recalls meeting Algonquin ecologist Carol Crowe at a conference about Indigenous models of sustainability. When Crowe requested funding, her tribal council asked about sustainability. She supplied the usual UN definition, only for one Elder to reply, "This sustainable development sounds to me like they just want to be able to keep on taking like they always have. . . . You go there and tell them that in our way, our first thoughts are not 'What can we take?' but 'What can we give to Mother Earth?' " (2013, 144). This invokes reciprocity and interdependence. Kimmerer writes, "The traditional ecological knowledge of indigenous harvesters is rich in prescriptions for sustainability" found in practices and stories, in philosophy and science. She calls this "the Honorable Harvest" whose practices "govern the exchange of life for life"—the ongoing back-and-forth between giving and taking, between humans and the natural world (2013, 137).

Algonquin dietician S. Kaitlyn Patterson objects to the dominant Western conception of food as "an object to dominate and control. . . . Food becomes 'it' rather than 'they,' thereby ignoring their living, diverse, multiple bodies" (2021, 26). Indigenous culinary sustainability recognizes relationships and looks at foods as subjects with agency rather than as objects to consume. Navajo chef Freddie Bitsoie argues it is impossible to talk about culinary traditions without considering the environment "and the spiritual relationship between Indigenous people and the foods that sustain us. Many of our most deeply held beliefs exist around planting, growing, harvesting, and cooking—honoring plant and animal spirits and giving back to the earth that gives to us" (Bitsoie and O. Fraioli 2021, 95).[9] Reciprocity does not necessarily feature in popular imaginations of sustainability but makes an essential contribution because it recognizes the needs of ecosystems and environments—of the Earth as a whole—alongside human needs.

Food studies scholar Kelly Donati argues that contemporary sustainability discourse mirrors "a deeply anthropomorphic view of the world" (2014, 137). She counters this by stating that sustainability is not a set of products, procedures, or politics: "Instead, it is a way of living that requires the creative forces of necessity, ingenuity, curiosity, passion, enchantment, hope and sometimes despair to propel us forward" (2014, 140). Sustainability also requires reckoning with the colonial past and present. Jeff Corntassel, an Indigenous studies scholar and member of the Tsalagi Cherokee Nation, writes, "When asked about living sustainably today, Indigenous peoples inevitably confront the ongoing legacies of colonialism that have disrupted their individual and community relationships with the natural world" (2012, 87). Colonial practices have contaminated with toxins "the medicines, water, and traditional foods that Indigenous peoples have relied on for millennia to sustain their communities." He continues, "As a refutation to a resource extraction-based economy, Indigenous peoples practice and honor their sustainable relationships. A Cherokee word that describes a sustainable relationship is *digadatsele'i* or 'we belong to each other' " (2012, 96). Belonging recognizes relationships and requires reciprocity.

Conclusion

Indigenous culinary sustainability, in short, centers human-nature relationships and reciprocity and resists the ongoing legacies of settler colonialism, which makes it important for sustainability at large and efforts to preserve the planet and the future of its food supplies. Swampy Cree scholar Tabitha Robin describes Indigenous food sovereignty as a movement that redefines food systems and revitalizes culture (2018, 11). Yet Indigenous culinary sustainability faces ongoing obstacles, such as the lack of access to land and water, contamination and pollution (examples of environmental injustice), and economic marginalization that makes it difficult to initiate and sustain Indigenous culinary businesses, as well as mainstream settler culture's continued exoticization and ignorance of Indigenous culinary cultures.

This chapter has argued that restaurants play a role in the Indigenous food movement. But since Silverbird, there have been no other Indigenous eateries in New York City, and too few in the United States, demonstrating the ongoing challenges Indigenous chefs face in entering the industry and sharing their food cultures. Sherman points out that other cities known for their culinary scenes, such as Los Angeles and Chicago, "have zero Native American restaurants that represent the same land they are built on" (2019b). He wants to change that, and so have restaurateurs before him, such as Silverbird and Oden. Sherman and his team are working "tirelessly toward the day we will be able to drive across this continent in any direction, stopping at Indigenous restaurants and experiencing all the richness of the varied original American cultures" (2019b). They are cooking toward a future where culinary sustainability also means cultural sustainability.

Notes

1. This figure was 111,749 in 2010.
2. The history of Indigenous restaurants in the United States deserves further attention. Other examples include Albuquerque's Pueblo Harvest, which was opened by the nineteen Pueblo tribes in New Mexico in 1976 and still operating today, and the Tiwa Kitchen in Taos, which opened in 1993.
3. See Gora 2020 and Gora 2024. For Indigenous foodways in the United States see Berzok 2005; Mihesuah and Hoover 2019; Mihesuah 2005; Pesantubbee and Zogry 2021; Wilson 1987; and Wise and Wallach 2018.
4. The article spells her name both Kavasch and Kavisch, although the former is correct. It also states that she "is not of Indian heritage."
5. This article was published in many newspapers: the *Berkshire Eagle* (Pittsfield, Massachusetts); the *Kilgore News Herald* (Texas); the *South Florida Sun Sentinel* (Fort Lauderdale, Florida); the *Signal* (Santa Clarita, California); *Tyler Morning Telegraph* (Texas); and the *York Dispatch* (Pennsylvania). According to the *New York Times*, it was scheduled to open June 15, 1986. However, another article says it opened May 29 (Miller 1986, C20; Rosenthal 1986, F1).
6. He later opened Mumbai's Indigo restaurant, which ran from 1999 to 2018.
7. For more about her childhood and culinary journey see Oden and Dooley 2024.
8. See also Sherman 2019a.
9. However, it is essential to avoid the stereotype Devon Mihesuah (2005, 21) identifies as "All Indians are Naturalists and Live in Harmony with . . . the Environment."

References

Albuquerque Journal. 1996. "Corn Dance Reopens," July 29.
———. 1997. "Santa Fe Advertisement," April 27.
Berzok, Linda Murray. 2005. *American Indian Food*. Westport, CT and London: Greenwood Press.
Bitsoie, Freddie, and James O. Fraioli. 2021. *New Native Kitchen: Celebrating Modern Recipes of the American Indian*. New York: Abrams.
Corntassel, Jeff. 2012. "Re-Envisioning Resurgence: Indigenous Pathways to Decolonization and Sustainable Self-Determination." *Decolonization: Indigeneity, Education & Society* 1 (1): 86–101.
Crawford O'Brien, Suzanne, and Kimberly Wogahn. 2021. "Bringing a Berry Back from the Land of the Dead: Coast Salish Huckleberry Cultivation and Food Sovereignty." In *Native Foodways: Indigenous North American Religious Traditions and Foods*, edited by Michelene E. Pesantubbee and Michael J. Zogry, 137–65. Albany: SUNY Press.
Daily Oklahoman. 2003. "Dining Guide," October 8.
Donati, Kelly. 2014. "The Convivial Table: Imagining Ethical Relations Through Multispecies Gastronomy." *The Aristologist: An Antipodean Journal of Food History* 4:121–43.
Dovalpage, Teresa. 2014. "Loretta Oden: Native Chef and Culinary Trendsetter." *Taos News*, December 4.

Dowell, Sharon. 1998. "American Indian Cafe Oklahoman's Creation." *Daily Oklahoman*, November 11.

———. 2003a. "Oden: Eager to Learn, Teach about Food." *Daily Oklahoman*, February 5, 2003.

———. 2003b. "Family Ties Bind New Shawnee, City Eateries." *Daily Oklahoman*, May 7, 2003.

Dullea, Georgia. 1986. "For Indians, Celebration and Sadness." *New York Times*, November 27.

Edmonton Journal. 1997. "Eating—Santa Fe Style," October 22.

Evans, Meryle. 1987. "Bison Returns to the Range and the Table." *New York Times*, January 7.

Ferlic, Katie. 2000. "Out to Lunch: Corn Dance Cafe." *Santa Fe New Mexican*, December 15.

Gabin, Vickie. 1994. "Corn Dance Cafe: Native Fare Creative, Well-Prepared." *Albuquerque Journal*, April 14.

Gora, L. Sasha. 2020. "The Muckamuck: Restaurants, Labour, and the Power of Representation." In *Proceedings of the Oxford Symposium on Food & Cookery 2019: Food & Power*, edited by Mark McWilliams, 104–14. London: Prospect Books.

———. 2025. *Culinary Claims: Indigenous Restaurant Politics in Canada*. Toronto: University of Toronto Press.

Hargreaves, Allison. 2016. "'The Lake Is the People and Life That Come to It': Location as Critical Practice." In *Approaching Indigenous Literatures*, edited by Deanne Reder and Linda M. Morra, 107–10. Waterloo: Wilfrid Laurier University Press.

Herzog, Karen. 2014. "The Next Craze in Exotic Cuisine? Native American." *Miami Herald*, October 30.

Kapadia, Jess. 2014. "New York's First Native American Restaurant Was Run by an Indian-American Chef." *Food Republic*, April 23. https://www.foodrepublic.com /2014/04/23/new-yorks-first-native-american-restaurant-was-run-by-an-indian -american-chef/.

Kimmerer, Robin Wall. 2013. *Braiding Sweetgrass: Indigenous Wisdom, Scientific Knowledge, and the Teaching of Plants*. Minneapolis: Milkweed Editions.

King, Lesley. 1995. "At the Nation's Table: Santa Fe, N.M.; Serving Indian Dishes with Ritual and Flair." *New York Times*, June 21.

Kormann, Carolyn. 2022. "How Owamni Became the Best New Restaurant in the United States." *New Yorker*, September 12. https://www.newyorker.com /magazine/2022/09/19/how-owamni-became-the-best-new-restaurant-in-the -united-states.

Levitt, B. Blake. 1985. "An Appreciation of Indian Foods." *New York Times*, November 24.

Lim, Sunamita. 2002. "A Native Thanksgiving: Chef Loretta Oden Stirs up an Indigenous Foods Feast." *Santa Fe New Mexican*, November 27.

Mares, Teresa M., and Devon G. Peña. 2011. "Environmental and Food Justice: Toward Local, Slow, and Deep Food Systems." In *Cultivating Food Justice: Race, Class, and Sustainability*, edited by Alison Hope Alkon and Julian Agyeman, 197–219. Cambridge, MA.: MIT Press.

Mihesuah, Devon A. 2005. *Recovering Our Ancestors' Garden: Indigenous Recipes and Guide to Diet and Fitness*. Lincoln: Bison Books.

Mihesuah, Devon A., and Elizabeth Hoover, eds. 2019. *Indigenous Food Sovereignty in the United States*. Norman: University of Oklahoma Press.

Mihesuah, Devon Abbott. 2005. *So You Want to Write about American Indians? A Guide for Writers, Students, and Scholars*. Lincoln: University of Nebraska Press.

Miller, Bryan. 1988. "Diner's Journal." *New York Times*, July 29, C20.

National Post. 2001. "To Santa Fe, for 'Food That'll Make You Howl.'" August 25.

Oden, Loretta Barrett, and Beth Dooley. *Corn Dance: Inspired First American Cuisine*. Norman: University of Oklahoma Press, 2024.

Parisi, Albert J. 1986. "New Jersey Journal." *New York Times*, November 30.

Patterson, S. Kaitlyn. 2021. "Who Are the Cattails? Stories of Algonquin Anishinaabe Food Systems." *Canadian Food Studies* 8 (1): 22–28.

Pentz, Michelle. 2001. "Corn Dance Café Charms Guests." *Albuquerque Journal*, January 19.

Peña, Devon G. 2002. "Environmental Justice and Sustainable Agriculture: Linking Social and Ecological Sides of Sustainability." Occasional Paper Series, Second National People of Color Environmental Leadership Summit, Washington, DC, October 23–27.

Pesantubbee, Michelene E., and Michael J. Zogry, eds. 2021. *Native Foodways: Indigenous North American Religious Traditions and Foods*. Albany: SUNY Press.

Pesci, Sasha, and Catherine Brinkley. 2021. "Can a Farm-to-Table Restaurant Bring About Change in the Food System? A Case Study of Chez Panisse." *Food, Culture & Society* 25 (5): 997–1018.

Preuss, Joanna. 1986. "FOOD: America's Native Legacy." *New York Times*, November 16.

Rao, Tejal. 2016. "The Movement to Define Native American Cuisine." *New York Times*, August 16. https://www.nytimes.com/2016/08/17/dining/new-native-american-cuisine.html.

Reder, Deanne. 2016. "Introduction: *Position*." In *Approaching Indigenous Literatures*, edited by Deanne Reder and Linda M. Morra, 7–17. Waterloo: Wilfrid Laurier University Press.

Robin, Tabitha. 2018. "Responsibilities and Reflections: Indigenous Food, Culture, and Relationships." *Canadian Food Studies* 5 (2): 9–12.

Rosenthal, John. 1986. "A Taste of Native America." *The Record* (Hackensack, New Jersey), August 31.

Santa Fe New Mexican. 1994. "Bites: Welcome to Two New Restaurants," January 12.

Santa Fe Reporter. 1994. "Visiting Chef: Loretta Barrett Oden—Santa Fe's Corn Dance Cafe, Native American Chef," November 2.

Schwartz, Arthur. 1986. "Please Fly Away, Silverbird." *Daily News* (New York), July 11.

Sherman, Sean. 2019a. "How a Feast for 1,000 Inspired an 'Essential' Dish from the Pacific Northwest." *New York Times*, November 6. https://www.nytimes.com/2019/11/06/reader-center/sean-sherman-native-american-recipes-the-sioux-chef.html.

———. 2019b. "Sean Sherman's 10 Essential Native American Recipes." *New York Times*, November 4. https://www.nytimes.com/2019/11/04/dining/native-american-recipes-sioux-chef.html.

Sherman, Sean, and Beth Dooley. 2017. *The Sioux Chef's Indigenous Kitchen*. Minneapolis: University of Minnesota Press.

Skinner, Kelly, Erin Pratley, and Kristin Burnett. 2016. "Eating in the City: A Review of the Literature on Food Insecurity and Indigenous People Living in Urban Spaces." *Societies* 6 (7): 1–17.

Silverbird, Reuben J. n.d. "Out of Body Experience." *Religionen.at*. Accessed February 21, 2022. http://www.religionen.at/irsilverbo1.htm.

Silverman, Jonathan. 1994. "Bringing Home the Flavor of Real Indian Cooking." *Santa Fe New Mexican*, August 18.

Sones, Melissa. 1986. "Native Gourmet: A New Style of Ethnic Dining Heads East, Hits the Big Time in New York." *Arizona Republic*, August 6.

The Sioux Chef. 2017. "James Beard House Dinner—The Indigenous Foods of Manhatta." Accessed September 10, 2021.

United Nations. 1987. *Our Common Future: Report of the World Commission on Environment and Development*. https://sustainabledevelopment.un.org/content/documents/5987our-common-future.pdf.

Van Buskirk, Audrey. 1998. "Discovering Food: The Corn Dance Cafe Shows Off Native American Contributions to the World's Cooking." *Santa Fe Reporter*, October 7.

Wahpepah, Crystal. 2019. Interview by L. Sasha Gora. April 15.

Wilson, Gilbert Livingston. 1987. *Buffalo Bird Woman's Garden*. Minneapolis: Minnesota Historical Society Press.

Wise, Michael D., and Jennifer Jensen Wallach, eds. 2018. *The Routledge History of American Foodways*. New York: Routledge.

Yarrow, Andrew L. 1986. "14 Reasons Why New York Is New." *New York Times*, October 3.

CHAPTER FIFTEEN

Interrupting Food Waste through Sustainable Cuisine in Ecuador

SANTIAGO ROSERO AND JOAN GROSS

Introduction

Santiago Rosero was trained as a chef at the gastronomic program of San Francisco University of Quito in Ecuador. He worked in various restaurants in New York City, Paris, and Quito before changing course and becoming a journalist and photographer. Santiago made his way back to cooking after being inspired by what chefs can do to interrupt food waste. Since 2018, he has been showing how this can be done.

Joan Gross is a professor of anthropology at Oregon State University who researches food activism, including that of freegans, people who reject the capitalist food system and prefer to live on food that is free, in other words, food that they find in dumpsters, fields, markets, and restaurants, most of which is destined for landfills. She has developed an Intercultural Learning Community, which is structured around a decolonial model highlighting Indigenous peoples and practices and food justice. Students, professors, and community members from Ecuador and Oregon spend two weeks in each country, exploring how people are working to create more equitable and environmentally sustainable food systems.

We met as participants in the 2019 Intercultural Learning Community on Food, Culture and Social Justice in Oregon and Ecuador. The idea of food waste had become increasingly more important since the first program trip in 2013. When the Learning Community first came together, food waste was addressed only within the context of composting. In the second iteration in 2016, we had a vegan participant from Oregon who helped start the No Food Left Behind program in Corvallis, Oregon. In 2019, we had the pleasure of cooking a dinner with Santiago in Quito and hearing about his Idónea project. When we originally proposed to write this chapter in 2020, Joan had planned to return to Ecuador to conduct ethnographic fieldwork on Santiago's Idónea project. The pandemic had just begun, but we had no idea how long it would last. By fall of that year, with COVID-19 still raging, Joan did not feel comfortable traveling and we decided to base the chapter on interviews. In general, Joan asked questions and Santiago answered, but it was not a typical ethnographic interview. Santiago shared some of his earlier writing on food waste and Joan examined Idónea's Facebook page. Sometimes our dialogue was written in e-mails and sometimes it was oral and recorded on Zoom. We are both bilingual and each agreed to write in our native languages, though our Zoom calls were in English. Joan rewrote her questions after reading/hearing Santiago's answers to make sure that the most interesting information was highlighted. Two Zoom conferences with other authors in this volume helped focus our conversations, and academic sources were added later.

What follows is a representation of this ongoing online dialogue between the two authors tracing the development of Santiago's work in Ecuador to create pleasurable dining experiences centered on saving food from becoming waste and spreading information about how to create a more sustainable food system. This work has progressed through various models and continues to morph as new situations arise. Joan's questions are in bold font and Santiago's answers follow in regular font.

The FAO reported that if only a quarter of the world's wasted food were saved, 690 million hungry people could be fed (FAO, IFAD, UNICEF, WFP, and WHO 2020) However, things are more complicated than that. If people think that they are being forced to eat garbage, they will rebel, but if discarded food is lovingly prepared and offered to them in an amicable way, they will be satisfied and perhaps even begin to change their ideas about food. Chefs can play an important role in changing people's ideas about food. How did you become interested in doing something about food waste?

I read an article in *Le Monde* about a restaurant called Freegan Pony when I was working as a journalist in Paris (Berteau 2015). I was really taken with its idea of working against capitalist consumerism and avoiding food waste in a restaurant setting. Freegan Pony was formed when a group of people occupied a former railway depot north of Paris. They got their supplies from the piles of discarded food at the central market of Rungis on the outskirts of the city. Much of the food was thrown out for minor aesthetic flaws that made it unsuitable for sale, according to strict market rules, but it was fine for human consumption. With what was rescued, the restaurant prepared around one hundred vegetarian meals every day from Friday to Monday. The food did not have a fixed price, but each diner contributed what their will dictated. A small part of the prepared food was shared with migrants who had come to Paris fleeing war conflicts and poverty in their countries in the Middle East and sub-Saharan Africa, but the vast majority of diners were young hipsters, professionals, and middle-class students. Although they recognized the political value of the restaurant's management, in large part they came because it was a fashionable place where you could have a good time and eat deliciously for a few euros.

After reading this article, I sent a message to the restaurant offering myself as a volunteer cook. That's how I returned to the professional practice of gastronomy after being away from it for fourteen years. Before I knew it, I was chef de cuisine, making decisions about how to prepare the discarded food coming into the restaurant and directing the other volunteer cooks. I became so involved that I decided to help get the word out. I wrote several articles for Latin American magazines such as *Vice* and *Late*, and for the Spanish journal *The Foodie Studies* (Rosero 2020a, 2020b), and I put together a radio program about this work for Radio France International. My research led me to FAO sites where I discovered that the global costs of food waste total about $2.6 trillion a year. This includes $700 billion in environmental costs and $900 billion in social costs (Gustavsson et al., 2011). In environmental terms, the disaster is undeniable. Producing food uses 40 percent of the land, 70 percent of the drinking water, and 30 percent of the planet's energy, so every piece of food thrown away takes a part of those resources. After cars, the food production system uses more fossil fuels than any other sector in the world economy. And food waste in landfills generates methane as it decomposes, the greenhouse gas that contributes the most to climate change.

Working at Freegan Pony, I was happy to be back in the kitchen and also intellectually immersed in such a progressive (and transgressive) political project. It inspired me to want to develop a similar kind of restaurant when I returned to Ecuador. A friend who organized a meeting for Ecuadorian students doing graduate degrees in Europe told me that he heard a presentation on food waste from Estefanía Gómez, a young Ecuadorian woman who was studying in Holland. Knowing that I was exploring that topic, he asked her for her e-mail address and then passed it on to me. I contacted her and we began exchanging ideas. That lasted for almost two years, and by 2018 we had both returned to Quito. We met in a cafeteria and after two hours of conversation, energetically clarifying our ideas, we had the Idónea–Food Rescue project set up. That was in November 2018.

So, tell us how your ideas developed into Idónea–Food Rescue once you were back in Ecuador?

Idónea–Food Rescue was born as a sociogastronomic bet focused on the fight against food waste. The word "Idónea" defines the state of the food that, despite its aesthetic imperfections, is completely "suitable," even "ideal" for human consumption. We set out to rescue discarded food from markets, fairs, shops, and other outlets, to transform it into tasty dishes and give it a worthy destination. We wanted this effort to be aimed at people in vulnerable situations, but also at the general public. We started with the conviction that food waste is a scourge that concerns us all and that the more people who understand its implications, the more actions can be taken to combat it.

In December 2018 we accomplished our first action, with a few foods recovered from a couple of greengrocers in our neighborhood. We processed the food in my kitchen with a group of friends who volunteered to help. We prepared simple things such as salads and dips to eat with raw vegetables and bread. We shared the food with people attending a craft fair in a cultural center. Their reaction, when we explained the origin of the food and the intentions of the project, was enthusiastic and motivating. It was then that we understood that the project had been born.

Previously, I had visited a couple of municipal markets to try to understand the dynamics related to food waste. The most suitable source turned out to be the Quito Wholesale Market, similar to the market that supplied the Freegan Pony in Paris. In the early morning of a Saturday in January 2019 we arrived at the market in two cars around five in the morning. The market is made up of several sheds with uncovered stalls organized by product. We divided ourselves up according to the different areas, explaining the project to the vendors and hoping they would donate the products that they were no longer going to sell. Their response was encouraging. Many gave us damaged food that they had separated out. Some gave us part of what they thought they were not going to sell because they had too much, and others simply gave us food in good condition because they identified with the goals of the project. After an hour and a half we had the trunks of our cars full of enough food to feed about three hundred people. We continued like this for the following months.

How do the ways in which food is wasted differ between France and Ecuador?

One thing that is different is where most of the waste occurs. The FAO distinguishes between food loss and food waste (Gustavsson et al. 2011, 2). The first category refers to the losses that occur postharvest up to, but not including, the retail level. Food waste results from decisions and actions by retailers, food service providers, and consumers. In developing countries, such as Ecuador, the biggest problem is food loss due to financial, administrative, and technical reasons. Harvests might rot if the roads are impassible, for example. Much of consumer waste, on the other hand, is diverted into animal food in Ecuador. In rural areas, it is common to see a bucket or barrel in the kitchen where scraps for pigs are thrown.

In developed countries, such as France, the problem is food waste related to consumer habits (Gustavsson et al. 2011, 14). Here we can talk about "bad management of the refrigerator" and the desire for picture-perfect fruits and vegetables. People throw food away because they buy in excess, because they become victims of expiration dates (which actually indicate a period of optimal quality but do not imply health risks), because they dislike its worn appearance, because they do not know how to put it to a worthy use, and because they are not aware of the impact of waste. Combining food loss and waste, the FAO estimated that in Europe and North America 250–280 kg of food is lost or wasted per person per year compared to 225 kg in Latin America. Looking specifically at food that is wasted in the home, the difference is more striking with the average rate of 90 kg for each individual in Europe and 25 kg in Latin America (Gustavsson et al. 2011, 5).[1]

Practices such as vendors taking unsaleable food home for their own consumption or for feeding animals, or donating it to various foundations or charitable associations, occur in both regions. Another Ecuadorian practice that reduces waste is the employment of peelers in the markets. Generally, it is the job of young women who dedicate hours to this work and are paid next to nothing. Beans or peas with battered pods, for example, are shelled and sold in plastic bags. Damaged potatoes are peeled and sold clean, without any trace of decay. Home cooks are happy to be able to skip the time it takes to prepare these vegetables for cooking.

I understand the attraction of buying prepared vegetables at the market because procuring, preparing, and cooking food takes a lot of time. Freegans often choose to spend their time rescuing free food, rather than working for wages in the capitalist system in order to buy food (Gross 2009). People who are working for money often don't have the time to spend foraging for food or volunteering at worthy projects. Were you able to find enough people to help you collect food and prepare it?

The project attracted people's attention in Quito because no one else was paying attention to this issue, neither the public authorities nor the professionals in the gastronomic sector. Their focus was on the use of local products that were, hopefully, environmentally responsible and bought directly from the producers for a fair price. Regarding production, farmers and chefs always work at producing more and better, but few wonder—or wondered, because fortunately things have changed a bit since we started—how to avoid waste in the production of food and how to take advantage of what has already been produced and is about to be wasted. As we began to ask ourselves these questions and take action, we attracted attention. We got support first from our friends and family and then from other people who identified with the project's values.

We presented it on our social media networks and called for volunteers to help us in food rescue, cooking, serving, and cleaning and the response was overwhelming. Some of the volunteers who collected food at the market also stayed to cook, and throughout the day others joined in to do whatever was needed. The general reaction was so enthusiastic that we felt we were doing the right thing.

This reminds me of how freegans cultivate themselves as activists and subjects of noncapitalist economies (Gibson-Graham 2006; Gross 2009). Freegan chefs offer the opportunity for others to try on this subjectivity, by eating in an equitable and environmentally sustainable manner. Were there any negative responses?

Only from the market bureaucracy. When I first tried to get official permission to collect food from the Wholesale Market, I spoke with the administration and told them about the project, but instead of being interested, they pointed out all the bureaucratic barriers that I would have to overcome to receive an official permit. It was then that we resolved to take on the task, and the risk, on our own without seeking official permission from the market administration. We went directly to the market vendors and explained the purpose of our project. They responded positively and gave us large amounts of food.

Once you had the food, how did you prepare and serve it? How did you find a suitable kitchen and customers?

I spoke with chef friends and restaurant owners in Quito to see if they would allow us to occupy their spaces for a weekend, calling the event Comida Idónea, or Ideal Food. Their support was immediate. They recognized in the project guidelines an urgency that not many of them were practicing in their culinary work, and they understood that it was necessary to provide a better destination for this food than the garbage dump. That's why stopping their operations for a weekend and making the spaces available to us was no problem at all.

From the Wholesale Market we went directly to the restaurant, and around eight in the morning the hard work began, first with the classification of the products and then with the creative application to devise what we would cook with what we had on hand: essentially, vegetables and fruits. The beginning of the creative process actually occurred at the moment of collection. As soon as I saw what we were getting, I began to shape the menu in my head. The chefs of the restaurants where we worked contributed their ideas. Working collaboratively and experimentally was also central to this project. We wanted to show what delicious meals can be made from rescued food, if only we make the effort.

News of the event spread through word of mouth and social media. People made reservations and began to arrive around 7:00 p.m. on Saturday evenings. After a presentation of the project with slides loaded with figures and hard data on food waste at a local and global level, we served dinner. Three, four, and even five courses of good food served with a flourish left no one indifferent. The delicious dishes in front of them were made with produce that had been destined for the trash. We were looking for an awakening of consciousness about food waste. The flavors, the shared information, and the collaborative and voluntary work succeeded in doing that.

We repeated the operation on Sunday at noon, often with other volunteers. On Sundays, we focused on people living in poverty. We contacted foundations, associations, and shelters. We were able to share meals with the Network of Waste Pickers of Ecuador, with the Venezuelan Association in Ecuador, with the Baca Ortiz Children's Hospital Shelter, and with other charitable organizations. We served fifty meals on Saturday night and fifty more on Sunday. We rescued so much food that we barely managed to cook about 25 percent. The food we didn't use, we put out so that the diners could take what they wanted and use it at home. In the first two years we did around ten events of this type and participated in another ten, smaller ones, related to food waste, such as distributing food to houseless people or those who work at night on the streets. We also participated in Slow Food's Disco Soup, an event celebrated around the world to raise awareness about the climate crisis and how we can have a positive impact by eating differently. People organize parties to collect wasted food, turn it into soup, and eat and dance together.

The type of food we prepared depended, first of all, on the variety of products we could recover, but also on the concepts of the chefs and restaurants that received us. This led to diverse results, some more successful than others. I was influenced by Massimo Bottura, who used his platform as one of the world's leading chefs to bring attention to hunger and food waste. In his book *Bread is Gold: Extraordinary Meals with Ordinary Ingredients* (2017), he includes a recipe for a cabbage soup with lime that I wanted to replicate, but it turned out to be very acidic and not very pleasant. Much tastier was a five-course menu in an Indonesian and Korean food restaurant where we prepared a red bean stew with fried tempeh, sautéed broccoli and a pumpkin puree, and vegetable rolls in cabbage leaves served with sweet and sour sauce and accompanied by cabbage-and-carrot pickles. For dessert we had fresh fruit, mango sorbet, and fried pineapple tempura.

The success of the meal also depended on who the diners were. On Saturday night, the meal I just described was a real success. The diners were educated upper-middle-class people open to the flavors of the world. The next day we served a similar menu to families of Venezuelan migrants in vulnerable situations and the reception was not so enthusiastic. The flavors were far removed from their customary food. We learned that we must always take into account the different groups of diners.

Even though we offered them a free meal, it did not provoke feelings of security and closeness that sharing food can generate when dishes are comfortingly familiar.

That's interesting. So, on Saturday nights you focused on educating about environmental issues through the lens of food waste, bringing a middle-class audience in through the taste sensations you created with discarded food. On Sundays the focus shifted to social justice and the recherché aspect of the food was not as appreciated as comfort food would be, like the hearty vegetarian soups that Food Not Bombs offers in parks around the world (http://foodnotbombs.net/new_site/). The middle-class diners at Idónea are not paying directly for the food, but they are supporting the idea of making our food system environmentally friendly and socially just. How did the model of moving the rescued food operation to different restaurants change through time and particularly after the pandemic became a reality?

When the COVID confinements began, access to markets was impossible for a long time, so our activity had to be limited to smaller amounts of food donated by a few agroecological producers, and with bread donated by a bakery. We had to stop making big dinners, and instead prepared simple meals to take away, sandwiches or other quick dishes, to give to needy neighbors and street vendors.

The itinerant model taught us a lot about organization and logistics, but it came to a point where we thought that a fixed space would allow us to carry out actions more consistently and more comfortably; people could come to our space, where we would have the necessary facilities. In January 2020 I was invited by an Italian named Matteo Rubbettino to a meeting to give ideas on how to revitalize a large, empty house with several rooms and patios in a working-class neighborhood in the north-central part of Quito. He wanted to do something related to gastronomy but had no clear ideas. I immediately realized that it was the ideal place for Idónea. Soon afterwards, we received a grant from the Global Greengrants Funds to install the Idónea kitchen in that house. I asked Rubbettino to join forces with me to create the gastronomic center. We came up with the idea of Fermento, a cultural and gastronomic laboratory dedicated to experimentation and collaborations in the gastronomic sphere. In addition to the Idónea kitchen, my partner installed a kitchen, which he called Humo, to prepare artisan pizzas, and we built a third kitchen that we called the Fermento headquarters, where we could invite chefs with interesting projects to work with us. Humo's production was completely conventional, but in Fermento's third kitchen we did seek to follow the practices of Idónea. However, because of the number and variety of projects that passed through there, it was not always possible to maintain those intentions. For example, most of them used conventionally produced ingredients and almost none of agroecological origin. Many also used processed and ultraprocessed products, with the consequent expense of single-use plastic. In the long run, I believe that the fact that Humo and the third kitchen of Fermento did not work within Idónea's framework of sustainability was one reason for the eventual decline of that project.

In March 2020 the pandemic arrived, but we were determined to move the project forward. By the end of May, we added a store that sold organic and artisanal products in the front of the house. The products they sold were not food waste, but whatever produce had passed its period of greatest freshness and aesthetic brilliance was donated for Idónea's events and actions.

In July of that year we started serving dinners to a reduced clientele in the outdoor patio. We began with two potato-centered dinners because we were given a big sack of potatoes. We planned for two days, one for me to prepare a menu, and one for my partner, Rubbettino. He made gnocchi au gratin and I made baked potatoes with a pesto of several leftover greens, and I fried the beet greens in a sourdough batter that I had left over from the bread I normally prepare. They were very elementary dinners in terms of their menus, but with quite a lot of concept behind them, and they also had that transgressive character for having been offered, almost secretly, in the middle of the pandemic. This gave me the idea to invite different chefs to develop menus based on a single main ingredient that we had available in large quantities because someone had donated it to us, or simply because we wanted to experiment with it. I called that concept Vicentina Clandestina (La Vicentina is the name of the neighborhood where the project house is located, and they started out as almost clandestine dinners with only a few guests from our immediate circles whom we knew were healthy.)

For the operation of Fermento, which existed independently of my project, Idónea, we put together a weekly program, sort of like a cinema, theater, or cultural center, but dedicated to food, which was not necessarily rescued. The idea was to have different types of cuisine, world cuisines, throughout the week. We had Mexican, Thai, Japanese, Brazilian, and "new Ecuadorian" food, among others. Also, we built a sort of gastronomic co-working space and we continued to create new concepts, cycles, and special events. For example, we invited chefs to make themed dinners for special dates (e.g., Valentine's Day, Mother's Day). We also made dinners bringing together two or more chefs. I even created a cycle based on home-cooked food prepared by the mothers and grandmothers of the guest chefs. This gave the project great visibility and appeal, even in the midst of the pandemic. When I participated in these programs, I always used at least a portion of rescued food. The rest of the participants in the Fermento programs used conventionally sourced products.

I understand that your initial attraction to this project was for environmental reasons, but we cannot live completely outside of a capitalist system, so how did this new model work economically? How was having your own place more comfortable and how was it more stressful?

In short, Idónea is a nonprofit project, but clearly we need funds to be able to pay a fair wage to those who put in the most work. As was the case at the Freegan Pony in Paris, we did not put a fixed price on the food. The diners gave a voluntary contribution to support the project and recognize the quality of the food. The funds raised served to cover the fixed costs of the project, from fuel to go to the market to the basic ingredients necessary to prepare the food: oils, condiments, cereals, and other things that are not available to rescue in the market. The only person who received an hourly wage was the one in charge of washing the dishes, a difficult job that requires long hours in front of the sink. The rest of the people in the kitchen and the servers, apart from myself and Estefanía Gómez (my partner in the project), worked as volunteers.

Idónea quickly attracted attention, thanks to the novelty of the project and its concern for a widely neglected issue in conventional culinary practice: waste. Its reputation grew and we began to receive offers of collaborations from companies, food ventures, and professionals in the food industry to donate leftover food from their operations or to ask us for help on what to do with the leftover food. We had to make sure that our partners shared our philosophy with regard to their own management and respect and care for the environment. We began to establish relationships with fair-trade, agroecological producers, and avoided dealing with large agribusiness companies, for example, in the meat or ultra-processed food industry. We always privilege fresh food and processed food from small businesses and enterprises. On another occasion, Conquito, an economic development agency related to the Municipality of Quito, asked us to research successful initiatives in the city to reduce food waste. We did that research and were able to create a map of people and projects working in that direction.

We were able to set up the Idónea kitchen thanks to a grant from the Global Greengrants Fund. We thought that a place of our own would allow us to carry out actions more frequently without waiting for permission to use other restaurants. We would charge enough to cover expenses and apply for grants from international organizations, but we did not count on the arrival of the pandemic, nor that I would also take charge of developing the parent project that was Fermento. While Idónea had a solidarity vocation and a nonprofit nature, Fermento was born as a business that had to generate income to sustain itself. Suddenly, I was more involved in the need to sustain a business (Fermento) than in consolidating a project and its ideals of sustainability and solidarity (Idónea). In other words, conventional capitalism overcame committed activism. It is true that the pandemic prevented us from moving forward with Idónea's regular actions, but it is also true that Fermento's complex management model took up my time and energy. Much to my regret, Idónea suffered the consequences of my becoming an entrepreneur because I had to give more time and attention to Fermento's conventional operations (creating events, convening participants, attending to its internal functioning, improving the operational and financial model) and I could not take as much care of activist and solidarity actions with Idónea (less food rescue, fewer gastronomic-pedagogical events, fewer links with people and organizations interested in working on these issues). As I said, this was also affected by the context of the pandemic, which hindered free mobility and the possibility of meeting.

Idónea was not designed to make money, but we came to understand the importance of economic sustainability. We needed a model that allowed us to generate payment for the management as well as the dishwashing because these are the functions that demand the most work. In our case, I am the manager and also head chef, and Fermento's tasks began to take up a large part of my time, to the point of preventing me from maintaining my paid work as a journalist and author. The rest of the participants in all the tasks, as I have explained, have been and still are volunteers, something that works as a sign of commitment on their part and is a pillar of the project.

Fermento was always thought of as a business, although its operating model and concept were highly experimental and unconventional. It was a space that housed several projects, some fixed (Idónea, Humo, the Fermento store) and others occasional (the varied events in the third kitchen). We devised a model in which Idónea and Humo had to contribute 10 percent of their income to Fermento's common fund, and the store paid a fixed rent for its space. The guest projects received 65 percent of the income , and 35 percent remained as income for Fermento. It seemed fair, but the profit margins were very small and with that we had to cover most of the expenses (basic services, supplies, salaries, rent). With so many variables in play, I, who was inexperienced in business and management, had trouble making it profitable and stable. We were especially concerned about being able to pay the salaries of the workers, who were almost all Venezuelan migrants in vulnerable situations who live in the same neighborhood.

It sounds like the economic sustainability that you were trying to achieve in Fermento was impacting social sustainability. Can you talk about the various ways you attempted to create social cohesion and improve the quality of life in the neighborhood?

La Vicentina is a middle- and working-class neighborhood that began to form in the 1940s with groups of internal migrants from the Ecuadorian countryside. There was a second migration flow at the beginning of this millennium with the settlement of Colombians, Cubans, and, more recently, Venezuelans. It's an active, lively neighborhood that benefits from the energy that the confluence of different populations gives rise to. It was always clear to me that I did not want Fermento to be implanted like an alien dissociated from the environment, so I sought integration with the neighborhood and its people from the beginning. Above all, I wanted to avoid anything that seemed like gentrification.

I contacted the president of the neighborhood and presented the project to her, asking her to help me establish relationships with the neighbors. In August 2020, the San Francisco de Quito University invited me to give a virtual talk called "The Future of Food." It was a virtual chat that at the same time was something of a cooking workshop. While I was talking with the moderators about the work of Idónea and the importance of taking advantage of the food that is wasted to ensure the feeding of the population that will increase in the coming years, I was preparing sandwiches with rescued food (bread donated by Cyrano, a great bakery in the city with which I have a good relationship, and vegetables from a couple of neighborhood stores that I then roasted). There was food for forty people that the president of the neighborhood helped me convene. Among the people who came were the elderly, children, and young adults, mostly Venezuelan migrants. In that group was Angie, a woman with her two children and her two sisters, twins with hearing and speech disabilities. There was also Efraín, a happy thirty-three-year-old man. That first event introduced us to the neighborhood in the best way: sharing food. More valuable still, it generated the contact that allowed Angie, her sisters and other members of her family, and also Efraín and a cousin of his named John, to work in Fermento as the service and cleaning team. Another neighbor devoted himself to parking and protecting customers' cars. In hiring local people, we had the satisfaction of having offered jobs to people who are migrants trying to insert themselves into a society where they do not always find open doors. We also frequently purchased items for our operations in the various businesses in the neighborhood.

I think that, at this small scale, we were successful in integrating a group of neighbors who needed work. However, we were not able to create a neighborhood customer base for our restaurants and store. The explanation is simple: in the neighborhood there are many small places where you pay between $2.50 and $3.00 for a simple lunch menu with soup, a main dish, and a soft drink. Most of the workers in the sector and neighbors who do not cook at home go to these places. At Fermento, lunch menus cost an average of $7.00, including those that I prepared on some occasions at Idónea, partly with rescued food. Instead of local customers, we attracted middle-class people from neighboring La Floresta, an area full of restaurants with a hipster atmosphere and, in prepandemic times, an active cultural scene. In short, neither the price of our food (which was comparable to that of restaurants in La Floresta) nor the type of food that we offered (world foods and reimagined local cuisine) connected with people in the neighborhood.

We had more success with our agroecological artisan food store. It faced competition from around ten other food stores on the same street that were conventional and had cheaper prices. But neighbors began coming in out of curiosity. When they did, they learned about the difference in how the foods were grown and some of them began to buy at least some of their food in our store.

Fermento only lasted one year. Now Idónea is in a third phase. It has become itinerant again, but now it is traveling outside of Quito into more rural areas. Tell us how this new model compares to the previous ones in terms of economic, social, and environmental sustainability.

It seems as if Fermento lasted longer than a year because of the amount of activity we promoted, but finally the differences in vision, values, and ways of working with my Fermento partner became too large. Perhaps one could say that since environmental sustainability was not forefronted throughout Fermento, the social and economic sustainability suffered. I decided to leave and dismantled the Idónea kitchen. Fermento ceased to exist and Idónea returned to its itinerant modality. Now, the current phase of the project, which we have called Idónea Ambulante, works as a kind of antiwaste minitour. We think of it this way because we decided to take the project out of Quito. We have traveled to three small cities in the country, two in the mountains and one on the coast, and worked together with agroecological producers and local social and gastronomic projects. In this phase, we are also working with two more people in the direct team, Carla García and Jazmín Buitrón, who are involved in various tasks, from graphic design and general production to kitchen assistance. At the same time, two other people are documenting the process on video, as we intend to make a short documentary of this phase of our work. It is economically possible thanks to another small grant from the Global Greengrants Fund. We couldn't survive without that, so we don't know whether it will be economically sustainable. Only two of the events generated a small income because we held dinners open to the public, who paid $15 in one case and $25 in the other (this was more expensive because for the first time in the history of the project we decided to use an animal protein, which was fish donated by a local producer). The third dinner was given for no charge to a group of poor Indigenous elders.

Part of the proceeds of the two dinners will be donated to organizations that work with people in poverty, and another part will serve to pay a minimum wage to those of us who are working on the project. The events carried out during our first two years of activity in Quito generated enough income to augment the general fund of the project, but now our economic resources barely cover all the production costs. We are putting all the resources into carrying out the tour, which, in addition to dinners, includes workshops on food waste and what we call optimization cooking—making the most of all parts and components of food (peels, skins, stems, leaves, roots) to reduce waste. At the same time, the additional investment in workshops requires more logistics and more interaction between agroecological producers and chefs. The agroecological producers allow us to harvest on their farms and they donate the food for the workshops and dinners. The chefs who work with us also work locally in various social and gastronomic projects, such as a cooking school and a foundation that feeds poor elderly people. This creates community participation and an interesting exchange of actions and knowledge. The project is very new, but we think that Idónea Ambulante will jump-start further interactions in these rural areas, leading to social sustainability within the movement.

Environmental sustainability lies at the root of these projects. Rural people are very aware of the problem of food waste and have always made efforts to reduce waste, mostly for economic reasons. Our contribution is to offer proposals from gastronomy, that is to say, we use rescued food as the main input for the gastronomic events we organize, as a way to show the value and potential of these foods with simple meals as well as with elaborate menus. In that sense, both realities complement each other. Neither food producers nor chefs can solve this problem independently of the other. What we are trying to do is spread our message and our actions outside of Quito so that, eventually, local groups or projects similar to ours will be formed and a national network born.

Eating is certainly one of life's great pleasures and chefs have an important role to play in creating pleasurable events around food. You have succeeded in doing this in a way that encourages environmental and social sustainability. Idónea is not a chef-centered project but one that is focused on enlarging the group of people who want to enjoy a socially just, environmentally sustainable life. The concept of alternative hedonism (Soper 2020) refers to people taking environmental and social sustainability into account when making their decisions about what to eat. How do you see this playing out in the events that you have created?

First of all, I want to say that we managed to create a model (without necessarily having consciously designed it that way) in which the economic costs are minimal. What is more important is the voluntary participation of people at all levels of the project. This is because people identify with the principles of the project and the way people work together. Already when I worked at Freegan Pony, I understood that the central public for this type of project, the people who allow it to maintain operations thanks to their faithful presence and their economic contributions, is a young, educated segment, connected to the trends of culture, food, and direct action, who are concerned about ecology and social justice in their daily lives. It is an audience similar to this one that provides part of the resources that have allowed us to keep the project afloat. By acknowledging this, I think we gained a greater commitment on their part, a commitment that allows us to allocate part of our time and effort to offering food to poor people. I think that alternative hedonism captures the way that this group of people seek pleasure that conforms to their social, environmental, and political concerns.

Pleasure should be thought about in a broader sense. If the food is delicious but has questionable traceability, for me the pleasure is not complete. We want to change people's habits and ideas more than their taste preferences. If diners understand that our raw materials are rescued foods and that we also use parts of the food that are usually thrown away (stems, peelings, roots, etc.), the palate also enters an experimentation phase. Diners enter a state of communion with us and with the project itself. Of course, this only happens if the food is satisfying. That's why we take great care with food preparation, since a bad meal wouldn't allow us to create the sensory and reflective experience necessary to grow the movement.

Notes

1. Later research shows that levels of household food waste between these areas are very similar, though confidence in the estimates is not high (United Nations Environment Programme 2021).

References

Berteau, Franck. 2015. "Freegan Pony, le restaurant squatteur." *Le Magazine du Monde,* November 25.

Bottura, Massimo. 2017. *Bread Is Gold: Extraordinary Meals with Ordinary Ingredients.* London: Phaidon Press.

FAO, IFAD, UNICEF, WFP, and WHO. 2020. *The State of Food Security and Nutrition in the World 2020. Transforming Food Systems for Affordable Healthy Diets.* Rome: FAO. https://doi.org/10.4060/ca9692en.

Gibson-Graham, J. K. 2006. *A Postcapitalist Politics.* Minneapolis: University of Minnesota Press.

Gross, Joan. 2009. "Capitalism and its Discontents: Back-to-the-Lander and Freegan Foodways in Rural Oregon." *Food and Foodways* 17:57–79.

Gustavsson, Jenny, Christel Cederberg, Ulf Sonesson, Robert van Otterdijk, and
    Alexandre Meyback. 2011. *Global Food Losses and Food Waste: Extent, Causes
    and Prevention: Study Conducted for the International Congress "Save Food!" at
    Interpack 2011, Dusseldorf, Germany.* Rome: FAO. http://www.fao.org/docrep/014
    /mb060e/mb060e00.pdf.
Rosero, Santiago. 2020a. "Comer de la basura." *The Foodie Studies*, October 16.
———. 2020b. "No hace falta producir más sino distribuir mejor." *Ojo público*,
    November 3.
Soper, Kate. 2020. *Post-Growth Living: For an Alternative Hedonism.* New York: Verso.
United Nations Environment Programme 2021. *Food Waste Index Report.* Nairobi.
    https://www.unep.org/resources/report/unep-food-waste-index-report-2021.

CONTRIBUTORS

Nanna Hammer Bech has a master's degree in anthropology. She is assistant manager and project leader of the Danish sustainable food think tank Tænketanken Frej, which works for a more sustainable food system in Denmark through dialogue, knowledge sharing, and collaboration.

David Beriss is an associate dean and professor of anthropology at the University of New Orleans. He is coeditor (with David Sutton) of *The Restaurants Book: Ethnographies of Where We Eat* (2007) and author of *Black Skins, French Voices: Caribbean Ethnicity and Activism in Urban France* (2004). He studies and writes about food and culture in New Orleans and south Louisiana and is editor of and a frequent contributor to FoodAnthropology (https://foodanthro.com/), the blog of the Society for the Anthropology of Food and Nutrition.

Rachel E. Black is an associate professor of anthropology at Connecticut College, where she also leads the Food Pathway. Black's areas of specialization are food studies, labor, and gender. She is author of *Cheffes de Cuisine: Women and Work in the Professional French Kitchen* (2021) and *Porta Palazzo: The Anthropology of an Italian Market* (2012). She is the coeditor of *Wine and Culture: Vineyard to Glass* (2013). Black's latest project, "The Taste of Climate Change," investigates the impact of climate change on cuisines in southern Europe. Black serves as an associate editor for the interdisciplinary journal *Food and Foodways*.

Carole Counihan is professor emerita of anthropology at Millersville University and editor in chief of the scholarly journal *Food and Foodways*. She has been studying food, gender, culture, taste, and food activism in Italy and the United States for forty years. She is author of *Italian Food Activism in Urban Sardinia* (2019, Italian edition 2020), *A Tortilla Is Like Life* (2009), *Around the Tuscan Table* (2004), and *The Anthropology of Food and Body* (1999). She is coeditor of several books on foodways, including, with Susanne Højlund, *Making Taste Public* (2018).

Lauren Darnell is executive director of the Made in New Orleans foundation. Since 2018 she has been leading the nonprofit organization in its work to create a transformative vision of the future of the hospitality industry in New Orleans. She has received the Ella Brennan "Stand Up for Your Hometown" Award and the *Essence* Essential Heroes Award. She holds a bachelor of arts from the University of New Orleans in anthropology and women's studies.

Jonathan M. Deutsch, PhD, is professor of food and hospitality management in the College of Nursing and Health Professions at Drexel University in Philadelphia and a Certified Research Chef (CRC®). He directs the Drexel Food Lab, a good-food product development and culinary innovation lab designing solutions to improve the health of people, the planet, and economies. He is the coauthor or coeditor of eight books, including *The Anti-Inflammatory Family Cookbook* (2021).

Michele Filippo Fontefrancesco is an associate professor of cultural anthropology at the Catholic University of the Sacred Heart in Milan, Italy, and an honorary fellow of the department of anthropology of Durham University, United Kingdom. His research focuses on food anthropology and economic anthropology, including fieldwork in southern Europe and East Africa.

Laura Garzón holds a master of arts in social studies from Universidad del Rosario in Bogotá, Colombia. She works on issues related to citizen participation and has centered her research on conflict and peace studies, gender, rurality, and agroecology in rural and urban communities.

L. Sasha Gora is a writer and cultural historian with a focus on food studies, contemporary art, and the environmental humanities. Since 2023, she has been based at the University of Augsburg, where she is the project director of the "Off the Menu: Appetites, Culture, and Environment" research group. Her research focuses on restaurant politics and cultural representation, the connections between cuisine and ecology, and all things fishy and salty.

Joan Gross, PhD, is professor emerita of anthropology at Oregon State University, where she taught courses in language and culture, folklore, and food anthropology and helped establish the Food in Culture and Social Justice program. She is the author of *Speaking in Other Voices: An Ethnography of Walloon Puppet Theaters* (2001) and editor of *Teaching Oregon Native Languages* (2007). Her recent research focuses on food sovereignty activism in Oregon and Ecuador.

Liora Gvion is a sociologist whose areas of expertise are the sociology of food and the body. Her works revolve around the social relationships embedded in food production and consumption. She is author of *Beyond Hummus and Falafel: Social and Political Aspects of Palestinian Food in Israel* (2012) and of many articles in major journals.

Susanne Højlund is an anthropologist working on taste and food culture, chef education and children's perceptions of taste. She is head of FOCUS, the Center for Food Culture Studies at Aarhus University, and initiator of the two interdisciplinary symposia, Creative Tastebuds. Based on fieldwork in Denmark and Cuba she has published widely on childhood, welfare, hominess, food, sugar culture, and taste, and has coedited several books, among them *Making Taste Public* (2018) with Carole Counihan, and *Sugar and Modernity in Latin America* (2014) with Vinicius de Carvalho, Karen-Margrethe Simonsen, and Per Bendix Jeppesen.

Elizabeth Hoover is an associate professor in the Society and Environment division of the Environmental Science and Policy Management (ESPM) Department at the University of California at Berkeley. Her work focuses on environmental justice, food sovereignty, and community uses of fire. Major publications include *The River Is Us: Fighting Toxics in a Mohawk Community* (2017) and a coedited volume, *Indigenous Food Sovereignty in the United States* (2019).

Jonatan Leer is a professor of culinary arts and meal science at Örebro University specializing in food culture. He has over fifty academic publications on the New Nordic cuisine, sustainable food design, food pedagogies, meat consumption, and the gendering of food practices, in journals such as *European Journal of Cultural Studies, Journal of Culture and Aesthetics, Feminist Review*, and *Food and Foodways*. He has edited the books *Food and Media* (2016) and *Research Methods in Digital Food Studies* (2021).

Raúl Matta, a full researcher at the Institut Lyfe Research and Innovation Center (Lyon, France), works at the intersection of anthropology, food, and heritage studies. He has conducted research in France, Peru, Germany, and Mexico, and held leading roles in projects funded by the German Research Foundation (DFG), the French National Research Agency (ANR), and the European Commission (HERA). He has published papers in *Social Anthropology, Gastronomica, Food, Culture & Society*, and *Food* *and Foodways*, among others. He is the author of *From the Plate to Gastro-Politics: Unravelling the Boom of Peruvian Cuisine* (2023).

Ole G. Mouritsen, PhD, DSc, is a physicist and professor emeritus of gastrophysics and culinary food innovation at the University of Copenhagen as well as president of the Danish Gastronomical Academy. His current work is centered on taste as a driver in the green transition. He collaborates with chefs and has authored books on fats, sushi, seaweeds, umami, mouthfeel, cephalopods, pickles, vegetables, and roe.

Marilisa Navarro, PhD, is an assistant professor of African American studies and a critical ethnic studies scholar at Thomas Jefferson University in Philadelphia, PA. Her scholarship analyzes the intersection of critical ethnic studies, critical food studies, popular culture, discourse analysis, and representations. She examines how foodways, food-related spaces, and culinary practices are sites in which racial and gender identities are constituted, expressed, and challenged.

Santiago Rosero is an independent writer, researcher, and cook in Quito, Ecuador. He holds a bachelor's degree in journalism and gastronomy and a master's degree in communication. He writes about culture, food, and the environment. He is the author of several non-fiction books, including *Una mesa más larga*. He is the director of *Disección de un plato*, a podcast that explores Ecuadorian gastronomy with an ethnographic and multidisciplinary approach, and is the founder and director of Idónea, a sociogastronomic project focused on the fight against food waste.

Klavs Styrbæk is an award-winning Danish head chef who owns and operates STYRBÆKS. Combining a high standard of craftmanship and sparked by curiosity-driven enthusiasm, he has created a gourmet center where people can enjoy excellent food, and where they can also learn and improve their culinary skills. Styrbæk has developed learning materials on food culture, sustainability, and food waste, and many of the recipes that appear in the books coauthored with Ole G. Mouritsen originated in the test kitchens at STYRBÆKS.

David Sutton is a professor of anthropology at Southern Illinois University, Carbondale. Since the early 1990s he has been conducting research focused on memory, historical consciousness, food, and cooking.

His most recent work, *Bigger Fish to Fry* (2021), develops a theory of cooking as everyday risk as a way of approaching questions of continuity and change in cooking practices.

Sarra Talib is a PhD candidate in food systems and a graduate fellow at the Gund Institute for Environment at the University of Vermont. Her transdisciplinary research explores the role of chefs as "change agents" for the transition to a circular economy for food. A DC native, Sarra also calls London and the Red Sea home. When she isn't exploring ways to design waste out of the food system, she likes to spend her time exploring nature, art museums, and the local cheese counter.

Amy Trubek, an anthropologist and a chef, is a professor in the Department of Nutrition and Food Sciences at the University of Vermont. She is the author of *Haute Cuisine: How the French Invented the Culinary Profession* (2000), *The Taste of Place, A Cultural Journey into Terroir* (2008), and *Making Modern Meals* (2017). She currently serves as the Director of the Climate Kitchen, a maker's space for collaboration and experimentation to help us reimagine the connection between food and climate change.

Ana María Ulloa is an assistant professor of anthropology at Universidad de los Andes in Bogotá, Colombia. She received her PhD in anthropology from the New School for Social Research in New York. Her work has focused on providing ethnographic accounts of how flavor becomes an object of knowledge and commerce and the formation of sensory skills in taste and smell laboratories, the flavor and fragrance industries, and restaurants. Her articles have appeared in *Senses and Society*, *Gastronomica, Food, Culture, and Society* and as chapters in the edited volumes *Capitalism and the Senses* and *Consumer Research Methods in Food Science*.

Dauro Mattia Zocchi is a research fellow in geography at the Department of Foreign Languages, Literatures, and Cultures at the University of Bergamo. He holds degrees in business administration and gastronomic sciences. In 2022, he earned a PhD in Eco-gastronomy, Education, and Society at the University of Gastronomic Sciences of Pollenzo, Italy. His primary research interests include food geography, food scouting, and the promotion of food heritage in rural and marginalized areas. He has contributed to research projects in Italy, Peru, Bolivia, Kenya, and Tanzania.

INDEX

menus during COVID-19, 166, 177n3; postindustrial, 59; transgressive, 64; urban, 224; of vegan dining experience, 55, 57, 65

development: community, 201, 228–30, 234; economic, 39, 239; infrastructural, 222, 223, 224; local, 6; of new products, 148, 150, 152, 157; rural, 39, 40, 41, 43, 244; social, 30; sustainable, 4, 40, 41, 66, 90, 203, 266. *See also* Sustainable Development Goals

diabetes: among Native Americans, 208, 209, 213

diaspora, African, 12, 219, 229–30

drinks: fermented, 78, 99, 101; made from avocado seeds, 157; organic, 99

E

EAT-Lancet Report, 4–5, 15, 69, 70

Eleven Madison Park (restaurant), 53–54

entrepreneurship, 220, 221, 222, 233, 238; and just sustainability, 228–30, 234. *See also* Black chefs

environmental ethics, 207

Equilibrio (foundation), 41

ethical eating, 91–92, 93, 104, 110, 112, 117, 238

ethics: of care, viii, 98; of vegans, 111, 112, 113, 116; of work, 90, 92, 93

Evans, Kurt (chef), 229, 233

Everybody Eats, 220, 227, 228, 231

F

FAO. *See* United Nations Food and Agriculture Organization

farm-to-chef, 11, 164–66, 175, 177

farm-to-table, 111, 122, 163–64, 165, 166, 265

fermentation, 74, 78

Fermento, 281–82, 282–83, 284–85

fieldwork, ethnographic: in Danish culinary schools, 10, 127, 128, 130; in Ecuador, 274; with Kenyan chefs, 239, 241

food activism. *See* activism

food apartheid, 220

food industry, vii, ix, 3, 23, 27, 146–48

food justice, 204, 212, 213

food loss, 277

food sovereignty, 7, 36, 202, 240, 250. *See also* Indigenous food sovereignty

food system: definition of, 5; global, 163; local, 163; as problem and solution, 3; unsustainability, 69. *See also* local food system

food waste, 71, 95, 97, 98, 128, 155; reduction in schools, 20, 25, 135–36

food waste in Ecuador, 13, 273; economic sustainability, 284–87; environmental sustainability, 288; extent, 274, 275; and food loss, 277; meals from, 275, 276, 279–81, 282; rescue of, 274–75, 276–77, 278–79; social sustainability, 285, 288

Freegan Pony, 274–75, 276, 283, 288

freegans, 273, 278

fry bread, 208–10

fungi, 72, 73, 76, 81. *See also* mushrooms

G

Gardens in Africa, 241

gastronomic reformism, 250

Geranium (restaurant), 53

Giusti, Dan (chef), 8, 19–23, 26, 28, 29–30, 31

Grand Central Restaurant (Paris), 96; menu, 97; seasonality, 97; waste avoidance, 97

Gray Horse American Eatery, 199, 213n1

foods, 114, 117–19. *See also* Israeli vegan chefs

J

Jacobs, Ben (Osage chef), 199–201, 205, 209, 212, 213
James Beard Award, xn4, 265
James Beard Foundation, 255
James Beard House, 255
just sustainability, vii, 7, 11–12, 220, 233–34; and collaboration, 220, 230–33; and collective agency, 222, 231; and community resilience, 222, 231; definition, 204, 221–22; and entrepreneurship, 220, 228–30; and food security, 220, 227, 228; and mentorship, 220, 230–33; and mutual aid, 220, 230–33

K

Kenya, 238; catering sector, 239; colonized cuisine, 239; traditional foods, 246, 250. *See also* Slow Food Cooks Alliance, Kenya
Kidz Meals on Wheels, 228, 230, 232
kincentric ecology, 203, 212
kitchen craft, 10, 41, 74–75, 140n1, 229; in Danish culinary education, 131–32; as practice of sustainability, 128–29, 137–40. *See also* craft
kitchen work, professional, 7, 13, 28–29; of chef apprentices, 129; combatting waste, 97, 122; conditions of, 10, 92, 99, 100–1, 105; in the food industry, 143, 144, 147–48, 149, 150, 151–53; transforming school food, 31; of women, 40. *See also* collaboration; kitchen craft; labor, in professional kitchens
kokumi, 77, 80, 81, 83

L

labor, in professional kitchens, 149, 169, 176; reskilling, 23, 26, 28–29, 31; shortages during COVID-19, 172. *See also* kitchen work, professional
La Maison Montreuil (restaurant), 98–101, 105n2; freshness, 99–100; local food, 99; menu, 99; "reasoned products," 100; sourcing, 100; taste, 99, 100
Le Vieux Belleville (restaurant), 101–4; fresh products, 102, 104; homemade cuisine, 102–3; menu, 101; taste, 103–4
local food system: sourcing from during the COVID-19 pandemic, 170–72; and sustainability, 175, 176–77; and trust, 163–64; and value chain, 164

M

Martínez, Eduardo (chef), 8; agronomy in Pacific region, 39; cooking, importance of, 41, 42; food story of, 38–43; interviews with, 38; women's cooking, influence of, 40–41, 47. *See also* Mini-Mal; New Colombian cuisine
meat, 70, 127, 134
Mini-Mal (restaurant), 8; aesthetics, 46–47; cuisine, 42; and cultural awareness, 37, 48; flavors, 46–47; history, 36, 38, 42; local ingredients, 36, 37, 42, 43, 44–45, 46, 49; philosophy, 36–37, 42; pop-up version, 42; relations with producers, 43, 45–46; sustainability, 37, 40, 43, 44, 48; twentieth anniversary, 35–36, 49. *See also* Colombia; Martínez, Eduardo; New Colombian cuisine

mentoring, 210, 230–33
mushrooms, 62, 76, 78, 81, 114, 118, 157. *See also* fungi

N
Native American chefs, 11; interviews with, 202; mentoring of, 210. *See also* Indigenous chefs
Native American Culinary Association (NACA), 202
NATIFS (North American Traditional Indigenous Food Systems), 206
National School Lunch Program (NSLP), 20, 21, 22, 29
Network of Waste Pickers of Ecuador, 280
networks: of Black chefs, 223; of chefs with community, 7, 45, 167, 175, 176; of Kenyan chefs, 240–43; of New Orleans chefs, 188–89; of chefs with producers, 11, 175, 177; of Slow Food, 240–42; through social media, 90, 278; Terroirs d'Avenir, 100; Vermont Fresh, 166
New Colombian cuisine, 38
New Nordic cuisine, 19
New Orleans culinary culture, 11; Black chefs, 183–84, 189–92, 193; local food in, 185, 188–89, 193; seafood in, 184, 185; sourcing food, 183, 186; sustainability of, 182–83, 189–94; white chefs, 183–84, 190, 191, 192
New Orleans restaurants: economic concerns, 189; relationships with fishers, 187–88, 189; role in sustainability, 186–87, 193; seafood in, 187, 188; supply chains, 188; value chains, 188
newspapers, 262, 263, 268n5; analysis of, 12, 13, 183, 219–21, 223–24, 234,

256. *See also New York Times; Philadelphia Inquirer*
New York Times, 224, 256, 257, 259, 260, 264, 268n5
Noma (restaurant), vii, viii, 13–14, 19, 53, 144; veganism, 53

O
Oden, Loretta Barrett (Potawatomi chef), 207, 210, 259–63
Oliver, Jamie (chef), 23, 237, 238
Olunloyo, Shola (chef), 229–30, 231–32
One Health, 14
optimization cooking, 13
organic food, 91, 100, 111, 121–22, 262
Our Common Future (United Nations report), 4, 133
Owamni (restaurant), 206, 264–65

P
pandemic. *See* COVID-19
Parker, KeVen (chef), 232–33
Parisian chefs, 9–10, 92–105; study of, 92–93; sustainability of, 93, 96; waste avoidance, 95, 97, 98. *See also* Grand Central Restaurant; La Maison Montreuil; Le Vieux Belleville; Paris Institute for Advanced Study
Paris Institute for Advanced Study (PIAS), 93–96; local food at, 94; lunch at, 93–96; menu, 94–95; refined collective catering of, 94. *See also* Parisian chefs
Peruvian Gastronomic Revolution, 238
Philadelphia Inquirer, 219–20, 222–24, 226, 227, 228, 230, 231, 232, 233, 234; cultural studies analysis of, 222–23; representation of Black chefs, 220, 223, 224, 234
planetary menu, 70

plant-based diets. *See* veganism

plant foods, 72; and sustainability, 72; and taste, 73–74; and umami, 73–74

Polanyi, Karl, 164, 167, 177

polycrisis, 3

R

Redzepi, Rene (chef), 13, 144, 145

regenerative food systems, 14, 14n2

research chefs, 10; advocates for sustainability, 150–51, 154–56; anonymity, 150; definition of, 143, 144–45; educating consumers, 152; equity concerns, 153–54; history of, 146–48; impact, 157; and ingredient selection, 150–53, 156; interviews with, 143, 145–46; multiple challenges, 149; products created by, 145, 148, 150, 153, 157; scale, 149; sustainability for, 144, 149–56; triple bottom-line framework of sustainability, 149, 154–55; upcycling, 151; waste reduction, 156. *See also* chefs; Culinologists®; Culinology®; Research Chefs Association

Research Chefs Association, 144, 148

restaurants: and hierarchy, 96, 100; industry, 3, 9, 93, 111; instrumental values, 164; labor challenges, vii–viii, 100–101; midscale, 92–105; relational values, 164, 174–75; and sexual abuse, viii; as third spaces, ix; working conditions, 100–101, 130, 172. *See also* Bellies; Grand Central Restaurant; La Maison Montreuil; Le Vieux Belleville; Mini-Mal; New Orleans restaurants; Parisian chefs; Paris Institute for Advanced Study; Tocabe; vegan restaurants

Rio Summit, 40

S

scalability. *See* research chefs

School Breakfast Program (SBP), 22

School Dinners (documentary), 23

school food: bad quality, 22–23, 31; in Britain, 23; and chefs, 23, 24; and ethnic food, 27; and hegemonic nutrition, 24, 26; influence of industry, 23, 27, 31; and learning, 23–24; and neophobia, 27. *See also* Brigaid

scratch cooking, 22, 26, 27, 28–29

SDGs. *See* Sustainable Development Goals

seafood, 11, 181; as animal feed, 79; bycatch, 188; overexploitation, 78; source of umami, 78–79; threats to, 79, 181, 182, 186

sensory ethnography, 57–58

Sherman, Sean (chef) (Lakota), 206, 255, 264, 268

Silverbird (restaurant), 255–56, 256–59, 263, 267

Sioux Chef, The (catering company), 206, 264

Sioux Chef's Indigenous Kitchen, The, 255

Slow Food movement, 12, 239, 240

Slow Food Ark of Taste, 43, 240, 242, 248

Slow Food Cooks Alliance, 240, 242, 243

Slow Food Cooks Alliance, Kenya, 12, 90, 239, 241–45; decolonizing food, 245–46, 250; ethnography of, 239–40; inclusivity of, 242–44, 247–48; raising awareness, 246–47, 248; relationships with small farmers, 242; sustainability, 242, 249; traditional foods, 244–45, 246, 248

Slow Food Presidia, 241, 242

Smag for Livet. *See* Taste for Life

Vermont chefs: creativity during COVID-19, 174, 177; interviews with, 164, 166, 177n3; and social sustainability, 173–75. *See also* COVID-19

Vermont Fresh Network (VFN), 166

Vittles Food Hall, 220, 227–28, 231

W

Wahpepah, Crystal (chef), 263–4

Wahpepah's Kitchen (restaurant), 264

waste. *See* food waste

Wild Bearies, 205

work ethics, 92, 93, 96, 98

work, in professional kitchens. *See* kitchen work, professional; labor, in professional kitchens

workshops: of Equilibrio Foundation, 41, 43; of Idónea, 285–86; of Kenyan Slow Food Cooks Alliance, 246; on optimization cooking, 13, 287–88

Z

Zenú, 35; agroecology, 35–36; cooking, 35; corn varieties, 35; cuisine, 36; cultivation practices, 49; foods, 36; food sovereignty, 36

Zero Hunger, 90